DEADLY DOZEN
2

Also by Robert K. DeArment

Bat Masterson: The Man and the Legend (Norman, 1979)
Knights of the Green Cloth: The Saga of the Frontier Gamblers
   (Norman, 1990)
*George Scarborough: The Life and Death of a Lawman on the Closing
   Frontier* (Norman, 1992)
(ed.) *Early Days in Texas: A Trip to Hell and Heaven* (Norman, 1992)
Alias Frank Canton (Norman, 1996)
Bravo of the Brazos: John Larn of Fort Griffin, Texas (Norman, 2002)
Deadly Dozen: Twelve Forgotten Gunfighters of the Old West (Norman,
   2003)
(ed. and anno., with William Rathmell) *Life of the Marlows: A True
   Story of Frontier Life of Early Days* (Denton, Tex., 2004)
Jim Courtright of Fort Worth: His Life and Legend (Fort Worth, Tex.,
   2004)
*Broadway Bat: Gunfighter in Gotham : The New York City Years of Bat
   Masterson* (Honolulu, Hawaii, 2005)
Ballots and Bullets: The Bloody County Seat Wars of Kansas (Norman,
   2006)

Twelve Forgotten

Gunfighters

of the Old West, Volume 2

DEADLY DOZEN

ROBERT K. DeARMENT

UNIVERSITY OF OKLAHOMA PRESS · NORMAN

Library of Congress Cataloging-in-Publication Data
DeArment, Robert K., 1925–
Deadly dozen : forgotten gunfighters of the old West, volume 2 /
Robert K. DeArment.
p. cm.
Includes bibliographical references and index.
ISBN 978-0-8061-3863-3 (hardcover : alk. paper)
1. Outlaws — West (U.S.) — Biography.
2. Frontier and pioneer life — West (U.S.) 3. West (U.S.) — Biography.
4. West (U.S.) — History — 1860–1890.
5. West (U.S.) — History — 1890–1945. I. Title.
F596.D385 2007
978′.020922 — dc22
[B]   2007005593

1   2   3   4   5   6   7   8   9   10

Contents

Illustrations

Acknowledgments

All of the people listed below have contributed to the research and preparation of this volume, and I would like to express my thanks to everyone.

Bob Alexander, Maypearl, Texas; Susan K. Anderson, Larry Ball, Jonesboro, Arkansas; Jim Bradshaw, Nita Stewart Haley Memorial Library, Midland, Texas; Donaly E. Brice, Lockhart, Texas; Eric J. Brock, Shreveport, Louisiana; Larry K. Brown, Cheyenne, Wyoming; Thomas R. Buecker, Curator, Fort Robinson Museum, Crawford, Nebraska; Susan C. Callaway, Deputy Clerk, Cochise County, Arizona; Woody Campbell, Spokane, Washington; Robert H. Carlock, Mesa, Arizona; Domenica Carriere, Louisiana State University Archives and Special Collections, Shreveport; T. Dudley Cramer, Oakland, California; Christopher Daly, Butte-Silver Bow Public Archives, Butte, Montana; Kay Dargitz, Department of Corrections, State of Arizona; Lori Davisson, Arizona Historical Society, Tucson; Harold L. Edwards, Bakersfield, California; Jane Watson Ellis, Bald Knob, Arkansas; Donna Ernst, Ocean City, New Jersey; Gary Fitterer, Kirkland, Washington; Joel Frandsen, Elsinore, Utah; Chuck Hornung, Lubbock, Texas; Jed Howard, Carlsbad, New Mexico; Richard Johnston, Carson City, Nevada; Donald R. Lavash, New Mexico State Records and Archives, Santa Fe; Belvadine Lecher, Dawes County History Museum, Chadron, Nebraska; the late Evelyn Linebery, Midland, Texas; Marion Marshall, LaJolla, California; Rick Miller, Harker Heights, Texas; Roger Myers, Larned, Kansas; Bobby Nieman, Longview, Texas; Bill O'Neal, Carthage, Texas; Ruth Owens, DeKalb County, Missouri; Chuck Parsons, Luling, Texas; Barbara Procarione, Price, Utah; Don Ringle, Homesteader Museum, Torrington, Wyoming; Gary Roberts, Tifton, Georgia; J. Richard Salazar, New Mexico State Records Center and Archives, Santa Fe; Arthur Soule, Deer Lodge, Montana; Elaine Way, Deer

Lodge, Montana; Jeanine Wilbarger, Toledo-Lucas County Public Library, Toledo, Ohio; John P. Wilson, Las Cruces, New Mexico; Roy B. Young, Apache, Oklahoma.

The research has been conducted over many years, and if I inadvertently omitted someone who also assisted, I apologize.

DEADLY DOZEN
2

Introduction

My book *Deadly Dozen: Twelve Forgotten Gunfighters of the Old West*, published in 2003, was greeted favorably by general readers and out-law-lawman-gunfighter buffs, many of whom may have tired of the apparently endless stream of volumes devoted to the well-publicized gunfighter characters of the American West. Academic reviewers also recognized that the book was not simply another recitation of "shoot-'em-ups," but provided some insight into conditions on the frontier that created the legendary western gunfighter.

"More than just a collective biography of dangerous gunfighters, this book functions as a social history of the gunfighter culture of the post–Civil War frontier West," wrote one reviewer. "The combined stories offer an intensive look into the lives of figures who helped shape the legends of the old West."[1]

Said another: "The author has selected twelve of the literally hundreds of lesser known gunmen of the frontier period. Based on newspaper accounts, court records and other original sources, he presents a thoroughly researched and well written account of these individuals. In addition to the biographical information, the work provided some interesting insight into the turbulent times of a developing nation."[2]

The book, wrote another reviewer, "provided tremendous insight into what caused hundreds of grassroots gunfighters to straddle both sides of the law without hesitation."[3]

"A lively social history of the gunfighter culture of the post–Civil War frontier West," said a book reviewer for a magazine devoted to western culture. "The imposing figures represent the thousands of homegrown pistol-packers who inhabited the late-19th century and early-20th century West."[4]

"Once viewed with simplicity, Western violence has been plumbed with vastly greater insight by historians in the last generation," wrote another. "This recently accumulated scholarly repository has gone far to explain the phenomenon, and this compilation of biographical sketches is a noteworthy addition."[5]

As pointed out by Richard Maxwell Brown in his 1991 study of American violence, *No Duty to Retreat*,

> there were two types of Western gunfighters: grassroots gunfighters and glorified gunfighters. The glorified gunfighters were those who became regionally and nationally famous: Wild Bill Hickok, Wyatt Earp, John Wesley Hardin, Billy the Kid, and many others. . . .
>
> The grassroots gunfighters of the West were kith and kin to the glorified ones, and they were socially significant but in a different way. I refer to them as "grassroots gunfighters" because their exploits became little known beyond their own localities; they lived and made their reputations only at the grass roots. Also, the term "grassroots gunfighters" suggests one of the most important facts about Western gunfighting; its pervasiveness. There were thousands of gunfighters and thousands of gunfights. The social institution of gunfighting was not at all restricted to the famous gunfighters but was all too often a feature of daily life in the West. Both the grassroots and glorified gunfighters adhered to the Code of the West, a cluster of social values that mentally programmed typical Westerners to use their guns, often in allegiance to the ideal of no duty to retreat. Grassroots gunfighters were the most numerous examples of the western proclivity to violence. As such they were exemplars of the ubiquitous gun culture of the West.[6]

There were, indeed, thousands of "grassroots gunfighters," as Brown has dubbed them, or "forgotten gunfighters" as I have called them, and the stories of many of them deserve preservation. Encouraged by the positive response to my initial presentation of the lives and careers of twelve of them, I here offer a second dozen for consideration.

The gunfighters chronicled in these pages were active in all parts of the American West. The states and territories of the Southwest — Texas, New Mexico, and Arizona — have long been recognized as the stage upon which many famous gunfights were enacted, and that section is well represented in these accounts. Nine of the twelve gunmen here chronicled — Jim Currie, Jack Watson, Joel Fowler, Jesse

Rascoe, Burk Burnett, Jim Sherman, Zack Light, Tom Tucker, and Ed Scarborough — played roles there. The central western states of Kansas, Colorado, Utah, Wyoming, and Montana saw plenty of six-shooter play also; Currie, Watson, Sherman and Light were active there, as were Jim Moon and John Owens. Moon, Sherman, and Jack Jolly enlivened the gun-fighting history of the great Northwest and Pacific coast region of Washington, Alaska, and California.

The stories of these men have been largely overlooked by encyclopedists. *The Album of Gunfighters*, published in 1951 by J. Marvin Hunter and Noah H. Rose, a seminal work in this field, mentioned none of them. Ed Bartholomew's *Biographical Album of Western Gunfighters*, published in 1958, contained sketches of only two, Joel Fowler and Zack Light. Bill O'Neal's more comprehensive *Encyclopedia of Western Gunfighters*, appearing in 1979, still had only one listing, that of Tom Tucker. Dan L. Thrapp's monumental *Encyclopedia of Frontier Biography*, published in four volumes, 1988–94, with thousands of bio-sketches, included five of this dozen: Burk Burnett (for his ranching fame, with no mention of his gunfights), Jim Currie, Joel Fowler, Jim Sherman (under his alias Jim Talbot), and Tom Tucker. *Encyclopedia of Western Lawmen and Outlaws*, brought out by Jay Robert Nash in 1992, also had five entries: Fowler, Sherman, and Tucker, as well as Jack Watson and Zack Light. The latest encyclopedic publication in the field, Leon Metz's *The Encyclopedia of Lawmen, Outlaws, and Gunfighters*, appearing in 2003, had sketches of three of the twelve: Jim Currie, Joel Fowler, and Ed Scarborough. None of these volumes contained entries for Jim Moon, John Owens, Jesse Rascoe, or Jack Jolly, all of whom had interesting careers worthy of mention in any consideration of the western gunfighter.

Here, then, are the stories of twelve gunmen, notorious in their time and place, who have long been forgotten, but whose stories are well worth telling.

— I —

JIM MOON
ca. 1840–1881

He died a natural death. That is, it was perfectly natural for Jim to die as he did. He was not bloodthirsty when he was sober. Most of the time he was bloodthirsty.
— *Denver Daily Times*, June 17, 1881

As modern chroniclers of Wild West history have ably demonstrated, the killing records of notorious gunfighters have been greatly exaggerated, first in the contemporary press, and later in exciting novels and supposedly factual accounts. The death tolls of Wild Bill Hickok, Billy the Kid, John Wesley Hardin, Bat Masterson, and other celebrated gunfighters have been shown to total in the single digits rather than the dozens — and even scores — once claimed.

But the formidable reputation of Jim Moon, feared as a deadly gunfighter throughout the frontier during his lifetime, may well have been the most overblown in all western history. In a fifteen-year career in the West, he developed a wide reputation as a fighting man, a bully who terrorized towns from the Midwest to the Pacific coast, a fearsome gunman who made known killers hunt their holes.

And yet not a single instance has been found where this redoubtable gunman ever shot another man.

This is not to say that he never killed anyone, for the big Colt's sixshooters he carried were deadly weapons indeed. But Moon preferred to use them as bludgeons rather than shooting irons. In Denver, where he spent his last years, he is known to have battered one — and perhaps two — people so badly with his revolver that death resulted.

When a reporter for a Denver paper approached this notorious pistoleer and asked about "the motives and sensations of border shooting scrapes" in which he had been involved, Moon responded: "The first man you kill, it goes pretty hard with you for awhile, but after the second or third you don't mind knocking over one of these gunfighters any more than you would a sheep. The man who pulls a gun on you when you have nothing in sight is a cur. All you need to do is to walk right up to him, take it away and beat him over the head with it, so he won't try it again. Nearly all my men came for me. Of course, I went after some of them — had to."[1]

This bulldozing tactic evidently worked well for Moon in many confrontations during the course of his career, but eventually he ran up against a man who used the gun in his hand and wrote finis to the life of the bully.

The best physical description of Moon was given by a Denver reporter who, viewing his body stretched out on the undertaker's cooling board, waxed almost poetic in his admiration:

> From a medical standpoint there has seldom passed under the dissecting knife a finer specimen of humanity than James Moon — six feet in height, his proportions were as nearly perfect as possible, and when stripped his form resembled more that of an ancient Roman gladiator than of a man belonging to our present age — especially was this magnificent development noticeable in the chest, which was deep and square and measured forty-four inches. The upper and lower extremities were models of muscular development and symmetry, while the feet and hands were small, the former arched and the latter delicately shaped. The head was not in keeping with the magnificent proportions of the rest of the body. It was of bullet shape and covered with a red shock of hair cut short. The brow, though high, was lowering. The eyebrows, of a sandy color, were inclined to shagginess and helped to give a forbidding expression to the face. The eyes were small, ferret-like and grey. The nose short and inclined to turn upwards. The mouth, of medium size, with thin lips which were generally drawn tight, the upper lip being covered with a short, stubby mustache of a sandy color, otherwise he was clean shaven.[2]

Jim Moon, as depicted by a Denver newspaper artist in the June 17, 1881, edition of the *Denver Republican*. From the author's collection.

Most of what we know about Moon's origins and early years comes from his wife, who was interviewed extensively by the Denver press in 1881, when he was killed. She said his name was actually John Erba Wilcoxon, that he was born in Philadelphia about 1840, ran away from home at the age of fifteen, and changed his name to Jim Moon so his parents could not trace him.

Moon reportedly served in the Union army during the Civil War, but his penchant for belligerence inevitably led to trouble.[3] Three Denver papers published on the same day gave three rather different accounts of his problems in the military service. One said that "he was in the army, but made an unruly soldier and was put in irons."[4] Another said he got in a fight in the army, seriously injured his opponent, and arrived in Memphis in irons. Somehow he avoided a court-martial and received an honorable discharge.[5] A third paper said he was arrested for attempting to kill another soldier; the intended victim was no less than the lieutenant colonel of the regiment.[6]

After his military service, Moon settled in Dubuque, Iowa, where he ran a saloon. But his violent nature led to another "bad scrape," and he had to "skip."[7] He turned to professional gambling for a vocation and over the next dozen years became a prominent member of the western sporting crowd. In the turbulent Reconstruction years, he was active in Louisiana, Texas, and other southern states, and even spent some months dealing monte in Cuba.

When railroad lines stretched into Kansas in the late 1860s, opening up a viable market for Texas cattle and triggering the great longhorn trail drives to the Kansas railheads, Moon, along with a horde of other members of the sporting element, was on hand at Abilene, Newton, Wichita, and Ellsworth, the early cow towns. He caught the attention of a correspondent for the *Topeka Daily Commonwealth*, writing about the sporting crowd at Newton in 1871. Moon, said the newsman, had "more the style of the New York gambler than anyone in town." He described Moon as a "well proportioned, athletic man, with brown hair and mustache," the owner of a "*tout ensemble* that is decidedly prepossessing."[8]

In the Kansas cattle towns Moon mixed with such sporting crowd notables as Dick Clark, "Rowdy Joe" Lowe, and Joe's paramour, "Rowdy Kate." For a time in Newton he partnered with Clark, keeping cases at the celebrated gambler's faro game, or dealing monte, but

Clark soon realized that Moon was too hotheaded to go long without stirring up trouble, so he dissolved the association.

Lowe was about as volatile a character as Moon and was recognized throughout the sporting fraternity as a dangerous gunfighter, but on one occasion, according to a newspaper report, Moon made him hunt his hole.

> [Lowe] went after Jim Moon, the faro dealer, but it is not believed he was very anxious to find the gambler. Moon had a reputation of being mighty handy with shooting irons himself, and when he heard that Lowe was after him, he sent around a tip that the vicinity was full of dangerous germs of the lead variety and Mr. Lowe might save some repairs to his hide by keeping out of reach. It was currently believed that this message completely bluffed the avenger of the vigilantes for he suddenly expressed a desire to make terms with Moon.[9]

At Ellsworth, Moon met the woman who would become his constant companion the rest of his life and, ultimately, the cause of his sudden death. Emma DeMarr was only about sixteen years old when Moon first saw her at Ellsworth, where she was working in a hotel. Swedish by heritage, she was born in Lubeck, Germany, on March 15, 1857. Described as a blonde "with fair, clear skin, high cheek bones, very pretty teeth, and rather delicate hands," she spoke in a "broken, musical Swedish accent."[10] At the age of fifteen (the same age as Wilcoxon/Moon when he ran away from home) she left her family, then residing in Leipzig, Germany, and went to Hamburg. There she boarded a ship for the United States. Landing in New York, she made her way to Ellsworth, Kansas, where she had friends. She later claimed she first met Moon at "picnics," adding, "It was love at first sight on his part, I think, at least he has often told me so."[11]

It may not have been love at first sight for the Swedish girl, but she was inexorably attracted to the dashing, powerfully built gambler. The two began living together in Kansas, and when he left the cow towns to seek greener pastures in Colorado, she soon followed.

They remained for some time in Denver, always a good gambling mecca, and Moon worked the local gaming emporiums and went on frequent side trips to the mining camps and railroad towns of Colorado and Wyoming. In 1875 at Cheyenne he got into a fight, as was his wont, and had to leave town hurriedly.[12] Having about worn out his welcome in that part of the country, Moon decided to move on west. He and Emma traveled together as far as Salt Lake City, where they separated. She went on to Los Angeles, while he worked the tables of Reno, Carson City, and Virginia City in Nevada, and San Francisco in California. They teamed up together again at Los Angeles, where he invested some of his winnings in a saloon called the Woodbine.[13]

In November 1876 the two were married in Los Angeles by a Swedish Lutheran priest named Carl Peterson. The ceremony was performed "at the point of a pistol," or so Emma claimed in one of her moments of anger toward Moon.[14]

There is no question that Moon was extremely jealous and could fly into one of his murderous tantrums if another man paid Emma any attention. A gambler named Cal Somers who knew the couple in California later testified that Moon "was considered a bully and a fighter. Do not know of his killing anyone, but have seen him have his gun out many times. . . . He was always in trouble and people dreaded him. . . . He kept a gambling place, called the woman 'his girl' and kept her locked up in a room with chains on the doors and paid $5 a day for keepers."[15]

Predictably, Moon's volcanic temper got him into brawls in which he usually acquitted himself well. In one he reportedly took on twenty adversaries, "seriously injuring some," but the incident cost him his gambling saloon, and again he had to pull stakes and leave.[16]

By 1878 Moon had acquired a sizable quantity of cash, $12,000 by Emma's estimate, and she informed him that she wanted to spend some of it on a trip to Europe to see her family. Moon, with all his faults, was never a tightwad, and he agreed. In the spring of that year the couple came back east as far as Cheyenne. There they separated, Emma going on alone to New York and an Atlantic liner. In Ireland, she took another vessel to Sweden, where her parents had moved. Moon joined her there later. After spending some time with Emma's family, the couple took in the Paris Exposition and a tour of Europe. Emma said that Moon spent $7,000 on the trip. "He bought me everything I wanted, and we had an awful good time. Besides making me several presents, he also gave my mother, sisters and other relatives money and valuable presents. Oh, he was very good to all of us."[17]

Jim and Emma returned from their European sojourn in July 1878 and went once again to Denver. There he invested some of his remaining capital in a combination saloon and restaurant he called the Oyster Ocean. As a partner in the enterprise he took in John Bull, another veteran of the western gambling circuit.

An Englishman by birth, Bull was four years Moon's senior, and had been living by his wits and dexterity with cards since before the Civil War. He was also known as a deadly gunfighter, having killed Langford Peel, another celebrated gambler-gunman, at Helena, Montana, in 1867.[18]

On the evening of October 14, 1880, Moon and Bull were in the Oyster Ocean with their womenfolk when two Denver police officers, Assistant Chief John Holland and a patrolman named Merrill, entered. They had been summoned by a man named Lamar, who complained that he had been abused and struck in the establishment by Moon, who was intoxicated. Seeing the officers, the always hair-triggered Moon quickly engaged in another of the donnybrooks that marked his career. But, as Moon later recounted the story, this one was more farcical than potentially fatal. "I was in the bar-room," he said,

> when the officers Holland and Merrill came in and Bull was standing by me counting some money. Our wives were sitting at a table eating. Nothing was said to the officers until they started to go out. . . . I heard Holland say to my wife, "It will make you sick."
>
> I stepped out and said I did not want my wife insulted.
>
> Holland replied, "I don't know that she is your wife."
>
> I then told him to get out of the house. After some words he pulled a gun and I jumped him and grabbed the gun. We had a scuffle and fell upon the floor. The women fired plates, cups and saucers, some of which hit me.[19]

The officers finally beat a retreat from the shambles of a restaurant littered with shattered furniture and broken chinaware. According to a Denver newspaper report, Holland was "dragged out bleeding profusely about the head from the deep wounds and taken to Comfort's on the opposite corner, where he was put to bed seriously injured."[20]

Officer Merrill called for reinforcements, and a paddy wagon arrived. "Whistles were blowing on every corner and finally a majority of the night force was assembled at Moon's."[21] No arrests were made, however. A large crowd that had gathered watched as Jim Moon, armed with "a small howitzer," stood in the doorway of the Oyster Ocean and held the police at bay. He kept his revolver "at full cock" and leveled at the officers as he, Bull, and their women climbed into a hack. "The driver whipped up his horses and the party was off, having defied fifty citizens and a whole platoon of police!"[22] Later Moon and Bull surrendered to authorities and paid fines.[23]

This relatively minor ruckus was often exaggerated in later published accounts of Moon's misdeeds. A dispatch from Denver printed in several newspapers throughout the West some months later asserted that at the time of the Oyster Ocean fracas, Moon had "defied the whole Denver police force to arrest him, and whipped the whole force single-handed. When under the influence of liquor Moon was a perfect demon."[24] And a newspaperman would write that

> Moon, while seated with a friend and two women at a restaurant and having rather a merry time, was . . . insulted by a lieutenant and officer of the police. He beat both of them nearly to death with the chinaware and chairs, hurried his three companions into a hack, which he ordered to a halfway house outside the city limits, and held his impromptu blockhouse a week with a double-barreled shotgun against the combined police and sheriff's force. He surrendered only when liberty was guaranteed him.[25]

But the incident in the Oyster Ocean was merely a forerunner to other violent episodes in Denver involving Jim Moon. Only two weeks later, on October 31, a serious race riot broke out in Denver. When rumors spread within the city about attacks on white women by Chinese, drunken mobs moved into the Chinese section, attacking all Asians in sight. Denver's chief of police at the time was David J. Cook. As founder and head of the Rocky Mountain Detective Agency and general of the Colorado militia, Cook was the most highly respected law enforcement figure in the state. But when the disturbance broke out he was hard-pressed to bring it under control.

At the height of the riot he came upon Jim Moon, standing in the doorway of a Chinese laundry, a six-shooter gripped in each hand.

"So you're in this, too," Cook demanded.

"Not by a damned sight," Moon retorted. "I'm here to guard my Chinamen. They do my shirts and do 'em damned well. I've got a dozen Chinks in here and anybody who tried to get 'em will have to do it over my dead body."

Nobody attempted to go through Moon to get at those Chinese. A newspaper report said that at the Chinese laundry, Moon, "revolver in hand," faced down a mob of about a hundred rioters. "Knowing his record the crowd fell back."[26] When the mob moved on to other sections, Moon volunteered to assist the police in their efforts to quell the disturbance and, as General Cook later admitted, "acquitted himself most creditably."[27]

For the part he had played in the Chinese riot, Moon was lauded as a hero, especially in the sporting community, but his newfound heroic celebrity lasted only a week. In the early morning hours of November 8 he went into one of his fits of murderous rage and committed the only homicide that can be attributed to him with certainty.

As newspaperman E. D. Cowan told the tale some years later, "a bad man from Breakenridge pulled a six-shooter on Moon in a gambling room. He captured it and hit his assailant over the head with the butt. The blow knocked the Breakenridge killer down a flight of stairs, and when the body was taken to the morgue the neck was found to have been broken."[28]

This account was badly distorted and differed substantially from eyewitness testimony presented at the coroner's inquest into the death of one Samuel Hall, the "bad man from Breakenridge." According to that testimony, Moon in the early hours of November 8 was standing at the bar of the Arcade, a prominent saloon and gambling house on Larimer Street in the heart of Denver's tenderloin district, drinking with Henry Scott, Frank Marshall,[29] A. McPhee, George Bunch, and Samuel Hall. Said to be "a quiet man when sober, but very foul-mouthed when a little tipsy," Sam Hall announced loudly that "he had often heard of Moon and was disappointed at seeing him. He went on using abusive epithets and telling how many men he knew who could lick Moon. The latter was also under the influence of liquor and resented these insults by giving worse ones in return." The dispute moved to the street outside the saloon and soon escalated into violence. In blind anger, Moon pulled a revolver from his coat pocket and struck Hall on the head, at the same time shouting, "God damn you, fight! Get your pistol!" Hall staggered, but did not go to the ground at once. Moon struck him again with his gun, and Hall fell to the gutter, but in a moment struggled to his feet. Moon then delivered three more blows to Hall's head, and he went down for good. When Marshall attempted to interfere in the beating, Moon turned the pistol on him and threatened to shoot him if he did not stand clear. Police arrived, but no arrests were made at that time. Hall's friends carried him to his room, where he was attended by a physician, who determined that Hall's skull had been fractured.[30]

More than two weeks later Hall's doctor announced that his patient was almost certainly going to die, and, based on this report, a warrant was sworn out for Moon's arrest. On November 24 Moon appeared before a justice of the peace, waived examination, and was released after posting bonds of $5,000.[31]

On December 2, 1880, Sam Hall died from his injuries. A coroner's jury found that "Samuel Hall came to his death . . . from injuries received on the morning of November 8, 1880 about one or two o'clock, from being beaten over the head with a revolver in the hands of James Moon in front of the Arcade saloon." Moon was indicted and charged with murder.[32]

Sam Hall may not have been the only victim of Jim Moon's brutal attacks in Denver. The same paper that reported the murderous assault on Hall remarked rather offhandedly that a woman remembered only as "Indian Lou" had been beaten and kicked so badly by Moon that "she was laid up for months and died at last from her injuries."[33] Evidently "Indian Lou" was a denizen of the lower echelons of the Denver demimonde, and city officials did not believe the circumstances of her death warranted investigation.

Before Moon ever came to trial for the Hall killing, he became embroiled in a row that would be his ultimate undoing. This time he employed his bulldozing tactics against the wrong man, and paid with his life for his error in judgment.

In the early months of 1881, following the death of Sam Hall, Moon and Emma had a series of domestic fights. This was not unusual, of course. Both had violent tempers; Emma could be a virago, and Moon was a notorious wife beater. The previous summer, after a particularly vicious thrashing administered by Moon, Emma had left him. Slipping out of town, she went to Salt Lake City to stay with her eighteen-year-old sister, Perl.[34]

But as she was leaving she made a serious mistake. Well aware of Moon's penchant for uncontrolled jealousy, in a fit of spite she decided to inflict even more pain on him than that created by her departure. She gave a newsboy a dollar to tell her husband that she had been taken to the depot by another man, a handsome fellow with a light-colored mustache. When he received the message, Moon "went about the streets for two days more mad than sane," looking for anyone who answered the vague description.[35]

Emma returned after a few weeks, and the two patched up their differences, but the seeds of insane jealousy always present in Moon's mind took deeper root and grew rapidly.

During this period, he was managing the gambling rooms on the second floor of the Arcade. One of his faro dealers was a gambler and sometime con man named Clay Wilson. A native of Lancaster, Ohio, Wilson was thirty-seven years old, but looked ten years younger. He had taken up professional gambling as a teenager and had toured the boom camps of the West for twenty-one years, appearing in many of the same locales as did Moon. In 1875 he came to Colorado and was active in Leadville before transferring to Denver. He had an innocent, honest-appearing countenance that was a great asset in his extracurricular confidence game activities. A very intelligent man, he was well-read and fluent in several languages, with an extensive knowledge of literature, music, and the theater. He also had a light-colored mustache.[36]

Emma on occasion visited her husband's gaming rooms above the Arcade saloon. Perhaps Moon saw, or thought he saw, a coquettish glance exchanged between Emma and Wilson, but something put the idea in his head that his own employee, faro dealer Clay Wilson, was carrying on with Emma behind his back. Moon started drinking, and the more he drank, the more convinced he became that his suspicion was true. He and Emma had several loud rows over the issue, resulting in another of their frequent separations.

Late in the evening of June 16, 1881, Moon met his wife on the street, berated her verbally with accusations of infidelity, and slapped her around, blackening an eye and making her nose bleed. Hearing her screams, police officers Ryan and Belcher ran up and pulled Moon away. Emma ran in panic, jumped into a hack, and had the driver take her to the outskirts of town, where she hid under a tree and spent the night. About five in the morning she returned to her rooms.

During the night, Moon continued to drink heavily, his anger mounting. Finally, he went to a room occupied by Clay Wilson and another gambler named Charles Lundin.[37] There he threatened both men, shouting so loudly that he was heard throughout the rooming house in which they lived. Wilson was in bed, and Moon "called him hard names, jammed a six self-action shooter into his face and breast several times [and] told him to get up and defend himself." When Wilson protested that he did not have a gun, Moon turned to Lundin and spat: "Give him a gun and let him defend himself like a man." Lundin did not comply, "knowing Moon would kill him if he made a move with his hand." Moon issued a final warning to Wilson: "I will get you yet. The town is too small for us." Then, cursing Wilson, he turned to leave. As he was going out he said to Lundin: "That God damned bastard has got to fight every time I meet him or leave town, or I will kill him."[38]

Clay Wilson got up the next morning about eleven o'clock and set out for the Arcade. He went armed, "a .45-calibre Colt's navy, barrel cut off to five inches," in his hip pocket.[39] He met Lundin on the street, and together the two entered the saloon. They passed Moon, who was having his shoes shined outside the building. He glowered at them, but said nothing at that time. Wilson and Lundin were having a beer at the bar when Moon came in and said, apparently as some kind of joke, "I want a doughnut." Wilson ignored him and walked away, but Moon turned on Lundin and snapped, "I came in here to make a fight!" Reaching his right hand behind his back as if to draw a weapon, he slapped Lundin twice in the face with his left. Lundin retreated, walking quickly out the front door.

Turning to Wilson, Moon barked: "I mean you too, both of you, and if you don't want to fight, get out of here!"[40]

He then advanced on Wilson, who was standing about twelve feet away. His right hand was still behind his back, hidden from view. As Moon closed the distance between them, Wilson drew his pistol.

Remembering that Moon had once told him he had taken revolvers away from more than a hundred men, Wilson gripped his weapon in both hands and fired. The .45 bullet slammed into Moon's chest, but the big man, hardly flinching, kept on coming.

Frantically, Wilson thumbed back the hammer of his single-action and fired again. A second bullet ripped into Moon's chest, but he still lurched forward.

Moon grabbed Wilson in a viselike grip, so strong that Wilson had a sudden flash of fear that somehow he had missed his target with both shots. As Wilson later explained,

> His object seemed to be to throw me on the floor, as he reached for my legs. I backed toward the side of the room, he following and clinging to me. Then I fired a third time, the bullet, I think, taking effect in his leg, as he fell to his knees. In the tussle I got against the wall, and he getting hold of my left hand, my position was such that I could not shoot without putting my arm behind my body. Consequently the last shot was fired from around my back, the pistol discharging close to his face. Moon then fell on the floor, dead.[41]

Wilson walked calmly out of the saloon, where he immediately met Chief of Police Dave Cook, who had come running at the sound of the shots. Barney Black, a witness to the shooting, pointed to Wilson, saying, "That is the man you want. He has just shot Jim Moon." Chief Cook took Wilson into custody and asked for his gun. The pistol was so hot, the officer later said, that it burned his hand when he took it.

Before Cook and a Sergeant Phillips of the Denver police department arranged for the transfer of Moon's body to George Brown's undertaking parlors, a large crowd gathered outside the Arcade, and many of the curious shouldered into the place to view the now lifeless remains of the man who had once been a terror to the community. Among those who had a look was Emma, who had been nearby when she heard the shots. Her first thought was that her husband had killed another man, and she rushed to the scene. When she couldn't get through the crowd at the front door, she went around and entered the rear entrance. After gazing at the dead body of her husband for a few moments, she turned and left without saying a word to anyone, "apparently little concerned regarding the fate of the man who had been in every sense of the term, her master."[42] Perhaps she had long known this day would come.

When the body was removed to undertaker Brown's quarters, a curious crowd followed and remained outside while Brown stripped the body. He found that Moon had been shot four times. Two bullet entry wounds to the left breast below the heart were within one and a half inches of each other. Another bullet had gone through the pelvis. The last, entering under the right ear, was believed to have caused instant death.

In the man's pockets were found "over two hundred dollars . . . in greenbacks, a fine gold watch and chain, a bottle of whiskey, which had been broken in the fall, a small phial which had contained morphine pills, a bunch of keys, a shoe buttoner, a scarlet silk handkerchief, a pair of kid gloves, a small pocket glass, a pocket knife, two or three cigars and some unimportant memoranda." Amazingly, no weapon, other than the small pocketknife, was reported found on Moon's person.[43]

Later Brown threw open the doors of his establishment to the crowd gathered outside and allowed them to enter and view the body. There followed "a scene that beggars description," as a reporter for the *Denver Republican* put it. A long line of people formed on the sidewalk and one by one entered the building and walked down the stairs into the basement where the body lay.

> A man was stationed in the basement to prevent the crowd from congregating around the body. When some more bold and curious than the rest would linger, he would break out in the oft repeated and suggestive refrain: "Don't stop, gentlemen, the weather is hot and the body is already getting bad." A second invitation such as this was not necessary. . . . So morbidly curious were many that they came in . . . five or six times before they were satisfied. . . . The number of people who viewed the sight was not less than 3,000. The steady passage to and fro of visitors continued for several hours, and presented a scene that once seen by one who could appreciate it under the circumstances, would never be forgotten. The prediction of the sentinel was fulfilled, the odor arising from the body before it had thus lain two hours showing that decomposition had set in. From the moment this fact was discovered, the crowd began to decrease and an hour later the visitors were all stragglers.[44]

Coroner Thomas Linton quickly assembled a jury to view the body and take testimony. After identifying the body as that of her husband, Emma gave her story.

Charles Lundin testified as to the previous night's altercation with Moon and the circumstances of the shooting in the Arcade. Chief of Police Dave Cook described Wilson's admission that he had killed Moon and his subsequent arrest. The jury came to the obvious conclusion that Moon had met his death at the hands of Clay Wilson. After a preliminary examination, Wilson was charged with killing "John E. Wilcoxon, otherwise known as James Moon, with malice aforethought."[45] (Besides ridding the city of a notorious bully and troublemaker, the killing of Moon seemed to have prompted Dave Cook and the Denver police to crack down on some of the pistol-packers walking the streets. A dispatch printed in several western papers said that the day after Moon's shooting some fifty arrests were made for the carrying of concealed weapons.)[46]

Wilson's trial before District Court Judge Victor A. Elliot opened on September 16, 1881. Representing Wilson were General Samuel E. Browne and Captain Putnam. The prosecution team was led by Arapahoe County Assistant District Attorney I. E. Barnum and Judge G. W. Miller. Interestingly, one of the witnesses for the defense was Charles L. Baggs, who testified, as did several others, that he heard Moon threaten the life of Wilson on the morning of the shooting. Charles L. "Doc" Baggs was one of the most notorious con men of the American West, who in later years would partner Wilson in a series of elaborate confidence schemes.[47]

The case was given to the jury at half past twelve on September 17. The jurymen enjoyed a leisurely lunch and then, after only twenty minutes of deliberation, reached a verdict of "not guilty," and Clay Wilson was released from custody.[48]

Four days later a woman tried unsuccessfully to shoot Wilson.[49] Whether the woman was Emma or even if the motive for the assassination attempt was revenge for the Moon slaying was never determined.

Although a Denver paper alleged that Moon had a wife back in Dubuque who might claim his estate,[50] nothing more was heard of this possibility, and Emma ended up with the money Moon had accumulated. When a reporter interviewed her shortly after the killing, he was impressed with the jewelry she wore: "On three fingers of the left hand she wore two elegant cluster diamond rings and a magnificent solitaire which she took no pains to conceal. From ears depended a pair of elegant diamonds and over her breast hung a diamond cross of great value."[51]

Emma remained in Denver, and her notorious husband and the part she had played in his violent end were generally forgotten. Many years later a reporter for the *Denver Post* discovered her, "a white-haired, dignified lady keeping a respectable boarding house in East Denver, the best part of town."[52]

Not forgotten was Clay Wilson, whose name appeared frequently in the Colorado newspapers as a successful confidence operator taking marks in ever bigger and better swindles.

In March 1882 he and Cal Somers, one of those who had testified for Wilson in the Moon murder case, were arrested for pulling off a gold brick swindle on the president of the Merchants and Mechanics Bank of Leadville and taking him for $20,000. A Denver newspaper referred to them as "the noted confidence men [whose] exploits would fill a good-sized bound volume." Together with Charles Lundin, another Wilson pal who had figured largely in the Moon case, they had earlier trimmed a Denver hatter named Edgar Leonard to the tune of $1,800.[53]

A true bill of indictment was brought against Wilson and Somers for the Leadville caper, and they were released on $10,000 bail. At a February 1883 trial in Leadville, they were acquitted.[54]

In later years Wilson worked with the Soapy Smith swindling gang of Denver and Doc Baggs. He eluded the clutches of the law until he was sixty-nine years old, when he and Baggs conned L. H. Taylor of Philadelphia out of $15,000, and Taylor blew the whistle on them. Police who arrested him in Rochester, New York, were baffled by a tattered notebook he carried in which were coded entries they could not decipher. Appealing to university professors for help, they learned that the inscriptions were names of swindling victims, dates, and amounts taken, all recorded in Greek, Arabic, and Sanskrit.

Clay Wilson was convicted and sent to prison, but was released after three years due to his failing health. He was seventy-four when he died at San Francisco in 1917, thirty-four years after he snuffed out the life of the notorious bullyboy known as Jim Moon.[55]

— 2 —

JIM CURRIE
1841–1899

Jim Curry was one of the most depraved specimens that ever visited the western country. He was the embodiment of everything bad and disreputable, the very quintessence of all wickedness, and a living personification of crime in its worst forms, without a single redeeming quality. No person was safe against his attacks; his murderous weapons were aimed at all alike.

— A. T. Andreas and W. G. Cutler, *History of the State of Kansas*

Jim Currie . . . was a ruffian of the type occasionally developed on the frontier. He had none of the redeeming qualities of chivalry and generosity that sometimes accompany a violent life. He was simply a cutthroat, one of the "devil's own."

— James H. Beach, "Old Fort Hays"

Although James H. Currie cut a murderous swath across the frontier with his deadly six-guns, he would be completely forgotten today, no doubt, had he not turned his batteries loose on a pair of stage actors at Marshall, Texas, in 1879, killing one and critically wounding the other.[1] When the latter victim of his attack survived and went on to found the foremost royal dynasty of the American theater, Jim Currie became a footnote to that story.

W. B. "Bat" Masterson, heralded widely himself as a prominent western gunfighter, classed Currie with such virtuosos of the six-shooter as Ben Thompson, Wild Bill Hickok, Wyatt Earp, Bill Tilghman, Charley Bassett, Luke Short, Clay Allison, and "Rowdy Joe" Lowe. All, said Masterson, were "men with nerves of steel who had often been put to the test—any one of whom would not have hesitated a moment to put his life as the stakes to be played for."[2]

Born at Ibrecken, County Clare, Ireland, in October 1841, Jim Currie was one of five boys parented by James and Mary Griffin Currie. When he was about nine, he and two of his brothers, Michael and Andrew, sailed from Cork to Boston, leaving their parents and other siblings back in Ireland. The boys lived first in New York City and then in Niagara Falls, presumably with relatives, for several years, and then went their separate ways.[3]

About 1859 Jim Currie, who had developed into a strapping teenager (a newspaper twenty years later would describe him as "a fine specimen of physical manhood—straight, square-shouldered, deep-chested and powerfully built, weighing over 200 pounds")[4] turned up in Cincinnati, Ohio, where he found work as a fireman on the Little Miami Railroad.[5] Trains seemed to fascinate him. Eventually he became an accredited locomotive engineer and was employed throughout much of his adult life by various railroad lines.

But something in Currie's character kept him constantly in search of violent action. He was a youth of twenty in April 1861 when Southerners attacked Fort Sumter, South Carolina, and President Abraham Lincoln issued a call for volunteers to preserve the Union. Only a few days later, on April 20, 1861, at Morrow, Ohio, Currie enlisted as a private in Captain J. D. Wallace's Company A, Twelfth Ohio Infantry. Six months later Currie was promoted to sergeant. He saw action in western Virginia and at the battle of Antietam in Maryland. He later served on provost duty at Charleston, South Carolina. After more than three years' service, he was mustered out at Columbus, Ohio, on July 11, 1864.[6]

He did not remain long in Ohio. One of his railroad bosses would later allege that Currie fled Ohio to escape punishment for a crime, but no evidence has been unearthed to support this claim.[7] He next turned up in Kansas, working as a locomotive engineer for the Kansas Pacific Railroad, but within a few years was discharged, reportedly for bad conduct.[8]

Currie first gained notoriety as a dangerous gunman in the mushroom towns springing up along the newly laid tracks of the Kansas

Pacific. At Ellsworth, Hays City, Coyote, Sheridan, and Kit Carson, he mixed with prominent members of the sporting fraternity: Wild Bill Hickok, John Malone, brothers Charlie and Frank Johnson, Barney Bohan, Steve Mulligan, Isaac "Ike" Thayer, Tommy Drum, Cy Goddard, Paddy Walsh, John Bitter, Chris Riley, and "Rowdy Joe" Lowe, along with their female followers, Joe Lowe's paramour, "Rowdy Kate," "Calamity Jane" Canary; brothel madam Ida May; and a horde of whores.[9]

We hear of him at Sheridan, a community so rough, according to one who was there, that Sodom and Gomorrah would look like church towns in comparison. "All the tough element that had been following the building of the road collected here," he said. "There is a grave yard on the hill back of the town called Boot Hill, [with] over one hundred graves of men and women, mostly men, not one of [whom] died a natural death."[10]

At Ellsworth, another Currie stop, "there was no night as far as the town was concerned, money was plenty [and] the town was filled up with gun men."[11]

Miguel Otero, an early visitor to the town and later governor of New Mexico, described Ellsworth as

> almost wholly a town of tents and small, rough, frame buildings, but it was as busy a place as could be imagined. There were at least a hundred business houses in the town, many of them conducting their business in tents. . . . It seemed as if nearly every other house in the town was a drinking place, while gambling rooms and dance halls and other questionable resorts were most common. Shooting scrapes were every-day occurrences, and the nights were frequently made hideous by drunken men firing off pistols promiscuously and shouting like bands of wild Comanches.[12]

Hays City, a carbon copy of Ellsworth, was "without doubt a wild and wooly town from start to finish. Main Street was almost a solid row of saloons, dance halls, restaurants, barber shops and houses of prostitution. . . . The saloons, dance halls and gambling rooms all did a thriving business. They never closed."[13]

Currie was described as "a desperado from Hays City"[14] when, on August 28, 1868, he was one of fifty "first-class frontiersmen" employed by Major George A. "Sandy" Forsyth at Fort Hays to serve in a company of scouts for the U.S. Army in a campaign against hostile Indians.[15] Signing up with Currie were a number of notable plainsmen and Indian-fighters, including Abner S. "Jack Sharp" Grover,[16] Simpson E. "Jack" Stilwell,[17] Isaac "Ike" Thayer,[18] and Chauncey B. Whitney.[19]

Enlistment for the recruits was to the end of the year with pay at $75 a month. Those enlistees who could provide their own mounts were to be allowed thirty cents a day extra and $3 if their horses were lost or killed; army mounts were provided all others. The scouts were equipped with blankets, tin cups, bridles, and saddles. They were issued seven-shot Spencer repeating rifles, Colt's .45-caliber six-shooters, and ammunition — 140 rounds for the rifle and 30 rounds for the revolver. They were to be accompanied by four mules laden with rations and medical supplies, as well as 4,000 additional rounds of ammunition.[20]

The day following Currie's enlistment, the company, led by Major Forsyth, with Lieutenant Frederick Beecher second in command,[21] and Dr. John H. Mooer as surgeon, moved out on a scout. On September 17 they were attacked by a combined war party of several hundred Sioux, Arapaho, and Cheyenne warriors. The "Forsyth Scouts" made their stand on a dry riverbed island of the Arickaree Fork of the Republican River and there fought one of the most dramatic battles of the Indian wars. For a week the scouts threw back repeated assaults by the Indians even as they suffered from wounds and lack of food. The officers had been among the early casualties. Major Forsyth was the first to be hit. A bullet struck him in the hip, and as he fell another shot broke his leg below the knee. Lieutenant Beecher, also hit twice, crawled over to Forsyth, mumbled "I have my death wound," and died. Dr. Mooer was shot in the head, but lingered three days, blind and speechless, before he, too, expired.[22] Twenty men in the party were hit; four died. By the end of the week the survivors were reduced to eating putrid horse meat. Chauncey Whitney, who kept a diary, scribbled on the 24th: "My God! Have you deserted us?"[23] Jack Stilwell and another scout, Pierre Trudeau, had slipped away during the siege to seek reinforcements. They were successful, and on August 24 a rescue party from Fort Wallace appeared at the river. The Indians disappeared, and the Forsyth Scouts received badly needed medical assistance and nourishment.

Since Currie's name is missing from a monument honoring the

Two accused murderers in jail at Marshall, Texas. Jim Currie is at left, wearing hat. His cellmate is Abe Rothschild. From the author's collection.

participants in the Beecher Island fight, some have questioned if he was even there. However, Cal J. Bascom, a railroad man who was in the area at the time, listed him among those Forsyth Scouts with whom he was personally acquainted.[24] Sigmund Shlesinger, one of the scouts, offered an explanation for the omission: "When we left Fort Wallace, two men joined our company. One was Jim Curry, whose name does not appear anywhere as a member of Forsyth's scouts or as a participant in the battle of Beecher's Island; but he was with us, of that I am sure, for I was well acquainted with him and knew him better than anyone else. The other was Jack Sharp Grover."[25]

Since Grover's participation in the Beecher Island fight has never been doubted, one might ask why Currie has been ignored. Perhaps people believed the man's later unsavory record disqualified him for inclusion on the list of heroes of one of the classic battles of the Indian wars.

The harrowing Indian fight on the Arickaree apparently did not daunt Currie in the least, for following the disbanding of the Forsyth Scouts, he signed on as a scout under Lieutenant Silas Pepoon. He even accepted a pay cut to $50 a month. Pepoon seems to have held Currie in high regard, for when seventeen former Forsyth Scouts were transferred to Fort Hays to serve with Pepoon, the lieutenant approved a pay raise from $50 to $75 a month for Currie and scout William H. H. McCall.[26] Currie's duties at Fort Hays included the hunting down of thieves, as indicated by this report of Lieutenant Pepoon: "James Curry and O. P. Johnson, Scouts, will proceed to-morrow morning to Ft. Harker, Kansas, by way of Ft. Larned and Zarah and endeavor to recover Government horses and mules stolen from the vicinity of Medicine Bluff Creek, Indian Territory, and capture the parties having them in possession, after using every exertion to accomplish this objective, they will return to Fort Hays, Kansas."[27]

Currie was discharged on March 23, 1869.[28] Other reports have him scouting for George Armstrong Custer's Seventh Cavalry and General Philip Sheridan's Nineteenth Kansas Volunteer Cavalry, but records have not been found to support this.[29]

After leaving army service, Currie returned to his job as an engineer on the Kansas Pacific. An item in a Lawrence, Kansas, paper a month after he left the army remarked on his handling of a chronic problem of railroad men on the Kansas plains:

BUFFALO ON THE TRACK.

On Thursday afternoon while the paymaster's train on the Kansas Pacific Railway was coming east at the rate of twenty-five miles an hour, a herd of thirteen buffalo attempted to cross the track in front of the engine, which five of the herd failed to do in proper time, and as a consequence were unceremoniously butted off by the advancing train. One was killed outright and the rest were more or less disarranged anatomically. By the skillful management of the engineer, Jim Curry, the engine came out with no more damage than three slats broken out of the cowcatcher, and one or two slight breakages.[30]

By May 1869 Currie had left the locomotive cabs to take over a business in Hays City. The *Leavenworth Times and Conservative* of June 4 announced: "Jim Curry, one of Forsyth's famous scouts, has now settled down to keeping a restaurant. His place is well patronized by day boarders, who appreciate his efforts to provide them good fare."

The establishment, called The Star, located at the corner of Fort and Main, appears to have offered patrons more than just a meal; Currie's partner in the management of the place was notorious madam Ida May, and presumably the service her girls provided was not limited to waiting on tables.

Not surprisingly, Ida May, who had managed brothels in other towns along the Kansas Pacific line, shared more than a business partnership with Currie; she shared his bed as well. Although Ida has been described as beautiful, talented, and well educated,[31] a Kansas newspaper would comment rather ungraciously that "her face was so homely it made her back ache to carry it."[32] The latter depiction is hard to accept, as Jim Currie was not the only man attracted to her and, according to several accounts, tangled with other men over her affections.

Currie and Ida May had barely taken over ownership of The Star when the place erupted in violence. On May 3 some black soldiers of the Thirty-eighth Infantry stationed at Fort Hays came to town, and Currie denied them access to his establishment. Outraged, they returned later with reinforcements, vowing, it was later claimed, to burn the place to the ground. In the ensuing battle — there were as many as five hundred shots fired — Currie was reportedly shot through the cheek and arm, deputy U.S. marshal and saloonkeeper Joe Weiss received a thigh wound, and four other civilians and soldiers were hit. That night a mob of townsmen, which may have included Currie, murdered two black residents of Hays City.[33]

Later newspaper accounts charged Currie with the murder of a black man named Snow (or Show).[34] After the killing, Currie allegedly placed the body of his victim in a dry goods box in front of his business establishment for passersby to view, remarking that there was now "one damn nigger less, anyway."[35]

Appearing about this time was a wildly erroneous newspaper story reporting Currie's death at the hands of a deserter from the Seventh Cavalry named Charles T. Brady.[36] A decade later, when it was obvious Currie was still around, a Hays City paper published a report that Brady, and not Currie, had been the murder victim. Currie, it said, had cut Brady's throat and tossed his body into a boxcar, where it was found later in Kansas City.[37]

This later story was closer to the truth. Brady was a discharged officer of the Nineteenth Kansas Volunteer Cavalry who had shot and killed the sergeant major of the regiment, George G. Gunning, at the Hays City depot. After the killing, he caught a train out of town, but returned later. When he was apprehended in the act of holding up the saloon of W. H. H. McCall, a vigilance committee, which may well have included Currie, decided to get rid of him. Heeding his anguished pleas not to hang him, the vigilantes beat him about the head, stabbed him, shot him once in the thigh, slashed his throat with a hatchet, and, to avoid having to dig a grave, tossed his lifeless body into an eastbound boxcar.[38]

Currie allegedly killed a young man named James Estes, who, it was said, "incurred [his] displeasure by too great an intimacy with Ida May."[39] Meeting Estes on the street, Currie reportedly attacked him. The youth pleaded for his life, "but the villain, deaf to such appeals, placed a revolver to the boy's breast and sent a bullet through his heart, stepped over his dead body and walked away."[40]

Apparently to make Currie's alleged crime appear even more barbaric, Estes was described in this account as a "quiet, inoffensive youth," but one researcher has noted that James Estes was less than a model citizen, having been twice hauled into police court at Leavenworth several months earlier, charged with drunkenness, disturbing the peace, and carrying a deadly weapon.[41]

Other undocumented stories allege that during his stay in Hays City, Currie killed several men in separate shooting affairs. He reportedly killed his own bartender,[42] and gunned down a man named Bob Gillman in a dispute over a card game, shooting "him through the teeth, so that the ball came out the back of his head."[43]

In an article in the *Denver Field and Farm*, a writer forty-five years later described "a street duel" involving Currie and former fellow scout William H. H. McCall, who was running a saloon in Hays City at this time. The affair, according to this completely undocumented tale, took place before a large crowd outside the Star Restaurant. McCall and Currie "began popping at each other. . . . They were both good shots and when the smoke of battle wafted it was found by the resuscitating committee that McCall had been plunked two times while Curry had three holes in his hide. . . . Neither was killed but both were more or less mutilated and never looked the same thereafter."[44]

Whether these stories had any basis in fact is difficult to determine now, but there is no doubt that violence was rampant in Hays City during the period of Currie's stay. For example, on July 23, 1869, saloon man Joe Weiss, a one-time state penitentiary inmate, former deputy U.S. marshal, and unsuccessful candidate for county sheriff, was shot dead by Alonzo B. "Ab" Webster. Weiss had been deemed an "undesirable" by the local vigilance committee, and Webster, a leader in the association, had delivered the message ordering Weiss out of town. When Weiss objected, Webster jerked a pistol and "shot him through the bowels." Weiss's companion in that altercation, Samuel O. Strawhun, a saloon hanger-on, was also ordered to leave. Ignoring the demand, he fell victim two months later to Wild Bill Hickok's unerring aim.[45]

However many Jim Currie may have contributed to the death toll at Hays City, he is best remembered today for the man he did *not* shoot. Cock of the walk in Hays City was the celebrated James Butler "Wild Bill" Hickok, recently elected Ellis County sheriff and Hays City town marshal. Since the publication of a glowing article extolling his exploits by George Ward Nichols in *Harper's New Monthly Magazine* in 1867, Hickok had gained national celebrity as the premier pistoleer of the plains.

Late-nineteenth-century newspaperman E. D. Cowan, who made a point of following the careers of salty western characters like Hickok and Jim Currie, wrote that "Curry at one time was reckoned among the bravest of the happy bad men of the Kansas frontier," and that he became "the peace-loving protégé" of Hickok and John Malone, Wild Bill's partner, but he "sort of went bad when he got beyond the pale of their influence."[46]

At least one newspaper reported that in the Kansas railroad towns, Currie "became identified with the 'Wild Bill' gang."[47] An early Hickok biographer disagreed with that characterization, saying Currie was "a reckless and dangerous man and the enemy of Wild Bill by instinct."[48] But whether Hickok and Currie were ever close or allied, they quickly became adversaries when Hickok took a shine to Ida May, Currie's paramour.

C. J. Bascom, who was also at Hays City, gave an eyewitness account of what then transpired. He had gone into Currie's place, Bascom said, to have a meal. When he finished, Currie suggested they take a walk together. They strolled the streets for a time as Currie steeled himself, perhaps, for the confrontation he planned. Finally, they entered Tommy Drum's saloon, Hickok's favorite hangout.

The famous gunfighter, well known for always choosing a seat facing the door, for some reason was sitting at a table in Drum's with his back toward them. Seeing this, Currie wasted no time. Said Bascom:

> Curry slipped up behind and pressed his cocked revolver against [Hickok's] head, saying, "Now, you son of a gun! I've got you!" Bill did not move a muscle. He showed no concern. He realized his danger but said in a casual way, "Jim, you would not murder a man without giving him a show!" Jim replied, "I'll give you the same show you would give me, you long-haired tough!" Everyone present knew the peril in which Bill stood, and the suspense was awful. Tommy Drum's oath was "By the boot!" He was running about the saloon in great perturbation, exclaiming "By the boot! By the boot!" Bill was really the only cool, self-contained man in the room, and remarked, "Jim, let us settle this feud. How would a bottle of champagne all around do?" The manner in which Bill had taken the whole incident, and the unconcern with which he made this remark relieved the tension, and all burst out laughing. Tommy Drum opened a pint bottle of champagne for everyone present. Curry and Bill shook hands and the feud between them was over.[49]

So Jim Currie did not shoot Wild Bill Hickok in the back of the head at Hays City in 1869, as Jack McCall did so infamously at Deadwood, Dakota Territory, seven years later. But the noted scout Tom Ranahan quoted Hickok as saying, "Jim Curry was the only man he dreaded,"[50] and a newspaper would later assert that " 'Wild Bill,' the most desperate man in the Black Hills, and who was killed there, used to state that he was afraid of but one man, and he was Jim Currie."[51]

Some time late in the year 1869 Currie quit Hays City. Perhaps like the late Joe Weiss, he had been deemed "undesirable" by the town's vigilance committee. He returned to work on the railroad, running the locomotive of a construction train between Ellsworth and Junction City.[52] By this time he had already become a legendary figure in that part of Kansas. Adolph Roenigk, who would later write a history of Kansas, was a young track worker laboring near Hays City in 1869 and remembered hearing the lurid accounts of Currie's exploits. At that time and place, said Roenigk,

> there were many hard characters who were "bad" simply for the glory of it. They found the new west a good place in which to give reign to their vicious tendencies and yet escape the consequences through sheer bravado. As a bad man, Jim Curry was one of the most notorious of that time. . . . It was said of him he had killed more than a dozen persons. We had heard so much about him that the first time his train came to our station to take water [my friend] Cook and I made a pretense of having some business about the engine, just to get a look at him. On our way back to our dugouts Cook remarked, "I would not be afraid of him."[53]

Cook may have been unimpressed by the ordinary-appearing man-killer, but as the attractions of booming Ellsworth drew Currie back to the fast life of saloons, bagnios, and gambling deadfalls, more stories were related of his bloodletting.

At Ellsworth, he is said to have gotten into a squabble with the brother of his Civil War company commander and killed him. Then, in January 1870, at a dance hall run by the rowdy ones Joe and Kate Lowe, he reportedly went on a drunken rampage, shooting two men and two women, killing two of them outright.[54] In another version of this tale, he "quarreled with his mistress, killed her and two men beside."[55] Two of the women said to be mortally wounded in this bloody affair were prostitutes Het and Nettie Baldwin, but Het survived and later told Cal Bascom that a man named Henry Whitney had shot her at Ellsworth.[56]

Most of the stories agree that the Ellsworth vigilance committee was moved to action by Currie's violent behavior. "To rid the world of the red-handed fiend, [the vigilantes] permitted him to ride out of the state in his water-tank, with his head only above the water."[57]

Several Kansas papers in October 1870 reported that Currie had again attacked women, shooting his former mistress Ida May and a woman named Vina Knapp in Wichita.[58] This was apparently another of the unfounded tales that seemed to attach themselves to Currie, and its authenticity was vehemently denied in an editorial in a Wichita paper:

> We copy elsewhere, from the *Emporia News*, *Topeka Commonwealth* and *Leavenworth Bulletin*, what purports to be accounts of the murder in this city of two courtesans by the notorious Jim Curry. The story originated in Emporia . . . and is the most insane and driveling attempt to create sensation out of nothing we ever came across. . . . This story of Jim Curry killing two women here is the most stupid lie of all the lies told by some citizens of Emporia to direct trade and travel from [Wichita] and throw it to Arkansas City, every lot of which is owned by Emporia men. . . . The story of the killing of Ida May and her girl here [is] a miserable and malicious lie. Ida May lives in Emporia and keeps a fancy house in that delectable burg. Jim Curry never was in this city.[59]

Whatever the truth of the repeated reports of the shooting of women by Currie, the very allegation disturbed nineteenth-century Kansans, many of whom otherwise totally ignored stories of hardened men gunning down each other in the rough border towns. In recounting several of these Currie stories, a Leavenworth newspaper opined:

> Jim Curry, who has lately shot two girls at Wichita, is deserving of some notice, not so much because he is a ruffian, but because the law should in some way be agitated so that he be brought to justice. There are lots of ruffians in the border

towns, but we cannot now bring to mind any man who has shot many women without in some way being called to account. The general plea if a man is killed is that there was provocation, or if there was no provocation, that he was a bad character anyhow, and that the community was no worse for the loss. . . .

We are not in a position to give any evidence as to any of the murders which Jim Curry is said to have committed, and for anything we know he may have killed all his victims, women included, in self defense. We only know that he has, in our opinion, killed an excess of antagonists within a very limited period, and we think that it is possible he has extinguished some of them under circumstances which should be the matter of judicial enquiry.[60]

The sensational reports of Currie's sanguinary exploits were picked up and copied in the eastern press, which elicited the following tongue-in-cheek response from another Leavenworth periodical:

The latest reports about Jim Curry in the Eastern papers lead us to believe that he has killed about thirty-one persons, with four or five counties yet to hear from that gave large majorities last year.

Perhaps it would be well for these Eastern editors to be informed that Western men are perfectly competent to supply the demand for border fictions and that when we send them anything startling they can stake all they have that the thing won't bear any more pressure than we give it. Western editors are not so devoted to bare and stupid facts as a great many people seem to think.[61]

At the base of all of this smoke there must have been some fire. Currie no doubt shot some people in Ellsworth and Hays City — including women, it would seem from the recurring accusation — but the tally of his victims grew like toadstools in the retelling. By 1879 a newspaper would state that "the villain has murdered his men into the teens."[62]

On April 12, 1870, Jim Currie, apparently having his fill of the Sunflower State, gave power of attorney to William M. Curry,[63] a lawyer of Leavenworth, to dispose of his property in Hays City, and disappeared from Kansas. He next turned up in Memphis, Tennessee, following his old trade as a locomotive engineer. He is said to have worked for the Memphis and Charleston; the New Orleans, St. Louis and Chicago; and the Little Rock railroad companies.[64]

By 1873 he was in Texas, working as an engineer for the Texas Pacific Railroad.[65] If a story published in a Kansas paper many years later can be believed, in Texas he resumed his lethal ways. F. M. Lockard, writing in the *Goodland News-Republic* in 1927, said: "At one time the railroad tried the experiment of using colored men for fireman. Curry announced that if they ever sent a 'nigger' out with him he would kill him. Sure enough, a 'nigger' was sent. Curry killed him, then put the body in the fire box of the engine and consumed it. He boasted of this but was never arrested for it. Killing negroes was not considered criminal in Texas at that time."[66]

Lockard lost much of his credibility when he added that this murderous engineer was later killed in a railroad wreck at Troup, Texas, and buried at Tyler, assertions known to be untrue about *this* Jim Currie. Perhaps the story related to another of the railroading Jim Currys, or perhaps it had no basis in fact at all.

When the Kansas Pacific Company experienced a high incidence of car and station thievery, Currie was removed from his engineer's cab and assigned the job of railroad detective to handle the problem. By all accounts his tough, hard-handed approach achieved satisfactory results, and company officials were pleased with their choice.

On April 4, 1878, members of the notorious Sam Bass gang held up a Texas Pacific train at Eagle Ford, Texas, and lawmen of all stripes converged on the area to engage in the hunt for the outlaws. Detective Jim Currie, who was reputed to know Sam Bass by sight, was called upon to assist. The next day he and Texas Express detective Sam Finley led a posse that included telegraph operator Ed Smith and former Dallas policeman William Edwards. They followed the trail of the bandits to a farm some three miles from Denton, where they found several horses tied outside. As the posse cautiously approached the building, two men, who it was later determined were gang members Frank Jackson and Harry Underwood, began shooting at Currie, who returned the fire. No one was hit in the exchange, and Finley called out to Currie, asking if either of the men was Sam Bass. He replied that they were not and the posse withdrew, allowing the two men to escape.[67] Thus Currie missed his opportunity to be a Texas hero, rather than the villain he was about to become.

On March 19, 1879, Currie was in Marshall, Texas, a station on the Texas Pacific Railroad. Following the events transpiring that night, he burst on the national scene, and his name became known across America.

The Warde-Barrymore Combination, a touring theatrical troupe, had a one-show engagement at Mahone's Opera House in Marshall on March 19, presenting the play *Diplomacy* by the popular French dramatist Victorien Sardou. Advertisements and broadsides proclaimed it "a play of powerful interest and novel construction, produced by a magnificent cast of characters, and received everywhere with most flattering attention by the public and greeted by the press with recognized encomiums, which stamp it at once as The Greatest Play of the Day." Featured thespians with the company were Maurice Barrymore, a partner of Frederick B. Warde in the Warde-Barrymore Combination; Benjamin C. Porter; Ellen Cummins; Barrymore's brother-in-law, Jack Drew; Josephine Baker; Mrs. E. F. Baker; and Harry Rees Davies.

The company concluded its performance that night about eleven o'clock and then had a three-hour wait to catch the train to Texarkana, the next engagement. Two of the male members of the cast, Maurice Barrymore and Ben Porter, took advantage of the time to investigate the recreational facilities available in the town at that late hour. They could not imagine they were about to be principal actors in a real-life drama rivaling anything they had ever portrayed on the stage.

Maurice Barrymore had arrived in that small western frontier town by a very circuitous route. He was born Herbert Blythe in an old dungeon room at Fort Agra, India, in 1847. The son of a British diplomat, he was educated at Harrow and Oxford, where he studied law. A handsome, athletic young man, he took up boxing. In 1872 he won the Queensbury Cup and claimed the amateur middleweight championship of England. When he lost interest in the law, he emigrated to the United States in 1875, adopted the name Maurice Herbert Barrymore,[68] and began a career on the American stage. In 1876 he married Georgiana Drew, a woman from a well-known theatrical family. The marriage would produce three leading stage personalities in America — Lionel, Ethel, and John Barrymore — and provide the beginning of a Barrymore theatrical dynasty that continues to this day.[69]

Benjamin C. Porter was thirty-seven, a native of Massachusetts, and a Union veteran of the Civil War. He was in the process of divorcing his wife and was planning on marrying the actress Ellen Cummins after his divorce was final.

Finding the gambling house of a man named Norton open, the two actors entered and ran into Jim Currie, who said he was looking for someone to join him in a friendly game of cards. Barrymore and Porter obliged, and when they got up from the table some time later, saying they wanted to get a bite to eat before catching the three o'clock train, they had relieved Currie of some $30. Although he had been drinking and growing increasingly querulous as his bankroll shrank, Currie said he would accompany the actors to the White House, a combination restaurant and saloon adjoining the railway station.[70]

The White House, open around the clock, was deserted at that early morning hour, except for the proprietor, Nathaniel A. Harvey. The three men entered the restaurant section, separated from the saloon area by a screen. The counter, backed by a long mirror, extended the length of the room, passing past the screen to serve as a bar in the saloon.[71] Shortly after they arrived, Barrymore disappeared for a few moments and returned with Ellen Cummins, who had been waiting with the rest of the company at the depot. The three show people had a light lunch together while Currie, restless and irritable, wandered back and forth between the restaurant and the saloon. At one point he also ordered a lunch. His remarks, as later reported by Harvey,[72] seemed to be completely irrational. When he paid for the lunch and Harvey tendered change, Currie growled, "Keep that. Don't you want to buy a dog?" He then walked into the saloon area, called for a glass of ice water, and added, "I guess I had better take a little budge [shot of liquor] with it."

Harvey warned him to go slow, that he had enough to drink, but Currie insisted. "No, I must have some," he said. "It is too good a thing around here."

Harvey poured a shot. Currie tossed it down and, pointing to the lunch room, made a vulgar comment about the woman seated there.

"Jim," Harvey remonstrated, "you don't know whether she is a lady or not; she has behaved herself, and I would rather you wouldn't make any such remarks."

"That's all right, partner," Currie responded. He then walked back into the lunchroom. As he passed Porter he turned and spoke sharply: "You threw up your hand this way when I passed you awhile ago. You can't give me any guff of that kind."

"My friend," Porter responded, "if you alluded to me, I hadn't thought of you; I was talking to this lady here."

But Currie was obviously spoiling for a fight. "If you say that," he snapped, "you are a damned liar."

Porter rose to his feet. "I'm in company with a lady and would prefer you wouldn't make remarks of that kind in her presence," he said calmly, "and if you want a difficulty you can see me anywhere you like outside the house."

"Damned fine lady!" Currie spat, and repeated his vulgarity.

Nat Harvey, seeing the situation escalating rapidly, cried, "Jim, Jim, stop that," and began to climb over the counter.

Maurice Barrymore also stood up. The former boxer quickly pulled off his coat, raised his clenched fists, and assumed the prizefighter's stance. "Go away," he told Currie. "There's a lady here."

As Porter hurriedly rushed Ellen Cummins from the room, Currie whirled on Barrymore. "Maybe you want to take it up, you damned son-of-a-bitch!" he roared.

"I will protect a lady anywhere," Barrymore replied gallantly.

"What are you going to do about it?" sneered Currie, as he drew two pistols from under his coat.[73]

"I'm unarmed," Barrymore said quickly, "but if you will lay down those pistols and come outside with me, I'll give you a chance to find out what I'm going to do about it."

Currie then opened fire. A bullet struck Barrymore in the upper right arm, passed through the muscle, and entered his chest.

Barrymore staggered out of the lunchroom into the saloon. Currie snapped off another shot, hitting him in the heel of his boot. Barrymore continued on through a doorway and collapsed near a water barrel. A third shot from Currie missed his target and struck the barrel.

Porter, at the door of the lunchroom, was shouting at Currie not to kill an unarmed man. Currie swung around and dropped him with a single shot to the stomach. "God damn you!" he bellowed, "I can kill the whole lot of you!"

As Ellen Cummins knelt sobbing by the side of her husband-to-be, other members of the stage company came running from the Texas Pacific waiting room. Stepping over the body of his victim lying in the doorway, Currie paced up and down outside, firing his two pistols into the air and vowing drunkenly that he would not be arrested.

In a highly exaggerated story, a newspaper said that Currie, "not content with the hellish work already done, . . . began firing with both hands, first at one of the ladies, whom he fortunately missed, and then at a little boy, whom he also missed. Then, rushing out of the restaurant, he opened fire at several people on the platform."[74]

This same paper in another issue said that after shooting Porter, "Currie fired at Miss Cummins with both pistols, and missing her, advanced and placed the muzzles of both weapons to her bosom. The afrightened woman shrank back and evaded the deadly discharge. The brute then turned and fired several times at a boy, and then at someone else; and then when he saw no one else he decided to murder, to show his utter lack of feeling walked up to a dog lying on the floor and stamped his head."[75]

This was typical of some of the distorted press coverage in the days following. The *Daily News* of Denison, Texas, for instance, reported erroneously that the altercation took place in the Texas Pacific sitting room, where Currie, "in a beastly state of intoxication," insulted "the wife of Mr. Barrymore." When Barrymore "gave the rowdy a well-merited thrashing," he left and returned with a loaded revolver and shot Barrymore, "wounding him it is thought fatally." Porter was "instantly killed" by another shot. "Not satisfied with two victims, Currie fired again and wounded a third party . . . , inflicting a wound which will probably cause his death."[76]

Clifton Seymour, who was a youngster in Marshall in 1879, claimed to have witnessed the shooting. In an account written more than fifty years later, he said that "Currie put up his gun, and taking hold of Miss Cummings [*sic*], jollied her around with a drunken air of braggartism."[77]

Station agent R. W. Johnson took charge of the wounded men and with the aid of others carried them to the Depot Hotel, where they were attended by Drs. Elan Johnson and B. F. Eads. There was no saving Porter; he died in excruciating pain within forty minutes.

The doctors found that Barrymore's shoulder blade was broken. They surgically removed the bullet and stemmed the bleeding. When they presented the patient with the extracted slug, he said, "I'll give it to my son, Lionel, to cut his teeth on."[78]

Meanwhile a crowd of some forty people gathered in the street outside the depot and watched as the Texarkana train came and went without the Warde-Barrymore troupe while Jim Currie strutted around the platform, waving his pistols, and defying anyone to arrest him. No one seemed anxious to take on that job, even Harrison County Sheriff Solomon R. Perry. The sheriff sent for his best deputy, Arch Adams, "one of the bravest men that ever wore shoe leather," according to Clifton Seymour, and delegated the task to him. Adams loaded a shotgun "with about fourteen buckshot in each barrel, put on a fresh pair of caps, and went to the depot to disarm Currie and bring him to jail. . . . Currie gazed at the determined and steel-blue eyes of Adams and his drunken air of grandiloquence disappeared."[79] Adams took the suddenly subdued Currie into custody without incident and locked him up in the county jail.

The story went out on the news wires, and soon the shootings in Marshall provided front-page articles in newspapers across the country. Said the *Waco Telephone*:

> Currie's pistol shots, fired at Marshall last week, re-echoed throughout the Union. The smoke that betokened the murder of an unoffending man had scarcely died away, ere the telegraph wires were bearing the tidings north, east, south and west. The great metropolitan papers of New York, Philadelphia, Chicago, St. Louis, and even San Francisco, laid the details of the murder in a few hours after it happened. . . . So brutal was the murder, so notorious had the wires made its details that the Union took a spell and turned for a look at Texas. The response in this State was prompt and proper. From press and people went a shudder of horror at the crime that had stained our soil. Texas disowns Currie, and the friends and companions of the murdered man have been afforded every possible evidence of the detestation entertained for the deed, and the sympathy felt for the dead and those who mourn.[80]

The reaction in the Texas press was almost universally similar to that of the *Waco Telephone*. The *Marshall Messenger* called the shooting "a most unprovoked, dastardly, cowardly murder,"[81] while the *Mar-*

shall Tri-Weekly Herald found it "gratifying to state that Currie is not a Texan, not a Southern man. Like three-fourths of the murderers that have disgraced our State, he comes from abroad."[82]

In an editorial on March 23, four days after the shooting, editor Buckley B. Paddock of the *Fort Worth Daily Democrat* stated unequivocally that Currie and his kind should be lynched. In later accounts the paper referred to Currie as "the red-handed murderer" and "the desperado who so wantonly murdered the actor, Ben C. Porter."[83]

The *Daily Democratic Statesman* of Austin castigated the Texas Pacific Railroad for hiring Currie. "The brutal detective, accustomed to wear arms and thus to contemplate murder," it said, "snatched out of this coward's pocket on the hip the fatal repeater and a bullet was dispatched on its errand of death. . . . The wonder is expressed that a great railroad company that has been nourished so well by Texas should give employment in our midst to such a brute."[84]

Papers nationwide gave the case featured coverage over the following months and commented in like vein.

The editor of the *St. Louis Globe-Democrat* noted that Currie had already killed four men without punishment, and the chances were good that he would again escape unscathed. It is, he opined, "to be greatly regretted that some enterprising citizen of Marshall did not fill the miscreant full of buckshot as a reward for his crime."[85]

The *Atlanta Constitution*, quoting the *Memphis Avalanche*, called Currie "the able professor of hip-pocket languages in the Texas college of murderers" who had relieved Porter "of the cares and responsibilities of life."[86]

Many predicted Currie would never be punished for his crime. Said the *New Orleans Picayune*: "When Jim Currie murdered Porter he killed an unarmed man, but he will doubtless be able to show by witnesses who were not there that he did it in self defense."[87]

"Jim Currie, the Texas murderer, will doubtless be turned loose again," said the *Chicago Tribune*. "The only thing to do, perhaps, is to quarantine against him."[88]

Texas, already notorious for its gunfighters, vigilante actions, and bloody feuds, came in for some criticism, especially in New York City press. The *New York Telegram* suggested the affair would "teach actors to omit Texas in future tours," and the *New York Sun* urged that

Texans should never be permitted to carry pistols after this unfortunate affair.[89] But a writer for the *Spirit of the Times* spoke out in the defense of Texas and Texans:

> We have been astonished at the various morals deduced from this sad affair. There has been some loud talk of lynching, broiling over slow fires, and otherwise mutilating the murderer; but the talkers have kindly concluded to permit the law to take its course, and Jim Currie will probably hang without the intervention of his New York denouncers. . . .
>
> If the whole party had been in any other state, or even in this blessed city of New York, precisely the same outrage would have occurred. If poor Porter and Barrymore had been tourists, traveling for pleasure, or businessmen returning from an inspection of stock farms, they would have been shot at just the same. There was nothing peculiar to Texas, or to the theatrical profession, in the affair.
>
> We have, unfortunately, plenty of drunken ruffians, armed with pistols, right here in New York. We can count up our Jim Curries by the score. There is scarcely a theatre, hotel, or saloon from Central Park to the Battery, the floor or the threshold of which is not stained with blood. There is scarcely a theatrical company or a theatrical audience assembled in this city which does not contain at least one person known to have killed his man or his wife, or notorious as having been accessory to the killing.
>
> Think over the facts, gentlemen, before casting the next stone at Marshall, Texas.[90]

A coroner's inquest was held on March 21. Barrymore, still in a critical condition, could not testify, and Ellen Cummins, "prostrated from excitement," was not in attendance. After listening to the testimony of Nat Harvey, the only other witness to the shooting, the coroner's jury concluded that Currie had committed "an unprovoked and cowardly murder."[91]

Shortly after the news of the shooting had gone out across the country, a battery of lawyers assembled in Marshall to conduct Currie's defense. Currie's brother, Andrew,[92] the mayor of Shreveport, Louisiana, sixty miles to the east, arrived by train with M. and M. S. Crain, the best criminal attorneys of Caddo Parish. The counsel for the Texas Pacific Railroad, James H. Turner of the Turner and Lipscomb law firm, was on hand, as was Alexander Pope, a Marshall attorney.[93]

A reporter for the *Marshall Tri-Weekly Herald* visited Currie in jail, where he was housed in a cell next to that of another prominent defendant, Abe Rothschild, scion of a wealthy Cincinnati family who was under indictment for the murder of "Diamond Bessie," his common-law wife, at Jefferson, Texas, three years previously. A *Herald* photographer took a picture of the two accused murderers; both were well dressed and looked supremely confident. To the reporter, Currie expressed "no regret at what he had done, but alleged that he had been insulted and he only regretted that he had not killed the whole party."[94]

On Monday, March 24, Harrison County Attorney W. H. Pope held an investigation into the affair before referring it to the grand jury. Currie, brought from the jail, waived examination, and the state introduced testimony from Harvey, H. Rees Davies, and Ellen Cummins, who had presumably recovered enough of her composure to appear.

Georgiana Barrymore arrived in Marshall on March 21 and helped nurse her husband until he had recovered sufficiently to travel. The two left for the East on April 15.

The grand jury on May 5 brought an indictment for first-degree murder against Currie, and the trial was set for June 17 in the district court. Extended hearings in the Rothschild case delayed the Currie trial a few days, but on June 23 Barrymore arrived, evidently fully recovered from his injuries. Cummins, still "very ill and laboring under severe mental and physical prostration," did not appear on the advice of her doctors, but sent a deposition. Nat Harvey had left town, and his whereabouts was unknown. Lawyers for the state and defense agreed on a request for a continuance, which was granted by Judge A. J. Booty. "This reminds me of our performance in England," Maurice Barrymore remarked to the judge, "We commence with a tragedy and end with a farce." Judge Booty had no comment.[95]

As they were leaving the courtroom, W. W. Spivy, of the district attorney's office, told Barrymore they were all fortunate the continuance had been granted. "Just as well the trial was continued," he said. "There are so many of Currie's stamp in the town and vicinity it was not possible to impanel a decent jury. The first panel contained no fewer than eleven murderers."[96]

When rumors spread that Booty was about to release the prisoner from custody on a habeas corpus appeal, the editor of the *Tri-Weekly Herald* expressed outrage. Since it is evident, he said, "that the courts of Marshall have determined to turn Currie loose, the citizens of that town could not make a better investment than to buy a strong rope and organize themselves into a vigilance committee and hang Currie on one end and that cowardly judge on the other."[97]

The case was continued again in the fall, when Harvey could not be located and returned to Marshall to testify. Currie's lawyers asked again for a habeas corpus hearing, and Currie appeared in court. Described by a court reporter as "neatly dressed, and looking well," he seemed not to have suffered from his months in confinement. The newsman thought him "a fine specimen of physical manhood [with] a good face [and] no appearance of the desperado."[98]

Finally, Harvey was tracked down and brought back to Marshall under arrest. The trial began on Thursday, June 10, 1880. W. W. Spivy and Major William Stedman represented the state. Currie's original battery of lawyers had been augmented by Major Crawford of Dallas and Judge Scay of Shreveport. Testifying for the state were Harvey; Barrymore; Cummins; Dr. Elan Johnson, who treated the victims; and Colonel T. E. Whitaker, who had witnessed Currie's rampage following the shootings. The defense called twenty-three witnesses.

Some time during the presentation of the state's case, it became apparent to the defense team that the ancient plea of self-defense would not work, so the argument was switched to a plea of insanity brought on by extreme intoxication. Testimony was concluded on Saturday, June 19, and closing arguments began immediately. William Stedman spoke for two hours, summing up the state's case, followed by James Turner and M. S. Crain for the defense. The jury listened carefully when, in his instructions, Judge Booty told them: "You are instructed if you believe from the evidence that at the time of the killing the defendant was laboring under *delirium tremens*, the remote cause was intoxication and be reason of so laboring under *delirium tremens* the defendant did not know he was doing wrong, then you should have acquitted the defendant on the grounds of insanity."[99]

The jury then retired to consider its verdict and, after only ten minutes of deliberation, returned. The foreman, T. A. Moore, announced to stunned spectators: "We the jury find the defendant not guilty on the grounds of insanity."

Judge Booty quickly ordered Currie released from custody and given over to the care of his brother, dismissed the jury, and declared court adjourned.

Editorial reaction to the verdict was irate and vehement.

Said the *Cincinnati Star*: "Currie is crazy. If any man cherishes an abiding faith in the intelligence of the jury it is Currie."[100]

The *Sherman Chronicle*: "The affront done to the peace of Texas by the endorsement of a jury of citizens of Texas, of the butcher Currie, will rebound to the eternal shame of this commonwealth."[101]

The *Dallas Herald*: "The result astounds this people, and disappointment sits on every brow, and is heard from nearly every tongue."[102]

The *Denison Herald*: "This news will not only startle but alarm people in this and other states. Life is not safe in Texas."[103]

The *Daily Arkansas Gazette*: "*What* a wretched farce our criminal prosecutions are getting to. . . . This verdict does great violence to the public sentiment of the people of Texas and disappoints public expectations. . . . It is a good thing for Currie that he didn't steal a 'two-bit Mexican pony.' If he had, the jury would have convicted him. It is all right to shoot a man, but you must not steal. Texas jurymen seem to have a very high idea of property and a very low idea of life. If the order were reversed, it would be much better for Texas."[104]

The *Dallas Times*: "The jury of Harrison County, be it remembered, announced to the world that there are moments in intoxication when the intoxicated man has a right greater than all sober men; the right to shoot down whomever he sees fit."[105]

Editorial remarks in the *Galveston News* were most intemperate. After the Currie acquittal, it said, "Law-abiding men will have to shoot such a man down like a rabid dog."[106]

Many in Marshall and around the state voiced their belief that in order to bring in such an unpopular verdict so quickly, the jury had to have been bribed. Typical was the comment of Henry Greenwald, manager of the Tremont Opera House in Galveston: "The acquittal is due entirely to the jury, who were most unquestionably bribed. . . . In order that a verdict of not guilty might be had, Currie's brother, the Mayor of Shreveport, has expended almost his entire fortune."[107]

Apparently, there was some circumstantial evidence to support this suspicion. One of the prosecution lawyers told newsmen that "money was probably used with the jury." He said that a Marshall merchant was willing to testify that the night of the acquittal, one of the jurors bought a quantity of goods in his store "without as much as asking the price," and pulled out "large rolls" of five- and ten-dollar bills to make payment. Another juror got a shave in a barbershop that evening and paid with a ten-dollar bill from "a roll of greenbacks he took from his side pocket." Another merchant reported that "an hour after Currie's acquittal, one of the jurors, purchasing some candy and other notions, offered in payment a $10 greenback" he peeled off a large roll of bills. This juror was quoted as saying he had not been on the jury "for nothing; that he made all these $10 bills during that time."[108]

In a letter to the editor of the *Marshall Messenger*, however, juror John Park defended the jury and its verdict. "I will attest to my fellow citizens of Harrison county and of Texas," he said, "that we did what we thought was just, both to the State and defendant. Both the defendant and his victim were strangers to us, and we acted just as we would do again with the same evidence and law before us, and we cannot see wherein our county or State can be injured by the acquittal of Currie."[109]

Andrew Currie lost no time in removing his brother, adjudged insane, from the state of Texas and taking him to the Currie home in Shreveport.[110] How long Jim remained there is not known. Ten months passed before we next hear of him in the press. Then, in early April 1881, a report went out on the wires that he had been shot to death in Albuquerque, New Mexico.

The *Fort Worth Daily Democrat* welcomed the news: "The notorious Jim Currie whom the courts of this state refused to punish has met his death by the same weapon with which he took the life of his victim at Marshall. It is a consolation to know that justice has overtaken this red-handed murderer in some shape."[111]

"Jim Currie is dead," said the *St. Louis Republican*. "Jim died in a saloon at Albuquerque, N.M., yesterday, after having been perforated by a bullet from a saloon-keeper's revolver. . . . A jury acquitted Currie on account of his 'sanity,' but as everybody expected, he finally ran against a man who would take none of his nonsense."[112]

Had Jim Currie been as witty as Mark Twain, he might have said, "The reports of my death are greatly exaggerated." The reported shooting did not take place in Albuquerque, and the victim was not Jim Currie of Kansas and Texas notoriety, but James H. Curry, another railroad man, who on March 23, 1881, was shot and killed by Joseph Enright (or Ebright), bartender in Bertha's Parlor Saloon, a house of ill repute in Las Vegas, New Mexico.[113]

Many papers that had printed the false report did not later correct the error. The *Fort Worth Daily Democrat* was an exception, inserting a single line, albeit regretfully, in an issue a few days later: "It wasn't Jim Currie of the insanity dodge who murdered the actor Porter, but another desperado who died with his boots on at Las Vegas a short time since."[114]

In 1881 Currie reportedly was at Durango, Colorado, involved in some kind of mining operation. Never long away from the railroad, in 1882 he surfaced in New Mexico towns along the new line of the Atchison, Topeka and Santa Fe. At San Marcial, he held positions as city marshal and Socorro County deputy sheriff.[115]

According to Chester D. Potter, an editor at the *Socorro Sun* during this period, Currie's reputation as "a fearless individual" got him the city marshal position at San Marcial. "He certainly was a wonderful shot," Potter remembered. "In order that his supremacy might not be disputed, [Currie] was in the habit of standing with his back to a tent pole, walking from it a distance of ten paces, drawing his revolver and shooting over his shoulder, placing three of six bullets in the four-inch wooden pole. He was as quick on 'the draw' as any of the territorial terrors, with the possible exception of 'Billy the Kid.'" Potter implied that Currie's quickness and accuracy with his six-shooters resulted in a few deaths at San Marcial: "After several affairs in which the party of the second part was registered in a local burying-ground, [Currie] became nervous [and] resigned his position."[116]

There are no contemporary records of these shootings, however, and other reports had it that railroad men ran Currie out of town after he attempted to kill J. M. Buckley, another officer.[117]

Currie went north to San Antonio, another stop on the Atchison, Topeka and Santa Fe, where he opened the Mountain Queen Saloon.

Again he became involved in a dispute that led to violence. According to one story, he became enraged at his bartender for spending his pay in a rival saloon, cracked a revolver barrel over the man's head, and fired several shots at him as he fled. The barkeep got a rifle and began pumping rounds into the saloon. Currie took refuge behind a whisky barrel and was only grazed by the barrage.[118]

Chester Potter left a different version of this shooting incident. A bunch of local cowboys, he said, enraged at losing their rolls at the "brace faro" tables in Currie's saloon, sent word from their camp that at a certain time they would ride into San Antonio and shoot up the Mountain Queen.

> Curley [Currie] thought this was a bluff. He was mistaken. This he realized when twenty or thirty range riders commenced to pump lead into his saloon. Gathering all his ammunition, he got behind a barricade of whiskey barrels and settled down for a siege. Knowing his cleverness with rifles and revolvers, the cowboys did not close in. Curley fired a shot now and then just to let them know he was still alive.
>
> Word of the battle reached Socorro and the sheriff sent a posse to rescue Curley. The cowboys did not interfere, and Curley was perfectly willing to leave.[119]

Returning to San Marcial, Currie opened another saloon and again accepted appointment as city marshal in August 1883.[120]

By 1884 he was spending a great deal of time in Socorro, where his hangout was Texas Ed's Saloon, the rendezvous of the proprietor, Ed Rousseau, "Colorado Charley" Utter, "One-Armed Jim" Reed, and other friends and supporters of Joel Fowler, a recently lynched rancher and gunman. In November 1883 Reed had purchased Fowler's ranch, an act that inadvertently precipitated the murder of an inoffensive drummer by Fowler and Fowler's own lynching death.[121] Colorado Charley, the compadre of Wild Bill Hickok, helped bury his friend after his 1876 assassination by Jack McCall. He and Jim Currie, who almost put out Hickok's light back in Hays City in 1869, must have had some fascinating discussions in Texas Ed's Saloon about the legendary gunfighter.[122]

The town's vigilance organization, proudly proclaiming itself the "Committee of Safety" but reviled as the "Socorro Stranglers" by its enemies, was still in a state of excitement and agitation over the Fowler lynching. The members watched Currie as he "strutted about town wearing two large six-shooters, drinking hard," and figured he was just another "undesirable" with whom they would have to deal. According to the story related by vigilance committee member Chester Potter, the problem of Jim Currie was handled for them by a local sign painter of diminutive proportions named Bob Sommerville and in a manner that was absolutely destructive of Currie's bad-man reputation. When the two met in a barroom, Currie, well in his cups, began to bully the little fellow and shove him around.

> In an instant Sommerville was all over him, smashing, clawing, and biting like a wildcat. He yanked [Currie's] two revolvers from their holsters, threw them on the floor, and continued his pommelling, which the big fellow apparently made no effort to resist. At last, realizing that neither a jab in the solar plexus nor a jolt to the jaw would bring down his man, Sommerville picked up the revolvers and told [Currie] to "hike" for the railroad, and [Currie] demurred not. A big crowd watched Sommerville march the bully to the station.[123]

After that humiliating experience, Currie quit the towns along the route of the Santa Fe. In June 1887 he showed up at White Oaks, a remote camp in Lincoln County, New Mexico, and took employment as an engineer at the North Homestake Company mill. He and a man named John W. Foley shared a cabin near the mill.[124] On February 21, 1888, he quarreled with Foley, and in one of the fits of rage to which he was subject, stabbed his roommate to death. Tried in September 1888 at the county seat at Lincoln, he entered a plea of not guilty be reason of self-defense. The jury did not believe him and found him guilty of murder in the third degree. Judge E. V. Long sentenced him to six years in prison, and he entered the territorial penitentiary at Santa Fe on September 17, 1888.[125]

The western press viewed the outcome of the trial with approval. Typical was a dispatch from Albuquerque:

> James Curry has been convicted at the Lincoln county court of the killing of Foley, at White Oaks, last winter, and his sentence to six years in the penitentiary ends for the time the public career of one of the most notorious criminals in the West. It was

he who killed Actor Ben Porter in the saloon row at Marshall, Texas, and he has figured in several other bad scrapes since his arrival in this country. He is a good engineer and was acting in that capacity for the North Home Stake company [*sic*] at White Oaks when he committed this last murder. He was gentlemanly and pleasant when sober and had many friends, but he was a riotous character when intoxicated.[126]

While still incarcerated, Currie applied for a pension from the U.S. government for his military service during the Civil War and as a scout in Kansas after the war. On May 17, 1890, he filed the application, claiming that at Antietam he had "lost the sense of hearing in his right ear, which loss was occasioned by concussion due to heavy artillery firing and the bursting of a shell in close proximity to his person." In addition, he said, he had contracted malarial fever, which had later developed into chronic kidney disease.[127]

Two months later, on July 22, 1890, he filed a duplicate application, and on February 5, 1891, perhaps at the request of the government, he underwent a physical examination by Dr. A. S. Frick, who found that Currie complained of deafness and rheumatism of the back caused by his war and scouting experiences, but, except for a slight deafness of one ear, Currie was "sound and healthy."[128]

The pension was not forthcoming, but efforts by Currie's influential brother, Andrew, to secure his release were successful. On March 27, 1891, New Mexico governor L. Bradford Prince granted Currie a pardon, and he walked out of the penitentiary.[129]

Governor Prince appended three conditions to the pardon: Currie's friends were to see that he got medical attention for his evident mental illness; they were to ensure that he would pose no further threat to the lives of innocent citizens; and he was to depart New Mexico Territory within ten days.[130] Currie agreed readily to these terms, but the only one he seems to have obeyed was the New Mexico departure admonition.

Currie spent the rest of his life in the Pacific Northwest. Writing in 1898 newspaperman E. D. Cowan said that the old "hero of the throttle . . . wandered around the mountain and Pacific coast country like a lost spirit, knocking at the walls of Paradise." In 1892 he "appeared like an apparition" at the Tacoma, Washington, rooms of John Malone, the old partner of Wild Bill Hickok back in Kansas days, and asked to borrow money. Currie may have returned to his railroad detective profession and engaged in further gunplay, for Cowan said that "while standing off train robbers and picking off men who thought themselves as desperate and clever with a six-chambered gun as he, Curry had the satisfaction of judicial duty well done."[131]

Currie reportedly lived for a time in Portland, Oregon, where he was a member of the Elks.[132] From 1895 to 1899, destitute and ailing, he lived in the home of Annie Sommert of Spokane, Washington, who cared for him on the promise of a forthcoming veteran's pension. When the pension was still not granted in early 1895, he filed a third application on March 10. This was followed up on July 6 by a letter written by a friend, W. H. Briggs of Spokane, and directed to President William McKinley. It pleaded for a monthly pension of $12 for Currie, who was impoverished, sick, and near death. "He can not live long and his case is justtable [*sic*] in the extreme."

On August 6 Currie completed another questionnaire, affirming that, having never married or fathered children, he had no immediate family. Another physical examination was ordered and conducted on August 23. Currie now claimed, according to the doctor's report, that he suffered from "deafness in both ears, weakness of vision, hernia in right groin, lumbago, and weakness of chest," and that he was "unable to do any work of any kind." Following the examination, the doctor confirmed there was "total deafness in right ear," and "direct inguinal hernia of right side," but that all other organs were normal, with no evidence of vicious habits.

Less than three weeks later, on September 11, 1899, one month before his fifty-eighth birthday, James Currie was dead. The following December Annie Sommert and her lawyer submitted a letter to the government requesting compensation for four years of boarding, nursing, and caring for Currie on the promise of a pension. Another letter was sent on July 14, 1900, but there is no record that a pension was ever approved.[133]

— 3 —

JACK WATSON
1843–1898

I killed at least six men since I rote [sic] you at Crested Butte a few years ago.

—John A. Watson, May 27, 1898

Cyrus Wells "Doc" Shores was one of the most outstanding lawmen of the frontier West. For more than thirty years he served as sheriff of Gunnison County, Colorado, deputy U.S. marshal, special investigator for railroad and express companies, and chief of police at Salt Lake City, Utah. In his long and eventful career, he knew and worked with many better-known frontier peace officers, including Wild Bill Hickok and Tom Horn. But none impressed him more than a tough Texan named John A. "Jack" Watson, whom he employed as a deputy when he was the chief law enforcement officer in the Colorado western slope county of Gunnison. Reckless, hard drinking, and hard fighting, Jack Watson, like many of his breed, had operated on both sides of the law, but when it came to a real showdown, he was a man upon whom Doc Shores could rely.

"During the time I was sheriff of Gunnison County, Colorado," Shores wrote in his memoirs, "I received a telegram from the Coroner of . . . the town of Crystal. . . . The Coroner said: 'Four men killed way up on the head of the muddy. Please come at once and bring several of your best men.' I turned round to old Jack Watson, an old deputy of mine, a man who had been shot and wounded several times and was willing to be shot at a few more times, and said: 'You are "several" of my best men, Jack.' "[1]

Born November 5, 1843, in Tennessee,[2] Jack Watson as a young man drifted into Texas and was there when the Civil War broke out. He was not yet eighteen when he enlisted in Company D, Ninth Texas Cavalry, the Ross Brigade, at Fort Worth in 1861.[3] On May 20, 1863, he joined Alexander Watkins Terrill's Thirty-fourth Texas Cavalry Regiment at Carthage with the rank of corporal.[4] Wounded several times during the war, the last and worst of his injuries was caused by a Yankee bullet that ripped through his foot, ended his military service, and crippled him for life.

The injury, Doc Shores remembered, "caused one leg to draw up crooked, crippling him, and making one leg much shorter than the other."[5] Watson limped badly the rest of his life, but in the saddle, with one stirrup pulled high to accommodate his shortened leg, he was a match for any rider. The disability may have served to heighten his pugnacious and aggressive nature. He was, as Doc Shores described him, an imposing figure of a man, "very well-built, large, square built, strong and quite muscular. His hair was very black, and his whiskers very long and black and came out very close under his eyes, which did not leave very much of his face in sight, as the cheeks and face were covered with a heavy growth of black whiskers. He had blue eyes, and was naturally a good looking man."[6]

Watson was a skilled blacksmith, a trade he probably learned in his years with the Confederate cavalry and perhaps accounted for his powerful upper body. After the war he practiced his trade off and on, but an innate combative temperament and love of adventure led him always back to work in law enforcement.

Little is known for certain regarding Watson's activities during the first decade following the Civil War. He may have been with the Hell-on-Wheels crowd, the motley group of whiskey sellers, gamblers, and prostitutes who followed the Union Pacific railroad construction crews from one end-of-track town to another. Veteran frontiersman and cattle rancher Ed Lemmon recalled that Watson was a prominent figure at Cheyenne, Wyoming, in 1867, when that town was the booming end of track and attracted gunmen by the droves, including Watson, who, Lemmon declared, was already recognized as one of the fastest and straightest shots on the frontier.[7] Based on his long experience, Lemmon would later list Watson as the six-shooter equal of much better publicized western figures Wild Bill Hickok, Bill Tilghman, "Bear River" Tom Smith, Wyatt Earp, Bill McDonald, Bat Masterson, Jim Bridger, and Kit Carson.[8]

The following year, when the tracks of the Union Pacific had extended beyond Cheyenne to a camp called Bear River City, Watson was a central figure in a famous shootout there, said Lemmon.

> The Bear River Riot was staged by Tom Smith who had some grievance at the town authorities and mounted a body of tie men (haulers) working for Coe & Carter and rode to town and . . . begun shooting at every town citizen who showed his head and Jack Watson, Coe & Carter night watchman, took charge and with the help of A. K. Beckwith, a splendid hunter and trapper, rallied the town element and vanquished Tom Smith and his adherents. As I recall, about 15 men were killed with about equal numbers on each side. Jack Watson at the time was conceded a superior shot to Wild Bill.[9]

Whether this gunman was the Jack Watson of this sketch is open to doubt. Because of the similarity of names, Lemmon may have confused Watson with gunman and outlaw Jack Watkins, who was active in Cheyenne, Laramie, and other Hell-on-Wheels towns during the railroad-building period.[10]

After the spring of 1874, the activities of John A. Watson become clearer. In response to continued Indian depredations and heightened outlaw activity in the northern counties of Texas during this period, Governor Richard Coke established the Frontier Battalion of the Texas Rangers under the leadership of Major John B. Jones. Six companies were formed. The first, Company A, with Captain John R. Waller commanding, began recruitment in May. One of the first to join Waller's company was John A. Watson, who on May 25 enlisted at Stephensville, Erath County.[11] It was a very large company; the muster payroll filed on that date enumerates three officers (Captain Waller and two lieutenants), twelve noncommissioned officers (six sergeants and six corporals), and fifty-two privates, a total of seventy-seven men in all.[12]

Captain Waller had hardly organized his company than he was ordered to Comanche County, where an outbreak of the long-developing Sutton-Taylor feud had erupted in new violence. On May 26, the day after Watson signed on with Company A, the notorious killer John Wesley Hardin gunned down Deputy Sheriff Charles Webb at the town of Comanche, and the entire area seemed about to explode in violence. Waller and fifty-five Rangers went to Comanche, arriving there on the 27th. They found that Hardin and most of his adherents had fled the town, but Waller arrested a number of the gunman's sympathizers, including his father and mother, his wife, and his brother.

"I commenced scouting at Comanche, Comanche County, the 28th day of May," Waller wrote in his monthly report. "Three fourths of my Command was kept in constant service until the 12th of June, during that time I made over twenty-two arrests. Seven of the Parties arrested I sent to DeWitt County, supposed to belong to John Wesley Hardin's gang of outlaws, the other Parties arrested I turned over to Sheriffs of different Counties."[13]

Jack Watson was a member of one of the scouting parties out searching for the wanted desperadoes. As reported in a Corsicana newspaper, this combined posse of sheriff's deputies and Texas Rangers located Ham Anderson and Alec Berekman, two Hardin cohorts, concealed in the brush about twelve miles north of Comanche. "They discovered each other about the same time," said the story, "and Anderson and Berekman opened fire upon the posse, who returned it, killing both desperadoes. . . . The killing of these two men was purely an act of self-defense, as they had evidently made up their minds to die rather than surrender."[14]

Captain Waller's report confirmed the story and identified Jack Watson as the slayer of one of the outlaws: "Barekman [*sic*] and Anderson, two of Hardin's [gang], fired on some of my men and several citizens. My men returned the fire, killing both Barekman and Anderson. . . . The Notorious Ham Anderson was killed by Private Watson of Co. A."[15]

Doc Shores first met Jack Watson later that year near Hays City, Kansas. After driving a small herd of Texas longhorn cattle to Kansas in 1871, Shores had remained in the area, buying and selling stock. One day in the fall of 1874, a lone stranger rode into his winter cow-camp on the Saline River. Introducing himself as Jack Watson, he inquired about a Williamson County, Texas, cattleman named J. C.

"Cul" Juvenall, whom he had trailed all the way from Texas.[16] While passing through the northern counties of the Lone Star State with a large herd of cattle bound for the Kansas markets, Juvenall and his cowboys had added fourteen head of loose horses to his remuda, and the owners had employed Watson to recover their missing stock. Shores shared a meal with his visitor and directed him to the Juvenall camp farther down the Saline.

About a week later Watson showed up again, this time driving the fourteen horses ahead of him. Stopping to thank Shores for his help in locating Juvenall, he spent several hours at the camp. He never explained how he single-handedly rescued the fourteen stolen horses from Juvenall's remuda, and Shores did not inquire, simply putting it down to what seemed quite obvious: Jack Watson was a singularly determined and intrepid man.

In a talkative mood, Watson regaled Shores with stories of his days in the Confederate cavalry and the Texas Rangers. Shores remembered one tale in particular, as it demonstrated Watson's tenacity and cold-blooded efficiency when on the trail of a wanted man.

Watson related how he had trailed a horse thief across northern Texas for many miles without food, and when he finally caught up with his quarry one morning, he was famished. He slipped up to the outlaw's camp to find him preparing breakfast. Watson watched, his mouth watering, as the smell of frying bacon drifted from the camp. When the bacon and biscuits were done and the coffee hot, Watson calmly shot the horse thief dead and then sat down by the body and ate the breakfast himself. "From the way he told it," Shores recalled, "I believed he had done just as he said he had. It was a very natural thing to do along in those years, in that country."[17]

Shores would not see Jack Watson again for ten years. During those years, Watson drifted throughout the northern counties of Texas. His game leg probably kept him from participating in the great buffalo hunt of the time, but he did make some money hauling hides at Fort Griffin.[18] He later returned to his blacksmith trade, working in that capacity for Charles Goodnight on the famous cattleman's JA ranch in the Texas panhandle.[19]

Like many tough frontier characters, Watson's weakness was alcohol. After taking on a load of tanglefoot whiskey, he often became belligerent and very dangerous. On one of these binges, he attacked a

Jack Watson. Drawing by Joan DeArment Hall from a photograph courtesy of Jane Watson Ellis.

man named Ab Griffin in Cooke County, Texas, on December 1, 1876. He was indicted in that county for assault with intent to murder on May 9, 1876, and his name began appearing on the fugitives from justice lists published by the Texas adjutant general's office.[20]

On August 1, 1878, Major John B. Jones wrote to Lieutenant G. W. Arrington, commander of Company C, Frontier Battalion, then stationed outside Fort Griffin, requesting information concerning his former Ranger:

> I wish you to ascertain from Joe Woods if J. A. Watson was with the party who escorted the prisoners from Comanche to DeWitt in 1874. His name was not given in the list you sent all though [*sic*] I am quite sure he was on the detail. If such was the case, ascertain if possible where he is now. This you can probably do at Griffin as he was there engaged in hauling hides the last I heard of him. Watson was a cripple and shod horses for the men. Your inquiries must be managed so as to create no suspicion that Watson or any of the rest are wanted. If Watson can be found I wish you to keep the run of him and Ables[21] as it is probable you will have papers for both of them before long.[22]

In April 1885 officers arrested and jailed a man named John Watson in Gainesville, Cooke County, charging him with the assault on Ab Griffin nine years earlier. In a letter to the district judge written from jail on May 14, 1885, Watson adamantly proclaimed his innocence. The letter was signed "J. T. Watson" and the handwriting was not at all similar to that of John A. Watson.[23] It seems the authorities had arrested and charged the wrong John Watson. They evidently realized their mistake eventually, for he was released and the case continued.[24]

By 1885 John A. Watson had long departed Texas. In February 1883 he showed up in Deming, New Mexico Territory, went on one of his alcoholic tears, got into a saloon brawl, and suffered another gunshot wound. "A woman was at the bottom of the trouble," remarked the editor of the *Lone Star* of El Paso.[25]

He recovered from this affair and a year later appeared in Montrose, a small town in a county of the same name on Colorado's western slope, where he again put on a display of drunken belligerence. Arriving in town on February 6, 1884, he left his horse, saddle, and six-gun at Dad Baird's livery stable and hobbled over to the nearest saloon to wet his whistle. In a few hours his whistle was more than saturated, and he was disturbing the tranquility of the town. The Montrose city marshal, a man named Murphy, arrested him and tossed him in the hoosegow to sober up overnight. In the morning, Marshal Murphy took Watson before a police magistrate and charged him with being a public nuisance. The justice found Watson guilty and asked him how much money he had in his possession.

"Eighty-five dollars," Watson replied.

"Then the fine will be eighty-five dollars," intoned the magistrate.

Watson considered the fine exorbitant for a common drunkenness misdemeanor and concluded the magistrate and the marshal had conspired to rob him. Retrieving his horse, saddle, and pistol from Baird's stable, he rode down the main street of Montrose, looking for the city officials. When he spotted the magistrate, he shot him through the side, inflicting a painful but not life-threatening wound. Hardly behaving like a valiant peace officer, Marshal Murphy ran before Watson's wrath and crawled under a board sidewalk. Bullets spattered all around him, wounding him slightly in the arm and heel. Watson rode to the end of the street, reloaded his revolver, and galloped back, firing indiscriminately. In short order the street was cleared.

The district judge, who happened to be in town at the time, was outraged and called on the citizens of Montrose to corral the wild man from Texas, but other than a few shots by townsmen from upstairs windows, no action was taken, and Watson rode off.

He had not escaped completely unscathed. Both he and his horse had received minor bullet wounds, but he made it back to his camp on Surface Creek in Delta County. Montrose officials posted a reward for his arrest, but no one appeared anxious to attempt collection of the bounty.[26]

A few weeks later Doc Shores, then sheriff of neighboring Gunnison County, rode into Montrose County, working another case. He had heard about the rampage recently staged by the wild Texan in Montrose and concluded from the description given that the perpetrator was the crippled Texas Ranger who had so impressed him years earlier in Kansas. When in the course of his investigation Shores inadvertently learned the location of Watson's camp, he thought it his duty to report the information to a fellow officer. On his way back home, Shores stopped in at Montrose and told Johnson, the county sheriff, what he had learned. But that officer was uninterested. "He said such a long time had gone by and the excitement had died down," Shores remembered, "and they would not pay the reward." Shores offered to go along to make the arrest, but nothing could change the sheriff's mind. It was obvious to Shores that Johnson had no desire to go after the Texas hellion. Shores shrugged and returned to Gunnison.[27]

But a tough character and notorious horse thief named Howard who had a cabin up in the mountains near Watson's camp was made of sterner stuff than the Montrose sheriff. Deciding that he would capture the wanted man and collect the reward, Howard set a trap. He invited Watson over to his cabin for Sunday chicken dinner. That sounded good to Watson. When he arrived at the Howard cabin, he found that in addition to Howard and his wife, another young man was also a dinner guest. As soon as the meal was finished, Howard and the other man suddenly jumped Watson. After a fearful struggle, they subdued him, bound his arms, and started with their prisoner for Montrose, about thirty-five miles away.[28]

During most of the trip, Watson was silent and seemingly resigned to his fate, but as the party crossed the Gunnison River in a small skiff, he suddenly threw himself violently about in an effort to overturn the boat and drown himself and his captors. After another struggle, the two bounty hunters managed to hold him down until they got across.

At Montrose, they turned their prisoner over to Sheriff Johnson and received the reward. Watson was convicted and sentenced to a few months in jail.[29]

Watson was out only a short time when he again got into trouble. He was among the Christmas celebrants at the flourishing mining camp of Crystal when the festivities turned ugly. During a saloon melee, he slashed another man across the midsection with a knife. The man's friends jumped in and beat Watson badly.

Crystal was in Gunnison County and therefore in Doc Shores's jurisdiction. Hearing about the cutting, Shores had his deputy in Crystal arrest the knife wielder and bring him to Gunnison. Watson was in bad shape from the beating. "His eyes were black and blue all round," Shores said. "I did not know him until he told me who he was, and then we had a sort of reunion."[30]

At a district court hearing, witnesses described the Crystal saloon ruckus as a general drunken brawl in which Watson was no more to blame than others involved. The man who had been cut recovered and did not press charges. Watson was released.[31]

Doc Shores saw an opportunity to help rehabilitate a man he had once admired and at the same time strengthen the sheriff's office by the addition of a fearless, resolute deputy. He offered Watson a job. Many eyebrows were raised when word got out that the sheriff had taken on a deputy most people believed was nothing but a drunkard and a troublemaker, but Shores was convinced Watson had once been a fearless, resolute officer of the law and could be again. Believing the man's good qualities outweighed his obvious weakness for alcohol, Shores was willing to risk his own reputation on that conviction.

Jack Watson worked as Doc Shores's chief deputy most of the eight years Shores held the office of Gunnison County sheriff and, as Shores himself was quick to admit, contributed greatly to his success. Responding to the faith and confidence Shores placed in him, Watson remained relatively sober and made an effort to stay out of trouble while serving as deputy.

He was not always successful. While on an assignment in Ogden, Utah, in June 1890, he had a bout with his old friend John Barleycorn. "John Watson, John Sutherland and Joe Lusk will each spend the next ten days in jail for imbibing too freely," noted the *Ogden Standard* for July 1, 1890.

But he quickly recovered, and his boss forgave him. It was only a month later that Shores received the message from the coroner at Crystal telling of the killings there and the urgent need for the sheriff and "several of his best men," and Shores's remark that Jack Watson *was* several of his best men.

The high esteem in which Watson was held by Doc Shores is all the more remarkable when one considers some of the other deputies the sheriff employed. Brothers Charlie and George Marlow, late of Texas, now living in Ouray, were two of the toughest and most courageous fighting men a lawman could hope to find. The story of how they had fought off a Young County, Texas, lynch mob back in 1889 while shackled to two dead brothers killed in the gun battle had gained for them nationwide celebrity. After the brothers relocated on Colorado's western slope, Doc Shores recruited them as deputies and called on them, as he did Jack Watson, for particularly difficult and dangerous assignments.

One such operation came about because of a strike of the miners at Crested Butte, a coal-mining town northwest of Gunnison. On December 11, 1891, Sheriff Shores received a telegram from William Grant, superintendent of the Colorado Coal and Iron Company at Crested Butte. It read: "Fans have been stopped by striking coal miners. Mines rapidly filling with gas. Explosion imminent which will blow up much of town as well as the mine. Your help needed immediately to protect life and property."[32]

Armed with a handful of warrants for the strike ringleaders, Shores immediately recruited a force of twenty-five special deputies, which included his "best gun fighters,"[33] Jack Watson and the Marlow brothers, and went to the scene of action. A Denver newspaper reported that Sheriff Shores arrived at Crested Butte with "such well known men as the Marlow boys of Telluride [sic], Colo., who are wanted in Texas but whom Governor [John L.] Routt refused to extradite, John Watson of western Colorado, who has the reputation of having killed several men and of having held up the town of Montrose, and several other well known gentlemen who are very handy with firearms in an emergency."[34]

When their train arrived in Crested Butte, Shores and his deputies walked from the depot into town through a hostile crowd lining both sides of the street. It was a tense situation, Shores recalled.

> We walked two abreast, each of us carrying a Winchester rifle. . . . My deputies and I held our rifles in both hands as we entered town, prepared for any emergency. . . .
>
> By this time nearly a thousand people lined the street watching our progress with interest. When we came to John Follette's saloon, I went inside, carrying my rifle in one hand and a warrant in the other. Follette was a prominent man about town, and the spectators for the first time began showing excitement. As they closed in around the posse to better see the show, Jack Watson and the Marlow boys raised their guns and ordered the onlookers back.[35]

One by one the warrants were served, and Shores and his deputies returned to Gunnison with a number of prisoners. There had been a few anxious moments, but the arrests were carried out without a shot being fired. "Perhaps," said Shores, "this was due to the well-known fighting men who accompanied me, since they presented quite a show of force."[36]

After serving eight years as Gunnison County sheriff, Shores left the office in 1892 to relocate in Grand Junction and accept appointment as special investigator for the Denver and Rio Grande Express Company. He later took similar jobs with the Denver and Rio Grande Railroad and the Globe Express Company. In 1915 he was appointed chief of police at Salt Lake City.[37] He left Jack Watson in Gunnison, but he never forgot the tough Texan with the crippled leg who, as a trusted deputy, had contributed a great deal to his own success as sheriff.

In 1897 one of Shores's friends, a prominent Utah cattleman named Preston B. Nutter of Salt Lake City, was suffering heavy losses to his herds, and local law enforcement officials seemed powerless to crack down on the rustlers preying on his stock. The Provo correspondent of the *Eastern Utah Advocate*, published in Price, reported in July: "Preston B. Nutter was in Provo securing the services of detectives to operate in connection with his extensive stock interests. . . . Mr. Nutter says he has been losing a great many head of stock recently, and he attributed the loss to a gang of thieves."[38] When Shores heard of Nutter's plight, he immediately thought of Jack Watson and recommended the former Gunnison County deputy as the detective Nutter needed to deal with the problem. Shores suggested that Nutter hire Watson as an undercover agent to drift into the rough country north of Price, where the losses had been most extensive, to see if Watson could identify and expose the thieves.

Nutter liked the idea. In order to maintain secrecy, he deliberately avoided a personal meeting with Watson and asked Shores to make all the necessary arrangements. Shores wired Watson to meet him in Grand Junction and told him of the plan. Watson agreed and a few days later, outfitted for a lengthy encampment, took a roundabout route to the Nine Mile Creek country of the Uintah Reservation, where he found an old, abandoned dugout and moved in.

Soon hard cases like Joe Walker, a former Texas cowboy turned Utah outlaw, and C. L. "Gunplay" Maxwell were dropping by to check out the new arrival in the desolate area. They saw a man as tough looking as anyone who might have been an outlaw himself. But after listening to Watson's tales of his former life as a Texas Ranger and his adventures chasing bad men across the plains of the Southwest, his visitors suspected he was a lawman of some sort. He was, they concluded, a man with whom they would rather not tangle, and they decided a change of location would be wise.

"It was not long before the cattle thieves . . . began to leave that country," recalled Shores. "They did not like the looks of him and the way he talked. . . . They saw he had been wounded a few times, and didn't mind being shot a few times more."[39]

Preston Nutter soon became aware of the outlaw exodus. Delighted that Watson had been able to accomplish his mission without firing a shot or making arrests that would have led to lengthy and expensive legal prosecutions, he asked Shores to send for Watson so he could personally thank him for his work. Shores arranged to meet Nutter in Price on a certain date and sent word for Watson to be there. At the designated time, Nutter and Shores waited all evening, but Watson failed to appear. Making inquiries the next morning, Shores learned that Watson, after arriving in Price a few days earlier, had toured the saloons, gotten drunk, and then disappeared. When he conveyed this information to Nutter, the rancher laughed off the incident and returned to Salt Lake City. But Shores, embarrassed by the behavior of his former deputy, was angry. "I wrote Jack Watson a letter and roasted him good and plenty," he said.[40]

Shores arranged to bring Nutter to Price again and received assurances from Watson that he would surely be there this time. Recalled Shores:

> So Mr. Nutter and myself went over to the town of Price again, which is 100 miles away from Salt Lake City, and [went] down to the stockyards again and stayed round a long time and no Jack Watson there. Mr. Nutter said: "What do you suppose is the matter this time?" I said: "I suppose he has come in and got drunk again. . . ." Still Mr. Nutter only laughed over it. . . .
>
> We got up in the morning . . . to leave for Salt Lake . . . and went over to the old depot and there lay Jack Watson, on his back, with his head cramped up against the wall, dead drunk, of course. I took him by one shoulder and gave an awful jerk, and he yelled out: "What's the matter?" And I said, "You are just drunk again."[41]

Shores made Watson lie out in the hot sun all morning without water until he sobered up enough to talk sensibly. Meanwhile, Nutter and Shores delayed their departure, and in the afternoon the Utah cattleman finally had a chance to thank his hired detective personally.[42]

Price, the county seat of Carbon County, Utah, seemed to hold a particular attraction for Watson — perhaps it was the town's gin mills — and he stayed on there after his work for Nutter was finished. His decision to remain may have been due to the fact that the rustlers he had scared off Preston Nutter's range — Joe Walker, Gunplay Maxwell, and company — had not gone far, nor had they abandoned criminality. Most still operated in the Price area, where they had hooked up with the Robbers Roost outlaw gang led by George Leroy Parker, alias Butch Cassidy, and his pal, William Ellsworth "Elzy" Lay.

In his sober moments, Watson found opportunity to chase these bad men as a deputy for Carbon County Sheriff Charles W. Allred. Watson's most notable law enforcement exploit in Utah was as a member of the posse that closed the career of Joe Walker. For months Walker had been stealing horses in the vicinity of Price, focusing especially on the fine stock owned by the wealthy horse-breeding family of J. M. Whitmore. On one occasion, when a posse led by Emery County Sheriff Azuriah Tuttle tracked him down, Walker engaged them in a pitched gun battle, shot Tuttle in the thigh, and escaped.[43] He was believed to have participated with Cassidy and Lay in a payroll holdup of the Pleasant Valley Coal Company of Castle Gate. Walker's name was added to a list of Robbers Roost outlaws for whom Utah governor Heber M. Wells offered $500 rewards. At Price, Carbon County commissioners added another bounty of $250 for Walker, dead or alive.[44]

This amount of money interested Jack Watson, and when in May 1898 J. M. Whitmore offered to finance an expedition to run down the outlaw, he quickly signed up. Armed with warrants for Walker's arrest, Sheriff Allred led an eight-man posse from Price that included rancher Whitmore; his ranch foreman, Bill McGuire; Carbon County Prosecuting Attorney J. W. Warf; Price City Marshal Pete Anderson; Jack Gentry; Jim Inglefield; and Jack Watson. In lauding the posse members, the *Eastern Utah Advocate* noted that Watson was "reputed to be a first class man in such emergencies."[45] Another paper described

Watson as "a criminal hunter from Colorado carrying eleven bullet scars."[46]

The posse left Price on May 8. Four days later they crossed the Green River at Desolation Canyon, climbed Book Cliffs with great difficulty, and at dawn on Friday the 13th closed in on the outlaw camp. Sheriff Allred shouted an order to surrender, but the four men in the camp grabbed rifles and began firing. Bullets from the posse cut down two of the four, and the others then threw down their weapons and gave up.

One of the dead outlaws was quickly identified as Joe Walker, and the other was believed to be the long-sought bandit leader Butch Cassidy. The possemen were elated. They had gone after Joe Walker and had been successful; they knew his body was worth at least $750. But Butch Cassidy was an even bigger fish; the Pleasant Valley Coal Company had put a $4,000 reward on his head for that payroll robbery.[47] In addition, one of the two men taken prisoner was believed to be Elzy Lay, for whom a large reward was also outstanding.

The posse stopped at Thompson Spring on the way home that night, and two telegrams were dispatched to Governor Wells. "Have killed Joe Walker and Cassidy and captured two others," read one. "Came up with the outlaws at 5 o'clock this morning. Killed Joe Walker and Cassidy. Captured Lay and one other man, Have prisoners and dead men here. Sheriff Allred and Posse did noble," read the other.[48]

Arriving back in Price on May 14, the posse members were welcomed by the largest crowd ever assembled in Carbon County. A coroner's jury met that afternoon, witnesses identified the dead bodies as those of Joe Walker and Butch Cassidy, the possemen were cleared of any wrongdoing in the deaths, and the deceased outlaws were quickly buried.[49]

But Watson and the other possemen, waiting in gleeful anticipation for their share of the large Butch Cassidy reward, were in for a rude disappointment. When rumors spread that the man believed to be Cassidy was in fact another man, Uinta County Sheriff John Ward, who knew the outlaw chieftain well, came in and had the body dug up so he could make positive identification. After the body was exhumed, Sheriff Ward stated positively that the dead man was not the noted

Butch Cassidy, but a minor Robbers Roost outlaw named Johnny Herring. It was also determined that neither of the prisoners was Elzy Lay. They, too, were lesser outlaws named W. J. Schultz and S. H. Thompson.[50]

In the end, the governor's $500 reward for the apprehension of Joe Walker was divided into nineteen portions, with each posseman receiving only $26.30 for his arduous and dangerous service. Jack Watson was especially disappointed by the turn of events, as he was dead broke.[51] Two weeks after returning from the Joe Walker expedition, on May 27, he wrote Benjamin Franklin Sylvester Watson, a brother he called "Vesta," asking for money.

> Dear Vesta Watson:
>
> I received yours of May 1 and was glad to hear from you yet sorry to hear of the death of our parents. Still I new of Pa's death some [time] after it took place. But was calculating to see Ma again before she died. . . . I suppose you no by this time what I am doing. I have bin in the Detective business 8 years. I killed at least six men since I rote you at Crested Butte a few years ago. I told you I was going to Alaska. That was after a desperado I got. Since I got your letter have got 4, killed 2 and got 2 others alive & have them here in jail waiting trial for robbery and murder. Their trial will come of in about 2 weeks. Then I am going to quit the business for awhile any way.
>
> Well, Vista, you said you had some money for me. If you will send it to me I will come home and stay a while. You will have to send it by express. No more at present. Your Brother, J. A. Watson.
>
> P.S. I got a letter from S. M. today.[52]

Watson also expressed his need for money to J. W. Warf, the county attorney and fellow posse member. On June 8 Warf wrote Governor Wells, asking the cause of the delay in distribution of reward money, as a "great many are in need of the money and one man, J. A. Watson, wants to start for home and has been waiting several days to receive his portion." That same day Watson's patience was completely exhausted, as Warf wrote the governor on another letterhead: "Since I wrote you today, J. A. Watson has sold his interest in the rewards offered for Joe Walker and I enclose you a copy of the assignment."[53]

Warf and Watson were apparently on friendly terms on June 8 when the county attorney wrote these two letters on Watson's behalf, but that all changed the very next day. Warf was involved at the time in a dispute with Clarence Marsh, the editor of the Price newspaper, the *Eastern Utah Advocate*, over a town irrigation project. Apparently in fear of his enemies, Marsh employed Watson as a kind of bodyguard to watch his backside. On the evening of June 9 Marsh, accompanied by Watson, walked to the water canal outside town to turn on the water. According to the obviously prejudiced story as it appeared in the pages of Marsh's paper, the two men were confronted by a man named Youngberg, who threatened them with a shotgun and ordered them not to turn on the water. Marsh was in the act of defying the man and releasing the water, according to the account, when his wife appeared on the scene "with a babe in her arms" and persuaded her husband to return home with her.

After Marsh left, Watson remained, evidently to see that no one interfered with the free flow of water. As he sat quietly on the embankment, said the story, two men, J. W. Warf and Alpha Ballinger, approached. Both carried rifles. As Ballinger covered Watson with his rifle, Warf circled around, "pulled his six-shooter and without warning dealt Watson a vicious blow on the side of the head. This was followed by others until the poor man fell insensible from the beating." The paper continued:

> Next day when Watson pulled himself together sufficiently to count the cost, he found himself carrying around a badly split ear, the right side of the . . . bone was laid bare, while a glance at his forehead would suggest that he must be a member of the Red Cross Society. He was badly injured about the ribs and the body, and for several days his stomach, as an assimilator and digester of food was a complete failure, the result of a well placed vicious kick by one of his assailants. Dr. Richmond was called and dressed his wounds, and in doing so found it necessary to put several stitches in his head and ear. Jack is slowly convalescing.[54]

Warf and Ballinger were arrested and, on a change of venue, had an examination on June 18 before Justice of the Peace J. Thomas Fitch of the neighboring community of Helper. Fitch, who was known to be sympathetic to Warf on the irrigation issue, found both men innocent of any crime. Clarence Marsh fumed. "IT WAS A FARCE" he headlined his account of the acquittal.[55]

Doc Shores, over in Salt Lake City, had followed these developments in the papers with interest. "There was," he remembered,

> one newspaper man there [Clarence Marsh] that had a lot of trouble over some irrigation business and the whole town had gotten down on him and the District Judge [J. Thomas Fitch] and everybody else, and the fellow had no friends at all, so Jack took him up and helped defend him, and he helped him out. They framed on Old Jack afterwards and held him up with rifles and beat him up terribly. But that did not drive him out of Price, he still hung around. I went over to see him and had a talk with him and said: "You are going to get killed here and I want you to leave here." Well, he said he would go when he got ready. . . . While I was there talking to him, we were sitting out in front of a bank, on the sidewalk, and along came a bunch of his enemies, and he commenced to spit at them and call them all kinds of names. I said: "I want you to behave yourself. You want to get killed and get me killed. Behave yourself while I am here."[56]

Shores talked to Watson as if he were still his deputy and could be ordered around, but the stubborn old fighting man said he would not be driven out; he would only leave when he was good and ready. Shores gave up and returned to Salt Lake City. On July 22 one of his agents at Helper reported that rumors were flying; Watson's enemies were believed to be conspiring to have him killed the next day. But if there was a conspiracy afoot to assassinate Watson, the intended victim certainly played into the plot.

On the morning of Saturday, July 23, Watson followed Warf into a Price drugstore and confronted the man who had so viciously beaten him. When Warf refused to talk to him, Watson blasted him verbally with vile epithets and threats. Although no weapons were produced, witnesses believed the old gunman was deliberately trying to force a violent showdown. Ignoring the vituperative attack, Warf turned, walked out of the store, and entered his office in the building next door.[57]

Throughout that day Watson visited the town's saloons, imbibing heavily and fulminating against his enemy. Shortly before six that evening he was in the Senate Saloon when Warf entered. Seeing an inebriated Watson at the bar, Warf turned and started to leave.

"That's right, sneak off like the dirty, cowardly —— you are," Watson was reported to have shouted. "Go to feeling for it," he challenged, at the same time drawing his revolver. Warf also pulled a pistol, and shots were exchanged. Watson missed, but one of Warf's bullets struck Watson in the groin and smashed the hipbone. He went down.

Warf ran from the saloon and across the street to the Price Trading Company Store, where he got a rifle. Emerging again, he saw Watson, gravely wounded, but still full of fight, staggering out of the saloon, pistol in hand. Using the cover of a wagon in front of the store, Warf opened up with his rifle. Outgunned and fainting from pain, shock, and loss of blood, Watson collapsed again and began crawling back into the saloon. A rifle bullet struck him "in the rectum, lodged just below the rib in front, on the left side." Watson was carried into the back room of the saloon, and Dr. Richmond was summoned. The physician extracted two bullets from Watson's body, but the damage had been severe, and he died about four hours after the shooting.[58]

The next day, Sunday, July 24, a corner's jury officially recorded that Watson had come to his death from gunshot wounds inflicted by J. W. Warf. Arrested and charged with murder, Warf predictably took a change of venue again to the court of his friend, Justice J. T. Fitch of Helper, who, also predictably, found Warf's action self-defense and justifiable.[59]

And so, at fifty-five, well advanced in age for a gunfighter, Jack Watson passed from this world. He had lived a violent life, and he died a violent death. As Doc Shore recognized, he had many good qualities, the foremost of which was utter fearlessness in the face of danger. But his old nemesis, John Barleycorn, did him in at the end, dimming his eye and unsteadying his hand when the moment of truth came. He left no immediate family, for he had never married. He was buried at county expense in the cemetery at Price, but any marking has long since been lost, and today nobody can determine for certain the location of his bones.[60]

— 4 —

JOHN OWENS
1843–1927

I doubt very much if Owens ever shot a man in the back. He was not that kind. He was not "trigger happy." He gambled, he was immaculate, he ran saloons and dance halls, but always shot on the side of law and order and self defense.

— Russell Thorpe

It has been written repeatedly that there were twenty notches on John H. Owens's gun, representing the twenty men he had killed, but none of the writers making that assertion have supplied documentation.[1] Like the lethal records of many other gunfighters of the West, this figure appears to be greatly exaggerated, although Owens was undoubtedly a deadly gunman who killed several men in gunfights. His marksmanship and skill in the use of six-shooters made him a legendary figure around Newcastle and Weston County, Wyoming.

"John Owens, without question, was the greatest pistol shot of any peace officer or individual in Wyoming," said one old-timer who knew him.[2]

"He always carried two guns, one for 'reserve,'" recalled another. "It was said he never aimed in his life. Those who knew him claimed that, as a gunman, he was far superior to Wild Bill Hickok."[3] Owens reportedly outshot the nationally famous pistoleer Hickok in a shooting match at Cheyenne in early 1876.[4]

A slender, handsome man of average height and weight, John Owens during his eighty years on the frontier pursued many careers.

He was an Indian scout, teamster, stagecoach driver, rancher, saloon keeper, whorehouse proprietor, professional gambler, and lawman.

Born at Marshall, Texas, August 11, 1843, he was with his father, John E. Owens,[5] at West Plains, Missouri, when the Civil War broke out. Although still in his teens, John enlisted in the Missouri State Militia and saw very limited service with the Confederate army.[6]

By 1862 he had ventured into the western wilderness, working for the government as a scout. In a letter to a friend in 1915 he wrote:

> We came up the Platte River in 1862. I was scouting on that trip and we had things very interesting. We had troubles all the way, lost a good many of our party, but finally got to Fort Laramie. . . . We had an attack made on us east of Scott's Bluff and I was wounded there but not laid up on the shelf. I was shot through the left arm and it was pretty bad for several weeks. . . . It was certainly great sport scouting. It was a good deal like fishing or hunting after you are at it a while.[7]

For the next nine years Owens worked out of Fort Laramie, scouting for hostile Indians and outlaws preying on travelers on the Emigrant Trail running between the two Platte rivers. He hunted game for the garrison's commissary, trapped in the winter, felled logs for construction crews, bossed the horse and mule corral, and did a little gambling, especially following the soldiers' monthly payday. At times he drove the stage between Fort Laramie and Fort D. A. Russell. In 1867, in preparation for the arrival of the Union Pacific Railroad building west, he helped lay out the town of Cheyenne.[8]

In the winter of 1867–68 he and eight other trappers were at a place called Rock Ranch when they were attacked by a large party of Indians. Owens told about it years later:

> Six were inside when the Indians tackled us. [Bert] Jessup, [Jack] Alsup [sic], and [Bill] Milligan were out looking after traps and our saddle horses. . . . We battled all day there. We shot only when it counted as there were eighty of them red devils and only six of us. [Jessup, Allsup, and Milligan were killed.] They were scalped but they dropped, I think it was, 17 Indians. . . . All of our horses were taken by them and we were left afoot. We had venison, antelope meat and some coffee and corn meal. We stayed at the ranch for nearly three weeks, then

two of the boys walked to old Fort Laramie at night and they sent some soldiers down after us with mules. Our saddles were stolen and we had to ride the mules bareback.[9]

Legend has it that about 1873, Owens and the wife of one of the officers at the fort fell in love. Since the officer was a close personal friend, Owens, rather than betray that friendship, abruptly broke off the relationship and left Fort Laramie.[10]

Owens filed a claim on a parcel of land on Reshaw Creek, in the Chug Water valley, north of Cheyenne, bought some cattle, and began ranching. Two of his brands, IO and DE, were registered that year in Laramie County.[11] By 1875, apparently recovered from his ill-starred love affair with the army officer's wife, he married "the former Miss S. Conley of Louisiana."[12] Sadly, this marriage did not last long, for the bride died in April of that year.[13]

About the only recreation for the scattered ranchers of the area was to found at a log roadhouse a man named Patton had constructed at Chug Springs back in 1871. There a man could cut the dust with a drink and pass the time with a friendly game of cards. The place livened up considerably in 1876 when the discovery of gold in the Black Hills of Dakota triggered a rush north out of Cheyenne and right past the Chug Springs roadhouse. When stagecoach service was begun to Deadwood and the other new mining camps in the Dakota country, the roadhouse became a stage station on the road.

The year 1876 also proved to have personal significance for John Owens. One evening early in that year he sat down at the card table in the Chug Springs roadhouse with several others, including C. P. "Dub" Meeks, one of the first freighters into the Black Hills, and the stationmaster and proprietor, Patton. It turned out to be a memorable game, going on all night for increasingly high stakes. Owens had a remarkable streak of luck, as one by one he drove all the players from the game until only he and Patton remained. When Owens rose from the table the next morning, he had won everything Patton had, including the roadhouse, the stage station, and the saloon with its entire stock of wet goods.[14]

Recalled Dub Meeks: "When the stage went through there that day the former landlord climbed aboard and Owens put on the white apron and proceeded to dispense choice liquors and western hospitality in a real frontier style. Owens made the former owner of the place a present of $50 for a grubstake when he pulled out."[15]

Owens found himself hard-pressed to manage both his ranch and the busy roadhouse and stage station, so he hired W. F. Barry and his wife to help him care for travelers at Chug Springs. He also plucked a woman named Maisie Mathers from another roadside establishment and brought her in to assist.

Maisie Mathers was a veteran employee of the trailside brothels that sprang up in Wyoming and were indelicately dubbed "hog ranches" by the frontiersmen. Of late, she had worked at the notorious Three Mile Hog Ranch, a collection of buildings three miles from Fort Laramie (hence the name) that housed facilities for the three frontier vices—drinking, gambling, and whoring. A notorious rendezvous of outlaws and desperadoes of all stripes, the establishment had been founded originally in 1873 by Julius Ecoffey and Adolph Cuny as a trading post, saloon, and inn. The following year these frontier entrepreneurs expanded their operation, constructing eight two-room shacks to accommodate women imported from eastern red-light districts to provide sexual release for soldiers stationed at Fort Laramie and travelers along the road. Always a rough place, it was the scene of many brawls, shootings, and cuttings.[16]

After visiting the Three Mile Hog Ranch, U.S. Army lieutenant John Gregory Bourke described it as a den of iniquity, "tenanted by as hardened and depraved set of witches as could be found on the face of the globe. [It was] a rum mill of the worst kind [with] half a dozen Cyprians, virgins whose lamps were always burning brightly in expectancy of the coming of the bridegroom, and who lured to destruction the soldiers of the garrison. In all my experience I have never seen a lower, more beastly set of people of both sexes."[17]

Although Mathers was one of those "hardened and depraved witches," more than one resident of the Wyoming frontier found her very desirable. Isaac Bard, operator of another stage station on the Deadwood road, noted in his diary on May 12, 1876: "Ed Carrington went in town to marry Mrs. Mathers, but J. Owens got ahead of him and got away with her."[18] If the intentions of Ed Carrington, a neighbor of Owens on the Chug Water ranch, were matrimonial, those of Owens were not. No record of a marriage to Mathers has been uncovered, and she evidently disappeared from his life after he disposed of the Chug Springs roadhouse.

The year 1876 was notable also for a number of raids by Sioux warriors along the Chug Water valley. In August a band of Indians made off with the horse herds of John Owens and Ed Carrington. One day at nearby Goshen Hole, Owens discovered the body of a man slain by the Indians. It proved to be the younger brother of another neighbor, John Hunton, and Owens had the sad task of carrying the body to the Hunton ranch. Troops were called out to protect the settlements, and Owens and other ranchers joined them in several skirmishes with the raiding parties.[19]

Disposing of the Chug Springs property (and Mathers) in 1878, Owens confined his energies to building up his ranch on Reshaw Creek. He may have planned on moving his ranching operation to the Black Hills, for he registered brands there that year.[20] He did not leave Wyoming, however, and in 1880 married again. Although described by all accounts as a great beauty, his new wife, Serena E. Bolt, was no innocent maiden. Thirty-six years of age, a year younger than Owens, she was another inmate of the infamous Three Mile Hog Ranch.[21]

In 1881 Owens sold his ranch on Reshaw Creek and moved to Cheyenne, where he ran a billiard parlor and saloon in the Masonic Temple on Sixteenth Street and gambled professionally. The next year he sold out and moved again, this time to a ranch five miles from Fort Laramie. He continued to gamble, a practice to which Serena Owens objected strenuously. The issue destroyed the marriage. In 1884 Serena obtained a divorce and in the settlement took possession of the ranch. Owens went off to purchase the Three Mile Hog Ranch where he could gamble to the limit of his bankroll and gambol with as many Cyprians as he desired.

Although his clientele at the Three Mile Hog Ranch represented some of the toughest characters in the territory, there is no record that Owens ever had to unlimber his pistols to maintain order in his resort. He seemed to get along well with all. A story from this period of his life has survived and illustrates how he ingratiated himself with the lawless types who frequented the place.

William Chambers, better known as "Persimmon Bill," was a top hand on the cattle ranges but had a weakness for alcohol. He drifted into outlawry and on one of his binges killed a soldier.[22] Arrested in Rawlins, he escaped and soon thereafter turned up at Owens's roadhouse. He was still disporting there a couple of days later when a Laramie County deputy sheriff rode in and began inquiring about the wanted man. Malcolm Campbell, a rancher who would later gain fame as a fearless Wyoming sheriff, related the rest of the tale.

When he learned the lawman was looking for him, said Campbell, Persimmon Bill approached Owens and inquired: "I understand you have a pack of hounds here that you use for hunting."

"Yes," replied Owens, "but I don't seem to get much time around here to keep them trained. They haven't had a run for months."

"Well, that's too bad," said Bill. "I haven't a thing to do. What would you say if should take them out for a while? Maybe we could scare up a few jack-rabbits or even an antelope."

Owens agreed, and soon the hunted man was "galloping out of danger surrounded by the frolicking pack of baying hounds."[23]

And John Owens avoided having blood spilled on his saloon floor.

But Owens could move on the side of law if he believed the situation warranted it. He picked up a lot of outlaw information from the habitués of his saloon, and when he learned that road agents were planning to hold up the stage and steal the Fort Laramie payroll at Eagle's Nest, the next stop north, he determined to prevent them. Grabbing a rifle, he saddled his best horse and raced fifteen miles to Chug Springs Station to catch the stage before it moved on to Eagle's Nest. He arrived as the horses were being changed. He waved at George Lathrop, the driver, and told him to tell the soldier riding as guard to get inside the coach, and he would take his place. Knowing that Owens would not make such a demand without good reason, Lathrop and the guard complied. Owens tied his horse behind, climbed up on the boot, and settled himself with his rifle across his knees.

As the stage went up a rise near Eagle's Nest, three armed men stepped out. "Halt! Throw up your hands!" one of them demanded.

John Owens responded quietly: "Not tonight, boys. Drive on, George."

When they recognized him, the road agents hesitated, and then backed off, and the stage and the payroll went on through to Fort Laramie.[24]

By early 1886 Owens had disposed of the Three Mile Hog Ranch and moved farther north to the new town of Lusk on the line of the Burlington and Missouri Railroad. J. K. Calkin, editor of the *Lusk Herald*, proclaimed proudly in his premier issue of May 20, 1886: "Lusk is on the line of the new railway pushing into this territory from the east. The new town is only two months old and has 40 business houses." In Calkin's second issue, a week later, came the announcement: "Johnny Owens has opened a large dance house on the east side of the creek."

Owens brought with him a gaggle of women from the Three Mile Hog Ranch to work his dance hall, including Mamie Dixon, with whom he was living at the time. Behind his imposing dance hall building he constructed a row of shacks, one for each woman. Locals began calling the place the "Street Car Line" because the row resembled a string of streetcars.[25]

"Doc" Cornett, another denizen of the frontier sporting world, soon provided competition for Owens when he opened another combination dance house–saloon–gambling hall featuring a monte game backed "with a $500 bank roll."[26] Following Owens in his various relocations, Cornett would later be a key figure in one of Owens's lethal encounters.

Violence erupted in Lusk in October 1886, when Charles V. Trumble, who had been appointed as a Laramie County deputy sheriff in the new town, shot and killed Charles Miller (or Milley), alias "Red Bill," a suspected horse thief. According to editor Calkins of the *Herald*, it was a deliberate murder. Trumble, he said, "shot Red Bill in cold blood in Whitaker's saloon. Afterward Ed Cerns and a man named Ketchum took the gun from Trumble and . . . took him out on the street. Several persons—John Owens in the lead—followed to arrest them. The Cleveland brothers [Larkin and Harper], [Peter] Sweeny and Watson helped Owens secure both Cerns and Trumble, who were bound over to district court and taken to Cheyenne."[27]

Later that month Laramie County Sheriff Nate Craig appointed Peter Sweeny to replace Trumble as his deputy in Lusk. Charles Gunn, a man very popular with Lusk residents, was made special constable, or town marshal. The appointments, said the *Lusk Herald*, met with "general satisfaction," as Sweeny was "a sober, resolute man," and Gunn, although he might not have "the little white wings attached to the messenger of peace, [possessed] all the other necessary requisites and Lusk will henceforth be the banner frontier town."[28]

Following the elections in November, the county commissioners approved construction of a jail at Lusk, removed Sweeny, and awarded Gunn with a deputy sheriff commission to go along with his local police authority. Perhaps aware that this was too much law enforcement responsibility for one man to handle in the rapidly growing town, the next month they also appointed John Owens a deputy sheriff at Lusk, and at the age of forty-three Owens pinned on a badge for the first time.[29]

In January the lid blew off Lusk, as a cowboy calling himself Bill McCoy turned violent. McCoy, a very tough customer and escape artist, was wanted for murder in Texas under his real name, Dan Bogan, and another alias, Bill Gatlin. He and Charlie Gunn had a couple of run-ins before the morning of January 15, 1887, in Jim Waters's saloon, when McCoy dropped the deputy sheriff with a pistol shot to the midsection. He then deliberately placed the muzzle of his revolver close to Gunn's head and fired "a second shot which splattered his brains over the floor and set fire to his hair."[30]

Smoking pistol in hand, McCoy ran from the building, leaped on a horse, and headed for the tall timber. His mount had taken only a few jumps when the form of John Owens loomed in his path. Owens, holding a double-barreled shotgun, ordered McCoy to rein up, and fired a shot into the air to show he meant business. Hesitating only a second, McCoy ignored the command and spurred his horse on.

Owens hesitated not at all. Whipping the shotgun to his shoulder, he turned loose the other barrel, striking McCoy in the shoulder and tumbling him from the saddle.

The fall knocked the pistol from McCoy's hand. Lying in the street, the weapon only inches away, the murderer watched Owens approach with the shotgun trained on him. In the excitement of the moment McCoy did not remember until after the officer had reached him and picked up the pistol that Owens had fired both barrels and the scattergun was now empty. Whatever opportunity he had to escape was gone.[31]

When Owens, who had been ill and confined to his bed for several days, asked McCoy why he had killed Charlie Gunn, the desperado replied, "I would not have done it if I hadn't supposed that you were at home and abed."[32]

At a hearing before Justice of the Peace Roe Kingman, McCoy was held without bail to be tried for murder in Cheyenne. The Lusk jail was still unfinished, so Deputy Sheriff Owens held McCoy, shackled, in the back room of a saloon. Rumors spread throughout the day that a lynch mob would deal with the slayer of popular Charlie Gunn that night, but when Owens let it be known that he would fight to protect his prisoner, no one could be found to lead the lynch party.

According to one account, when Owens heard that Sterling Ballou, one of McCoy's friends, was making threats against the man who had shot and arrested his pal, he called Ballou out of a saloon and said: "There has been enough killing, Ballou — or else there hasn't. I don't like your talk. If you are in town two hours from now I'll shoot you on sight."

"Well, I'll go if you say so, Johnny," Ballou said sheepishly.

"I say so," replied Owens.

And Ballou made tracks out of town.[33]

Some time after midnight Owens, still not fully recovered from his illness, and weak and tired from the events of the day, went to bed, leaving his prisoner in charge of Tuck Jester and Quint Pennick, two cattlemen he had sworn in as special deputies. His trust was misplaced, for during the night the cowboy guards allowed McCoy to escape, and he rode off into a blinding snowstorm.

Owens did not follow. Knowing that the blizzard would quickly obliterate the fugitive's tracks and that with his gunshot wounds he could not go far, Owens rightly concluded McCoy would hole up in one of the nearby cattle range line camps. He posted guards on the roads and waited.

Two weeks later McCoy, burning with fever and in desperate need of medical attention, sent word he was ready to surrender, but still was fearful of a lynch mob. By prearrangement, Owens and four special deputies met him at night outside of town. Each officer wore two pistols and carried a shotgun. Owens handed McCoy a pistol to use in his own defense if they were attacked by a mob. The entry into town was uneventful, and Owens held McCoy in irons in a back room of Peter Sweeny's saloon until morning, when he took him by stage to Cheyenne and placed him in the Laramie County jail.[34]

Dan Bogan, alias Bill Gatlin, alias Bill McCoy, was found guilty of the murder of Deputy Sheriff and Constable Charles Gunn on Sep-

John Owens. Courtesy of the American Heritage Center, University of Wyoming.

tember 7, 1887, and sentenced to death. But McCoy was a very slippery character indeed, and before the sentence could be carried out, escaped custody as he had done many times before. He was never recaptured. John Owens thus joined a long line of notable western peace officers, including Pat Garrett, Jim East, Frank Canton, Nathaniel Boswell, Malcolm Campbell, T. J. Carr, and Charlie Siringo, who had pursued and often jailed the elusive outlaw, only to see him slip away.[35]

John Owens had barely returned home from his trip to Cheyenne with the pestiferous Bill McCoy when he was met with a serious personal problem. On February 25 the *Lusk Herald* reported:

> A lamp exploded Tuesday evening about 10 o'clock in Deputy Sheriff Owens' house and, no one being home, the contents were soon on fire. Mamie [Dixon] discovered the fire and, unassisted, extinguished it before it could burn through the roof. Everything was charred and blackened but not consumed, probably because the closed room kept everything in a smoldering condition until discovered. Much of their best clothing was consumed and loss will probably reach $300. Lucky it was discovered in time before it spread, as the whole town is without protection.

Owens, who was particular about his clothes and always dressed in the best of style, had to replace his damaged wardrobe. A few months later he lost his live-in girlfriend also. In September the *Herald* reported that Mamie Dixon had married Archie Crawford at Hot Springs, Dakota Territory.[36]

About this time a controversy developed regarding Owens's position as deputy sheriff at Lusk. John Hunton, who was then a member of the Laramie County Board of Commissioners and had pushed for the initial appointment of Owens, noted in his diary on May 27: "Cheyenne: Many persons objecting to Owens remaining deputy sheriff at Lusk. Investigating the matter and find some cause for complaint, but do not believe we can help the matter at present." Hunton talked to Owens, who was in Cheyenne to testify at the murder trial of Charles Trumble. The next day Hunton wrote in his diary: "Still investigating the Owens matter. Asked him to resign, which he did."[37]

Perhaps the problem was of a political nature; it seems to have been resolved after Seth K. Sharpless replaced Nate Craig as sheriff. If

Owens did indeed tender his resignation, he was quickly reinstated by Sheriff Sharpless and was soon back on the job. The *Cheyenne Leader* of October 5 reported that "Deputy Owens received messages from Sheriff Sharpless and Prosecution Attorney [Walter R.] Stoll about 10 o'clock Wednesday morning that some outlaws were headed toward Lusk. He immediately procured and equipped three parties of five or six each, leading one himself and placing one respectively in charge of John Steffan and P. F. Sullivan. These officials were all cool and started out with the intention of not allowing the fugitives to pass this way."[38]

And on February 17, 1888, the *Lusk Herald* reported that "Deputy Owens started for Cheyenne with the 'Long-Haired Kid' and Dick Charles last Friday. The former got 50 days for vagrancy and the latter will serve 60 days for petit larceny. Owens returned yesterday."

Throughout his life John Owens was a great admirer of fine racehorses. He owned many of them and often entered them in races around that region of the country. Part of the allure of the track was his gambling proclivity, which apparently extended to betting on human races, a sport frowned on and deemed illegal in some places. John Hunton remarked in his diary on May 19, 1888: "Went to Fort Laramie with Oscar Sharpless. Foot races and Jno. Owens arrested, but released."[39]

In addition to his business interests in Lusk and his duties as the deputy sheriff there, Owens about this time accepted employment by the Wyoming Stock Growers' Association as an inspector, with responsibility for protecting the members' interests throughout the cattle ranges of northern Wyoming and western Nebraska. It was during this period that one of the legendary stories developed about his gun-fighting prowess. As the tale was told and retold, a shooting affair took place in Crawford, Nebraska, a little town just outside Fort Robinson. Owens was said to have walked into a Crawford saloon one day to find the town marshal backed against the wall by "some negroes," presumably black soldiers from the nearby fort. "Johnny quickly went to his aid and when he and the marshal walked out together, five negroes were dead and Johnny carried a pistol slug under the skin in his left side. His heavy leather belt had prevented the bullet from going deeper. He had the scar the rest of his life."[40]

Although Owens's son, Sterling, "verified certain facts of the story," saying he had heard it from his father years earlier,[41] it had no basis in fact and evidently was just another of those sanguinary yarns that attached themselves to celebrated western gunfighters.[42]

In the late summer of 1889 Owens sold his Lusk property and moved to Newcastle, a swiftly developing town in northeastern Wyoming on the line of the expanding Burlington and Missouri Railroad. In June 1890 he purchased a store on a central corner and two adjoining lots. The store he converted into a saloon called The Jumbo. Later he sold the saloon to finance a new place he had constructed on the third lot from the corner. This building was a combination saloon and gambling house he called The Castle. It was no sooner erected than he built an addition, a theater and music hall, an entertainment center that a Newcastle newspaper enthused would be "a metropolitan adjunct to the city."[43]

The theater was twenty-four by sixty-six feet in size with a large gallery and a stage sixteen by twenty-four feet. When it opened on July 19, 1890, it was the only theater within a radius of one hundred miles. Box seats were fifty cents and general admission a quarter. The featured act that opening night was "The Allen Sisters Company, a first class combination from Denver."[44] Later attractions were "Diablo, the Fire Fiend," who drank flaming liquids; "Young and Leclaire, sketch team," direct from Kansas City; "John Obee, the Human Serpent," and his contortionist act; "Miss Hazel Dendee" and her vocal renditions; and "Miss Ella Jones, the Giantess," who would wrestle four men.[45]

The combined buildings, officially called the John Owens Saloon and Music Hall, in time came to be known throughout that part of Wyoming as The House of Blazes, presumably "because the guns often blazed behind its scarred walls."[46]

The first recorded gunplay in the Owens establishment and the first documented killing by John Owens took place in the early hours of January 2, 1891, when celebrants of the New Year, after many hours of alcoholic intake, engaged in a wild melee. It started between three and four o'clock in the morning, according to newspaper reports and testimony before a coroner's inquest, when a dispute broke out at a gambling table between Doc Cornett and Jim Davis, operators of the game, and Mike Pendergast, one of the players.[47] As the argument grew heated, everyone leaped up. Cornett, very intoxicated, pulled a gun and struck Pendergast over the head. When Maude Rivers, a woman with Pendergast, screamed, Cornett struck her also, knocking her to the floor. Bartender A. M. Anderson rushed up and tried to calm Cornett, but Davis grabbed the bartender from behind and pulled him away.

Anderson testified that at this point, John Owens ran in from another room and, as he "tried to quell the racket," Davis drew a gun.

> Owens told him to put up his gun and that he could not run that place or hurt anybody there. Davis said he would not have it that way and made the remark that he was a fighting man. He then stepped back from the bar. Owens went over to him and told him again to put up his gun. He said, "I don't have to." Doc Cornett stepped between Davis and Owens and told Davis to put up his gun. Davis kept pointing his gun at Owens. Cornett grabbed Davis and Davis pushed his gun under Cornett's arm at Owens and Cornett took a step back towards Owens, still facing Davis, when Owens pulled his gun and fired. Davis fell to the floor and Doc Cornett picked up his gun. Owens then told Cornett to give up his gun, which Cornett did by handing it to me.

At an inquest held the next day before Justice of the Peace Henry Leppia, acting coroner, it was shown that a bullet from Owens's gun struck Davis in the left side of his face and ranged upward, passing through his head and killing him instantly. After hearing the testimony of witnesses, the coroner's jury ruled the death a justifiable homicide.

Commented the *Newcastle News*: "John Owens, the man who did the shooting, is a fine-looking man about 35 years of age [he was a youthful-appearing forty-seven] and is well known throughout the Black Hills. . . . Mr. Owens is known as being far above the average man of his class and the community had learned to overlook his business for his many qualities as a citizen and the generous nature of the man. We all feel sad that the life of a human being stands between him and eternity."[48]

When Newcastle was founded in 1889, it was in Crook County, but in March 1890 the Wyoming territorial legislature voted to form a new county called Weston from the southern half of Crook. At an election in May, Newcastle was voted in overwhelmingly as the county seat, and Edward Stack was made sheriff.[49] In 1892, at the urging of many admirers, Owens ran for sheriff and at the general election was elected handily. He would serve seven terms, a total of fourteen years in the office.

On July 11, 1894, just one month short of his fifty-first birthday, he married again. His bride, Addie Augusta Parker, was thirty-one, and, like his former wives, a dance hall girl.[50] The couple had been co-habitating for several years, and Addie had given birth to a son on December 5, 1891. John named the boy Sterling Robert after Confederate general Sterling Price, his commander in the Missouri Militia.[51]

In the fall of that year, he easily won reelection as sheriff.

Despite his reputation as a deadly gunman, John Owens avoided violence for the most part in the performance of his duties as sheriff. A story told by M. D. Quick, a Weston County old-timer, is illustrative of how he used guile and wit to capture miscreants.

He got on the trail of a wanted outlaw, but the fellow spotted him and high-tailed it for the Dakota line, where he knew Owens could not arrest him as it was beyond his jurisdiction. Owens gave chase, but the fugitive had a good start and kept out of rifle range. He galloped over the line a few rods, pulled up his winded horse, dismounted, dropped the reins, and, hunkering down, coolly rolled a cigarette.

Owens rode up, took in the situation, smiled, and said, "Well, I see you beat me all right."

"I was just a little too fast for you, Johnny," said the outlaw, chuckling. "But come on, have a cigarette and rest your horse a bit."

Owens squatted cowboy-fashion beside the man, and they smoked and exchanged stories. The outlaw, completely distracted, did not notice the grazing horses as they moved back across the boundary line into Wyoming. He was in the middle of an entertaining yarn when Owens arose and casually sauntered toward his mount. The rustler, laughing and talking, followed along.

They had picked up their bridle reins when Owens suddenly drew his pistol and snapped, "We're in Wyoming now, pard. I guess I was just a little too fast for you."

With a sheepish grin, the outlaw, knowing he had been outwitted, surrendered. In later years he often told the story on himself.[52]

In February 1896 Owens led a posse on an outlaw chase that was not resolved so peaceably. A gang of rustlers led by Fred Truax and

Fred Timms had moved into Weston County from Johnson County, and when Sheriff Owens received a tip that they were holding stolen stock between Newcastle and the Cheyenne River, he rounded up five possemen — Wyoming Stock Growers Association detectives D. C. Kelty and Joe LeFors, Miller Wiker, T. J. Hunter, and W. W. Mc-Clung — and took off in pursuit.

They found the rustlers about twenty miles southeast of Newcastle on Beaver Creek. They were holding twenty-eight head of cattle and about fifteen horses. Seeing the outlaws on foot, Owens, Hunter, and LeFors dismounted and, leading their mounts, worked their way up a draw to get nearer. As they came into view over the lip of the draw they were fired upon from about seventy-five yards by Truax and Timms. When Owens was later asked at a hearing into the affair if any of the bullets came close, he replied, "I thought they came very close. One of them knocked dirt in my face."

Owens, LeFors, and Hunter returned the fire, and Truax and Timms went down. A third gang member, William Thomas, galloped off, but Owens sprang on his horse, ran him down, and escorted him back to the others. He found Truax and Timms dead.[53]

The Owens posse arrived back in Newcastle on February 19 with the bodies of the dead men; the prisoner, William Thomas; and the stolen stock. The bodies of Truax and Timms were buried in a common grave that same day in Old Ridge Cemetery, and Coroner F. Horton held an inquest. After listening to the testimony of Owens, his possemen, and Thomas, the coroner's jury found that Truax and Timms had come to their deaths from Winchester rifle bullets fired by Owens, LeFors, and Hunter in the discharge of their official duties, and the officers were exonerated from all blame.[54]

The *Laramie Boomerang* commented that "Sheriff Owens is said to be the quickest man in the state with a gun."[55]

The voters of Weston County liked John Owens's style — avoiding gunplay when possible, but employing swift and accurate deadly force when necessary. In November 1896 they elected him to a third term as sheriff.

Nothing dramatic occurred during the next two years,[56] and Owens, perhaps suffering from complacency, failed to campaign for reelection to the sheriff's office in 1898 and was defeated by William Miller. He stayed on as Miller's chief deputy, but had to vacate the sheriff's quarters in the jail building. He moved with his family to a small house on the north edge of town and devoted more of his time to the management of his saloon and theater. Later he returned to ranching, building a house on Beaver Creek eighteen miles from town, and grazing a herd of cattle on a spread there.

Apparently content with his other interests, Owens did not contest the reelection of his good friend Bill Miller as sheriff in 1900 or 1902.

The year 1903 was a momentous one for Newcastle and Weston County. In April Theodore Roosevelt visited the little town, and Owens helped Sheriff Miller guard the president of the United States as he stood on a flag-draped platform in front of the Palace Saloon and addressed a crowd that had come from throughout the county to see and hear the popular president.[57]

The next month an event occurred that did not reflect as well on the town. W. C. Clifton, calling himself "Diamond L. Slim," was being held in the county jail, charged with the murder of a young married couple named Church. Some cowboys employed on nearby ranches, outraged by the brutal crime and fearful that Clifton might escape justice with a plea of insanity, assembled at the jail on the night of May 28, took the prisoner from his guards, marched him to a railroad bridge, tightened a noose around his neck, and shoved him off to his death. He was decapitated in the process.[58]

Then on October 31 the last pitched battle between Indians and whites in Wyoming took place on Lightning Creek, almost a hundred miles south of Newcastle in what is now Niobrara County. John Owens was involved, acting as one of a large posse of deputies Sheriff Miller had enlisted to arrest and take into custody a party of Sioux from the Pine Ridge Agency who were charged with killing livestock belonging to ranchers and slaughtering game in violation of the laws of the state.[59]

When the posse came up on the Sioux, a party of twenty-three men and forty women and children, Sheriff Miller led his deputies into the dry bed of Lightning Creek, and he and Owens, his most trusted aide, climbed up the embankment. Miller called out to the Sioux that he was there to arrest them and demanded their surrender. His command, repeated several times, was ignored. When his voice began to give out, the sheriff asked Owens to try.

As Owens shouted, repeating the demand, a shot rang out, and

Miller went down. A bullet had struck him in the leg, severing the femoral artery, and blood spurted. Owens returned the fire as the other deputies scrambled up the bank, and the shooting became general. Deputy Louis Falkenberg toppled over, a bullet through his neck, and died instantly. Sheriff Miller died about thirty minutes after he had been hit.

The Sioux had also suffered badly in the exchange. Owens saw Black Kettle, a warrior known for his animosity to whites, fire the first shot, striking Miller. He immediately centered the Indian in his sights and dropped him with a death shot.[60] Eagle Feather, who had been heard to brag that he would kill the sheriff, was shot through the legs and died from loss of blood. Two others Indians were killed, and a number suffered nonfatal injuries.[61] Many in Weston County believed that it was John Owens's rifle that accounted for all four dead Sioux.[62]

Although a citizens' petition requesting the appointment of John Owens to replace the deceased Bill Miller as Weston County sheriff was presented to the county commissioners, the board chose Fred Coates to fill the office until the November election.[63] Owens stayed on as chief deputy.

At the next regular election, Owens again ran for sheriff and was elected. He would remain in office through several election cycles, until finally being defeated in November 1910.

In November 1904 Owens was found guilty in police court of assault and battery on a man and fined ten dollars.[64] This may have resulted from an altercation in the House of Blazes, which he still operated, and not from his activity as sheriff. The Newcastle press thought the matter of so little importance that it did not mention it in its pages.

His arrest in February 1906 of a young man named Logan Blizzard on a horse-theft charge triggered a series of events that led to another killing.[65]

Blizzard was tried, convicted, and sentenced to five years in the penitentiary. It was still the dead of winter when Sheriff Owens set out by train in early March with his prisoner, handcuffed and shackled with leg-irons. The train derailed north of Sydney, Nebraska. Three men were killed in the pileup, but Owens and his prisoner escaped serious injury. Owens managed to board another train with his prisoner and proceed, but when Blizzard complained that he had hurt his leg in the wreck, Owens removed the leg-irons. At a point near Dix, three miles east of Kimball, Nebraska, Blizzard asked to have the cuffs removed also, as he had to visit the water closet. Owens complied and followed his prisoner to the facility. But there Blizzard slammed the door in the sheriff's face and locked it. Smashing the window, he leaped out of the swiftly moving train. Miraculously uninjured in the fall, he plunged through the bitter cold. He stole a horse and rifle from a man named Robert Gunderson and rode off to the G. W. Fetterman ranch several miles distant. Cold and wet, he holed up there.

Owens meanwhile had gone on to Kimball, where he enlisted the assistance of Kimball County Sheriff E. W. Bartholomew. The officers took another train back to the scene of the escape. There they met Gunderson with a team and buggy and Godfrey Pearson on horseback. Determining the direction Blizzard had taken from tracks in the snow, Owens, Bartholomew, and Gunderson followed in the buggy, and Pearson rode along on his horse. They headed directly for the Fetterman ranch, where they figured Blizzard had taken refuge.

Owens, mortified and angry that his prisoner had escaped, was determined to recapture him without delay. Growing increasingly impatient at the pace set by the buggy's team, he insisted on changing places with Pearson. Once mounted on Pearson's horse, he galloped on ahead and reached the Fetterman place before the others.

As he suspected, Blizzard was there. Owens confronted the young man with drawn pistol, but Blizzard refused his order to surrender. As Owens later testified,

> He stepped outside of the door, caught his coat and spread [it] open . . . and asked me to shoot him. He said he would rather die than to go the penitentiary because if he went there he would be there the balance of his life. He again insisted that I shoot him. I told him I would not do so unless he forced me to do it as I did not want to hurt him. Then he says, "If I break and run will you shoot me?" I said, "No, sir, I won't because there are three sheriffs coming and you could not get away anyway." Then he commenced to crowd me, backing me back. . . .
>
> He said, "If I had a gun I would kill you. . . . I'll die before I'll go to the pen." And he jumped at me and said, "Shoot!" and I did shoot.[66]

One shot from Owens's revolver struck Blizzard, and he died instantly. At an inquest held in the undertaking rooms of Coroner F. M. Woolridge at Kimball on March 13, 1906, jurors heard the testimony of Owens and the other witnesses to the shooting, Mr. and Mrs. G. W. Fetterman and their nephew, Tommie Elders. The jury's verdict was that the deceased "came to his death from a gunshot wound [and] that the gun was fired by John Owens, Sheriff of Weston County, while attempting to recapture the deceased, that said act was justifiable in his performance of his official duty and we completely exonerate him from any blame."[67]

The law had cleared him, but the killing of an unarmed man did not enhance Owens's prestige in Weston County; some folks there held the incident against him for the rest of his life. But around the state and Black Hills region, Owens's popularity was undiminished, as evidenced by a blurb in a January 1908 edition of the *Times* of Deadwood, South Dakota:

> John Owens, sheriff of Weston county, Wyoming, was in the city yesterday on business. Mr. Owens is serving his tenth year as sheriff of his county and is more popular than during his first years. While in the city he met many old friends whom he knew in Cheyenne and when he was freighting to Deadwood in the early days. Mr. Owens is not a very large man physically, but he is one of the truest men and friends that the west ever produced. His heart is the biggest thing about him.[68]

Less than a month after the unfortunate Logan Blizzard incident, Owens suffered a personal tragedy. His wife, Addie, who had been suffering for some time with several ailments, died on April 2, 1906. John was left to raise their fifteen-year-old son, Sterling.[69]

Then in 1907 the rising antisaloon, antigambling reformist movement sweeping the country reached even remote Newcastle. Although the citizens there were not yet ready to follow the hatchet-wielding Carrie Nation and her minions and close the saloons, popular opinion turned against open gambling. As an officer of the law, John Owens was in no position to buck the trend, and was forced to sell his saloon, gambling house, and theater.

In 1910 Owens, now sixty-seven years of age, ran for reelection. Some Weston County voters evidently questioned his capability because of his advanced years, but the *News Letter Journal* supported him, saying, "In answer to the statement that [Owens] is an old man, it can be said that, if so, he has grown old in his endeavor to make this a peaceful and law-abiding community where we are sure to be protected from the depredations of criminals who infest the Black Hills country. He is not half as old as his age and is the youngest man in the country."[70]

Nevertheless, Ralph Hackney, his opponent, defeated Owens by the slim margin of thirteen votes. Owens contested the election results, claiming that many recent arrivals in the county, mainly Polish immigrants, had neglected to register and had therefore voted illegally. He further claimed these people had voted in a bloc against him because, as sheriff, he had seized their livestock to settle unpaid mortgages.

Hackney remained in the sheriff's office for a year and a half as the case dragged on through the courts. Then, in July 1912, the courts installed Owens as sheriff for the remaining six months of the two-year term. In the final resolution of the case in early January 1913, each litigant was awarded one year's salary as sheriff, and each was required to pay his own costs and legal fees.[71]

Meanwhile, as the contested election case worked its way through the courts, Owens found himself without a job. An opportunity arose when a series of shootings occurred at the coal-mining town of Cambria, and the Cambria Fuel Company employed him in February 1911 as a watchman to put a lid on things. The previous November a tough character named John Feeney had shot and severely wounded Tom Jones, but nobody apparently had the nerve to arrest him. On his arrival, Owens rectified that failure. He collared Feeney and lodged him in the county jail.[72]

On the night of February 17 Owens's six-shooter spoke again, and another man died. At a coroner's inquest the next day, Owens related what happened. He said he had been in the pool hall until it closed at nine o'clock and then retired.

Had just got in a dose of sleep when I heard a gun shot. I jumped out of bed and come out on the top porch of the office building in my night clothes and bare-footed and while I was on the porch I heard some loud talk and another gun shot. I run in and put on part of my clothes. As I came out I still heard this loud talk and I started down toward it and met the night watchman, Jeppe Lavredson, and I asked him who was doing the shooting and he said he did not know. So I went right on by him in a hurry, and when I got right at the crossing of the railroad track I come up close to two men. One was [Bill "Bottle Ass"] Davis and the other was [Mike] Duffy and I said, "Hold up, there, who is doing that shooting?" and just at that time [Davis] pulled the gun off [fired] again as close as that machine [three feet]. So I just dropped back and said, "Stop that shooting and throw up your hands."

I said that to Davis about three times . . . and I heard the gun cock. I did not see the gun . . . and when I heard it cock I just shoved my gun out in that direction and fired.[73]

Owens said he called for Jesse Larson to fetch a light and then went after Duffy and brought him back. As a crowd gathered, Owens said, a man sidled up to him and whispered, "You had better look out for Tom Jones, and if I was in your place I would get away." Evidently Tom Jones, who had recovered from his earlier gunshot wound, was a particular friend of Bottle Ass Davis, and was considered a dangerous man. This advice "kind of excited me," Owens said, "and I went to Mr. Naysmith [superintendent of the Cambria Fuel Company] and asked him what I should do, as I was afraid of a mob."

Friends of Davis pressed for a charge of first-degree murder to be brought against Owens, which would have meant confinement in jail without possibility of release on bail, but County Prosecuting Attorney James O. Marts, after talking to Owens, decided on a second-degree murder charge and permitted Owens's release on bond. The following September Marts, with the concurrence of Assistant Prosecuting Attorneys Metz and Sackett and the county commissioners, after investigating "the conditions existing in Weston County . . . , and the probability of securing an impartial jury for the trial," decided "that a verdict of guilty against the defendant . . . cannot in all probability be had," and received the court's approval to nolle prosequi the case.[74]

Owens completed the disputed term as sheriff. Now seventy years old, he chose not to go through another campaign for office. With his famous saloon and dance hall a thing of the past, his sheriff job gone, his wife dead, and his son grown to manhood (in December 1912 Sterling married and moved to a house of his own), there was nothing to keep Owens in Newcastle. He took work for a time as a guard at the state penitentiary at Rawlins. When construction began on the State Industrial Institute at Worland using convict labor, he was put in charge of the workers.[75] He remained there as a guard until retirement in 1920 at the age of seventy-seven.

One day on a visit to Thermopolis he contributed to a collection being taken up for a woman who had been crippled in an accident. When he saw the woman in the wheelchair he recognized her immediately as Serena, his former wife who had divorced him many years earlier because of his gambling habits. Perhaps out of a remaining affection for his once beautiful bride, or perhaps simply out of human compassion, Owens proposed marriage to Serena again, and again they were wed. They lived together at Worland until he retired and then moved to Thermopolis.

John Owens died there on his eighty-fourth birthday, August 11, 1927. His son, Sterling, an officer on the Casper police force, took Owens's body back to Newcastle and buried him beside Addie in the Greenwood Cemetery. The gray granite marker over his grave has only one word: "Owens." It was his wish. "I'm only a plain, rough man," he said, "and when I die, just put a plain, rough stone at my head.[76]

— 5 —

JOEL A. FOWLER
1846–1884

Joe is not by profession a "bad man from Bitter Creek." On the contrary, when his deeds are not inspired by whiskey, a pleasanter or a squarer man cannot be found.
— *Santa Fe Daily New Mexican*, February 28, 1880

There was no question he was one of the most notorious bad men of the west of all time.
— Montague Stevens, January 27, 1953

Joel Fowler has always been controversial. In one of his biographies, prolific writer Richard O'Connor characterized Fowler as "a drunken apprentice bad man," which prompted Ramon Adams, that indefatigable critic of all outlaw-lawman literature, to sniff: "If Fowler was an apprentice I'd hate to tangle with a professional."[1]

New Mexico historian Harvey Ferguson was in the Adams camp, calling Fowler "a perfect specimen of the licensed killer at his worst . . . , a homicidal maniac."[2] It was the considered opinion of Frank Collinson, who personally knew many western gunfighters, that Fowler was "the worst killer there ever was in New Mexico."[3]

Although he was damned in the New Mexico press of the 1880s as "The Exterminator," "The Annihilator," and "The Human Hyena," those who knew Fowler and wrote about him couldn't concur on such basic facts as when and where he was born and even his Christian name. Western writers, deriving most of their information from confusing newspaper articles and the recollections of old-timers, have had the same trouble.

There has always been general agreement that Fowler was a small, wiry fellow, barely five feet tall and weighing little more than one hundred pounds. Montague Stevens, for instance, who knew Fowler in his latter days, remembered him as being "a little man with eyes close together . . . about five feet high [but] pretty strong."[4] A contemporary newspaper story called Fowler "a small man but as strong as a giant."[5] And yet to compound the confusion the very name Joel Fowler seems to engender, a recent encyclopedist described him as "a tall, striking man."[6]

Conflicting sources have led followers of the Fowler story to place his birth in the states of Indiana, Mississippi, Massachusetts, and South Carolina. A number of writers have followed early newspaper reports that he was born in Indiana in 1849, 1850, or 1851.[7] An Albuquerque newspaper, however, debunked this report in 1884, stating categorically that "Fowler was not a native of the Hoosier State," but was born and reared in Mississippi.[8] Rejecting these sources and citing a U.S. census report, one writer insisted in magazine articles that the "Harry Fowler" enumerated at Silver City, New Mexico, in 1880 was in fact Joel Fowler, and his place of birth was Massachusetts in 1854.[9]

Joel A. Fowler himself in sworn testimony taken in November 1883 said that he was born in Marshall County, Mississippi,[10] a statement confirmed by U.S. census records. He was four years of age when enumerated at Northern Division, Marshall County, Mississippi, on November 26, 1850, indicating an 1846 year of birth. His father was a thirty-three-year-old farmer, also named Joel A., and his mother was named Rebecca, age thirty-one. Residing in the family home were three siblings of young Joel, and two grown men—Archibald Fowler, twenty-two, an uncle; and Joel M. Fowler, thirty-two, apparently a cousin to his father.[11]

Young Joel seems to have been singularly attached to his uncle Archibald Young, generally called "A. Y." Born in South Carolina in 1828, A. Y. became a lawyer and in 1859 married Juliette Peak, daughter of Captain Jeff Peak and sister of Junius "June" Peak, later the renowned city marshal of Dallas and noted Texas Ranger captain. By 1861 A. Y. was well established in the legal profession at Fort Worth.

Joel seems to have followed him to Fort Worth and reportedly began studying law in his offices.[12]

A. Y. Fowler had a fierce temper and was known to resort to violence on little provocation, traits that later so distinguished his nephew, Joel. After a disputed election in 1856 over the location of the Tarrant County seat, he and a man named Hiram Calloway had an altercation that resulted in a broken arm for Fowler. John B. York, later sheriff of Tarrant County, sided with Calloway in the affair, and Fowler never forgave him.[13]

The feud between Fowler and York erupted on August 24, 1861, when the two men met on the Fort Worth city square. Fowler pulled a knife and began slashing as York reached for a pistol. York was cut in twelve places before he downed Fowler with a bullet through the chest. Then entered another combatant, identified in the press only as Fowler's nephew, but who was almost certainly young Joel. He turned loose a blast from a double-barreled shotgun, killing York instantly. A. Y. Fowler also died of his wounds.[14]

If, as seems likely, it was indeed Joel Fowler, then about fifteen, who killed John York at Fort Worth in 1861, the affair was probably his introduction to violent behavior. We are told that "at school he was a model student, and at church he was well-mannered and respectful. Everybody knew what he was: pious, soft-spoken, obedient, kind, friendly. He was no problem child." But the writer provides no documentation for his assertion.[15]

One of the perennial stories about Joel's early life also lacks authentication. About 1869 he is said to have married "the girl he had eyes on from the first grade" and begun the practice of law. All was idyllic until, goes the tale, he caught his wife in bed with another man and emptied his pistol into the fellow. This may have happened (if it happened) in 1875 or 1877; the writer cites both years in two versions of the tale.[16]

This event, according to the legend, was the decisive turning point in Joel Fowler's life. From that time on it is said he took to the owl-hoot trail in Texas, becoming a "rustler, highwayman, stagecoach robber and outlaw."[17] That Fowler in the 1870s became an outlaw and fugitive from justice in Texas is beyond dispute, but contemporary records seem to indicate that, rather than highway robbery or rustling, his criminal activities tended more toward crooked gambling and con games, spiced with a propensity for mayhem. It is also clear his criminal career in Texas began long before either 1875 or 1877.

As early as 1871 he was in trouble with the law in Longview, Texas. As an Upshur County old-timer named William Conley Matthews recalled, "hawks of prey, men like Joel Fowler," descended on Longview (which was then in Upshur County) when the railroad reached the town in 1871. Law enforcement was scant or completely lacking, so "Captain Campbell," a local merchant, assumed responsibility for protecting local citizens from the thieving scoundrels. When his firm paid a couple of farmers $2,200 in cash for their cotton, Campbell suspected they would be targeted by Fowler. As expected, Fowler was soon trying to inveigle the farmers into one of his braced gambling games. Campbell told Matthews, who was a callow teenager at the time, "to get his gat and come along." Together they interfered in the crooked play. Infuriated, Fowler drew a gun and swung it wildly, striking young Matthews on the head and knocking him to the ground. But Campbell tackled him, and Fowler got "his face beaten to a pulp and his head cracked no little."[18]

Whether related to this incident or another, Upshur County officials brought an indictment in June of that year against Fowler, charging him with assault to murder.

He was still wanted on that charge six years later when Texas Ranger Sergeant N. O. Reynolds arrested him in Lampasas on June 25, 1877. In his monthly report to Ranger headquarters Sergeant Reynolds noted that Fowler was also wanted in Travis and Williamson counties on similar charges.[19]

In Williamson County, he was charged with attacking one A. W. Grimes on August 6, 1876, and a grand jury brought in an assault to murder indictment on October 3. A month later Fowler made bond of $400, which was ordered forfeited by the court on September 23, 1878, when the defendant failed to appear to answer the charge. Fowler's lawyers claimed their client had been unable to make his court appearance because he had been ill at Round Rock on that date. Their request to set aside the court order was granted. This game was played again in 1879 and 1880, when the court grew tired and placed the case on the retired docket.[20]

Fowler was indicted again on September 22, 1877, in Williamson

County for assaulting Joseph Harris with "intent to kill and murder." This case, too, dragged through the courts without resolution for several years before finally dying a quiet and unnoticed death.[21]

The Travis County case also languished and eventually died. The fugitive from justice list issued by the adjutant general's office in Austin for 1878 still listed Fowler as a wanted man from Upshur County.[22]

According to a later newspaper report out of Dallas, Fowler lived in that town for a while, and during that period "shot and stabbed" a former city alderman named Leopold Bohny and was "regarded as the most desperate man in Texas." He was said to have "figured as a shooter in Dallas, Fort Worth, Round Rock, Austin, Taylor and San Antonio," and to have killed in total six men.[23]

"The number of [Fowler's] killings in Texas he took to the hangman's noose with him," one researcher has written. "He was on the loose for seven years."[24] Assisting him in his criminal activities during the Texas years was a man named John B. Barnes, reputed to be Fowler's cousin.[25] Barnes later rejoined Fowler in New Mexico and shared a jail cell with him. The two argued and fought, and Barnes reportedly accused Fowler of killing a man in Texas for twenty-five cents.[26]

Whatever the truth or falsity of the stories that have come down regarding Fowler's Texas years, his murderous career after he left the Lone Star State for New Mexico can be much better documented.

He turned up in Las Vegas in 1879 when that town was the end of track on the Atchison, Topeka and Santa Fe line and was regarded as one of the wildest hellholes in the entire West. There he is said to have opened a dance hall on Sixth Street and "married" (or cohabitated with) one of his girls.[27]

It was here that confusion with the two Fowlers, Joel and Harry, developed. Harry Fowler was a twenty-six-year-old actor and variety theater manager from Massachusetts who was married to an eighteen-year-old girl from Michigan named Josie, who also performed on stage.[28] These Fowlers were in several New Mexico towns at the same time as Joel and a woman named Belle, who had come from Texas with him.[29] Belle was described by one who knew her as "a very beautiful young woman whom [Fowler] introduced as his wife. [She] was an expert manipulator of the pasteboards and could hold her own against all comers in any game of chance."[30]

The local papers confused the two Fowler couples,[31] and later writers, drawing on the newspaper source, repeated the error.

Josie Fowler, the wife of Harry, was evidently a very colorful individual who seemed more fitted to be the consort of the equally newsworthy Joel than a mere actress. A year before the Fowlers turned up in Las Vegas, a Reno, Nevada, paper marveled: "Josie Fowler of New Haven snuffs candles and cores apples with a revolver. The young men are exceedingly respectful in their attentions to her."[32]

In addition to her theatrical work, Josie gambled professionally, as did Belle, which probably contributed to their being confused. Since they shared the same surname and traveled in the same sporting and theatrical circles, the four Fowlers undoubtedly knew each other and perhaps were quite intimate.

Despite the violence rampant in Las Vegas during the time he was there, Joel Fowler apparently managed his dance hall without incident of consequence. After six months he and Belle moved on to Santa Fe, then enjoying a boom. Early in 1880 he opened the Texas Saloon and Dance Hall on San Francisco Street.[33]

The other Fowlers, Harry and Josie, also resettled in Santa Fe, where Harry, in partnership with an actor named Dave McCoy, opened the Theatre Comique not far from Joel's establishment. McCoy and an actress named Grace Rallia took the leading roles in the theater's presentations, with supporting roles played by Josie Fowler and a woman billed as Belle LaMont.[34] (One wonders if "Belle LaMont" was the woman identified only as "Belle," who was passing as the wife of Joel Fowler.)

At Santa Fe on Friday, February 27, 1880, Joel Fowler put on one of the displays of drunken and violent exhibitionism for which he would become notorious. He started drinking Thursday evening and continued all through the night. As the *Santa Fe Daily New Mexican* reported, on Friday morning

he took his stand upon San Francisco Street, near the plaza, and with a breech-loading shotgun and a full supply of cartridges, bid defiance to all.

The time was between seven and eight, and when Fowler first made his appearance upon the street, it was crowded with people. However, this was soon changed, for when Fowler pointed his gun down the street, without seeming to care whether he hit a lamp post or an Apache, the just before busy street became as deserted as a graveyard, and as far as the eye could reach not a person was in sight.

Having thus cleared the neighborhood, Fowler began to load and discharge his weapon with extreme precision and rapidity, at one time aiming at the sun, at another at the new tank at the depot, occasionally varying the performance by putting the muzzle of the gun in his mouth and letting off a whoop which was heard by Manzanares [a small village fifteen miles south of Santa Fe] and there mistaken for a locomotive whistle.

Finally, after Fowler had held his position for about half an hour, a hundred or so of the boldest spirits in town held a council in Keyser's Saloon, and after hastily adopting resolutions of respect to the memory of those who might fall in the attack, boldly advanced upon the enemy.

In the meantime, a Mexican passed along the street on the side on which the man and the shot-gun were, and just as Fowler finished a wild and blood-curdling invocation to the pictured bills upon the wall of the Theatre Comique and discharged the gun as a sort of "Amen," he was leaped upon by the pedestrian and borne to the ground, where he lay panting and quoting all the maledictions from Shakespeare he could remember until the army came rushing down and secured him.

He was immediately taken to jail, that is, immediately as was possible under the circumstance. He struggled desperately, and when the jail was reached, he was carried in bodily while the procession followed behind bearing as trophies his coat, hat, pants, boots and suspenders.

Then he was put into a cell, and jailer Silva sat upon him and sang a lullaby to quiet his nerves.[35]

Perhaps aware that he had worn out his welcome in Santa Fe after this performance, Joel Fowler soon left town. He next turned up in White Oaks, a new community in Lincoln County, New Mexico, where he opened another saloon and gambling house. Veteran New Mexico cattleman Clement Hightower remembered Fowler's arrival in early 1880 with "a most complete gambling outfit and two rather good looking females, one of whom operated a faro game and the other dealt monte."[36] One of the "good looking females" was undoubtedly Belle; perhaps Josie was the other.

At White Oaks, Fowler had one of his rare experiences as an enforcer of the law and in the process killed a man.

On May 31, 1880, a pair of hard cases named Joseph Askew and Virgil Cullom got drunk and raced their horses up and down the street, shooting up the town. White Oaks, however, was full of hard cases, and the town's residents were not as inclined to accept such behavior as were the folks in Santa Fe when Joel Fowler put on a similar display. Some of them opened fire on the drunken shootists. A bullet struck Askew in the arm and knocked him from his horse.

Joel Fowler and Dave Riverhouse mounted up and set out after the pair. Finding Askew where he had fallen "with his arm lying beneath him," they dismounted, "straightened his arm in place, put his hat under his head and went in pursuit of Cullom." When they found him, Fowler jumped down from his horse, leveled his Winchester rifle across the saddle, and shouted for Cullom to surrender.

When the man did not drop his pistol, Fowler fired, shooting him in the chest. The bullet tore through Cullom's lung and, turning "pale in the face [he] fainted from internal hemorrhage. Cullom died at 6 o'clock next morning."[37]

With the profits from his saloon and gambling ventures, Fowler invested in a ranching operation in the Gallinas Mountains north of White Oaks. This new enterprise led to more killing, and once again Fowler became the central figure in a complicated and controversial affair. The story, as it appeared in the December 19, 1881, edition of the *Las Vegas Daily Optic*, was typical of the territorial press coverage:

> Joel Fowler, a White Oaks man, well known in Texas and New Mexico, has a large herd of cattle in the Gallinas Mountains. Last week he had forty head stolen by Jim Greathouse, Jim Finley and a man named Forrest.[38] Another rustler drove them to Georgetown, in Grant County, and sold them. Fowler and a fellow named Jim Ike took a train and met Greathouse, Finley and Forrest on their return at Shaw ranch near Socorro. They [Fowler and Ike] deceived them as to their intentions, camping with them for some thirty miles. Ike was riding fifty yards behind the wagon. Greathouse stopped for lunch and

pulled his gun on Fowler, saying, "I know your racket, but it won't work." Fowler had a double-barrel shotgun and was too quick for Greathouse. The rustlers died with their boots on.

Evidently cattleman Fowler and Ike, in defense of their lives, had simply dispensed rangeland justice to a trio of thieving rustlers. The press accepted this account, as did almost all later chroniclers of the Fowler history. But the story had only come from Fowler and Ike; all other witnesses to the shooting lay dead back on the trail.

There was, however, another version, recounted later by New Mexico pioneer Clement Hightower, who said he got most of the details from Jim Ike, whom he knew as "Ross," after Fowler's death.

Hightower said that Fowler, while running his resort at White Oaks, began an association with Greathouse, a notorious character with a long history of nefarious conduct. "He was," said the *Socorro Sun* succinctly, "known as the killer of many men."[39]

Described as "rather a tall man, with a heartless staring countenance,"[40] Greathouse was widely known on the frontier as "Whiskey Jim," for his illegal operations as a booze peddler to the Indians. It was said he had been especially targeted by General Ranald Mackenzie, who issued orders to his troops to kill or capture him if he was seen in the Indian Territory. Greathouse hunted buffalo and was with the hunters at the famous Yellow House Canyon fight with the Comanches in February 1877. At the Reynolds and Rath trading post he ran a scam, driving off hunters' horses, hiding them, and bringing them back to collect a reward. For a time he teamed up with "Larapie Dan" Moran and Dan "Little Red" McClusky, two notorious horse thieves who were hanged near Fort Griffin, Texas, by the vigilantes. Later he drifted on to New Mexico, where he became a part of the cattle-fencing ring that bought stolen cattle from Lincoln County rustling gangs. In partnership with a man named Joseph Kuch, he established a road ranch in 1880, some forty miles north of White Oaks. A horse-changing station and refreshment stop for travelers between White Oaks and Las Vegas, the place became known as Greathouse's Tavern or Red Cloud.

The only heroic act of Greathouse's disreputable career occurred at his roadhouse in November 1880, when the most wanted outlaw in the territory, Billy the Kid, and members of his gang holed up there and the place was surrounded by a posse. It was a standoff until a truce was called, and Greathouse came out of the building to offer himself as a hostage and allow posseman Jim Carlyle entry into the building to negotiate with the outlaws. Unfortunately, somebody broke the truce, and in the resulting gunfire Carlyle was shot and killed.[41]

Joel Fowler during 1880 and the early months of 1881 began acquiring small bunches of cattle under the COD brand. Perhaps recognizing in Jim Greathouse a kindred — that is, larcenous — soul, he entered into an agreement with Greathouse and a couple of his pals, Jim Finley and Jim Forrest (a man Hightower remembered as "Jim Conley"), to run his cattle with a herd they had collected in the Gallinas Mountains. Neighboring ranchers soon began to notice a suspiciously rapid increase in the size of this jointly owned herd, which quickly grew to an estimated ten thousand head. As the other ranchers muttered their concern, Fowler and his partners began a hasty and unannounced removal of the entire herd to a wild and isolated section known as Bear Springs in western Socorro County. The cattle were moved in small bunches, "each drive increasing in numbers as it reached its destination."[42]

About this time Fowler moved his gambling outfit and girls to Socorro, where he posed as the sole owner of the cattle at the Bear Springs ranch, representing Greathouse and his pals as employees. This arrangement was suggested by Fowler and agreed to by the others, who were willing to let fall on Fowler's shoulders the growing suspicion in some quarters that a large-scale rustling operation was going on.

Fowler found a ready market for beef at railroad construction sites and kept his "employees" busy moving cattle out to meet his commitments. He put off sharing sales revenues with them, however, claiming delays in payments by the purchasers.

Meanwhile, Fowler was preparing a trap for his secret partners. He arrived at the ranch one day to report that officers from Lincoln County were in Socorro with papers to arrest all of them, including himself. In order to save the stolen stock and themselves, he urged Greathouse and the others to drive the illegally acquired cattle off to another range, while he dealt with the officers.

He certainly "dealt with the officers," for the time had come to complete his carefully plotted double cross. Returning to Socorro, he swore out complaints against the three men, charging them with cattle stealing. He then led a posse to the Bear Springs ranch, where he "recovered" the combined Greathouse-Fowler herd, reportedly stolen. The scheme was so well planned and carried out that newspapers condemned Greathouse and his companions as cattle thieves and lauded Fowler for his energetic pursuit of the rustlers and congratulated him on recovery of his stock.

> After thus outlawing themselves, Greathouse and his companions began to see the light but still were unable to lawfully claim their own property. They decided there was only one way out: to really steal their own stock, drive them away, sell them and change climate. . . .
>
> Hastily gathering something like 100 head of cattle, they trailed them southward [to the Alamo] Ranch, long since abandoned, where . . . they decided to make a stand and if necessary fight it out.[43]

Greathouse rode to the ranch of Joe Stinson, a beef contractor, and arranged the sale of the cattle. On his return he was surprised to find Fowler and a man named Ross (Jim Ike) in peaceful conversation with his two pals. All had "laid aside their arms and cartridge belts in token of good faith while Fowler told a weird story."[44]

Once again employing his con game skills, Fowler explained that to save his own skin, he had played along with the officers, but reminded his "partners" he had forewarned them of the posse's coming, thus allowing them to escape arrest. He now proposed that they all return to the Bear Springs ranch, round up the cattle remaining there, and bring them to the Alamo. From there they could sell the entire bunch to Stinson on Greathouse's contract, after which they could split the profits and each follow his own trail.

Greathouse and his buddies bought it. In doing so, they agreed to their own death warrants.

The next morning they moved out, Finley and "Conley" in a chuck wagon pulled by a span of mules, Fowler, Greathouse, and "Ross" behind, driving a small remuda of remounts. All had recovered their firearms. Fowler packed a six-shooter on his hip and carried a sawed-off shotgun across his saddle.

About noon a halt was made for dinner. . . . Conley was busy unhitching the team while Finlay [*sic*] gathered wood to build a fire; while they were thus engaged the other three arrived. This was the very situation Fowler had planned: separated and unsuspecting. Fowler fired one barrel of the shotgun into Greathouses's [*sic*] breast and quickly turning, emptied the other into Conley's body and before the astonished Finlay could account for himself, a shot from Fowler's pistol dropped him in his tracks. Thus quoth Ross, who also fired at Finley, but, because of his excitement, probably failed to hit the mark.

After taking their money and other things of value, Fowler and Ross hitched up the team, leaving the bodies of the murdered men where they fell, and drove into Socorro and reported to the Court officials a thrilling story of a fight to the death with the three rustlers. The Socorro paper again printed fulsome accounts of the bravery and unerring marksmanship of Citizen Joe Fowler.[45]

Clement Hightower's editors remarked that his "account of Whiskey Jim's end is based upon the account of a willing but ineffectual accessory thereto, to which Hightower gave credence, and should settle this homicide for all reasonable purposes."[46]

So in one bold and cold-blooded stroke, the wily Fowler had disposed of his three ranching "partners" and gained complete control of their mutually owned herds, augmented by stolen stock. For the next year and a half he continued to manage his ranch without recorded incident, although his duplicity in dealing with Greathouse had evidently made his name anathema to other shady dealers in cattle. In August 1882 a New Mexico paper reported that "rumors of the assassination of Joel Fowler are again rife on the streets. It is a well known fact that thieves and rustlers would kill him if given the chance."[47]

Then, in September 1883, there was another eruption of violence on his range. As reported in the *Albuquerque Daily Democrat*, when Fowler discovered that one of his ranch hands, a man called George "Pony" Neal,[48] was actually the brother of "Jim Forrest," one of his victims in the triple slayings of December 1881, he suspected Pony might be bent on revenge, so he promptly fired him. If the man had previously planned on murdering Fowler, the thought now became an obsession. To help him in this aim, he sought out "Butcher Knife Bill" Childes, "a gambler and a bad man,"[49] and together they rode from Socorro to Fowler's Alamo ranch at Bear Springs and waited for Fowler to return from a cow hunt.

On the morning of September 17 Fowler showed up, accompanied by several of his ranch employees, including John Barnes, Francisco Vigil, and a man named Rogerio. Butcher Knife Bill immediately opened fire, but in his anxiety to accomplish his mission, shot too quickly and missed. Fowler swung around his ever-present shotgun and killed his assailant with a single blast. Pony Neal sprinted toward a nearby house, emptying his pistol without effect as he ran.

The house belonged to a man named McGee, described as "a good, peaceful man and highly respected."[50] McGee "went to the door of the house and called to Pony to come out of the house. Receiving no reply, he broke the door and looked in, when Pony shot him in the head, killing him instantly. Fowler then asked Pony to come out and fight it out with him. Pony refused to do so, and Fowler set fire to the house to drive him out, when Pony shot himself through the head. The three men were buried on the spot."[51]

The stories in other New Mexico papers were in much the same vein. The *New Mexico Weekly Review* called the incident "one of those terrible tragedies in West life which occasionally occurs."[52] A Silver City paper noted that the latest bloodshed made a total of "six men that Fowler has killed within a period of two years. . . . Joe Fowler is a dare-devil fellow, and the only man that bluffed John Gilmo [a tough Silver City gunman] while marshal of this city."[53]

This latest shooting spree by Fowler received considerable attention in the New Mexico press and was picked up and disseminated nationally.[54]

Publisher C. A. D. Conklin of the *Socorro Sun* allowed Fowler to make his own "personal statement concerning the late tragedy" at the Alamo ranch. His account provides a rare and interesting description of a gunfight by a personally involved gunfighter.

Fowler said he approached the Alamo ranch on that fateful morning and saw two men cooking breakfast over a camp stove. One he recognized as Pony, the man he had discharged; the other was a stranger to him.

When I got up within about ten steps of the camp fire . . . , one of the men jumped up . . . and sprang behind a post with his six-shooter in his hand, and the other jumped up and turned and made a break for his six-shooter.

The one behind the post about this time fired a shot. In return I fired a shot at the other, he being nearest to me. After this I exchanged shots with the other party behind the post. The party after firing from behind the post retreated around the house. I jumped off my horse and went around the house the other way, we both meeting at the corner, he firing at me and I trying to reload my shotgun, he getting in his shots too fast. I dropped my gun and pulled my six-shooter. I fired five shots from my six-shooter. He acted as if he was hit and ran back around the house and into the door. I broke around the other way to meet him, loading the shotgun at the same time. When I got around the house he fired two shots at me from the door casing, and I fired one load of buckshot into the door. This was the last shot that I fired, and he firing ten or twelve shots afterward from port holes.

About fifteen minutes after this exchange, McGee, who lived in the house, rode up with two neighbors, Hiram Brown and Robert D. Lippard, and Fowler told them what had happened. McGee volunteered to get the man out of the house. He approached the door and called out, but received no answer. Finally he kicked the door in and started to enter, but "when a shot from within killed him instantly," Fowler decided to smoke the man out.

The dirt roof was set on fire and during the burning of a couple of hours he would fire a shot now and then from the door and port holes. About half an hour after the roof had smoldered and the rooms had got full of smoke and long after he had ceased firing could be heard inside the last shot. We guarded the house that night and the next morning I went into the house and found the man lying flat on his back dead, with a six-shooter in his hand.

Fowler said he came into Socorro and "delivered myself up to Sheriff Simpson who took me before a justice of the peace for examination. The forenoon of the 19th [I] was tried and acquitted." He said there were strong indications that this shooting affair was initi-ated by those who wanted "to avenge the death of parties I had trou-ble with two years ago."[55]

Fowler may have believed that the hearing in the court of Justice of the Peace W. N. Beall had cleared him of all charges in the shootings at the Alamo ranch, but he was mistaken. Later he and two em-ployees, John Barnes and Francisco Vigil, would be arrested and charged with the murders of Pony Neal and William Childes. Even in the days immediately following the initial hearing, many residents of Socorro were fed up with Fowler's murderous acts.

One was a livery stable owner named "Turk" Kerrafin, who ap-proached Fowler aggressively on the street with a rifle in his hands. Fowler whipped out his six-shooter and pistol-whipped the man severely, according to newspaper reports.[56] In a "card" inserted in the *Socorro Sun*, Fowler defended his actions and denied any pistol-whipping: "As S. Kerrafin, called the Turk, spread reports about me yesterday, that I shot at him and wounded him with a pistol, I will say that he has told what is untrue. He provoked a quarrel with me Sun-day afternoon by drawing a rifle on me, to which I slapped him in the face."[57]

With attacks against him mounting both in the street and in the press, Fowler decided to seek another clime. Only three weeks after the shootings at the Alamo ranch, he sold all of his cattle operation to James D. Reed, a wealthy cattleman of Fort Worth, Texas,[58] and his partner, Wes Bruton. The price was $52,000, paid in cash,[59] a huge amount of money in 1883. When Reed and Bruton showed up in Socorro with the cash on November 6, Fowler met them and imme-diately deposited the funds in the Socorro County Bank.

After checking into the Grand Central Hotel with his "wife," he went to the offices of the *Socorro Sun* and asked the editor, Chester D. Potter, to insert a notice in the next edition of the paper that he had sold his ranch and would leave for Texas the following night. He said that all persons holding claims against him should present the same at the Socorro County Bank by noon the next day. Then, in the words of Editor Potter, he "started to take a census of bartenders."[60] He went on a grand celebratory binge, moving from saloon to saloon, waving two six-shooters, and getting drunker and meaner as he went. Potter has left a vivid account of this drunken exhibition:

A group of weapons-brandishing young men of Socorro in 1882, when Joel Fowler was prominent there. The photographer, Joseph E. Smith, participated in the lynching of Fowler, and his subjects may well have also. From the author's collection.

During his rounds of the saloons, Fowler met the Rev. Doctor J. H. Robinson of the Methodist Church, South. He surprised the Divine by asking him if he knew how to dance. He refused to accept a negative reply and insisted that Doctor Robinson was mistaken, emphasizing his conclusion with a fusillade of bullets, which, though they did not hit the Dominie's feet, persuaded him to do a jig.

Fowler met Justice of the Peace Daugherty a little later and gave him, also, a dancing lesson. After the Judge had performed he was taken by Fowler to the Monarch Saloon for a "bracer." It was at this time that I caught up with the procession. As I entered the place, Fowler was standing, his back to the bar, facing the entrance. In either hand he was twirling a revolver, pointing them at every person who attempted to leave. I tried to back out but he insisted that I must be thirsty. However, he kept the "drop" on the crowd while I was "quenched." That he had no soul for music was evidenced when he refused to compromise and accept a song instead of a dance. So I went through the motions while the crowd cheered.

Ed Cutler . . . , the proprietor of the "Monarch," was so much pleased with my exhibition that he climbed up on the bar behind Fowler and clapped time.[61]

When Fowler directed his attention to Cutler and ordered him to do a few "double shuffles" Potter "faded away."

Having "faded away," Potter did not actually witness the dramatic events later that night, but it was his recollection that after Fowler had continued his high jinks for some hours, City Marshal R. M. "Bob" Monroe and Guy Cox, his deputy, rather belatedly showed up with a man named Cale, who had been sent by Belle Fowler to help induce Fowler to quiet down and return to the hotel. Potter said the officers disarmed Fowler and accompanied him and Cale to the Grand Central, where Fowler insisted on having "just one more drink before he joined his wife."[62]

Cattleman Montague Stevens, who was staying at the Grand Central at the time and claimed to be an eyewitness to what then transpired, told it differently.

I was sitting out in front . . . with some friends smoking. . . . Suddenly we heard a terrible racket and we jumped up. . . . We looked in [the bar room] and there was Fowler with a couple of six-shooters in his hands. . . . He was making [an old man] dance and he was dancing. And Cale was standing at the bar looking on. Finally the old man sat down on the chair — he was played out.

Cale said to him, "Come on, Joe, and have another drink," and winked at the bartender. Joe came up to the bar, laid the two six-shooters down on it, and picked up the drink. When he did that the bartender suddenly grabbed the two six-shooters and put them behind [the bar].

Fowler said, "Give me back my six-shooters."

"No, Joe, I won't," he says, "I'll give them to you in the morning. I won't give them to you now because you've drunk too much and you'll only get yourself into trouble."

So then Fowler turned around to Cale and says, "It was you that told him to take those six-shooters." He says, "Take this." And he runs his hand forward and Cale fell to the ground. I never saw it but Fowler had taken a penknife out of his pocket and opened it and thrust it into Cale's heart. . . .

Well, then . . . I grabbed hold of Fowler with one hand and, I think it was the bartender grabbed him with the other, and we just held him between us. He began kicking around so that I began twisting his arm to keep him quiet. And he turned round and tried to bite me. So I said, "If you bite me I'll twist your arm off." And he quit trying to bite. In the meantime someone . . . sent off for the deputy sheriff in town and he came in a few minutes. . . . We held [Fowler] there several minutes and in came the sheriff who picked him up and put handcuffs on him and took him off to jail.

Well, Cale was taken and put . . . on a little sofa . . . and we took his shirt off. . . . We sent for a doctor. He just had a small little cut like a penknife will make but it had pierced the heart sac. It didn't kill him but he lived until the next day in the afternoon and then he died.[63]

This last victim of Joel Fowler's homicidal aggressions signed an affidavit hours before he died:

J. E. Cale, being duly sworn, disposes and says: That he is 36 years old, and was born at Jerico, Vermont: was at the Grand Central Hotel on the night of the 6th of November; Joel A. Fowler was with me; I was holding him from a stockman when he struck me with a Spanish dagger; I had no trouble with

Fowler; I was taking a gun from Fowler; he was drunk and swinging [it] around; I was afraid Fowler would shoot somebody else.[64]

The identity of Fowler's last victim has engendered as many conflicting statements from chroniclers as the early history of his murderer. He was said to be James E. Cale, a traveling salesman or drummer.[65] Perhaps his name was John Cole, and he was "a cowman and old-time friend" of Fowler's.[66] His name might have been Joseph Cale as reported by a contemporary newspaper and a knowledgeable historian.[67] Clement Hightower believed he was "an inoffensive miner named Kale."[68] One researcher thought he was a saloon owner from Engles, New Mexico,[69] a conclusion agreed to by Eugene Manlove Rhodes, who claimed to know the man well, but said his real name was Yale. "The man killed was Jim Yale, saloon keeper at Engle. If it wasn't Jim who was killed, that is a joke on Jim for we buried him. Curious mistake."[70]

But regardless of the dead man's identity, the citizens of Socorro County had about enough of the murderous Joel Fowler. Only a week after the death of Cale, Fowler and two of his cowboys, John Barnes and Francisco Vigil, were arraigned in the court of Justice of the Peace Beall in the matter of the killings at the Alamo ranch two months earlier. Judge William Tell DeBaun and Isaac S. Tiffany conducted the prosecution, and attorneys Neil B. Field and W. A. Leonard represented Fowler and his employees.

Just as the hearing began, DeBaun announced that charges against Vigil were being dropped in exchange for his testimony. Vigil took the stand and said that Fowler shot Bill Childes once in the side, inflicting "a large wound," and Barnes shot him once in the head. He said that Fowler shot at Pony Neal "many times" as he ran for the house. Under orders from Fowler, he and Rogerio had set fire to the house. To ensure his appearance before the grand jury, the court placed Vigil under a $500 bond.

The neighbor, R. D. Lippard, was called and testified that he had heard Fowler offer a $500 bounty to anyone who could tell him where he might find Pony Neal and that when he found Neal, he "would kill him before sun-down."

Fowler took the stand, and his testimony under oath was quite similar to what he had written to the *Socorro Sun* earlier. He admitted offering Lippard $500 for information as to the whereabouts of Pony Neal, who he had learned was a cousin of Jim Forrest,[71] one of the men Fowler had previously killed, and had sworn revenge.

The testimony of John Barnes, who gave his age as nineteen, corroborated Fowler's in most details.[72]

Fowler and Barnes were bound over to await the action of the grand jury. That body, after hearing prosecution reports of the shootings two years earlier resulting in the deaths of Greathouse, Finley, and Forrest, and the more recent killings of Neal and Childes, on November 22, 1883, brought in indictments charging Fowler with the murders of all these men.[73] The next day John Barnes was indicted as an accomplice in the murders.[74]

The two were confined together under heavy guard in the Socorro County jail, an adobe building next to the courthouse, but, somehow, despite the guards' vigilance, Fowler obtained a pistol. When the weapon was discovered, Fowler flew into a towering rage, directed primarily at his cellmate Barnes, whom he suspected of tipping off the jailers about the gun. Dissension between the two escalated. Barnes accused Fowler of many murders, including one in Texas for twenty-five cents. Fowler then attacked Barnes with such ferocity that the guards were forced to chain him to a heavy boulder in the cell. Some believed this violent behavior was an attempt by the wily Fowler to establish grounds for an insanity defense at his trial.[75]

At his own suggestion, Barnes on November 27 signed a remarkable affidavit. Visitors to Fowler in the jail, he said, had been the man's wife, Tom Nickles, George Smith, and Jack Best. Fowler, he continued, had importuned Jack Best to send telegraphic dispatches to Luke Short and Wyatt Earp and other

> desperadoes and outlaws to come to Socorro to assist the said Fowler in his present emergencies; that the said Fowler desired the assistance of said outlaws to aid him in getting out of the county and that the said Best returned to said prison and informed the said Fowler that he had sent the telegraphic dispatches . . . ; that one Joseph Collins . . . informed the affiant that if the writ of habeas corpus were granted in this case . . . that he should have two horses in readiness at the Windsor Hotel . . . so the affiant and said Fowler might escape from custody and

that he and Fowler should ride to San Marcial this county and take the train on the ATSF RR [Atchison, Topeka and Santa Fe Railroad] and escape from the territory.[76]

Noted gunfighters Wyatt Earp and Luke Short did not come to Fowler's assistance, nor did the famous pistoleer Ben Thompson, who reportedly also received a telegraphic plea for help.[77] But quickly responding and hurrying to Socorro with several cohorts was "Texas Ed" Rousseau, a Fowler relative, characterized by some as a "desperate character."[78] Rousseau assumed management of the Texas Saloon, on the northeast corner of the plaza, from which location he issued warnings that if any harm came to Fowler, he and his friends would wreak havoc on the city. Rumors flew that he was assembling a crowd of Texas gunmen for the purpose of taking over the jail and freeing the prisoner.[79]

The leading businessmen of Socorro, who all happened to be members of the "Committee of Safety," as they called the local vigilante organization, took these rumors quite seriously. Pedro Simpson, sheriff of Socorro County, was a personal friend of Fowler's, they believed, and might conspire in his rescue.[80] They turned to Governor Lionel Sheldon for help. The governor ordered Colonel Ethan W. Eaton to mobilize elements of the New Mexico militia at Socorro to guard the jail and prevent either a vigilante hanging or a jailbreak and rescue by Fowler's supporters. Eaton himself was a leading member of the Socorro Vigilance Committee and, according to Chester Potter, the militia units who began guarding the jail on November 10 were entirely composed of vigilantes. Eaton is said to have reached an agreement with Fowler's lawyers. Fowler would be allowed to stand trial, but if found guilty, there would be no appeal.[81]

A strange state of circumstances developed. One party of men wanted to storm the jail and help Fowler to escape, another group was anxious to lynch him, and a third was determined to protect him until he had a fair trial.[82]

In the end, the third group prevailed. Fowler was brought to trial for the murder of Cale at the December term of the Socorro County District Court, Judge Joseph Bell presiding. The defendant's attorneys were two of the highest-priced lawyers of the territory, Thomas B. Catron, head of the politically powerful "Santa Fe Ring," and Neill

B. Field of Socorro. Fowler reportedly paid these two legal luminaries $5,000 to provide a defense that was basically a claim that he was so drunk at the time of Cale's killing, he did not know what he was doing.[83] Montague Stevens said he attended the trial and

> from the evidence given it appeared Fowler had killed twenty-three men — that was his record — murdered them all. He had his own way of killing people. For instance, if he wanted to kill a man, he'd go right up to him and say in a friendly sort of way, "You gotta chew of tobacco?" The man would put his hand to his hip pocket to pull out the tobacco and then Fowler shot him and say he shot [him] in self defense. The crowd that was standing around they saw the man put his hand back but they took Fowler's word for it that it was for his gun he was reaching. And then he was arrested and taken to the justice of the peace and he was let off on the score of self defense. Those were the sort of tricks that Fowler used to play.[84]

But in the Cale murder case, the *Territory of New Mexico v. Joel A. Fowler*, the jury on Saturday, December 8, 1883, brought in a verdict of murder in the first degree. In imposing the sentence, Judge Bell the following Monday addressed the defendant:[85]

> After a fair and impartial trial, you have been convicted of a most heinous and wicked murder. You have been ably defended by distinguished and zealous counsel. The jury in your case arrived at the only just verdict which in the judgment of the court the facts warranted. I am informed that you have been guilty of other homicides in this territory of equal ferocity and I refer to that fact now not for the purpose of adding additional reproach to you, but to warn you that in your case there should be no hopes entertained by you that there will be executive interference to in any way modify the stern course of justice.[86]

He then sentenced Fowler to death by hanging, the sentence to be carried out on January 4, 1884.

The indictment of John Barnes had been altered to a charge of accessory to the murders of Pony Neal and William Childes only. He later stood trial, was convicted of murder in the fifth degree, and sentenced to eight years in the penitentiary.[87]

The verdict and sentence in Fowler's case met with approval in newspaper editorials throughout the Southwest, but some editors feared that Fowler's clever lawyers, through legal trickery, would still find a way to subvert justice. An editorial headline in a Texas paper asked the question: "CAN A RICH MAN HANG?" Fowler, it said, had "committed a most dastardly and cowardly murder . . . one of those crimes that stir public feelings to the extent of frenzy." After Judge Bell's denial of a motion for a new trial, "everyone felt that the lesson would at length be taught that no man's wealth places him above the law. . . . Not so. Fowler's attorneys, Tom Catron and Neill B. Field, are preparing papers necessary to take the case to the Supreme Court of the Territory on a writ of error. . . . The case cannot be argued until the January term of 1885. If a new trial is granted, the witnesses will all be dead or out of the country." The tone of the article plainly indicated that the lynching of Fowler might be necessary and completely appropriate.[88]

Strangely enough, the decision by Fowler's lawyers to appeal the verdict sealed their client's fate. Leaders of the vigilance committee, or the "Socorro Stranglers" as they were known throughout the territory, thought that this was a breach of faith and voided the agreement reached earlier. They were determined that Fowler should die, and die quickly. If he was not to swing at the end of a hangman's noose provided by legal process, then he must swing at the end of the noose they would supply. On the night the news of the appeal was announced, the vigilance committee met and voted unanimously to lynch Joel Fowler.[89]

Their opportunity came when Governor Sheldon, responding to numerous editorial complaints about the cost to the territory of militia maintenance at Socorro to protect one man, ordered Colonel Eaton to disband his force on January 21.[90] Shortly after midnight on the morning of January 23, the Socorro Stranglers made their move.

The report of what transpired that night was rather succinct in the pages of the *Socorro Advertiser*:

> Between the hours of one and two o'clock this morning a man rushed excitedly into this office and exclaimed, "They've killed Joe Fowler." We made inquiry of the individual as to who and how and where the deed was done, but could find out nothing beyond the fact that Fowler had been lynched. Subse-

quently we found one of the men who had been on guard at the time the prisoner was wrested from the law and life, and learned that about one hundred men had "got the drop" on the guards at the jail, and they, seeing it was the height of folly to resist such an onset, had quietly submitted to the mob and allowed the prisoner to be taken out. The guard said that they were told that unless they dropped their arms every one of them would be killed. After taking Fowler from the jail the mob proceeded with him down the street running westward from the court house plaza and hanged him to a large tree near the residence of Mrs. Elder. Whether Fowler flinched when the final moment had arrived, we were unable to learn. Not a man in town knows anything of the particulars. . . .

Later — Since the above was put in type we learn from a gentleman who saw the body of Fowler hanging where the lynchers left it, that Fowler begged most piteously when the lynchers were taking him from the jail, shouting "murder" at the top of his voice, but all to no purpose, the mob was composed of unmasked, determined citizens. Fowler was dragged to his doom showing the most abject cowardice, our informant states.[91]

After a flurry of telegraphic messages back and forth between Las Vegas and Socorro, the *Las Vegas Daily Optic*, two hundred miles away, provided more details:

The city was startled this morning by the report on the streets that Joe Fowler . . . had been lynched at Socorro last night. . . .

Last night a large body of men, all in mask, met in the outskirts of the town, and there the arrangements which would send the soul of the murderer into eternity were perfected. The jail was visited about ten o'clock by one of the vigilantes and Fowler was found to be sound asleep. The guards . . . had almost all been taken away, and only a few men guarded the entrance to the outer door and two others paced up and down in the hallway.

The mob, consisting of about two hundred armed men, waited until twelve o'clock and in a quiet and orderly manner marched to the jail, arriving there about 12:20 this morning. They were halted by their leader and a committee delegated to wait on the jailer and ask for the keys. The guards, seeing that resistance would be useless, quietly withdrew and the door of Joe Fowler's cell was soon opened and the criminal, yelling, pleading, calling for help, was taken outside the enclosure. No demonstrations were made by the crowd, and all was as quiet and orderly. . . . On the way, Fowler called loudly on heaven to protect him, when some wag in the crowd called out: "It's a cold night for angels, Joe. Better call on someone nearer town."

He then protested that the law-abiding citizens should protect him. The same voice replied: "You're in the hands of law-abiding citizens, Mr. Fowler, and they'll see that you get your deserts."

Only about two hundred yards from the jail, a tree was found which someone remarked "was about his size," and a rope being thrown over one of the lower limbs, and the victim's neck being encircled by the dangling noose, everything was ready. Fowler, trembling in every limb, continued his entreaties up to the very last. When he saw that help was not likely to come, and realized that every moment occupied in endeavors to save his life was just that much time lost to his preparation for the grave, he became very quiet and said:

"Boys, you are doing wrong, but you will not listen to me. When I'm dead, do me a favor and send my body to my uncle at Fort Worth, Texas.[92] Good-bye."

The rope was tightened and four strong men taking hold of it, the body of Fowler was drawn into the air. The end of the rope was then wound around the trunk of the tree and as soon as his life was extinct the crowd dispersed.

This morning . . . the body, still hanging, was visited by at least three thousand people. About eight o'clock it was lowered to the ground and a coroner's jury empaneled to sit upon the evidence. . . . The jury decided that the "deceased came to his death at the hands of a mob of unknown persons, who placed a rope around his neck and hanged him until he was dead." Thus ended the career of a man who, had he left whiskey, cards and attending evils alone, might be alive today, highly respected and an honor to his relatives and friends.[93]

Other dispatches from Socorro emphasized Fowler's cowardly behavior as he was taken to his death. A special to the *Denver Republican* on January 24 said: "At one o'clock yesterday morning Joel Fowler, a notorious Socorro desperado, was taken from jail, and, in spite of his frantic appeals for mercy and cries for help, was dragged to a neighboring tree and hanged."[94]

Several men, while never admitting membership in the vigilante organization or taking an active role in their action, later claimed to have personally witnessed the lynching and provided more details.

Chester Potter, of the *Socorro Sun*, denied that Fowler displayed the abject cowardice described in other accounts. He said that the door of the jail was knocked down by "Big Bill" Elderton, the town blacksmith, "a man of gigantic stature and strength, benign of disposition, a church member, and withal, a man of peace," who was the one who administered the lashes to miscreants the vigilantes determined deserved whipping rather than hanging.[95] Fowler, chained to a big boulder inside, screamed "murder" several times, hoping that friends might come to his rescue, but "this was the only evidence of nerve-shortage shown by Fowler. He came laughingly up the steps, and as he passed me, said: 'Kid, I never thought you would attend my funeral.' . . . Fowler repeatedly requested that he be shot instead of 'strangled,' as he termed it. . . . He did not whine but presented his proposition in a cool and businesslike manner."

The procession moved up McCutcheon Avenue to a large cottonwood tree that the vigilantes had selected as the lynching site. There occurred a moment of levity, according to Potter, that has been mentioned by no one else:

> At the tree the leaders asked for a rope [and] Arthur Goebel gravely announced . . . that he would supply the hemp. The evening was cool and nearly all the "Vigilantes" wore overcoats. Goebel removed his, disclosing a rope wound about his body. Someone grabbed the free end while others caught hold and in an instant Goebel became a human reel. He rolled some distance before the rope was entirely separated from his person. Fowler heartily joined in the laughter which greeted this little by-play.

Potter said a noose was quickly formed and placed around Fowler's neck. The other end of the rope was thrown over a limb, and Fowler was asked if he had anything to say. "He inquired: 'Can I climb up, jump off and pop my neck?' The answer was 'no,' and then he said: 'It's a damn tough country where you have to climb for water, dig for wood, and they call corn "mice" (maize). I'll take my medicine like a little man.' These were his last words."[96]

Cattleman William French, who said he just happened to be in Socorro from his ranch near Alma that fatal night, saw the crowd assemble at the jail and a dozen men enter the building. About ten or fifteen minutes later

> the committee came out again, dragging the most miserable, contemptible object I ever saw. All of Mr. Fowler's bravado had gone. He was howling and begging for his life. He had so far lost control of his functions that he was loathsome to look at, and I felt glad that I was not one of those who had to drag him along.
>
> The rest of the proceedings went without a hitch. He was hustled into a wagon. The whole procession moved quietly to the edge of town, where a convenient tree overhung the road. There they strung him up and drove the wagon out from under him. Somebody fired a few merciful shots into him, but I think they were unnecessary. I saw his face as they did the work, and I believe he was already dead before they swung him loose. It was a horrible sight: the face of a coward.
>
> The crowd dispersed as quietly and mysteriously as it had assembled and we went back to the hotel, where it took something strong and ardent to mitigate the bad taste in our mouths.[97]

Montague Stevens also claimed to have witnessed, but not participated in, the Fowler lynching. In his account, he added a number of details not mentioned elsewhere. In his version, Fowler's aborted attempt to escape precipitated the lynching.

> We heard a big racket in the street. People were all running towards the courthouse. . . . Fowler had almost dug his way through the adobe wall with a knife or something and he was about to get out. There was a saddle horse outside that was left for him to get on and skip out as soon as he got out of the jail. The jailer . . . came into the cell . . . just in time, and grabbed him and shouted the alarm. People rushed down and helped the jailer. . . .
>
> Then somebody says, "Let's hang him. He's bound to get away if we don't do something, so we'll just hang him this time —make sure." They picked up Fowler and started him to a

tree . . . about 300 yards from the jail. . . . The tree had a limb running straight out from it, a good stout limb, and they hauled him up to the tree. . . .

He just pleaded and cried for mercy — so he was yellow after all. . . . I think four men had hold of him. . . . Another man climbed the tree and they put a noose around Fowler's neck and threw the other end of the rope to the man up on the limb. He caught it and they lifted Fowler up in the air. The man tied his rope to the limb [and] said, "All right, let him go." And they let him go but the loop stretched, it was a little too long, and his feet hit the ground and he was standing on the ground on his toes. Of course his weight on the rope had tightened the knot. The men lifted him up again for the man on the limb to loosen the knot but he couldn't do it. It was too tight. . . . So one of the men holding him says, "Well, never mind." He says, "We can hang him anyway." He says, "Boys, let's get on his body and we'll put all our weight on him and let him hang that way." And that's the way he was hanged with the body never swinging. . . . One of the men [said] afterward, "They looked like a lot of bees ahiving."[98]

According to a report in the *Las Vegas Daily Optic*, when Fowler's friends heard the news of his lynching, one of them ran out on the plaza, brandishing two revolvers and calling upon all Texas men to help him avenge the hanging. When he received no support, he soon quieted down.[99]

Potter said he had just finished writing his story of the lynching for the pages of the *Socorro Sun* when Texas Ed Rousseau and several of his followers burst into the paper's offices, demanding to know if the story was true, that Joel Fowler had actually been hanged. "I foolishly told them that I had just finished writing the story, but they could not see it until it was printed. After a blanket curse of the Sun's staff, the vigilantes, and the town in general, they left, promising to return and 'shoot up' the plant. Texas Ed and his gang were arrested, taken to the railroad station, placed on a train, and told not to return unless they wanted to join Fowler."[100]

Other accounts dispute Potter's story. Rousseau, they say, remained in Socorro for some time after the lynching, taking care of Fowler's body and arranging for his burial.[101]

Sheriff Simpson arrived back in Socorro from Silver City, where he had been on business, the morning after Fowler's death. (One suspects the lynching was timed to coincide with the sheriff's absence.) A newspaper reported that when he heard what the citizens had done, Simpson telegraphed the governor, expressing his horror at the hanging, and then sat down and wept.[102] Enlisting the aid of Alfred Hardcastle; Billy Minters, "a well known and highly esteemed 'gentleman gambler' "; and another man, Simpson cut Fowler's body down and took it to Rousseau's saloon, where it "lay in state for the whole day, much to the profit of the bar of that saloon."[103] A coroner's jury, made up, according to Chester Potter, entirely of vigilance committee members who had assisted in the hanging, found, predictably, that "Deceased came to his death by reason of strangulation at the hands of persons unknown to this jury."[104]

Montague Stevens remembered Fowler's friends had purchased for him a new suit and a new pair of boots, but they could not pull the boots on as rigor mortis had set in, so they went back to the shoemaker and got a much larger pair. "They were almost twice the size of Fowler's foot. And it looked so funny to see his little body there with this enormous pair of boots on it."[105]

Rousseau placed the body in the most expensive casket he could find. He shipped it to Jim Reed at Fort Worth. An attempt was made to follow Fowler's last request, to bury him beside his uncle, A. Y. Fowler. Reed, however, found that the uncle's body had been removed to the Masonic Cemetery at Dallas, so Joel Fowler was interred in the Old Cemetery at Fort Worth, and his last request went unfulfilled.[106]

In a letter to the *Austin Daily Statesman* some months later, Ed Rousseau complained that during his stay in Socorro, he had been threatened constantly with assassination, but had been determined to defend himself and had come through the ordeal unscathed.[107] This drew a response from the vigilantes, who disputed his remarks and denounced his conduct at Socorro.[108]

Newspaper editorial comment around the territory reflected approval of the action by Socorro's "Committee of Safety." Said one paper:

> The lynching of the murderer Fowler in Socorro was a healthy expression of dastardly crimes. Custom condemns taking the law into one's own hands, but if the people who are the

source of all delegated authority and whose sentiments vigilance committees express, cannot properly take the law into their own hands, in whom is such right naturally vested? Nothing so deters from the commission of crime as the swift and certain vengeance of the people visited upon criminals. The remedy is two-fold; directly as a fearful warning to the lawless offenders and indirectly as a wholesome rebuke to our knavish incompetent courts.[109]

At White Oaks, where the residents had some familiarity with the antics of Joel Fowler, the headline in their paper read: "MORE ROOM IN HELL THAN SOCORRO FOR FOWLER."[110] And the *Chloride Black Range* of February 1, 1884, opined that the news of "the hanging of Joe Fowler at Socorro proved to be correct, much to the satisfaction of this part of the country."

The *Galveston Daily News*, quoting a dispatch from Denver, noted that "Fowler was worth $100,000 and would use his wealth to purchase witnesses, and had done so in other cases. Having good reason to believe that the law's delay would result in a final release, the citizens took his execution into their own hands."[111]

Only attorney Neill B. Field appeared distressed by the outcome of the Fowler affair. When he had helped file papers to appeal Fowler's conviction and heard the lynching rumors, he had publicly stated that if his client were lynched, he would leave Socorro forever. When the vigilantes acted and Fowler died, Field kept his word and moved to Albuquerque, which reportedly prompted one of the vigilantes to remark that Field's threat to leave might have been incentive enough to provoke the hanging,[112] and the *Chloride Black Range* to comment caustically that if Field "was unable to bear the pain caused by the just death of a desperado, he should have gone still farther away."[113]

One writer contended that Fowler spent his last days blaming his "wife" for his plight, complaining that he had experienced nothing but bad luck from the day he married her.[114] There is no record, however, that Fowler and the woman known in Socorro as "Mrs. Fowler" were ever married, although she apparently ended up with his considerable wealth. The *Las Vegas Optic* of June 3, 1884, reported that she was dealing monte in Butte, Montana, and a month later the *Silver City Enterprise* made note: "The widow of Joe Fowler, the killer, recently hung at Socorro, is now living at Butte City, Montana. She is well known in this city, having dealt monte here. She went through with all the money her husband left her."[115] The same paper reported a few months later that "Mrs. Joel Fowler" was back in New Mexico, "dealing monte in Santa Fe."[116] There she teamed up once again with Josie, the other "Mrs. Fowler," in a successful tour of the gambling houses. A newspaper erroneously identified the two women as Joel's wife and sister. If a report that one of the Fowler women had placed her seven-year-old child with the Sisters of Loretto was true, it must have been Josie Fowler, for it is believed Belle Fowler never had any children.[117]

A woman who lived in Socorro during these years told a Fowler researcher that Belle Fowler spent much time in the town after her husband's death. "Why, I knew Mrs. Fowler very well," she said,

> not in the sense of intimate friendship, but we met often at our dressmaker's, for she had her gowns made at the same place I did. She was one of the most beautiful women I had ever seen. She had big, brown, wide-open eyes, set in a baby face that caused men to look at her twice. She was short and trim and wore nothing but the best. . . . [After Fowler's death] she remained right here in Socorro. She had to earn a living, and she did. She dealt Stud Horse Poker in Charley Udder's [*sic*] saloon. She had a title, too, for all her beauty. "Queen Gambler of the West," she was called, and her manipulation of the cards proved the title was not a vain one. In 1886, when I came to Socorro she was still here, the Common Law wife of one Sam Egginton. . . . The Fowlers had no children.[118]

Belle Fowler did not confine her gambling to Socorro, however. Several newspaper stories in August 1886 indicate her profession led her to experience a very eventful month with the sporting crowd in the northern sections of the territory. On August 17 she was fined $25 in Las Vegas for conducting a gambling table on the plaza.[119] On the 19th an assailant, identified only as "a saloon man," shot off the little finger of her left hand.[120] A few days later she was involved in a shooting at Montezuma Springs, in which two men were wounded.[121]

After this spate of reportable activity, Belle Fowler's name dropped from the pages of the New Mexico press, and her later history is not known.

Joel Fowler is remembered today primarily for the manner in which he left this world. That he was a vicious killer has never been doubted. Just how many men fell victim to his homicidal proclivities has never been accurately determined.

After his killing of Cale, a newspaper headlined its story: "KILLING BY INSTINCT. MONSTER IN NEW MEXICO WHO HAS JUST BEEN CAUGHT." It listed seven murders Fowler had allegedly committed in the territory: three at White Oaks, one at Georgetown, two at his Alamo ranch, and one in Socorro. No mention was made of any killings for which he might have been responsible in Texas.[122]

In estimating the Fowler death toll, Miguel Otero, who became governor of New Mexico, employed a politician's circumspection: "It was rumored that he had killed no less than a dozen men while under the influence of liquor."[123]

Alfred Hardcastle of Kent, England, who had been in Socorro at the time of the Cale murder and Fowler lynching, went Otero one better, writing that Fowler "was said to have killed thirteen men — not counting Mexicans." Hardcastle added that Fowler always carried a Wells Fargo sawed-off shotgun across his saddle, and it was believed he had originated the shoulder harness, "especially arranged scabbards under the armpits, out of sight under his vest."[124]

Harvey Fergusson followed Hardcastle's lead, saying that Fowler "was commonly credited with the killing of thirteen men and he killed most of them with little risk to himself. It is said that he killed two cowboys with a shotgun while they sat by a fire, that he killed men who worked for him to save their wages and as a deputy sheriff he shot unarmed prisoners. He liked to use a knife as well as a gun and always carried a sawed-off shotgun across his saddle."[125]

The Fowler killing total was upped one more by Harvey Whitehill, longtime sheriff of Grant County, New Mexico, who told his daughter, Ollie Bell, that Fowler had killed fourteen.[126]

But Montague Stevens topped them all with his insistence that evidence produced at Fowler's trial for the murder of Cale showed that he had killed twenty-three men, a claim not substantiated by the court record. Stevens also said that after Fowler's death, sixteen human skeletons were found in his ranch corral.[127] (He may have arrived at his total of twenty-three by adding the alleged sixteen Fowler victims to the seven reported in the press.)

Whatever figures were cited, someone always seemed anxious to raise the ante. Said Chester Potter: "Eighteen graves, it was claimed, were found on Fowler's range. Who filled them is not known."[128]

It is obvious that the tally of victims attributed to the gunman Joel Fowler, like similar totals credited to other notorious western gunfighters, has been grossly exaggerated. No one will ever know for sure how many men he put under the sod, but that he was a brutal, cold-blooded killer can hardly be denied. Most would agree with Ramon Adams that if Fowler was "an apprentice bad man," they would not want to tangle with a professional.

— 6 —

JESSE RASCOE
1848–1925

This town is too beastly peaceable to make life interesting for Deputy Sheriff Goodlett and Constable Rasco [sic].
                                        — *Eddy Argus*, February 1, 1890

It was not uncommon for gun-fighting lawmen to come to the profession by way of outlawry, but it was a rarity for one to pin on a badge after having lost an arm in a gunfight. Such a man, however, was Jesse Rascoe.

Born in Rusk, Cherokee County, Texas, July 10, 1848, the son of Laban and Francis Rascoe,[1] Jesse reached adulthood during the turbulent Reconstruction years in Texas following the Civil War and was drawn into the antisocial behavior and violence that marked the bitter sectionalism of this period of Texas history. Better remembered today are three other hot-blooded Texas youths, Joe Horner,[2] "Wild Bill" Longley,[3] and John Wesley Hardin,[4] all born within five years of Rascoe, who shared his hatred for "carpetbagger" Yankees and "bluebelly" blacks and allowed that hatred to lead them to murder and a life of outlawry.

In 1859 the Rascoe family moved to Corsicana in Navarro County, Texas.[5] Jesse was seventeen years old and living with his parents when the war ended in 1865. According to family tradition, his first acts of violence were precipitated by an unfortunate incident that occurred there that year. Like Horner, Longley, Hardin, and other proud, young, gun-wielding firebrands during those troublesome years in

Texas, Jesse Rascoe was bitterly offended by the Northern-imposed Reconstruction government and especially the actions of blue-clad black soldiers who enforced its edicts. When a black Union soldier pushed Jesse's mother off the sidewalk, so goes the family story, she fell and broke her ankle. Young Jesse swore vengeance and subsequently waylaid and killed several black soldiers.[6] Confirmation of this story cannot be found in the contemporary records and may simply be a distortion of a verifiable act of violence Jesse committed against a black man later.

Jesse Rascoe was unquestionably hot-tempered and prone to violence, but he was nonetheless a devoted family man. On September 2, 1866, he married Mary Jane "Mollie" Duncan. The marriage lasted more than half a century and produced eight children.[7]

Like many young Texans following the Civil War, Rascoe turned to the cattle ranges to earn a living, but in 1870, at the age of twenty-two, he made a tentative entry into the field of law enforcement when he accepted an interim appointment by Texas governor Edmund J. Davis as Navarro County sheriff.[8] This lasted only a few months, however, and Rascoe was on the opposite side in his next involvement with the law.

Almost a decade after the end of the Civil War, his animosity toward black people remained undiminished, and in 1874 this racial hatred led to the killing of two men and the stabbing of a woman.

On August 7, 1874, a black man named Aaron Gibbins, who had a home about two miles outside Corsicana, came into town and filed charges against Rascoe, claiming he had attempted to rape his wife the previous day. Before officers could arrest Rascoe, he learned of the charge and confronted his accuser on the street. According to the press account, Gibbins, seeing Rascoe approaching, grabbed up a "jug and a piece of iron with which to defend himself, whereupon Rasco [sic] pulled his pistol out and shot Gibbins through the head, killing him instantly." Rascoe then mounted his horse and galloped out of town, heading "for parts unknown." Later it was found that Gibbins's wife at some point had been stabbed. It was not clear whether the wound had been inflicted by Rascoe or her husband, but in any event it was superficial.[9]

A posse was organized and went after Rascoe. Three days later the hunted man shot and killed one of his pursuers, one Johnson Thompson, before getting out of the state into Louisiana. On March 18, 1875, a Navarro County grand jury brought in an indictment charging Rascoe with the murder of two men. When a year passed and he was still at large, E. J. Simkins, district attorney of Navarro County, wrote the governor of Texas for assistance:

> Corsicana, Tex., March 2, 1876
> To His Excellency
> Gov. Richard Coke
>
> Dear Sir:
> Enclosed I send a copy of indictment against Jesse Rasco [*sic*], who has committed two cold blooded murders in this county for which indictments have been found. He stays in Louisiana but I have just heard he returned home. If a reward is offered he will be caught and I would like to have one "effort" at him before I retire from the cares of the District Attorney's office.
>
> Respectfully,
> E. J. Simkins
> District Attorney[10]

Governor Coke acceded to the district attorney's request. On March 6 he issued a proclamation offering a reward of $200 for the arrest of Jesse Rascoe for the murder of Johnson Thompson. Five days later he rescinded that proclamation and issued another, this time offering $350 for Rascoe's arrest on the charge of murdering Aaron Gibbins.[11]

Despite the reward notices and efforts by the Texas Rangers to capture the fugitive, Rascoe remained at large for more than a year. Family tradition credits the assistance of Jesse's younger brother, William Preston "Bill" Rascoe, a corporal in Company C of the Frontier Battalion of the Rangers, in thwarting Ranger efforts to make the arrest.[12]

Eventually, however, Rascoe was apprehended and jailed. At the fall term of the district court in 1877, he stood trial on one of the murder indictments but came clear due to the absence of witnesses. His lawyers gained a continuance on the second indictment, and he was released on bail of $1,500.[13]

The smoke had still not dispersed from that court appearance when Rascoe leaped right back into the legal fire with another killing.

On the night of Saturday, December 29, 1877, he went on a tear in Corsicana and committed what one paper called "the most cold-blooded and dastardly murders on record."[14] The major target of his wrath was a man named Harry Lackey (or Lacky), who, during the recent court session, had "by his superior bravery and prowess," as a newspaper put it, taken a pistol away from Rascoe and had him fined for carrying it. Seething from that humiliation, Rascoe talked openly of violent reprisal, but Lackey, by reason of his "superior bravery" or his professed "prowess" with pistols, ignored the threats. When Rascoe finally braced Lackey in Smith's saloon on Benton Street, he wasted little time and few words. "Lacky," he snapped, "you are the cock of the walk here!" as he drew and fired. Lackey tumbled to the floor with a bullet through his torso and died within moments.

Rascoe ran from the scene, sprinting "the entire length of a ten pin alley," and bolted out the back door of the saloon. Meanwhile, his cousin, William G. Jackson, covered his escape, waving a pistol at the crowd and yelling, "If anybody wants anything, I'm the man." A city policeman and a deputy sheriff were in the saloon at the time, and the two officers ignored Jackson and pursued Rascoe into the back alley. They fired five or six shots at the fleeing figure without effect. Jackson was later arrested and jailed as an accessory to Lacky's murder.[15]

Captain John C. Sparks, commanding Company C of the Frontier Battalion of the Texas Rangers, maintained a home in Corsicana, and he happened to be there at the time. He organized a posse to pursue the gunman, but the wily and elusive Rascoe got away.

Once again Rascoe took refuge in Louisiana, and once again a Texas governor, R. B. Hubbard this time, offered rewards for his capture. On January 23, 1878, Hubbard issued a proclamation revoking all previous rewards and offering $300 for delivery of Rascoe to the Navarro County sheriff and an additional $200 payable on Rascoe's conviction for the Lacky murder.[16]

On January 25, 1878, G. M. Chalfee, a deputy sheriff of Waxahachie County, adjoining Navarro, acting on a lead as to Rascoe's whereabouts, wrote to Governor Hubbard: "You will please send me by return mail requisition on Gov. of Louisiana for the arrest of Jesse Rasco [*sic*], who killed Harry Lacky at Corsicana a short time ago. Hoping you will give the above your immediate attention. . . . Make me the agent and receiver." Hubbard scribbled a note on the request:

"Is there a Bill of Indictment here against this man? If not, can't issue requisition."

The matter was referred to N. W. Read, who now was district attorney of Navarro County. On January 30 he wrote the governor:

> In reply to yours of the 28th just to hand I have the honor to report that no term of the District Court having intervened since the killing of Harry Lacky by Jesse Rasco [sic], there is now no indictment pending against Rasco for that particular crime, but that there will be as soon as the next grand jury assembles as the crime was one of the most cold-blooded and dastardly ever committed in our midst. Rasco is, however, under indictment here in connection with others as will be seen by the enclosed certificate copy of indictment. He is under recognizance for this, but has fled the country. I would most urgently recommend to your Excellency that the writ of requisition issue if possible. I know nothing of Mr. G. M. Chalfee as I have never heard of him before. I know [Sheriff] W. D. Ryburn[17] of Ellis County to be an efficient and fearless officer in discharge of criminal business, at least so reports say, and suppose his deputies are efficient men. If your Excellency should not desire to commission him (Chalfee) as agent, I would suggest John C. Sparks of this place who knows Rasco well and who would doubtless take him if he can be found.
>
> P.S. The evidence against Rasco in the Lacky murder is convincing and overwhelming and we can not fail in my estimation if tried.[18]

On May 2, 1878, a grand jury did in fact bring a true bill against Rascoe and Jackson for the crime of murder.[19] The following month, on June 26, Navarro County officers, acting on a tip, slipped over the line into Henderson County in search of the fugitive. Early on the morning of June 28 a posse of five men, led by Deputy Sheriff G. B. Walker, approached the house in which Rascoe was reportedly staying and caught him outside, apparently relieving himself in the bushes. The officers called on him to surrender, but he turned and ran. The possemen opened fire, and a bullet struck Rascoe in the right side. He went down, got back up, and attempted to run again, but the officers closed in and quickly overpowered him. It was, Rascoe, told them, "the first time in years that he [had] ever been out of easy reach of his pistols," implying that if he had them, the outcome would have been different. The wound he received was not serious, and the officers returned him to Corsicana and that evening placed him in jail there once again.[20]

While still awaiting trial he participated in a general breakout from the jail on March 4, 1879. About five o'clock that evening, as the prisoners were being shackled for the night, Cole Hudson, alias Frank Cloud, being held for Ellis County on a horse-theft charge, managed to wrest a weapon from a guard named Powers and hold him at gunpoint while he freed Rascoe and the other inmates. They garnered other weapons from the guardroom, and made a break for freedom. G. B. Walker, who had led the posse that captured Rascoe eight months earlier, and other deputies reacted at once, and a gunfight ensued. Prisoners Hudson, George Ellison, and Robert Tickle were shot, but none of the guards and deputies received injuries. The prisoners were all recaptured with the exception of Rascoe, who managed to get to a saddled horse and thundered out of town. A twenty-five-man posse was formed and went in pursuit, but Rascoe, as he had done so many times in the past, got away again.[21]

The *San Antonio Daily Express* five weeks later reported that "Jesse Rascoe, the notorious murderer, who recently escaped from the Corsicana jail, has sent word to policeman Robinson that he is coming to Corsicana soon and will fill Robinson's hide full of lead ore. Rascoe is a bad one."[22]

If Rascoe ever made such a threat, it is unlikely he had any intention of returning to Corsicana of his own free will. On the run again, he not only left the state but also departed the country, crossing into old Mexico, long a haven for southwestern outlaws on the dodge.

But by 1882 he was back in the States. Using the alias "Peavey House," he took a job with John Galey of Cochise County, Arizona Territory, a mining man who in 1880 founded Galeyville, a town that soon became notorious as an outlaw rendezvous.[23] Later Rascoe established a home on the San Simon River, sent for his family, and cowboyed for the Triple C ranch.[24]

On Sunday, March 5, 1882, Rascoe was in Charleston, another tough town in the Tombstone mining district, when he got into a heated dispute with the bartender in a saloon. He left the place and was just about to mount his horse when the barkeep came out carrying a shotgun and blasted away. The charge struck Rascoe in the right side of his body, shattering his arm. Cowboy friends took him to Tombstone, where a doctor (probably George Goodfellow, who had worked on the shotgun-shattered arm of the well-known Tombstone lawman Virgil Earp only two months earlier) amputated his right arm at the elbow.[25]

For a time Rascoe was not expected to survive his ordeal,[26] but he was a very hardy and determined man, and gradually he regained his strength. Soon he returned to his home on the San Simon to complete his recovery. He would live, but the news of the shooting would get all the way back to Navarro County, Texas, and lead directly to his apprehension on the old murder charges.

When Navarro County Attorney Rufus Hardy learned on March 16 that Jesse Rascoe, alias Peavey House, was recovering from a gunshot wound in Cochise County, Arizona, he immediately wrote Oran M. Roberts, the new governor of Texas:

> We have information that one Jesse Rasco [sic], who is a fugitive from justice from this county is now in Arizona. He is a desperate character. There are two indictments against him for murder in this county, one for the murder of Harry Lacky, a most cowardly and dastardly act. In this case the proof is easy to come at and positive. In the other murder case there is only one witness I know of. I think the case is well worth a considerable reward and respectfully ask your excellency to grant a requisition for Rasco upon the Governor of Arizona.[27]

Navarro County Sheriff Ewing E. Dunn went to Austin and personally delivered this request to the governor. He also carried a certification signed by J. H. Southworth, clerk of the district court at Corsicana, that on March 18, 1875, Rascoe had been indicted for murder in Cause No. 1646 and had posted bond of $1,500, which had been forfeited on May 13, 1878, when he failed to appear to answer the charge. In addition, Dunn handed Governor Roberts a letter from R. C. Beale, Navarro County judge, asking that the requisition be issued. "Rascoe committed a most atrocious murder here several years ago, broke jail and escaped, going to Mexico and then to Arizona," said the judge. "I trust your Excellency will issue the necessary papers and do something in the way of assisting Mr. Dunn in the payment of the heavy expense necessary to bring the man here."[28]

Governor Roberts issued the requisition and authorized a reward of $400 for Rascoe's capture. The Navarro officials forwarded this information to an energetic and resourceful bounty-hunting detective from Dallas named John Riley "Jack" Duncan, who quickly agreed to make the journey to Arizona. According to other reports, Frank Jackson, the sole surviving member of the infamous Sam Bass gang that had been shot up by Texas Rangers at Round Rock, Texas, in July 1878, was also in the Tombstone area. Duncan knew that rewards totaling $2,500 issued by the state and railroad and express companies were still outstanding for Jackson's arrest. On March 28 Duncan boarded a westbound train in Dallas with high hopes that his trip to Arizona might well result in two lucrative captures.[29]

After a few days in the Tombstone area, Duncan determined that the Frank Jackson reports were unfounded, so he turned his attention to collaring the Navarro County fugitive, Jesse Rascoe, alias Peavey House.

On April 3 he hired a team and wagon and, accompanied by a man named Yearinger, the owner of the outfit, drove out to the Rascoe place on the San Simon. According to one newspaper account, as the two men pulled up outside the house, the wagon tongue suddenly snapped, producing a sharp report like a pistol shot. Rascoe came charging out, revolver in his only hand. Duncan, who had suffered a gunshot wound years earlier that required him to hold his fingers to his throat in order to talk, managed to calm him down. After a few moments of quiet discussion about the lack of dependability of wagon tongues, Rascoe pocketed his pistol. Seizing the opportunity, Duncan and Yearinger grabbed and disarmed him. Since handcuffs were useless as Rascoe had only one hand, they strapped his remaining arm to his body. Duncan guarded his prisoner while Yearinger repaired the wagon tongue. Then, leaving the family with the impression they were taking Rascoe to Tombstone, they headed directly for the nearest railroad station at Benson.[30]

Duncan arrived back in Dallas with his prisoner on April 6. News dispatches reported that Rascoe "acknowledges the crime, also several others, murders in Texas, mostly negroes, and is undoubtedly a hard case."[31]

Jesse Rascoe in later years as city marshal of Roswell, New Mexico. From the author's collection.

Navarro County Sheriff Ewing E. Dunn and two of his deputies, R. H. "Little Bob" Cubley and Wes Edens, took charge of Rascoe and conveyed him to Corsicana that same day.[32] A dispatch from that town said "he has been secured in jail, and extra precautions taken to prevent another escape, as he has money, relatives and connections in this county."[33]

While confined in jail, Rascoe, still suffering from his wounds and arm amputation, wrote a letter to the local paper thanking Jack Duncan for the humane treatment he had received while in his charge.[34]

Rascoe remained in the Corsicana jail until the following August, when he went on trial for the Lackey murder. Despite County Attorney Hardy's assertion that the proof of Rascoe's guilt was "easy to come at and positive," witnesses to the shooting disappeared or refused to talk. He was acquitted.[35]

Perhaps this close brush with the hangman's noose or a long prison sentence scared Rascoe, or perhaps the arrival of twin babies, William and Katherine, in January 1883 made him realize that with the responsibility of a wife and five children, it was time for him to get off the owl-hoot trail and settle down. At any rate, from this time on he seemed to renounce the life of a saloon tough and gunman.

After the trial he again left Texas, settling in the Pecos Valley of New Mexico. He drove stagecoaches out of Seven Rivers for a time, no easy task for a man with one arm.[36] During this period three more children, daughters Minnie May and Lydia and son George, were born to the Rascoes, making a total of eight, four boys and four girls. Tragedy struck in 1887 when one of the girls, three-year-old Minnie May, wandered off into the desert and died of exposure and exhaustion.[37]

In 1889 Rascoe and his large family settled in the spanking new town of Eddy on the Rio Pecos. Developed by promoters Charles B. Eddy and W. W. Hagerman, Eddy (later to be called Carlsbad) was established as a business center for an ambitious irrigation project then under way in the Pecos Valley. Charles Eddy was a strictly religious man, a prohibitionist who despised vice in all its forms, and his town was kept clean of the saloon, gambling, and brothel crowd that for fifty years had flocked to new boomtowns in the West.

But quickly springing up just outside the Eddy city limits was another community. Its founders and residents were members of the sporting element outlawed in Eddy. They called the new town Phenix, and their behavior was as bad as their spelling. Phenix soon became notorious throughout the Southwest as the worst sin city going, with shootings, stabbings, and strong-arm robberies commonplace occurrences.

When the first elections were held in January 1890, Jesse Rascoe, in his new role as an upstanding citizen, entered the race for town constable on the Independent ticket. He was opposed by W. L. Goodlett, the candidate of the People's Party. Rascoe was elected, receiving sixty-six votes to Goodlett's forty-two, and then pinned on a badge for the first time in twenty years. Goodlett had to be content with appointment by Sheriff D. C. Nowlin as a sheriff's deputy.[38] Although they had been opponents in the election, Rascoe and Goodlett seemed to work as a team in keeping the peace. Commented the *Eddy Argus* in its issue of February 1: "This town is too beastly peaceable to make life interesting for Deputy Sheriff Goodlett and Constable Rasco [*sic*]."

But a few months later Rascoe had the unpleasant duty of arresting his friend and fellow officer for complicity in murder. When coyotes dug up and partly devoured the body of a man on the Kimmel ranch just outside Eddy, an investigation disclosed that the victim was a man named Cofelt who had been killed and buried by Goodlett and other officers or purported officers as a common horse thief. An Eddy justice of the peace issued warrants, and Rascoe arrested and jailed Goodlett and his alleged accomplices, Sam Brown and Miles Stone.[39]

Despite having only one arm, Jesse Rascoe seems to have performed his law enforcement responsibilities well; the editor of the *Eddy Argus* in 1892 called him "a most trustworthy and efficient officer."[40] By that time he had assumed the position of Eddy city marshal. Eddy and its saloon suburb, Phenix, were loaded with quick-triggered mankillers during these years. The roster included Zack Light and the man who would kill him, Les Dow; frequent visitor John Wesley Hardin, who claimed to have killed some forty men; and Dave Kemp, the elected sheriff of Eddy County, who had served time in Texas for murder and in 1897 would gun down Les Dow in Eddy. City Marshal Rascoe dealt with these and many other hard cases without resort to gunplay.

This is more than can be said for his twelve-year-old son, William, who in 1895 shot another boy to death. William, or "Willie" as he was called, was playing with a group of five boys in a pool of water at Dark

Canyon, a quarter mile northwest of Phenix, when Willie fired a gun and killed one of his companions. He claimed it was an unfortunate accident. The fact that the victim was the only Mexican in the party might lead some to suspect that young William perhaps had displayed some of the racial bigotry that had blighted his father's early life, but the accidental death story was accepted, and no charges were filed.[41]

One of the tough Phenix crowd, a cowman named Martin Mroz, under indictment for cattle theft, left hurriedly for Mexico early in 1895. As he slipped back into the country at El Paso, Texas, on June 29 of that year, he was shot to death by lawmen. To assure New Mexico authorities of the fact of Mroz's death, Rascoe went to El Paso in early June to identify the remains. By the time he got there, interment had already taken place, but Rascoe was able to identify Mroz positively from photographs of the body.[42]

The Eddy and Phenix excitement waned in the later years of the 1890s. By 1900, when Eddy changed its name to Carlsbad in an effort to exploit the nearby mineral springs, many of the original townsmen, including Jesse Rascoe, had moved on. The Rascoe family — Jesse, Mollie, and their seven surviving children — relocated some seventy miles north in Roswell, Chaves County, where in 1904 Jesse again assumed the duties of city marshal.

Paid only $55 a month as Roswell city marshal, Rascoe managed to more than double that amount, augmenting his income with license fee collections and a share of police court fines. Highly respected in the town, in September 1905 he was elected an officer of the Old Settlers Society of Chaves County.[43]

Rascoe was a striking figure patrolling the streets of Roswell, as an early resident recalled:

In performing his duties in Roswell, he always rode a very fine sorrel horse. He had scabbards strapped to either side of his saddle. In one he carried a sawed-off double-barreled 12-gauge shotgun; in the other he had a Winchester .30-30 repeating rifle, known to old-timers as a "saddlegun" because it had a shorter barrel than the ordinary high-powered hunting rifle. Around his waist he wore a cartridge belt, always completely filled. On his left hip, because his right arm was missing, he wore a regulation double-action Colt .45. . . . Mr. Rascoe was a most efficient officer.[44]

Rascoe served five years as Roswell city marshal. He retired in 1908 at the age of sixty because of poor health. In April 1911 he and Mollie moved to Bakersfield, California, to live with a married daughter. In 1922 Mollie died.[45]

Jesse Rascoe had lived through a number of violent episodes, had killed men, and had lost an arm in a deadly encounter. But he had always been a loving husband and father. Twice the specter of death, sudden and unexpected, visited his children, first when little Minnie May wandered off into the desert, never to be found, and again when son Willie shot and killed another boy. Jesse would live long enough to see sudden death impact the life of one of his children again in 1924.

Daughter Katherine, twin sister of Willie, had married a man named Mack Fletcher, foreman of the Turkey Track ranch,[46] and had lived with him at the ranch for twenty-one years before finally obtaining a divorce. In November 1923 she married Fred Halsey, a prominent rancher who had a spread southwest of Artesia, in Eddy County. Only five months later, on the night of Sunday, March 20, 1924, Halsey, returning from church services, was closing the gate to his ranch when he was killed instantly by a load of number six birdshot. On Monday officers arrested two men, Luther Foster and Claude B. "Cottonwood Bill" Archer, and charged them with the crime. The following day officers also arrested Katherine Halsey as an accomplice. The theory of the prosecutors was that Katherine and Foster were lovers and that they had conspired to employ Archer to murder Katherine's husband. Payment to the triggerman was to be made after receipt of a heavy insurance policy on Halsey's life. All three suspects were indicted and, after a change of venue, tried in Chaves County in June 1924.[47]

The jury was out only fifteen minutes before finding the three defendants guilty of murder. On July 3 Judge Charles R. Brice sentenced them to hang and set August 1 as the date. A stay of execution was granted as the defense attorneys appealed the case to the New Mexico Supreme Court. In January 1925 that judicial body affirmed Archer's conviction, but ordered a new trial for Katherine and Foster on a technicality. Judge Charles R. Brice, who had heard the case, called the supreme court's decision "the most flagrant miscarriage of justice I have ever come in contact with in this or any other jurisdiction." In subsequent separate trials, Foster was convicted again and sentenced to a long prison term. Katherine was also convicted and again sentenced to hang, but won another appeal and a court order for a third trial. At this point witnesses had disappeared, and the prosecution decided the case was hopeless. After five years in jail, Katherine Halsey was released and disappeared. On January 1, 1933, New Mexico governor Arthur Seligman pardoned Luther Foster and later also granted a pardon to Cottonwood Bill Archer.[48]

Jesse Rascoe did not live to see his daughter's melodrama play itself out. On January 25, 1925, just about the time the New Mexico Supreme Court was ordering Katherine's first retrial, he died at the age of seventy-seven at his home in Bakersfield. Funeral arrangements were made by the local lodge of the Odd Fellows, an organization to which he had long belonged, and the one-time gunman and outlaw turned respected peace officer was buried in the Union Cemetery at Bakersfield on January 28, 1925.[49]

— 7 —

BURK BURNETT
1849–1922

Had not Burnett fired certain death awaited him. The event causing the loss of human life is greatly to be deplored, and none regrets the fact greater than Mr. Burnett, who was forced to the act only by the knowledge that a moment's delay would cost him his own life's blood.
—*Henrietta Journal*, June 14, 1879

The inclusion of Samuel Burk Burnett in a book devoted to the careers of a dozen man-killing gunfighters of the Old West may raise some eyebrows in Texas historical circles, where Burnett is remembered and widely revered today as a pioneer cattleman and trail driver who later became hugely successful in both the ranching and oil businesses. A leading figure in the history of Fort Worth, a capitalist and a millionaire many times over in a day when a dollar was a dollar and millionaires were rare, Burnett had a town named for him. His life is one of the great success stories of the American West.

But almost forgotten today is the fact that Burk Burnett was a gunfighter, as skilled with a six-shooter as he was with a bank ledger. In his long and tumultuous rise from trail-driving cowpuncher to wealthy capitalist, he was involved in at least two standup gunfights and killed his adversary in both encounters. He was unique, the only multimillionaire in the annals of western gunfighters. His is a remarkable story.

The first of ten children born to Jeremiah and Nancy Burnett, he entered this world on the first day of the year 1849 in Bates County,

Missouri.[1] He was christened Samuel Burk, after his grandfather, but throughout his life family and friends called him simply "Burk." The first years of his life were marked by the violence that swept Missouri and Kansas in the period leading up to the Civil War.

According to an early historical account:

> He witnessed the raids of ruffians and jayhawkers on the Missouri and Kansas border in 1857 and 1858, and while young in years he became old in experience. He witnessed the wreck and destruction of his father's home during these raids, and with him and the other members of his family started on the long journey through the Indian Territory to Texas in search of peace and quiet, finally reaching the place on Denton Creek. In that section scholastic advantages were few, and when the Civil War began Burk Burnett's chief education consisted in what his common sense and nature had taught him.[2]

When the Civil War erupted in 1861, Jerry Burnett joined the army of the Confederacy, leaving his oldest son, Burk, only eleven, as the male head of the family. Burk held that responsibility for the next four years during his father's absence.[3]

Denton County, on the northern frontier of Texas, where Jerry Burnett homesteaded, was cattle country, and young Burk grew wise in the ways of cattle before he reached his teens. When his father returned from the war, Burk hired on with the Wiley Robin outfit as a hand at $30 a month and in 1866 helped drive one of the first herds of Texas longhorns up the Chisholm Trail to the Kansas cow towns. He went along on another drive the next year and by the spring of 1868, at the age of nineteen, had gained enough experience to boss a trail drive himself. Throwing together a herd of fifteen hundred longhorns, he hired a crew of drovers and started up the trail to Abilene.[4]

During those memorable trail-driving years, Burnett drove other herds to the Kansas markets, always pouring his profits back into the purchase of additional longhorn stock. The way he handled a seemingly disastrous financial setback in 1873 demonstrated his remarkable business acumen. Arriving with a herd in the new cow town of Wichita, Kansas, that year, he found that a national financial panic had so deflated market prices that he could not sell his trail-wasted steers at a profit. "There I was," Burnett later recalled, "with a bunch of cattle on my hands that I could neither sell nor give away, but my expenses going on all the time and eating off the heads of several steers a day. I saw that would not do, so I dropped back to the Osage Reservation and wintered there, trading and operating as best I could, and finally sold out in the fall of 1874, having a year's age on the cattle. I did very well and came home with a $10,000 profit."[5]

Burnett was one of the first to realize the benefit of delivering fattened cattle to the northern markets. In the winter of 1874 he bought thirteen hundred steers on the Rio Grande ranges of southern Texas and took them north to graze and fatten in lands he held in northern counties, before trailing them on to the Kansas markets. Soon other Texas cattlemen were following his lead.

Burnett had begun acquiring ranchland in northern Texas as early as 1870. That year he bought the stock and brand of cattleman Frank Crowley and grazed the herd on a ranch in Wichita County. The brand was 6666, and the "Four Sixes" ranch, as it was commonly called, soon became one of the most prosperous and famous in Texas. Legend has it that Burnett won the herd and ranch in a poker game with a winning hand of four sixes, but the story appears to be apocryphal.[6]

Burnett's shrewd business maneuvers did not escape the attention of Martin B. Loyd, a Texas banker and capital investor. Soon he was helping finance many of the young man's projects. The relationship grew even stronger when Burnett wooed and won the hand of Loyd's daughter Ruth, whom he married on February 9, 1871.[7]

When Loyd established the First National Bank of Fort Worth, Burnett was appointed to the board of directors and became the largest stockholder. With the financial assistance of his father-in-law, Burnett began purchasing land south of the Red River at twenty-five cents an acre, eventually expanding this 6666 range to some 40,000 acres.[8] In coming years he would acquire additional ranch land in King, Cottle, and other north Texas counties, and the 6666 would cover some 252,000 acres.

In February 1877 Burnett joined other storied pioneer northern Texas cattlemen, including Dan and W. T. Waggoner (father and son), the Millett brothers, the Ikard brothers, the Curtis brothers, James C. Loving, C. C. Slaughter, C. L. "Kit" Carter, and John N. Simpson at Graham to form the Texas and Southwestern Cattle Raisers Association, the oldest and largest organization of its kind in the United States.[9] He would hold several offices within the association, including that of treasurer, and was a member of the executive committee for forty-five years until his death in 1922.

H. H. Halsell, a longtime association member, recalled a meeting of the executive committee in which the perennial problem of cattle rustling was brought up for discussion:

> Burk Burnett made a motion that the executive committee hire a certain notorious cow thief as cattle inspector for the Association. Tom Waggoner said: "Burk, that man is the biggest cow thief in West Texas." Burnett replied, "Yes, that's the reason we want him. He is on to the job, or rather on the inside, and can break up the stealing." This man was hired, became the most useful inspector in the Association, and was the means of cleaning up a vast amount of cattle stealing.[10]

Burnett's rather unusual logic was also evidenced when it came to providing beef to feed his family and employees. Since before the annual roundup cattle from various ranches mingled together on the range, he thought it perfectly logical when butchering a beef for the table to choose someone else's animal. He was not alone in this practice. "It became a custom to kill everybody's beef but your own," veteran cowman Charles Goodnight recalled. "Within a mile of my ranch lived a widow who got to be a cattle lady. . . . She said she 'would as leave eat one of her little children as one of her own beeves.' . . . When fellow rancher Dan Waggoner was invited to dinner at the 6666 ranch one time, Burnett told him he would serve something Waggoner had never before eaten. Seeing nothing unusual on the table, Wagoner reminded his host of his promise. Burnett passed him the meat platter, saying, 'Taste a piece of your own beef.'"[11]

Over the years Burnett grew in wealth and prominence as one of the foremost cattlemen of north Texas, but he remained a working cowhand. Much of his time was spent astride a horse, with a Winchester rifle in a scabbard under his knee and a Colt's six-shooter belted on his hip. As he demonstrated on more than one occasion, he had the sand and skill to use his weapons to protect his life and property. At least two hard cases with claims as gunmen made the mistake of taking on Burk Burnett and paid for their error with their lives.

A cowboy named Jack King was the first to fall before Burnett's deadly fire. After fleeing Montague County, where he had been indicted on four counts of assault with intent to kill,[12] King, described by a contemporary newspaper as "a noted desperado, a man of bad habits, a terror on the frontier,"[13] went to work on the Millett brothers' spread and was soon promoted to foreman. Cattle ranchers "Hi," "Cap," and "Lon" Millett were notorious for employing desperadoes and brand-burners,[14] but apparently King was too tough even for the Millett brothers, for he was soon fired.[15]

King then began accumulating a herd of his own, overbranding any cattle he could find on the range and driving them across the Red River into Indian Territory. In June 1879 Burk Burnett learned about this and, together with a few of his hands, rode across the river to see if any of his stock had been taken. When he found some twenty head with King's brand, 818, burned over the 6666, Burnett drove the cattle back to his range and sent word to King that if he wanted to argue ownership, he should come to see him.

On Saturday, June 7, King, accompanied by two pals, Pat Walford and Jim Garrison, rode over to the Burnett camp. It was evident when he found Burnett that he had not come to negotiate the dispute. Burnett's attempts to reason with the man were met with "a tirade of abuse." Finally King dismounted and, with his hand on his pistol, walked toward Burnett, growling, "I will kill you, anyhow."

Burk Burnett had heard and seen enough. He "drew his revolver and as quickly stepped out, firing instantly four successive shots, the first shot taking effect immediately over the left eye, passing through the brain and causing death instantaneously." When one of King's companions made a move for a weapon, Phoenix M. "Fene" Burnett, Burk's younger brother, whipped out his pistol and covered the pair. Deciding that discretion was the better part of valor, Walford and Garrison put spurs to their mounts and galloped off.[16]

Burnett surrendered to the law, posted $3,000 bond, and awaited trial. The editor of the *Henrietta Journal*, in his account of the affair, made it plain where he believed responsibility for the unfortunate affair resided. King was characterized as "a man of bad reputation and one that was quick to anger, and when aroused was a dangerous character." Burnett, on the other hand, "one of our most extensive stock men," was "a quiet, unassuming gentleman and an industrious worker.

Samuel Burk Burnett. Courtesy of the Archives Division, Texas State Library, Austin.

Public sentiment justifies Burnett in the act, for it is conceded by those who knew King that had not Burnett fired certain death awaited him. The event causing the loss of human life is greatly to be deplored, and none regrets the fact greater than Mr. Burnett, who was forced to the act only by the knowledge that a moment's delay would cost him his own life's blood."[17]

There was no doubt that public opinion strongly favored Burnett, and in such instances the wheels of justice turned swiftly in Texas courts of the period. Only eight days later Burnett was tried for murder at Henrietta, and a jury took less than an hour to return a "not guilty" verdict. On June 15 Martin B. Loyd, who had attended the trial in support of his son-in-law, wired a friend in Fort Worth: "Burk Burnett was tried and acquitted for the killing of Jack King. I will try and start home tomorrow." Editor B. B. Paddock of the *Fort Worth Daily Democrat* printed this telegram with a personal editorial comment:

> The readers of the *Democrat*, most of whom are acquainted with or know of Mr. Burk Burnett, our esteemed citizen, will be pleased to learn of the happy termination of his trial by jury at Henrietta, charged with the murder of Jack King, a "boss" cattle man, in the employ of the Millet [*sic*] Bros. . . .
> The *Democrat* was satisfied that Burk was acting in self defense, and so expressed its conviction, well knowing the gentleman and his reputation as a peaceable, law-abiding and honorable citizen, and in the result of the jury's investigation, none will extend the hand of warm congratulations with more pleasure than the writer.[18]

A story later circulated in the cow camps that another Millett employee, a man named Clark, seeking revenge for the King slaying, rode onto the Burnett range in search of the owner. As old-timer Tom Roberts told the tale, Clark hid behind some underbrush at a Burnett ranch gate, "and all that could be seen was his eye." But, said Roberts, Burnett saw the eye, drew, and fired one shot, "and [Clark's] eye was where the fatal shot struck." No contemporary evidence has been found to substantiate this story; it may have been only a distortion of the Jack King killing.[19]

Another story that went the rounds of the north Texas range concerned Cal Suggs, a cowman who became enraged over a cattle deal with Burnett that fell through. In one version of the tale, Suggs pulled a gun on Burnett, who was in shirtsleeves and unarmed. Suggs triggered off a round, but missed when Burnett dodged. " 'You're a coward for shooting an unarmed man,' Burnett said coldly. Suggs winced. Burnett pressed his advantage. Soon he had talked Suggs into putting his gun away, a superb demonstration of cold nerve."[20]

In another version (or perhaps it was a different confrontation) "Burnett and Cal Sugg [sic], the dark-haired giant from the San Angelo country, were continually at loggerheads over fence lines and lease boundaries. . . . On one occasion, after a particularly bitter quarrel, they met in the lobby of the Delaware Hotel [in Fort Worth] and both men drew revolvers at the same time. Tom Waggoner, so the story goes, stepped between the two and averted what possibly might have been a tragedy."[21]

Unlike the Millett brothers, who made a practice of hiring outlaws and gunmen, Burnett prided himself on employing only honest, law-abiding cowboys to work his vast spreads. He was therefore chagrined when one of his hands turned bad in 1896. Foster Crawford, line rider for the 6666, entered into a criminal partnership with Elmer Lewis, alias Foster Holbrook, alias Younger Lewis, alias "The Mysterious Kid." Lewis was an experienced desperado who had ridden in the Indian Territory with the notorious Christian brothers and veteran outlaws "Red Buck" Weightman and Hill Loftis. In a holdup of the City National Bank of Wichita Falls on February 25, 1896, Crawford and Lewis shot and killed cashier Frank Dorsey. Texas Rangers under renowned Captain Bill McDonald soon captured the pair and jailed them at Wichita Falls.

Frank Dorsey had been very popular in the town, and feeling against the murderers ran high. Sensing that a lynch mob was forming, Foster Crawford begged his captors to bring Burk Burnett to the jail. Asked if he expected his employer to free him, Crawford shook his head. In a fit of rage because one of his men had turned criminal, Burnett would shoot him, Crawford said, and he preferred to die from a Burnett bullet than a lynch mob's rope. Burnett did not come, however, and Crawford did not get his wish. On the night of February 27 a mob took the two bandits from the jail and strung them up.[22]

Thirty-three years passed after the killing of Jack King before Burk

Burnett again resorted to the six-shooter in a deadly encounter. During those years, even as he continued to expand his cattle holdings and grow increasingly wealthy, Burnett remained the gruff, tough, plain-spoken man he had always been, a man of the range, a cattleman. His loud, booming voice, grown rough from years of shouting to other riders across the range, impressed a visiting Englishman, who, on meeting Burnett, described him as "devilish noisy, but a deuce handsome chap."[23]

The marriage of Burk and Ruth Burnett produced three children, Tom, Francis, and Anne, but Francis died in infancy. Following the death of Ruth, Burk remarried. On September 13, 1892, he took as his second wife Mary Couts Barradell, a widow. One child, Samuel Burk, Jr., born to this marriage, was his father's favorite. The old cattleman had plans for this boy to follow in his father's footsteps and suffered a great blow when young Burk died at the age of twenty following an automobile accident.[24]

In 1907 the town of Nesterville in Wichita County was renamed Burkburnett to honor the owner of the nearby 6666 ranch, and a few years later this town boomed when oil was discovered in the area. Many of the wells were drilled on Burnett property, and cattle mogul Burk soon became an oil baron also. In 1908 Burnett was elected president of Fort Worth's annual Southwestern Exposition and Fat Show, the largest livestock exhibition in the country, and served in that capacity until his death fourteen years later.

Having developed a close friendship with the celebrated Comanche chieftain Quanah Parker and other leaders of the Comanche and Kiowa tribes, Burnett drew on that relationship to lease some three hundred thousand acres of prime grazing land in the Indian Territory. There he established horse- and cattle-raising operations in what came to be called the Big Pasture. In 1905 he hosted President Theodore Roosevelt at a wolf hunt on his range in the Indian lands. Among the western celebrities taking part in this hunt with Burnett and the president were Quanah Parker, Texas Ranger captain Bill McDonald, and Jack Abernathy, who greatly impressed Roosevelt with his ability to catch wolves with his bare hands. Figuring that a man with that kind of skill should be equally adept at nabbing outlaws, Roosevelt the following year appointed Abernathy U.S. marshal for Oklahoma Territory.

In 1912 Burk Burnett was sixty-three years old, one of the wealthiest and most respected men in Texas, when once again he was forced to unlimber his six-shooter in a deadly encounter.

Neighboring rancher Farley P. Sayers, age thirty-three, married with four children,[25] had been giving Burnett trouble for years. Burnett had raised the familiar charge of cattle stealing against him and succeeded in getting Sayers indicted for stealing 6666 steers. On a change of venue the trial was moved to Benjamin, Texas, and Sayers was acquitted, but carried a grudge against Burnett thereafter. An irascible and violence-prone man, Sayers openly threatened his neighbor's life. A year or two prior to the final Burnett-Sayers showdown, Sam Graves, one of the 6666 cowboys, tangled with his boss's enemy, and pumped a bullet into him. But Sayers recovered, and the incident only served to heighten his hatred of Burnett.[26] In December 1911 Sayers quarreled with his own brother and at Dumont, King County, shot and killed him with a Winchester rifle. He was under indictment for this murder when he went gunning for Burnett in the spring of 1912.[27]

At Fort Worth in March for the annual Southwestern Exposition and Fat Show, Sayers voiced threats against the life of the organization's president. Jim Barkley, who was Burk's brother-in-law,[28] and several others close to Burnett heard the threats and warned the old cattleman to be on the lookout. Burnett began carrying a gun at all times and went to Mayor W. D. Davis and requested protection. During the run of the show, uniformed police and city detectives kept Sayers under constant surveillance, and he never found an opportunity to carry out his threat.

In May Burnett left his Fort Worth home to spend a week at his King County ranch. Constantly at his side as a bodyguard was Tom Pickett, a Wichita Falls constable and former Burnett ranch hand.[29] On May 21 a farmer named George rode twenty miles to warn Burnett that Sayers was waving a gun around and voicing renewed threats against the cattleman's life. Two days later, Thursday, May 23, Burnett and Pickett, together with King County Sheriff Garrison W. Moore and Jim Barkley, drove from the 6666 ranch to Paducah, where Burnett was to catch a train to Fort Worth and Pickett for Wichita Falls. On arrival at Paducah about ten o'clock in the morning, Sheriff Moore went about his business while the other three repaired to the Goodland Hotel for a bit of lunch in the dining room. As Burnett, Pickett, and Barkley made their way to the hotel, several citizens approached them, warning that Sayers had been in town a few days earlier, buying cartridges and loudly proclaiming his determination to carry out his murderous plan. No one had seen Sayers that morning, however.[30]

It was a little early for lunch, so Burnett and his party spent an idle hour conversing in the lobby of the hotel. Shortly after eleven o'clock Farley Sayers and four other men — Walker Morgan, Willis Evans, Fred McDonald, and Walter Edwards — entered the room. It was later reported that as they passed by the Burnett group, Sayers or one of the men with him muttered, "There is the old S.O.B. now."[31]

Sayers, McDonald, and Edwards immediately went into the washroom. Signaling to Pickett to follow him, Burnett got up from his chair and headed for the lavatory, Pickett at his heels.

Sayers was washing his hands as they entered. Glancing up, he saw Burnett, and his right hand immediately flashed to his hip pocket, where he carried a .25-caliber Colt's automatic pistol.

Wet hands do not make for a fast draw. Before he could get the gun out, Burnett whipped out the weapon he had carried for four decades on the range, a single-action .45 six-shooter, thumbed back the hammer, and fired one shot. The bullet struck Sayers on the left side of his chest and came out below the right shoulder blade. Sayers tumbled to the floor, gasping his final breaths.

Tom Pickett, behind Burnett, also had his gun out, covering the other two men. Walter Edwards had been bending over the sink, washing his face, when the shot was fired. He estimated that the bullet passed within six inches of his head. He and McDonald lost no time in exiting the premises. "I didn't run out of the wash room," Edwards later testified, "but came out in a pretty peart[32] walk and kept up the pace until I was a block from the hotel." Fred McDonald stayed right with him, and Walker Morgan and Willis Evans were not far behind.[33]

Burk Burnett walked calmly from the hotel to the First State Bank across the street and told the bank employees to telephone Cottle County Sheriff A. L. Backus and inform him of the shooting. Arrested, he posted bond of $15,000.

As an indication of the power and influence Burnett had in this part of Texas, officials of the Quanah Acme and Pacific Railroad that serviced Paducah held up their train to Fort Worth until he could arrange for his bond and board the cars to go home. The news of the sensational shooting had gone out over the telegraph news services, and before Burnett left Paducah he received more than thirty telegrams from friends across the state, offering support.[34]

When Burnett arrived back in Fort Worth, reporters descended on him, and he issued a statement. He said that for years he had been aware of Sayers's threats against his life. Only ten minutes before he entered the washroom a man came up to him in the lobby of the hotel and told him he had heard Sayers say he would kill Burnett on sight. When he went to Paducah, he did not know that Sayers was in town.

> Had I known that Mr. Sayers was at Paducah I would have done everything in my power to avoid meeting him. I know of no reason why he desired to kill me, and why he threatened my life to so many people [but] I believed him to be a dangerous man and I believed he was a man that would carry into execution the threats he had made. . . .
>
> I went into the washroom about 11:30 to wash my face and hands for dinner. As I entered the room I noticed three men, two of whom I did not know, and did not recognize Mr. Sayers until I was near the washstand . . . and when I did recognize him he was reaching with his right hand toward his right breeches pocket. I then realized that I was to be murdered or that I was to kill him. I jerked my pistol out and fired one shot. Did not have time to get my pistol hardly straight, shooting the moment I snatched it from my pocket.
>
> I regret very much, especially at my age, having any trouble, but it was absolutely unavoidable, as will be shown at the trial by the evidence of witnesses whose veracity cannot be questioned. I shall demand a trial at the first term of court.[35]

When Tom Pickett got back to his hometown of Wichita Falls, he, too, was cornered by reporters and asked for his version of the affair. He confirmed the stories of threats by Sayers. Burnett, he said, was in the lead when they entered the washroom. There they found three men. Sayers "reached in his pocket as if for a gun, but Burnett beat him to it." He fired, and "Sayers fell to the floor dead with a bullet through his heart." Pickett then "drew his own gun and covered the other two men who broke and ran out the door."[36]

The district attorney of Cottle County secured an indictment against Burk Burnett for first-degree murder. Another indictment charged Tom Pickett with being an accessory in that crime. Burnett's lawyers requested and obtained a change of venue for the trial, which was held more than a year later, at the July session of the district court in Seymour, Baylor County.

In the meantime, Rosa Sayers, Farley's widow, filed a wrongful death civil suit against Burnett, claiming $150,000 in damages. Two months before his criminal case went to trial, Burnett made an $8,000 settlement out of court with Rosa Sayers.[37]

A week before the case was called in Seymour, Burnett had an accident in Fort Worth. He fell and cracked several ribs. When he arrived in Seymour for the trial in his private railroad car on Sunday, May 20, 1913, friends noted that the sixty-four-year-old appeared drawn and pale and in obvious pain.[38]

The Burnett murder trial was a huge event in north Texas. Some 250 witnesses were subpoenaed to testify, and every hotel in Seymour was loaded. When District Judge Jo A. P. Dickson called the court to order at 10:15 in the morning on May 21, 1913, the courtroom was packed to overflowing, with representatives of the press, friends and relatives of the victim and his slayer, and the just plain curious. The Associated Press covered the event and reported that the seats were filled with "ranchmen, cowboys, bankers, merchants and representatives of every class."[39]

The prosecution was conducted by J. Ross Bell, county attorney of Cottle County; R. O. Newton, Seymour district attorney; and Bert King, county attorney of Baylor County. The defense team was extensive and impressive: J. F. Cunningham and J. H. Berney of Fort Worth; the firm of Brown and Hawkins of Paducah; A. J. Fires of Childress; the firm of Glasgow and Kenan of Seymour; and J. T. Montgomery of Wichita Falls, a jury selection consultant.

A jury was impaneled by 10:30 the following morning and, after brief remarks by District Attorney Newton and defense counsel Cunningham, testimony began. The state called as its first witnesses the four men who had been with Farley Sayers when he went into the Goodland Hotel: Walker Morgan, Willis Evans, Fred McDonald, and Walter Edwards.

Morgan testified that he thought Burnett had a gun in his hand when he entered the washroom, and he immediately fired. He never saw Sayers reach for a gun. Under cross-examination, he said that Sayers owned a .25 automatic and "always" carried the gun in his right-hand hip pocket. He also admitted Sayers could have made a play for his gun without the witness seeing him.

The testimony of the other three men was similar to that of Morgan, Willis Evans adding that Sayers's shirt had caught fire from the muzzle blast and he had put out the flame. Subjected to a tough cross-examination by Cunningham, Evans admitted that he was then under indictment in Cottle County for theft. As Cunningham skillfully led him on, Evans became an excellent witness for the defense. He admitted that he had been a witness for the state in the case against Sayers for killing his brother. He told of being with Sayers when he tried to shoot Sam Graves, the 6666 cowboy who had bested him in a gunfight. He related how Sayers and his wife had concealed themselves near the 6666 bunkhouse with the intent of ambushing Burnett, and had almost killed another man by mistake. His testimony was devastating to the state's case.

Other prosecution witnesses, a Dr. Alexander, who described the death wound and verified the burning of Sayers's shirt and body; undertaker L. Monroe, who merely confirmed the doctor's report; and Cottle County Deputy Sheriff T. A. Freeman, who searched Sayers's body and found no gun, provided a weak conclusion to the state's case.

The defense opened with a succession of no less than sixteen witnesses who swore to hearing Farley Sayers threaten the life of Burk Burnett. They included lawyers, cattlemen, farmers, and law enforcement officers. Typical was the testimony of Green Harrison, an attorney, who said that in his law office, Sayers had openly admitted making a failed attempt to murder his enemy. "I had one chance to kill Burnett, the damned old son-of-a-bitch, but would never let another opportunity slip by," he was quoted as saying. "I ought to go over to the 6666 and kill the whole Burnett outfit."

B. L. Winters, who had worked for Sayers, said that his employer had offered him a bonus if he would help bushwhack Burnett.

C. E. "Ed" Herndon, former sheriff of King County, said Sayers offered him $500 in 1909 to kill Burnett.

Notables on a wolf hunt on the Burnett range in 1905 included Texas
Ranger captain Bill McDonald (*standing, second from left*); John R.
"Catch-em-Alive Jack" Abernathy, who here holds a wolf by the jaw
(*standing, center*); Burk Burnett (*standing, third from right*); President
Theodore Roosevelt (*standing, second from right*); and Comanche chief
Quanah Parker (*kneeling, left of center*). From the author's collection.

J. M. "Bud" Barrow, ex-sheriff of Cottle County, related how a man named W. M. Coombs had told him as early as 1910 that Sayers had "asked him how he could kill Burnett and get out of it." Barrow had heard Sayers repeat his threats in Matador the day before the shooting and, seeing Burnett in the Goodland Hotel that Thursday, had given him this information only five minutes before the shooting.

W. D. Davis, who had been mayor at Fort Worth at the time of the cattlemen's convention in March 1912, recounted how Burnett had come to him demanding special protection because of Sayers's threats, and he had complied.

A total of six current and former sheriffs of Cottle, King, Knox, and Motley counties testified to their conviction that Farley Sayers was a hard and dangerous character. One of them, Sheriff J. E. Russell of Motley County, happened to be in Paducah the day of the shooting, and he had removed the .25 automatic pistol from Sayers pocket before the body was searched by Deputy Sheriff Freeman. It was Cottle County Sheriff J. L. Backus's expert opinion that the weapon was "as deadly as an old-fashioned 45-Colts."

Burk Burnett took the stand and testified for two hours in his own defense. He repeated what he had told the press shortly after the shooting, that he had been aware for years of Sayers's obsession with killing him, and that since the 1912 Cattlemen's Convention he had carried a gun. He said that when he suddenly confronted Sayers in the washroom and saw him reach for his pocket, he reacted instantly in defense of his life.[40]

Texas juries, even in the second decade of the twentieth century, looked favorably on the time-honored plea of self-defense, and this jury lost little time in bringing in a verdict of "not guilty." The accessory charges against Tom Pickett were then quietly dropped.

Burnett returned to the mansion he had constructed at Summit and Rio Grande streets in Fort Worth. The Sayers affair had been trying, but he put it behind him and concentrated his still formidable energies on real estate projects.

In 1915 he purchased the twelve-story American State National Bank building, then the tallest structure in Fort Worth. Two years later he built a second huge home at Guthrie, county seat of King County and the headquarters of the 6666 ranch. That same year he donated an extensive section of property he owned in downtown Fort

Worth to the city for a public park and provided $50,000 in his will for improvement and maintenance.[41]

When he died in the early hours of June 27, 1922, after suffering several strokes and a long illness, Samuel Burk Burnett, pioneer cowman, oil producer, merchant, financier, and banker, left an estate valued at between $6 million and $15 million, an immense sum for the time.[42] In 1969 he was elected to the National Cowboy Hall of Fame of Great Westerners.[43] In his seventy-three years he had proved to be one of the most successful cattlemen in Texas and an extraordinarily intrepid capitalist. As Jack King and Farley Sayers learned too late, he was also a man skilled in the use of the six-shooter, who, when provoked, was not afraid to use it.

— 8 —

JIM SHERMAN
1850–1896

The bold and fearless form of Jim Talbot was the center of the firing. He stood bravely in the front, with revolver in each hand, firing at the men he premeditated to kill.

— G. D. Freeman

Christened James Daniel Sherman when he was born into a notable Ohio family in 1850, Jim Sherman would turn to gun fighting and outlawry at a young age. Under the aliases "James Daniels" and "James Talbot" he would be hunted in Texas, Kansas, and Indian Territory and be a fugitive from justice for fourteen years. If the term "black sheep of the family" ever fit a man, Jim Sherman was that man.

Since the arrival of Samuel Sherman from Essex, England, to the shores of the New World in 1634, the men of the Sherman family had distinguished themselves in America. In 1805 one of those descendants, scholar and jurist Taylor Sherman, moved from Norwalk, Connecticut, to Ohio, which was then on the American frontier. In the following years he and his wife, Elizabeth, became the grandparents of two of the most distinguished Americans of the nineteenth century, brothers John and William Tecumseh Sherman. John would serve in both the U.S. House of Representatives and Senate, accept appointments as secretary of the treasury under President Rutherford B. Hayes and secretary of state under President William McKinley, and be a candidate for the presidential nomination in the campaigns of 1884 and 1888. William T. Sherman, a graduate of West Point in 1840, would go on to a brilliant military career in the Civil War.

While his first cousins were on their rise to national fame, Charles Sherman, another grandson of Taylor Sherman, was working his way west as a pioneering farmer. Charles, born in Vermont in 1812, followed his grandfather to the Ohio frontier and farmed for a time near the Ohio River town of Ironton in Lawrence County, Ohio. There he married Charlotte Crank, a daughter of neighboring farmer Sylvester Crank. One child, a son named Eugene, was born to Charles and Charlotte there in 1843. But a few years later Sherman and his family moved on west, homesteading another farm near Salem, in Henry County, Iowa. A second son, Edmund, joined the family there in 1847. The next year Sherman, ever following the advancing frontier, moved again, this time to northwestern Missouri, where he homesteaded farmland between Buchanan and DeKalb counties. Four more children — a daughter, Flora, and three more sons, Rollan, James, and Sylvester — were born there in the next four years. Other relatives — Sylvester and Polly Crank, Charlotte's parents, and the families of James and Jesse Sherman and Henry and Jacob Powell — joined in this western migration and established farms nearby.[1]

The decade of the 1850s was a chaotic time on the Missouri-Kansas frontier, with the free state–slave state controversy a burning issue. In the years leading up to the Civil War, outbreaks of violence over the issue were common occurrences in both Missouri and Kansas. The Shermans, staunch Republicans and free-state advocates, found themselves very much at odds with their neighbors in a state dominated by those of an opposing view. Charles Sherman, not one to remain silent, gave full voice to his opinions and engendered hatred among some of his more militant political foes.

One night three of these radical slave-state adherents, armed with shotguns, came to the Sherman house and banged on the door. Charles, followed by his ten-year-old son, James, hurried to the door. When he swung it open, the men blasted him with buckshot, and "his life blood spurted out all over his white-haired boy." Two years later Charlotte, "a victim of a broken heart," followed her husband to the grave.[2]

The orphaned Sherman children were distributed among relatives and friends. James went to live with Allen and Elizabeth Smith of Marion, Buchanan County.[3]

When all-out warfare finally broke out in 1861, the older Sherman brothers, although still teenagers, joined the Union army and went off to fight. James, only eleven years old, remained at home with relatives. For a time he lived in the home of his mother's sister, who had married one of the Powells. Her son, about the same age as Jim Sherman, was named, like Jim's younger brother, for their maternal grandfather, Sylvester Crank. Cousins Jim Sherman and Sylvester Powell spent many of their adolescent years together and became close.

Shortly after the end of the Civil War, a man named William Johnson Lingenfelter, who had married Flora, sister of the Sherman boys, arrived in Winslow, DeKalb County, and opened a school. Because of the tragedy that had befallen the Sherman family and the turmoil of the Civil War years, the education of the children had been sorely neglected, and Lingenfelter attempted to remedy that. Attending his school were his young wife and three of her brothers, Rollan, Jim, and Sylvester. It must have been difficult and embarrassing for Rollan, who had been only fifteen when he went off to fight in the war, but was now eighteen and a veteran, to sit in primary classes with much younger children. Nor could it have been easy for Flora, a married woman, and Jim, now a strapping youth of sixteen. But pedagogue Lingenfelter later praised them as exemplary pupils, eager to learn.[4]

For a time Jim Sherman lived in the Lingenfelter home and did chores to earn his keep. William Lingenfelter would later state flatly: "A kinder hearted, a better behaved, a more gentlemanly boy never lived in Missouri or anywhere else than James D. Sherman."[5]

In August 1868 Sherman's teacher and benefactor saved his life. The two were swimming in flood-swollen Lost Creek with a number of other boys and young men when Sherman's legs cramped. In response to his frantic calls for help, Lingenfelter swam to him, grabbed him by the hair as he sank in twenty feet of water, pulled him ashore, and, after some difficulty, revived him.[6]

Having worked on farms throughout his childhood, Jim Sherman decided as a young man that the bucolic life of a farmer was not for him. He thirsted for excitement and adventure, and in early 1869 set out to find it on the nearby frontier. He went to Leavenworth, Kansas, then a bustling center of western business activity, and took a job driving oxen to Wisconsin. But on the way an ox gored him severely, and he had to return by stagecoach to Leavenworth. Unable to work because of his injuries, he returned to Missouri.

While he was mending he lived in the home of Fannie Oldaker, a widow of Marion Township, Buchanan County. Down the road a piece from the Oldaker place was the home of a seventy-year-old farmer named James W. Talbot. Jim Sherman liked the name and stored it away for future use.[7]

As soon as he was physically able, Sherman went west again. The great buffalo slaughter of the 1870s was just beginning, and for a time he joined the hide hunters on the plains of eastern Colorado. But he soon gave up buffalo hunting to become a cowboy, working longhorn cattle on the plains of Texas and driving them up the trails to the newly developed cow towns of Kansas. It was a trade that perfectly fitted his restless nature.

In 1872 he helped trail a herd up the Chisholm Trail to Wichita, enjoying its first big shipping season that year. Years later he would say what he remembered best about cow town Wichita was the fun he and his fellow trail hands enjoyed in the notorious dives of "Rowdy Joe" Lowe and E. T. "Red" Beard. If, during these escapades, he had any contact with the top lawmen of the town, Sedgwick County Sheriff John Meagher or his twin brother, Wichita City Marshal Mike Meagher, both of whom would play leading roles in Sherman's story, he did not mention it.[8]

On July 9, 1876, Sherman married a woman named Allie Williams at San Antonio, Texas.[9] Despite troubles that would shatter many marriages, the two raised five children and remained husband and wife throughout his lifetime.

In the years following the Civil War, outlawry was rampant in Texas. The names of Texas outlaws and killers like John Wesley Hardin, Bill Longley, and Sam Bass became nationally known, and the celebrated Frontier Battalion of the Texas Rangers, formed originally to protect the outlying settlers from Indian raids, began devoting more of its efforts to hunting down desperadoes.

Sometime during this period the kind-hearted, well-behaved, gentlemanly youth of William Lingenfelter's recollection turned into a thief and a vicious killer and joined the ranks of the Texas outlaws.

According to later, unconfirmed reports, he murdered two black men in the Creek Nation,[10] killed two brothers while robbing a store in Texas, and slew two men and a woman in the course of a cattle theft in Kansas.[11] These stories may well have been exaggerated or even fabricated. Sherman himself later adamantly denied them under oath in a court of law. He did admit under cross-examination, however, that he had participated in a deadly gun battle with a band of what he called "horse stealing Mexican greasers" in which three of his companions and two Mexicans were killed. His only regret, he said, was that he did not get "the last of the greasers" before they made their escape.[12]

Whether the stories of bloodletting and violence attached to Sherman during these years were true or false, he was definitely gaining the attention of westerners who kept an eye on these things. Celebrated frontier peace officer W. B. "Bat" Masterson certainly had Jim Sherman in mind when, in a magazine article on gunfighters he had known, he mentioned "a near relative of the famous Sherman family of Ohio" who sharpened his marksmanship constantly on the range and, when in a city, practiced in shooting galleries by the hour. Masterson said that "Johnny" Sherman, as he remembered the name, was a "remarkably fine pistol shot" and "courageous as a lion," but when he became enraged at a St. Louis dentist for insulting his wife, "he emptied his pistol at the dentist without as much as puncturing his clothes [because he] was in too big a hurry to finish the job and forgot there were a set of sights on his pistol."[13]

While following the outlaw trail in Texas, Sherman dropped his surname and employed his first and middle names to adopt the alias "Jim Daniels." In April 1881 he was indicted under that name, together with cohorts John Ray and brothers Thad and Frank Williams,[14] on two counts of horse stealing in Hill County. Soon Texas Rangers were carrying wanted books containing the name "Jim Daniels."[15]

From Hill County, Jim Daniels, John Ray, and the Williams brothers, wanted fugitives now, rode northwest to Baylor County and the cattle range of the Millett brothers, a notorious sanctuary for outlaws on the run. A. P. Black, who worked cattle from Texas to the Dakotas, called the Baylor County ranch of Eugene, Alonzo, and Hiram Millett "one of the toughest spots this side of hell. . . . When the Millets [*sic*] run the spread there wasn't anybody but a rustler or gunman could get work with them. . . . The Millets were a tough outfit straight through and hired the toughest bunch of men I ever ran up against. They even paid bonuses to their cowpunchers for every cow or horse they stole."[16]

As one local historian put it: "When a man got so tough that he couldn't affiliate with civilization he would go to this [Millett] ranch and get a job."[17] Daniels and his pals fit right in with this crew.

One of the horses the outlaws had stolen back in Hill County belonged to a tough customer named Watt Perry. Not the kind of man to accept theft of his property without taking personal action, Perry trailed the outlaws more than 150 miles, past Fort Griffin in Shackelford County, on north to the Millett range in Baylor County. Satisfied that he had located his quarry, Perry doubled back to Fort Griffin and called on Shackelford County Sheriff Green Simpson to apprehend the fugitives. For the foray, Simpson enlisted his regular deputy, Henry Herron, and swore in as special deputies Perry and a man named A. B. Duty, who had lost a saddle to the thieves.

Unfortunately, Simpson, newly elected and with little law-enforcement experience, led a posse ill-prepared for a confrontation with outlaws of the caliber of Jim Daniels and his gang. The officers carried only six-shooters; not a one was armed with a rifle. The mistake cost them dearly.

Henry Herron left a vivid account of what transpired when this little posse approached the Millett headquarters:

> Perry had told us that there were four men in the gang who had gotten his horse. As we neared the ranch house, we saw four men holding a herd about one-half mile away. We figured these were our men, so we dropped down a ravine to make plans for their capture. I proposed that each of us pick one of them and arrest them in that way. Simpson thought best to go up to the house and ask for help. We stayed hid in the ravine, watching them, while he went to the house.
>
> When [the four cowboys] saw him going for the ranch they quit the herd and started after him. So hurriedly we mounted and rode hard for the same place. However, they beat us there, dismounted, and got behind a rock fence. Simpson appeared in the doorway with a shotgun and started shooting. It was not his gun, but one he picked up in the house and which happened to be

loaded with birdshot. He shot his man, Daniels, in the legs, but did not bring him down. I saw Simpson fall back in the doorway and thought they had gotten him. He was shot through both arms with a Winchester bullet. We had only six-shooters and were too far away for pistol shooting, but started shooting as we advanced. I emptied my pistol before they brought me down with a Winchester bullet through my right hip. My horse was shot first, hit in the forehead, and we both started falling at the same time.

Their first shot at Perry hit the cylinder of his pistol and put him out of action, although he stood his ground and tried to get his gun going. They killed his horse and shot him five times in various parts of his body, none being fatal. Duty claimed to have been shot in the neck, but he could not stand under fire and pulled his freight, and did not stop until he reached Young County. . . .

After Perry and I were down and helpless, one of them, Daniels, came out and asked me if I had any money. I told him I was broke, so he said, "I'll just fix you so you will not follow me any more." John Simpson, of Dallas, was there at the time, receiving cattle, as he had purchased the Millett cattle and bought their range for his outfit, the "Hashknife." He came out with Daniels and persuaded him not to kill me, saying that I was all crippled up and wouldn't ever be able to follow him again. I said nothing, knowing there was no use. But John Simpson no doubt saved my life.[18]

John Simpson and his cowboys ministered to the wounds of Sheriff Simpson and Deputy Herron, while others conveyed Perry, the most seriously injured, to Seymour, the nearest town with a doctor, for professional treatment. Eventually an army ambulance from Fort Griffin transported Sheriff Simpson and Herron back to Shackelford County. The *Fort Griffin Echo* reported late in May that the officers were recovering and eager to get after the desperadoes who had gotten away from them a month earlier.[19] Apparently they were not overly anxious to resume the pursuit, for when they heard an unsubstantiated report that all four outlaws had been killed shortly after the Millett ranch shootout, they dropped their plan.[20]

Authorities in Baylor County ignored the reports, however, and in

August 1881 filed cases in the district court at Seymour charging Daniels, Ray, and the Williams brothers with three counts of assault to murder Green Simpson, Henry Herron, and Watt Perry at the Millett ranch. The cases remained open for nine years, but were dismissed by order of the court on April 18, 1890.[21]

John Ray and the Williams brothers may well have met untimely ends, for they seem to have disappeared from the pages of history after the gun battle at the Millett ranch, but certainly Jim Daniels did not die in 1881. He remained on the vast Millett spread, working out of remote line camps, until later in the year, when he joined a cattle drive headed for Kansas.

When he struck Caldwell, he peeled out of the drover crew and remained in the new cow town that squatted on the Chisholm Trail just across the Indian Territory line in Kansas.

Jim Sherman, aka "Jim Daniels," was using the name "Jim Talbot" at the time, and that was the name by which he would become famous —or infamous— in Kansas. By December 1881 the name Jim Talbot would be on everyone's lips in Caldwell and Sumner County, Kansas. Years later Sherman would tell a newspaper interviewer: "Talbot is my middle name and the boys always called me 'Talbot.' "[22] This was only one of his many lies. He had used his middle name "Daniel" as an alias in Texas, but the name "Talbot" was borrowed from a neighbor back in Buchanan County, Missouri.

He had been to Caldwell before. The previous March, before he drifted down to Hill County, Texas, and took up with Ray and the Williams boys, he had been arrested there on a drunk and disorderly charge. Jim Johnson, then city marshal of Caldwell, ran him into the police court of Judge James Kelly, where he was fined.[23]

Despite this distasteful experience in Caldwell the previous spring, the town held a special appeal for "Jim Talbot." Even before returning in the fall, he had sent for his family to take up residence there. That family now consisted of his wife, Allie, and two children, a boy of three or four called Jimmie, and a one- or two-year-old daughter named Sarah. The son was described as "heavy set and fat, a little freckled, [with] light colored hair." The "Talbots" moved into a house on Chisholm Street owned by an all-around sport and sometime law officer, Dan "Red Bill" Jones.[24]

Mike Meagher (*at left*) fell victim to Jim Sherman's gun. Mike's twin brother, John (*at right*), swore to avenge his murder. Courtesy of the Kansas State Historical Society, Topeka.

The attraction Caldwell held for Talbot was the residency there of one man, Mike Meagher, the mayor of the town and proprietor of the Arcade Saloon.

Meagher, one of the early settlers of Wichita, had served well and honorably as city marshal of that town during its greatest days as a cattle-shipping point. In controlling the rough element drawn to every cow town, he had resorted to gunplay in Wichita only once; on New Year's Day, 1877, he had gotten into an altercation with a stage-coach driver named Sylvester Powell and, in an exchange of gunfire, had shot him dead.

Sylvester Powell happened to be the first cousin and boyhood chum of Jim Sherman, aka Jim Talbot, who thirsted for revenge.

Mike Meagher was a formidable foe, however, and Talbot bided his time, waiting for the right opportunity to exact his vengeance. He gathered around him in Caldwell a group of followers that became known as the Talbot Gang. Doug Hill, Bob Bigtree, Jim Martin, and Bob Munson, former Millett trail hands who had stayed on with him in Caldwell, were joined by three other cowboys, Tom Love, Dick Eddleman, and Tom Delaney, and a pair of saloon and brothel habitués, "Comanche Bill" Mankin and George Spear.

Jim Talbot, the undisputed leader of this crew, was described at this time as "about five feet, 10 inches high, weight about 170 pounds; light complection [*sic*]; light colored mustache and whiskers; light blue or gray eyes; broad face, high cheek bones; nose turned up a little at the end; low narrow forehead; his under jaw is the longest; when he shuts his mouth his under teeth project out past lower [upper?] ones."[25]

Although he was not an unusually large man, Talbot was known for his strength. "Jim Talbot was one of the most powerful men I had ever seen," said a cowboy who knew him then. "He could take hold of two ordinary men and handle them easily."[26]

The editor of a Wichita paper provided a rather unattractive description of the man: "Talbot is a slim, long-haired, cadaverous looking Texan, smooth faced and destitute of anything approaching a smile, with a coarse, rough voice and a cold dead looking grey eye." He was said to have a taste for the flamboyant, always seen wearing a white, broad-brimmed hat with a crown encircled by a rope band, the ends of which, ornamented with red ribbons tied in a bow, dangled to the shoulders.[27]

The Talbot gang roistered for weeks in Caldwell, drinking, gambling, and whoring throughout the nighttime hours and sleeping most of the day. Their favorite hangout was the Red Light Dance Hall, a notorious joint, scene of many shootings, kept by tough sporting woman Mag Wood, but they frequented every watering hole in the town, including Mike Meagher's Arcade Saloon. Everywhere they caroused they boasted of their outlaw pasts and made drunken threats against the city police officers. Most residents, including Meagher, shrugged off the talk as nothing but whiskey babble, but as the weeks went by, some in Caldwell grew increasingly apprehensive.

During this period Talbot gained some grudging admiration in Caldwell for the part he played in the J. S. Danford banking scandal, which rocked southern Kansas in the fall of 1881. When Danford suddenly closed the doors of his bank and slipped out of town, depositors were outraged. Jim Talbot took command of a mob of 150 and led them by special train to Wellington, the county seat, where Danford was being held. At the Phillips Hotel in Wellington, Talbot accosted Judge W. P. Campbell, one of Danford's attorneys. Campbell later told a reporter that Talbot "organized and led the advancing column that stormed the stairway at the hotel and gave the writer a genteel cursing, and jostled him off the sidewalk."[28] After much loud and angry negotiation, Danford agreed to return to Caldwell, where Talbot assumed responsibility for guarding him. Cattleman Oliver Nelson, who was in Caldwell at the time, said Talbot "was given the job of entertaining His Eminence at five plunks a day. One mourner said he'd give twenty-five dollars to anyone who would shoot him. Talbot pointed his .45 full cocked, and said, 'Out with your money,' but the fellow backed down. Then Jim said, 'I'll send him out for twenty dollars,' but no one would hand over that much."[29]

As might be expected, "Danford would get shaky during these discussions,"[30] but the wily banker managed to escape bullets, lynch ropes, and legal prosecution. He eventually fled, and his depositors recovered about twelve cents on the dollar.[31] In the end he may have been grateful to Jim Talbot for turning Caldwell into a shooting gallery a few days later and making people forget absconding bankers.

Some Caldwell residents speculated that the dramatic shootout of December 17, 1881, was planned by Talbot to cover an attempt to loot the Danford bank, but that seems unlikely, as Talbot and his followers were not bank robbers, and the bank had already been looted by its president.

The explosion that rocked Caldwell that Saturday was triggered by the hatred Jim Talbot felt for Mike Meagher, stemming from Meagher's shooting of Sylvester Powell back in Wichita, and Talbot's determination to avenge his cousin's death. That it took him five years to exact that revenge can only be explained by Talbot's innate cowardice. Afraid to face the former lawman, who had amply demonstrated his courage on many occasions in a man-to-man showdown, Talbot chose to surround himself with allies and set off a chaotic gun battle, during which he could achieve his goal, the death of Mike Meagher.

To the relief of many in Caldwell, Talbot and his cronies made it known during the second week of December that they were leaving town. They began a kind of departure celebration on the evening of Friday, December 16, by attending a performance of *Uncle Tom's Cabin* at the Caldwell Opera House. During the show, the men and "their prostitutes," as a paper bluntly termed their female consorts, disrupted the performance with loud and profane catcalls. When Tell W. Walton, editor of the *Caldwell Post*, rose and admonished them for ignoring the sensibilities of the women in the audience, Talbot responded with curses and threats.

After the play the toughs toured the saloons, boasting they would "fix Meagher and that editor."[32] Walton, not wanting to be "fixed," quietly slipped out of town.[33] Talbot, backed by his pals, boldly entered Mike Meagher's Arcade Saloon, sat down at a poker table, and played throughout the night. Meagher stayed out of sight and avoided a confrontation.[34]

The night passed without further incident, but then came the dawn. George Spear and other gang members welcomed the rising sun with a fusillade of pistol shots. City Marshal John Wilson appointed Mike Meagher a special deputy, and together they went looking for the troublemakers. Finding Tom Love in Ren Moore's saloon with a smoking pistol in his hand, they disarmed and arrested him and started for the jail. They were passing the Opera House when Talbot and the rest of the gang suddenly appeared and blocked their path. A crowd formed as Talbot shouted threats against Meagher. A wild melee ensued, and Meagher was knocked down. Red Bill Jones, a former city policeman, stepped out of the crowd to assist the embattled officers, and with leveled pistols he and Wilson held the enraged Talbot at bay while Meagher escaped up the outside stairway of the Opera House.

The gang, augmented by Love, who escaped custody during the excitement, retreated to the home of Comanche Bill Mankin, where they planned their next move.

City Marshal Wilson hurried to the telegraph office and sent an urgent wire to Cass Burrus, mayor of Caldwell, who was in Wellington, that hell was about to pop. Burrus in turn alerted Sumner County Sheriff Joseph Thralls, who began recruiting a twenty-man posse to take the noon train to Caldwell and preserve order.

When gang member Jim Martin, wearing a pistol, showed up alone on the street a little later, Wilson, after some difficulty, ran him in for carrying weapons and resisting arrest. A police judge fined Martin, but allowed him to leave in the custody of Wilson and Deputy City Marshal Bill Fossett to obtain the money. As they crossed the street, Talbot, Munson, and Eddleman accosted the officers. There was another scuffle, and Martin escaped.

Talbot led his followers in a slow retreat toward his home. By this time the entire town was aroused, and citizens were arming themselves. Stopping in the middle of the street, Talbot loudly announced that the ball was open and that the dancing had begun. "Hide the little ones!" he shouted, as he opened fire on the officers and other citizens. Caldwell resident G. D. Freeman, no admirer of Talbot or his kind, had to admit that he was awed by the daring displayed by the Texas outlaw in those moments.

> The bold and fearless form of Jim Talbot was the center of the firing. He stood bravely to the front, with revolver in each hand, firing at the men he premeditated to kill. Shots fired by the citizens were striking the buildings and tearing up the ground in all directions near the fearless leader who stood undaunted by shot or bullet, watching for the men who were to be his victims. . . . The bullets flew thick and fast, and still the daring Talbot stood as a target for the guns of many citizens. . . . I expected every moment to see the form of Talbot reel and fall. . . . But not so. When Talbot emptied his six-shooters, he called to his men and said, "Boys, let's get our Winchesters," and started to run for his house, followed by his gang of outlaws.[35]

Most of the gang members, after securing their rifles, ran to horses they had saddled and hitched to the rail in front of the Red Light Dance Hall. Their leader, however, intent on killing Mike Meagher, ran back, rifle in hand, toward Main Street.

Talbot and his quarry spotted each other about the same time and exchanged rifle fire from positions on either side of the Danford Bank. In an effort to outflank Talbot, Meagher, followed by Wilson and a man named Ed F. Rathburn, ran around the building. Talbot, in anticipation of the maneuver, was waiting with leveled rifle when Meagher appeared on the other side. Talbot squeezed off a single shot, and Meagher staggered back with a bullet through his chest.[36]

Ed Rathburn would later testify that he saw Talbot aim and fire, "saw the smoke issue from the gun, heard the report and saw Meagher begin to sink down." Catching his friend in his arms, Rathburn shouted: "Good God, Mike, are you hit?"

"Yes, I am hit and hit hard," Meagher gasped. "Tell my wife I have got it at last."

Talbot's rifle bullet had struck Meagher in the right arm, entered his chest, and passed through both lungs. He died in less than an hour.[37]

Having accomplished his murderous mission, Talbot ran for the Red Light, where he expected the horses to be waiting, only to find that every mount was dead or dying, shot down by an astute storekeeper named W. N. Hubbell during the general gun battle. The other gang members were frantically pulling saddles from the stricken animals and throwing them on other horses from a nearby livery. Bullets from pursuing officers and townsmen snapped around them. Hill, Munson, Martin, and Bigtree got mounted and shouted for their leader to join them. Spear was in the act of saddling a horse for Talbot when both he and the horse were struck by bullets. Spear was the second man to bite the dust that day in Caldwell.

Unable to find horses, Love, Eddleman, Delaney, and Mankin ran from the scene. Talbot jumped up behind Hill and double-mounted, raced out of town, with Munson, Martin, and Bigtree in his wake.

The battle of Caldwell was over. Hundreds of shots had been fired and, miraculously, only two men had been killed.[38]

About a mile out of town the fleeing outlaws came upon a farmer on his way to Caldwell with a load of hay and a saddle horse trailing behind. Talbot appropriated the horse and continued on, riding bareback. At the W. E. Campbell ranch farther on, they picked up a saddle for Talbot and fresh horses to replace two that had been wounded in the gunfight. Well mounted now, they swung south and headed for Indian Territory.

When news of the shootout went out on the telegraphic wires, the *Wichita Daily Times* announced in its afternoon edition: "As we go to press, hell is in session at Caldwell."[39]

Sheriff Thralls and his posse from Wellington arrived in Caldwell and immediately joined other hurriedly organized parties in the pursuit of the outlaws. By late afternoon scores of man hunters were in the country between Caldwell and the border.

Once into Indian Territory, Talbot headed for a horse ranch where he knew remounts could be obtained. There, closely pressed by their pursuers, the gang jumped down from their jaded horses and took to the brush. They found refuge in a canyon dugout tunneled out by earlier outlaws, threw up stone breastworks, and kept possemen at bay with a hail of rifle fire. It was now late in the day, and the outlaws took advantage of the fading light, silhouetting their targets on the canyon rim while they remained almost invisible in the deep shadows below. When a posseman named John Hall stuck his head up, a bullet immediately tore a hole through the crown of his hat. Rancher W. E. "Shorthorn" Campbell, who had joined the chase, was struck twice with bullets through the wrist and the thigh.[40]

Editor Tell Walton, who had also joined the chase and was one of a party of fifteen who cornered the gang, said that the accurate fire of their quarry "disconcerted the citizens to a certain extent."[41] Some of the more "disconcerted" returned to town, leaving six to guard the canyon. Four of those remaining went off to corral the ranch horses and prevent them from falling into the hands of the outlaws, leaving only two to keep watch.

It was not enough. By the time reinforcements arrived about ten o'clock that night, the gang had fled, a fact the possemen did not discover until they mounted an attack the next morning and found the dugout empty.[42]

After slipping out of the canyon, Talbot and his men walked on south, covering about eight miles that night and the following day. Their progress was slowed by Doug Hill, who had been shot in the leg, and by Bob Bigtree, who had a hip wound.[43] The well-mounted pursuers, had they followed, could easily have overtaken their quarry, but, chagrined by having spent a nightlong vigil over a deserted dugout, they lost their taste for man hunting and returned home.

On Sunday evening, December 18, the fugitives appeared at the camp of freighter J. K. Harmon and at gunpoint demanded horses, food, and blankets. They promised to return the horses, an assurance in which Harmon had little confidence. He was agreeably surprised, therefore, when a week later another freighter brought the horses to him, with a message from Talbot that "they were not horse thieves, if they were bad men otherwise."[44]

The shootout in Caldwell culminating in the murder of the town's former mayor attracted national news attention. The story went out over the Associated Press wires and was printed in newspapers across the country, often with inaccurate embellishments. The *San Francisco Examiner* of December 21, 1881, for instance, reported erroneously that Talbot had a finger shot off in the Caldwell fight. It passed the gratuitous and unsubstantiated information that the gang leader had previously killed the marshal at Fort Elliott, Texas, and two blacks "without cause" in the Indian Territory. He was said to be "one of the 'Billy the Kid' gang of cutthroats."

Another San Francisco paper carried an account of a bloody battle on December 22 between desperadoes and freighters in Clay County, Texas, in which two men were killed. It was "supposed" that this was the work of the Talbot gang, as "the villains escaped from Caldwell to the territory and were en route for Texas, and it is believed they have proceeded with their plunder to Mexico."[45]

The *National Police Gazette* of December 31 contained an even wilder account. Under the heading "Cowboys on the Loose: Storming a Kansas Town, Slaughtering Citizens and Stirring Up Judge Lynch to a Fury," it described the sacking of Caldwell by "a large troop of cowboys, about thirty, fully armed with rifles and revolvers and all drunk, [who] drove the citizens out, insulted the affrighted women and children, helped themselves to the goods in the stores and raised Cain generally." Owing Mike Meagher "a bloody grudge," they "rode him down in the street, riddled him with bullets and trampled him to a shapeless mass beneath their horses' feet."

In its issue of December 29, the *Caldwell Commercial* grumbled: "It is more than probable now that they have made their escape and by this time are in the Panhandle, where they will find plenty of men of their own stamp ready and willing to give them all the aid they require."

Talbot and his gang had not reached the Texas panhandle, but it was true that as they made their way south through Indian Territory, they were welcomed into the Chisholm Trail cattle camps, where the Texas cowboys had no love for the lawmen of Kansas. According to one of those cowboys, Laban Records, the five outlaws, after riding all night on the horses taken from the freighters, spent several days at his camp and that of H. Wheeler Timberlake. It was from these camps that Talbot returned the borrowed horses.

Of course, the big Caldwell shootout was the major topic of conversation throughout that country. Talbot displayed some coyness in telling the story of the Meagher killing to Records. He said he saw Meagher raise his rifle to shoot and then abruptly stopped his narration.

"So that is the way you got him," Records prodded.

With a wink and a smile Talbot responded, using one of his favorite expressions: "Somebody did, as sure as God made little apples in the summertime."[46]

Frank Stevens, one of the cowhands in the Records camp and a wanted man himself, volunteered to ride all the way to Caldwell to purchase ammunition for the Talbot bunch. "Since Bob Munson seemed to be a rather straightforward sort of fellow," said Records, "I let him take a $60 horse with the understanding the horse would be returned as quickly as he could. I haven't seen the horse since."[47]

The gang also stayed several days in the Charles Colcord cattle camp, where they felt so unhurried and secure that, despite their wounds, they helped put up a log cabin then under construction.[48]

When the outlaws reached the Red River, they camped on the Indian Territory side, across from Doan's Store, a major provisioning point on the Western Cattle Trail to Dodge City. They slipped over at night to get supplies. Corwin Doan remembered that Bob Munson "couldn't sit down for a week" after riding 120 miles bareback. Doan later claimed that Captain G. W. Arrington of the Texas Rangers was on the lookout for the Talbot bunch and offered him $1,000 to tell him where they were. "I had a wife and baby and my uncle's two daughters," said Doan, "and I couldn't afford to tell him and told Arrington so. He said I was right. They would have killed me." On one of his nocturnal visits Bob Munson asked him, "Corwin, you wouldn't give us away, would you?" Doan replied, "Not on your sweet life, Bob." In addition to his fear of gang retaliation, Doan confessed that, as a Texan, he was not overly concerned about the killing of a Kansas "marshal" by Texas cowboys, for "the Texans hated the Kansas people and the Kansans hated Texans."[49]

While hiding out in the breaks of the Red River, Talbot and his cohorts followed the accounts of their escapades as reported in the press. On January 12, 1882, they wrote an indignant letter to the *Kansas City Times*, denying many of the stories and presenting their version of the events of December 17 and thereafter:

> In Camp, January 12. — We have noticed through the columns of your paper the account of the so-called cut-throats. You are aware of the fact that every story has two sides, so we wish to inform the readers of the *Times* that we were not drunk at the time of the fight. In the next place we never rode into the city of Caldwell. We had been in town about one month and had always abided by its laws, and as far as helping ourselves to anything it is false. We never molested any thing that was not our own. As for Meagher when he was killed we were not mounted. He had two six shooters in his hands at the time he was shot, and more he went to Hubbell's store and borrowed the pistols. It seems to be the general opinion that Meagher was a leading man in Caldwell. Do you know his business? He was nothing more than a saloon keeper and ran a keno table. Just a few days before the row he was arrested and had to give bond for selling whisky in Caldwell. It has been published that the row grew out of the killing of George Flat,[50] this is also false. It never entered our minds.
>
> The very reason the row came up was that the honorable Marshal of Caldwell, John Wilson, was on a protracted drunk and stationed a posse of men in the Exchange saloon and told them to shoot every man that moved — that is, cowboys — then arming himself with two pistols, and then throwing them down on every one of the cowboys, telling them to throw up their hands, which we refused to do. He then withdrew his weapons and proceeded to organize a mob to take or kill us. We went and got our guns and marched to the front and engaged in a fight, which lasted about an hour. We then went and got our horses and started to leave town and then we were fired on from every and

all concealed places imaginable. The second skirmish lasted about thirty minutes and then we were forced to ride. We were pursued by about 100 armed men. They at length got us rounded up in a washout and there we stayed until night, then we got together and left. After the mob had dispersed Wilson turned to shoot one of the boys in the back, and this is why the row came up. George Spears was shot by the town mob. He had no hand in the fight whatever. He was a friend of the cowboys and that was the cause of his death. He was just as honorable a citizen as Caldwell had. The Assistant Marshal acknowledged that Wilson was drunk, and that if he (Wilson) had let things alone every thing would have been all right and there would have been no row.

We did take the freighters' horses and told them that we would return their horses in six or eight days, and on the seventh day we took them back. They told us that if they were situated in the same position that they would do the same thing and did not blame us. Caldwell citizens seem to think that Talbot was one of Billy the Kid's gang. This is a bare falsehood; he has never seen the Kid and has never had any acquaintance with him whatever. We notice that it was stated we had a fight on Wagon creek; this is a mistake; we never was at Wagon creek and took saddles and horses. We never took any horses but the freighters. We are willing to go and stand trial if we thought we could get justice, but this we know we cannot get. This is the true facts of the row.

[Signed] Jim Talbot,
Dug Hill,
Bob Munson,
Jim Martin,
Bob Bigtree[51]

After a fruitless weeklong search for the outlaws, Sheriff Thralls gave up the hunt and disbanded his posse. Meanwhile Caldwell was recovering from the traumatic events of December 17. At an inquest into the death of Meagher, it was concluded that he "came to his death from the effect of a gun shot wound from a gun in the hands of Jim Talbot," and that Bigtree, Martin, Munson, Hill, Tom Love, and Dick Eddleman were accessories. Spear's death was caused by a gunshot fired by "some person not known to the jury."[52]

Governor's Proclamation.

$1700 REWARD!

STATE OF KANSAS,

Executive Department, Topeka, Dec. 9, 1882.

I, JOHN P. ST. JOHN, Governor of the State of Kansas, by virtue of the authority vested in me by law, do hereby offer a reward of FIVE HUNDRED DOLLARS for the arrest and conviction of one Jim. Talbott, as principal, and THREE HUNDRED DOLLARS each, for the arrest and conviction of Jim. Martin, Bob. Munson, Bob. Bigtree, and Dug. Hill, as accessories, to the murder of MIKE. MEAGHER, in Sumner County, Kansas, on or about the 17th day of December, 1881.

In Testimony Whereof, I have hereunto subscribed my name, and affixed the Great Seal of the State, at Topeka, the day and year first above written.

[L. S.]

JOHN P. ST. JOHN.

By the Governor:

JAMES SMITH,

Secretary of State.

Kansas governor's proclamation offering rewards for the slayers of Mike Meagher. Courtesy of the Kansas State Historical Society, Topeka.

Officers arrested Love, Eddleman, Comanche Bill Mankin, and Tom Delaney. When it was shown that Mankin and Delaney had taken no part in the shootings, they were released, but Love and Eddleman were jailed at Wellington. At a preliminary hearing in January 1882, Love was acquitted and freed. Eddleman escaped from custody, enjoyed a brief period of freedom, but was caught and also released after a hearing.[53]

Soon after the "Talbot Raid," as it was coming to be known, rewards totaling $1,100 were posted for the outlaws.[54] Later the governor of Kansas upped the ante, offering $500 for the arrest and conviction of Talbot as principal, and $300 each for Martin, Munson, Bigtree, and Hill as accessories in the murder of Mike Meagher, and Sheriff Thralls published a public notice that the combined reward money offered by the city and state now totaled $2,400.

Meagher's body was taken to Wichita for burial, as glowing tributes to the man appeared in newspapers in both Caldwell and Wichita.[55]

The *Wichita Daily Times* scolded the city where Meagher died for allowing the conditions that led to the tragedy: "Caldwell sowed the wind and she reaps the whirlwind. . . . Wichita has had the cowboys. We could teach Caldwell many useful lessons. Talbot and his gang would have been driven from the city as vagabonds long ago in the cattle days of Wichita."[56]

Mike Meagher left a widow, Jenny, but, fortunately, no fatherless children. Jenny moved back to Wichita in January 1882, but it is not known if in her last weeks in Caldwell she ever confronted Allie, the wife of her husband's slayer. Talbot had left Allie penniless, with no means of support for herself and her two small children, and she found herself at the mercy of the residents of the community he had terrorized. A few days after the big shootout the *Caldwell Commercial* reported: "Talbot's family are in a destitute condition, but their immediate wants have been supplied by order of the mayor." The city was still supporting the family a month later.[57]

By that time Talbot had found a job with a cow outfit and was making arrangements to get his family out of Caldwell.[58] He hired a cowboy named Hank Smith to take a covered wagon to Caldwell for that purpose. Aware that officers were keeping a close watch on the family in anticipation of Talbot's attempt to reach them, Smith waited a day or two after arriving in Caldwell to make his move. When he found that the officers had become lax and did not watch the house at night, he contacted Allie, and together they laid plans. Late one night he drove the wagon to the house, helped Allie load the Talbot belongings under the canvas, and with the woman and children hidden inside, slipped out of town. The family was not missed for several days, and by that time Smith and his wagon were too far away for anyone to give chase.[59] Smith took Allie and the children to a ranch near Dodge City, where the husband and father was waiting. The family celebrated the reunion for a few days and then left for points west.[60]

Wanting to put as much ground between himself and Kansans as possible, Talbot did not stop his westward trek until he reached California. There he settled into a new life at Boonville, Mendocino County, about a hundred miles north of San Francisco.

With a new life came another name. Discarding the outlaw aliases "Jim Daniels" and "Jim Talbot," he reverted to the name his parents had given him and once again became James D. Sherman.

Mendocino County was sheep-raising country. Although he had always been associated with cattle, and cowmen were notorious for their hatred of sheep, Sherman hired on with the Marks and Newfield sheep-herding outfit, headquartered about eight miles out of Ukiah, the county seat. The owners quickly recognized his native intelligence and natural leadership ability and soon promoted him to manager. He also for the first time pinned on a badge, taking appointment as a township constable and later a deputy sheriff. Highly regarded by his neighbors and employers, his life went well for more than a decade, and his outlaw days were almost forgotten.[61]

But then Sherman's dark, violent side reemerged. In the early hours of Monday, June 19, 1893, he and George William Parker, a city councilman and jeweler of Ukiah, were drinking in Niepp's saloon when they got into a drunken dispute.

According to witnesses, each claimed to be the better marksman. As tempers rose, Parker shoved Sherman against the bar, produced a little knife, and threatened to cut him in two. Scott Howard, a bystander, jumped between the two, forcibly propelled Parker to the rear of the saloon, took away his knife, and attempted to quiet him. But Parker broke away and pulled a pistol. Shouting "Jim, I've got you dead, God damn you!" he started for Sherman.

Howard yelled, "Look out, boys!"

Then, "quicker than I can tell you," as one witness testified, Sherman "got his pistol out," brought it up over the shoulder of Dick Simmons, who was between Sherman and the advancing Parker, and turned it loose at Parker's head.

"There were four or five shots fired as fast as the pistol could be fired," said Gus Henry, another bar patron. "[It] looked like a stream of fire."

Felled with three bullets in the face, Parker collapsed and died within fifteen minutes. Sherman surrendered to Under Sheriff Fred C. Handy, who locked him up. At an inquest held that afternoon S. C. Poage, justice of the peace and acting coroner, found that Sherman had killed Parker "willfully and intentionally, but in self-defense," and released him from custody. But District Attorney J. E. Pemberton, dissatisfied with the ruling, had him rearrested immediately and held for a preliminary examination to determine if he should be charged with murder.[62]

The local paper editorialized that while most citizens concluded that the killing was "cowardly and unnecessary," no one believed Sherman would be convicted of murder.[63]

At a hearing held on June 21 before Justice Poage, attorney J. A. Cooper represented Sherman, and J. H. Seawell appeared for the people. Although the evidence presented was almost identical to that given at the inquest, Poage bound Sherman over for trial in the Mendocino County District Court and fixed bail at $3,000. Sherman's employers went the bond, and he was released.[64]

The trial began on November 16, 1893, and lasted only three days. After deliberating less than an hour, the jury found the defendant guilty of manslaughter. The *Dispatch Democrat*, reaffirming its original view that the killing was "cowardly and unnecessary," thought the verdict was "most righteous."[65] On motion of Sherman's attorneys, J. A. Cooper and J. Q. White, to delay sentencing until December 11, when another motion for a new trial could be entered, Judge McGarvey granted a delay until that date. On December 11 he denied the new trial motion and sentenced Sherman to a six-year term at San Quentin Penitentiary. The judge did grant a request by defense counsel for a forty-day stay of execution of sentence to allow time for filing a bill of exceptions and an appeal.[66]

Through the early months of 1894 extensions were allowed, and legal maneuvering continued. Meanwhile, a report reached San Francisco that a plot was afoot to take Sherman from the Ukiah jail and string him up.[67] The editors of the *Dispatch Democrat* scoffed at this story, saying it was based only on the babblings of a saloon drunk, who had loudly voiced his opinion that Sherman ought to be lynched.[68]

On January 27, 1894, the California Supreme Court granted Sherman a new trial, but he remained in jail pending the setting of a date for a second trial.[69]

Meanwhile, on January 22, 1894, a strange tragedy occurred that is one of the unresolved mysteries of the James Sherman story. On that night a man and his totally blind wife were brutally attacked in their home at Willow Ranch, near Petaluma, California. Someone fired a shotgun through a window, instantly killing the woman and severely wounding her husband. The vicious and apparently unprovoked attack outraged the community. Its pertinence to the Sherman history lies only in the names of the shooting victims: Mr. and Mrs. John Meagher.[70]

In the dozen years since relocating in California, Sherman had been plagued by the constant fear that John Meagher, twin brother of the man he killed in Caldwell, would somehow track him down and exact vengeance. It was something he would have done, and he expected no less from Mike Meagher's brother. Petaluma is in Sonoma County, only eighty miles south of Ukiah. The suspicion arises that Sherman, learning that a man named John Meagher was that close, struck preemptively before Meagher struck him. Although the attack on the Petaluma Meagher took place when he was ostensibly jailed in Ukiah, Sherman, as a former constable and deputy sheriff, was undoubtedly close with his guards, and may well have been permitted to leave the jail occasionally to conduct private business. A quick trip to Petaluma to dispatch a man named John Meagher would have been high-priority private business for Jim Sherman. And what better alibi, if one was ever needed, could a man have than his incarceration at the time of the crime? Whether Sherman actually was guilty of this horrendous crime will never be known, for the case was never solved, but if it was indeed his intention to murder Mike Meagher's brother, he was unsuccessful, for the John Meagher of Petaluma was not the John Meagher of Kansas.

After the death of his brother, John Meagher of Kansas lived for a time in Caldwell, where he occasionally took work as a special law officer.[71] Then, for a decade, he moved about the West, living for a time in New Mexico and ranching in Colorado. Many back in Kansas were convinced the real reason for his restlessness was a relentless search for his brother's killer. The *New York Times* would later report that "for twelve years John roamed the West with a picture of Jim Talbot in his pocket and murder in his heart."[72]

In the summer of 1894, while Jim Sherman still awaited his second trial for the killing of George Parker, someone contacted Mendocino County Sheriff J. R. Johnson that the man in his jail was known in Kansas as Jim Talbot, and that he was wanted for another killing and large rewards were offered for him.

Of course, the mention of rewards aroused Sheriff Johnson's interest. He wired Sheriff S. S. Woodcock of Sumner County, Kansas, requesting confirmation of the report. Woodcock replied that Sherman, alias Talbot, was definitely wanted, and he would be coming to California with a requisition for him.

It is not known who informed on Sherman. He had gone to great pains to keep his former identity a secret in California, and it is unlikely anyone there, even his closest associates, was aware of his previous history. His wife, Allie, was the only one in California who would have had full knowledge of her husband's dark past. Perhaps, having had her fill of his murderous disposition, she blew the whistle on him; her later behavior might tend to support this theory. John Meagher was a prime candidate for informer — the *New York Times*[73] even stated positively that he had traced his brother's killer to California and arranged for his return to Kansas — but John never publicly took credit for the capture, and the identity of the informer remains another of the mysteries of the Sherman story.[74]

On September 6, 1894, Sheriff Woodcock set the wheels in motion to secure Sherman's return. Appearing before Justice of the Peace W. E. Cox at Wellington, Kansas, he filed a formal complaint on behalf of E. H. Henderson, "a concerned citizen," charging "James Talbott et al" with the murder of Mike Meagher.[75] Cox issued a warrant for Talbot's arrest, and two days later Woodcock and Deputy Sheriff William Lee secured a requisition from the governor at Topeka for Jim Sherman. When they arrived by train in Sacramento, California, Governor Henry H. Markham issued the necessary papers, and in Ukiah Sheriff Johnson turned his prisoner over to the Kansas officers, who set out on the long ride home with their charge. Happy to leave the fate of the pestiferous Sherman to the Kansas authorities, District Attorney Pemberton quietly dropped the charges in the Parker shooting case.[76]

The return of Jim Sherman, aka Talbot, to Kansas after thirteen years was a hot news story in Sumner and Sedgwick counties.[77] One Caldwell paper printed a sensational report that the officers bringing Sherman back would be in for a "hot time" as "desperadoes all through New Mexico, Colorado, Arizona and Southern California" in sympathy with the murderer were organizing to prevent his return.[78]

Nothing of the kind ever happened, of course. After reaching Wichita with their prisoner on September 17, Woodcock and Lee admitted there had been some talk in Ukiah that Sherman's friends might attempt a rescue, but they had slipped out of town at night and ridden in a buggy thirty-five miles to Santa Rosa, where they caught the train. The remainder of the trip had been uneventful. They said Sherman had at first denied that he was Talbot, but when confronted by Deputy Lee, who knew him well back in Caldwell, he admitted his true identity.[79]

Wichita reporters interviewed the notorious fugitive while he was held overnight in jail there, awaiting transfer to Wellington. A *Beacon* newsman found him dressed in dark pants, vest and flannel shirt, about five feet ten inches in height, with auburn hair and mustache, blue eyes, and a rather high forehead. The reporter thought him quite intelligent and "the last man that one would suspect of being a desperado."[80]

The man from the *Eagle*, who remembered Sherman from thirteen years earlier, thought he had "rather improved in his looks" and no longer appeared to be the rough-looking cowboy he recalled.[81]

The *Caldwell News* described him as "a bright, shrewd looking man, who when roused, fears nothing human and yet can be brought to tears in a moment."[82]

On November 20 Sherman appeared in court at Wellington and was bound over for trial without bond. Prosecutors said they would seek a first-degree murder conviction and the death penalty. Editors opined that a death sentence was unlikely, but that Sherman would "certainly be convicted of manslaughter and be given a term in the penitentiary."[83]

The trial began on April 8, 1895, before Judge J. A. Burnette.

County Attorney Harry L. Woods prosecuted, assisted by his father, Judge John G. Woods, and C. E. Elliott. Representing the defendant were Ivan D. Rogers and William J. L. Crank, Sherman's first cousin, who had come from Denver to defend his relative. Arriving with Crank was another Denver resident, Sherman's brother, Rollan.[84] William Lingenfelter, Jim Sherman's brother-in-law and one-time teacher, also was in attendance.

The *Wellington Daily Mail* noted that an attentive spectator at every session of the ten-day trial was John Meagher: "One of the prominent figures in the case will be Johnnie Meagher. . . . He is taking a deep interest in the prosecution, for he was more than a brother to the victim of Talbott's bullets; he was a twin brother. It is said of him that after Mike was killed he followed Talbott for eleven years and over that many states and territories, and that if he had laid eyes upon him either a Talbott or another Meagher would bite the dust."[85]

Harry Woods asserted in his opening statement that James D. Sherman, then known as James Talbot, planned and carried out the cold-blooded murder of Mike Meagher, and his motive was revenge for a previous altercation with the ex-mayor and law officer. Woods apparently did not know the actual motive for the murder, retaliation for Mike's killing of Sylvester Powell five years earlier.

A parade of witnesses who had been present on that dark day in Caldwell in 1881 testified. (One key witness was unavailable; John Wilson, city marshal at the time, had been shot to death at Wellington in December 1884.)[86] Possemen who had pursued and battled the outlaws recounted their tale. Even Mag Wood, the old madam of the Red Light, returned to tell her piece.

The testimony of Ed Rathburn, who had been at Meagher's side when he was shot, appeared to be most damaging to the Sherman case. He related "with great minuteness and positiveness" how Talbot fired the fatal shot. "His recollection of the smallest details of the whole encounter seemed to be as vivid as though the shooting had just occurred."[87]

Two members of the old Talbot gang, Doug Hill and Tom Love, testified for the defense. Hill admitted taking part in the shooting spree back in December 1881, but was exempt from prosecution, having plea-bargained a fourth-degree manslaughter conviction and a six-month jail sentence in 1886. Love had been arrested in 1881, but had convinced the court he did not participate in the shooting and was released. The substance of the testimony of both men was that there had been so much excitement in Caldwell that fateful day no one could be sure who shot Mike Meagher.[88]

Jim Sherman took the stand in his own defense. Giving his version of the commotion over the arrest of Jim Martin that precipitated the shooting, he said he was unarmed when City Marshal John Wilson ran up, waving two revolvers. As he was walking away, Sherman said, someone handed him a revolver and suggested he "shoot it a couple of times and see how the crowd would scatter." He said he "took the revolver and fired it twice in the air and the scattering commenced." Then he began to receive fire from housetops and business buildings. He ran home, and "shots went clean through his house." Grabbing his rifle, he went back out and returned the fire. He said he was so close to George Spear when he was hit that he could hear the ball strike him. His account of the escape from town and flight from the posse closely approximated that told by previous witnesses.[89]

Under sharp cross-examination by C. E. Elliott, he did not waver. Asked to explain large discrepancies between his story and that of others, he "stated positively and unhesitatingly that their evidence was not correct. . . . Cross examination . . . did not seem to disturb him in the least."[90]

Rebuttal witnesses were called to refute Sherman's story further, closing arguments from prosecution and defense were heard, and Judge Burnette delivered his charge to the jury on April 17. The jury deliberated twenty-four hours before announcing that it was hopelessly deadlocked. Although on the first ballot ten jurors voted for a first-degree murder conviction, two held out for acquittal. A lesser offense compromise could not be reached; those favoring a guilty verdict would not accept anything less than second-degree murder, and "not guilty" proponents would not agree to anything stiffer than third-degree manslaughter.[91] Deputy County Attorney John G. Woods cleverly remarked: "We started out to hang one man and hung twelve instead."[92]

The comment did not strike John Meagher as humorous. The *Caldwell News* noted in its edition of April 18 that he was "probably the most disappointed man in the state. For eleven years he followed the man who he believes killed his twin brother." The *New York Times* would report that "the twin brother of the dead Mayor of Caldwell" vowed that Talbot would "either swing for that killing" or he would "shoot him on sight."[93]

Judge Burnette dismissed the jury and held the defendant over for a second trial.[94] When lawyers for the defense raised the question of bail for their client, Burnette angrily "put a quietus on the whole subject by stating that he would not admit him to bail under any circumstances whatever."[95] So Sherman remained in the Sumner County jail at Wellington through the summer months of 1895, waiting to go on trial for his life again.

The second trial, beginning on September 4, was simply a reprise of the first, with no new evidence of any substance. Like the first trial, it lasted ten days. Judge, prosecutors, and defense attorneys were the same individuals, and the same witnesses gave the same testimony.

And yet a different jury, after only four hours of deliberation, part of which was spent in eating a meal, returned a unanimous verdict of acquittal. The press reported there was only one "guilty" vote on the first ballot and eleven "not guilty." Observers believed the quick acquittal could be attributed to the passage of time since the killing, Sherman's generally commendable conduct in California, and sympathy for the defendant's wife and children.[96]

Sherman, of course, was elated by the verdict. He pumped the hands of his attorneys and each of the men on the jury.

The *Kansas City Star* commented editorially that the lesson to be learned from the case was that anyone accused of a crime should face the courts rather than run away to live miserably as a hunted man. "Talbot was captured at last, only to be acquitted and freed from the haunting fear which had shadowed his life for so long. It is better to face the music and have done with it."[97] The editor ignored two important facts: first, that the public mood in Sumner County had been entirely different fourteen years earlier, and Sherman almost certainly would have been convicted if brought to trial then; and second, that the "haunting fear" would never be lifted from Sherman's head as long as John Meagher lived.

The verdict, of course, appalled John Meagher, who, as a newspaper reported, strode across the courtroom at the completion of the trial and informed the celebrating Sherman that although the jury may have acquitted him, he had not, and that he would "kill him if he had to follow him to the end of the earth."[98]

Charges against "Jim Daniels" were still open in Texas, and rumors spread that Rangers were in Wellington to arrest Sherman if he was acquitted. But if the stories were true, the Texas Rangers missed their man, for following his dismissal by the court Sherman lost no time catching a westbound train.[99]

Seemingly incapable of escaping notoriety and controversy, Sherman, soon after his arrival back in California, was the center of another sensational story. He had returned to his home just outside Ukiah to find his wife and children gone. Allie, presumably anticipating her husband's conviction and lengthy sentence, had taken up with twenty-nine-year-old John Vallele, an old Sherman acquaintance who had been in Niepp's saloon the night of the Parker killing and had testified at the Mendocino County trial.

Sherman immediately headed for Covelo, near Round Valley, where he was told Vallele, Allie, and the children had gone. Soon the San Francisco press was publishing sensational reports that he had stabbed Vallele to death.[100] No doubt some heated words were exchanged when Sherman confronted his wife and Vallele, but in the end Allie and the children returned to Ukiah with Sherman, and Vallele, unharmed, remained in Covelo.

A bitter range war marked by many brutal assaults and murders was raging in Round Valley and Covelo at this time. Not surprisingly, the violence-prone Jim Sherman soon was drawn into the fray.

Among the opposing combatants in the conflict were Jack Littlefield, a popular cowboy, and Joe Gregory, a former convict and hired gunman. The two tangled on several occasions. When Littlefield's bullet-riddled body was found hanging from a tree in a remote section of nearby Trinity County, Gregory was an immediate suspect. He was one of six men arrested and charged with complicity in the murder.[101]

Mary Williamson, the mother of Joe Gregory, in an effort to uncover evidence that would clear her son, employed Jim Sherman, known to have much experience in the murder line, to come to Covelo and investigate the case. In early 1896 Sherman rented a house about two miles from Covelo, moved his family there, and began his detective work.

The violence continued. In the following months two men, Bill Williams and Charles Felton, were murdered. The word in town was that someone had hired Sherman to look into the Felton murder also. He was evidently helping Mendocino County Sheriff J. R. Johnson in his investigation of the crimes, for in August 1896 that officer presented Sherman with "a fine large revolver" as an expression of appreciation for his assistance.[102]

Many residents of the area, made jittery by the series of murders, were carrying weapons in their travels. Little notice was taken, therefore, when a stranger turned up one day in Covelo driving a buggy and toting a long gun across his knees. The few he spoke to remembered little about him other than he was from Kansas.[103]

About eight o'clock on the evening of Tuesday, August 11, 1896, Jim Sherman returned home from town. He was riding a mule and carrying a sack of flour across the saddle in front of him. As he neared the gate a single shot rang out. A rifle bullet struck Sherman in the neck and severed the spinal column at the base of the brain. He tumbled from the mule, dead before he hit the ground. John Bishop, a neighbor, found him lying there moments later.

Coroner Joel Eveland conducted an inquest on August 13. Bishop and another Sherman neighbor, Brady Tuttle, testified they heard the shot. J. H. Rohrbough found a cartridge case near the body. According to Dr. C. R. Rogers, who examined the body, the death wound was caused by either a .38- or .40-caliber rifle bullet. Jacob Wattenburger told of the trouble between Sherman and John Vallele some months earlier. Allie Sherman said that her husband had told her after returning from Kansas about John Meagher's vow to avenge his brother's murder "if he had to follow him to the end of the earth." The coroner's jury found that James Daniel Sherman, age forty-six, came to his death from a gunshot wound at the hand of parties unknown.[104]

And so died James D. Sherman, alias Jim Daniels, alias Jim Talbot. For more than twenty years he had lived the life of a desperado, defying the law and thwarting every effort of the legal system to stop him. But someone, with a single gunshot, ended his career that night. Who that someone was is an enduring mystery, for no one was ever charged with the murder, and it is unsolved to this day. John Vallele, an early suspect, apparently had an air-tight alibi and was never arrested or charged, although some local people were convinced of his guilt.[105] Attempts to attach blame to one or more of the suspects in the Round Valley range war murders were fruitless. Evidently the local authorities never explored the possibility that John Meagher carried out his threat to avenge the murder of his brother. One gets the feeling that Sherman's death was not greatly mourned in Mendocino County, that many in the community felt his passing was good riddance, and that the authorities made no great effort to solve the crime. In reporting the killing, the *Mendocino Dispatch Democrat* called Sherman "a hard and dangerous character [who] should have no doubt been long ago behind prison bars."[106]

Many folks back in Kansas believed it was the hand of John Meagher that finally administered retribution on Sherman.[107] Wichita newsman David D. Leahy, who interviewed Meagher several times, affirmed that John Meagher had vowed vengeance and "pursued Sherman for nearly twenty years," but was very reticent about discussing the man's death. Since the statute of limitations never runs out on murder, it is not surprising that John Meagher, if he did snuff out Sherman's light, would be reluctant to admit it to anyone, especially a newspaperman.[108]

John Meagher, a Civil War veteran, entered the Soldiers' Home at Leavenworth, Kansas, in 1916. About 1925 he was transferred to the new veterans' treatment center at Battle Mountain Sanitarium, Hot Springs, South Dakota, where he died on February 22, 1930. If he was indeed the man who avenged his brother's murder and closed out the career of James Sherman, he took that secret with him to the grave.[109]

JACK JOLLY
1852–?

*The girls of the house, in décolleté which left nothing to the imagina-
tion, lined the stairway. . . . Jolly and Molly descended the staircase to
the strains of Mendelsohn's [sic] Wedding March, played by the professor. . . . The bridesmaids stood on their heads with delight.*
  — The anonymous judge who performed the mock wedding

The story of John H. "Jack" Jolly is a tale of the conversion of a hard-
working, well-respected, law-abiding citizen to a gun-wielding desperado and killer.

Jolly was born in New York City on January 3, 1852. About 1860 he
moved with his parents, John and Mary Jolly, to Syracuse, Onondaga
County, New York.[1] As a teenager he struck out for the West, going
first to Arizona, and then to Montana. In 1876 Jack Jolly settled just
outside the booming new mining town of Butte, Montana, and established a ranch a few miles away at Moose Creek. On July 16, 1878, he
married eighteen-year-old Ella Brush, from Clermont County, Ohio.
The union would produce four children.[2]

A burly man with blue eyes, curly black hair, prominent nose,
strong jaw, and cleft chin, Jolly was by trade a blacksmith, and a good
one. In Butte he entered into a partnership with a man named Black
and opened a blacksmith and wagon-making shop at the corner of
Main and Park streets in the hub of the rapidly expanding community. By 1881 he had bought out his partner and was the sole owner of
the largest shop of its kind in the city.[3] As a sideline, he concocted and

sold a panacea. His advertisements, decorated by two inverted horse-shoes over a large anvil, appeared daily in the local paper and read:

JOHN JOLLEY[4]

Blacksmith and Wagon maker, Park and Main St., Butte.

The best of iron and hard wood used. Skilled workmen employed. John Jolly makes a specialty of shoeing. The best in town. Makes all the shoes used. Treats and cures all cases of diseased feet in horses.

JOLLY'S LINIMENT

The most useful liniment for man or beast ever put up. For Rheumatism it has no equal. Put up and sold by John Jolly. One dollar per bottle.

Later he dropped his own ailment remedy, but peddled another with a personal testimonial sales pitch that appeared in the daily paper:

RHEUMATISM CURE.

My wife was helpless for over two years with inflammatory rheumatism. I tried the best remedies I could find, also the Boulder and Utah Hot Springs, but the only remedy I found for her was HARTZEL'S SURE CURE.

John Jolly

Jack Jolly was a busy man. In addition to his ranching activities, his blacksmith business, and his elixir promotion, he was active in the Butte City fire department.[5] In June 1883 he was floor manager for a "Grand Ball" for the benefit of Butte Fire Brigade #1. (Tickets cost $3 each.)[6]

In September 1883 Jolly ran for alderman of Butte's Fourth Ward on the Democratic ticket and received the endorsement of the *Daily Miner*: "Mr. John Jolly, Democratic candidate for Alderman, is an old resident of the city, intimately acquainted with its needs, and is otherwise thoroughly qualified to discharge the duties of the position. Mr. Jolly deserves, as he will receive, the support of the voters of the Fourth Ward."[7] The election was held on Saturday, September 22, and when the vote was canvassed by the city council the next Monday, it was found that Jolly and his opponent, Republican W. Pinkham had tied, eighty-six votes apiece. The problem was solved quickly by the city council. Said the *Daily Miner*: "Under a city ordinance which provides that in case of a tie vote for Mayor or Alderman, the election shall be decided by lot, the names of the candidates were written upon two sheets of paper and placed in a hat with a number of blank slips. One of the aldermen drew from the hat and the first slip drawn proved to be the one bearing Mr. Pinkham's name. He was therefore declared duly elected Alderman for the Fourth Ward."[8]

Boxing exhibitions were a popular form of entertainment in Butte, and Jack Jolly often took part in these events, not as a pugilist, but as a ring official. When men named Sorrenson and Grenier met in the city's Gymnasium Arena on December 8, 1883, before a packed house, "Marquis of Queensbury gloves were used and the rules of the London prize ring observed." Jolly acted as timekeeper as the gladiators fought fifty-four furious rounds in one hour and twenty minutes.[9] A month later he was the referee in a contest between Dave Cusick, a local favorite, and Pete McCoy, "champion of the middleweights of New York, of the [John L.] Sullivan combination." When Cusick could not answer the bell for the third round, Jolly raised McCoy's hand and declared him the winner.[10]

Life was looking good for Jack Jolly; his businesses were doing well, and he was a popular member of the community. But during the winter of 1885–86, tragedy struck in the form of an epidemic of diphtheria that swept through the mining district. His wife, Ella, and all four of his children contracted the terrible disease and died.[11]

With all those for whom he had labored so hard now suddenly gone, Jack Jolly tried to assuage his grief with alcohol and debauchery. He sold his ranch and his business, turned to the uncertain vocation of professional gambling for a livelihood, and became a habitué of the saloons and sporting houses of Butte's vice district.

His friends tried to straighten him out. They talked him into allowing his name to be put forward as a candidate for city marshal. Although as a businessman he had been well liked and respected, and folks in Butte commiserated with him over his terrible loss, his recent behavior made some voters dubious that he could handle the job of principal law enforcement officer of the town. He was elected in May 1887, however, by the slim margin of 136 votes.[12]

He held the job for a year and did a passable job, although many thought he spent too much of his time in the dives on Galena Street, Butte's red-light district. There he became, in the parlance of the vice world, the "solid man" of Molly Demurska, proprietress of one of the parlor houses. By all accounts, Madam Demurska was an attractive woman who ran an honest house, where the prettiest women were employed and the rolling of drunks was prohibited.

Word spread quickly throughout the Dardenelles, as Butte's sporting district was called, that City Marshal Jack Jolly and Molly Demurska, the red-light queen, were to be married. A grand ceremony was planned to take place in the Clipper Shades, a large concert hall at the corner of Park and Wyoming streets, run for many years by Pete Hanson, widely known as "The King of Galena Street."[13] The notoriety of the Clipper Shades was reputed to be so widespread that a letter addressed to the Clipper Shades without state, city, or street address, arrived at its destination.[14]

The judge who performed the wedding later described the event on the promise of anonymity.

> It was a wedding attended by a score of the leading men of the city. For the sake of their present conventional respectability it might be added that most of them were bachelors at the time, too busy with the engineering of their own fortunes to give much thought to domestic felicity. At least one of the guests was to become a United States senator. Others were to rise high with the building of Butte. For the moment they were at play.
>
> Jack Jolly was a popular man who had suffered a tragedy which stirred the sympathy of the entire town. . . .
>
> When he announced to . . . friends that he was going to marry Molly Demurska, they planned a ceremony suitable to his regeneration. Molly was popular. She ran an honest house, beautifully appointed, with beautiful girls as her boarders. A select list of guests was arranged. The grand staircase of the house was decorated with smilax and flowers. A wedding bell hung at its foot for the ceremony. Hampers of champagne and the finest delicacies obtainable in Chicago and San Francisco were provided for the wedding supper.
>
> . . . The girls of the house, in décolleté which left nothing to the imagination, lined the stairway. The guests were assembled below. Jolly and Molly descended the staircase to the strains of Mendelsohn's [*sic*] Wedding March, played by the "professor."
> . . . The bridesmaids stood on their heads with delight.[15]

Following the marriage ceremony, the wedding party was escorted outside, where the city fire wagon waited. Bride, groom, and the Cyprian bridesmaids climbed aboard, and the wagon led a procession of celebrants, whooping and hollering, through the streets of Butte.[16]

The judge who presided over the ceremony may not have had the authority to conduct a legal marriage. It appears that Jack Jolly and Molly Demurska were united only in a mock wedding. No official record of the marriage has ever been found, and following the ceremony and for several years afterward Molly continued to operate her brothel under her own name.[17] That was unfortunate, for had she been able to advertise and promote herself as "Jolly Molly Jolly," she might have become the most famous madam in the West.

According to one newspaper report, discord over finances within a year led to a split up of the marshal and the madam. While Jolly lost money to the point of bankruptcy, Molly "held a casket of diamonds of the high pressure pattern."[18]

Jolly served only a single one-year term as city marshal of Butte. In May 1888 he was again nominated to run for the office but declined, and J. E. Coulter succeeded him.[19] By now a well-known member of the sporting class, Jolly left Butte and traveled throughout the Northwest, following the gambling circuit. There is an undocumented report that, about this time, he got into a gambling row on a train and killed another man,[20] but true or not, many professional gamblers were deadly gunmen, and Jolly soon developed a reputation as a fighting man, dangerous with fists, gun, or dagger.

This reputation, together with his law enforcement experience as Butte city marshal, led to his appointment in the spring of 1894 as a special deputy U.S. marshal to help control the followers of Jacob S. Coxey. The nation had gone through a severe economic downturn in 1893, and many men were unemployed. On the West Coast, Coxey organized many of these hungry, disheartened, and desperate men into a band the newspapers called "commonwealers" or "Coxey's Army," and incited them to acts of lawlessness.

Yakima, Washington, was in a state of turmoil when the commonwealers stormed the railroad yards in great numbers and prevented the trains from moving. On May 9, 1894, Jolly was one of thirteen deputy marshals dispatched to the yards to protect railroad employees attempting to move a train. Shooting broke out, and a bullet struck Jolly.

The ball, passing through his side, lodged in his intestines, and for several days he was not expected to survive. Another deputy marshal, J. C. Chidester, and three Coxeyites, identified as Nick Weaver, "Seattle" Savage, and Joe McAlphee, were also wounded, but none as seriously as Jolly. The story was picked up by news services and transmitted by wire across the country.[21]

The others wounded were treated in Yakima, but Jolly was rushed to Tacoma, where better medical facilities were available. The story filled the Yakima and Tacoma papers, and a controversy immediately arose over the question of who was responsible for the shootings.

Under the headline "Who Shot Jack Jolly?" a Tacoma newspaper reporter quoted Jolly in a lengthy interview:

> I'll tell you it ought never to have happened, and never would have if the marshals had not got scared and were afraid to do their duty. The citizens up there are to blame, too. If it had not been for them the men would have stayed off of the train when they were put off. Chidester was on top of the cars when some deputies were trying to drive them off. The crowd around the cars were yelling and jeering and the deputies lost their heads and were afraid to put the men off. I was down on the ground at the time. . . .
>
> I got up on the car where Chidester was with a stick in my hand like that which brakemen use to tighten the brakes. I ran at the men, hitting them with the stick to throw them off. I did not mean to hurt them, for, poor fellows, they are so weak from hunger and fatigue that I could have whipped a half dozen at once. Chidester was right behind me with two or three of his marshals. As soon as I hit the first man with the stick one of them hit me on the side of the head with a club and three or four jumped on me. They were pushing me down when I heard a shot from behind me and at the same time felt a pain in my side and knew that I had been shot. I pulled my pistol out and turned to see who had shot, and saw Chidester with his pistol in his hand. I said, "What in hell did you shoot me for?"
>
> He made no reply and before I had hardly said it his gun went off again and he shot himself in the leg. There might have been some more shooting, but I did not see or hear it. I put my gun which I had drawn back in its case and never fired it off at all.
>
> The night I was shot I was delirious part of the time and said

a whole lot of things about Chidester, but I did not mean them. I don't think that he tried to shoot me, but he was so scared that he did not know what he was doing.[22]

Another Tacoma paper claimed Jolly gave them an entirely different account of the affair: " 'Any man who says Chidester shot me, or that I said anything of the kind, is a God damn liar,' said the wounded deputy with all the vehemence his condition would allow." Jolly went on:

I have been delirious since wounded, and may have said some wild things, but remembering the position of Childester [sic] and myself at the time I was shot, it was impossible for him to inflict the wound I am now possibly dying from. When the men would not get off the car and had set the brakes, I climbed upon the car and with a stick . . . proceeded to fight my way to the brake and throw it off. I had reached the brake and accomplished my object and had seized two commonwealers by the throat when I was struck a fearful blow with a club over the right shoulder which felled me. While I was down I felt the sharp pang of the bullet entering my side, but did not hear the sound of that particular shot, so intense was my interest in the fight on my hands, for when knocked down I had clung to the collars of the two men who had grappled with me and had drawn them over with me. I was shot from beneath and it is my opinion by one of the citizens who had congregated at the track.

Had it not been for the encouragement and cheering on of the commonwealers this would never have happened, but with the constant egging on of the individuals by the citizens, the mob were led to believe they could do as they pleased with the railroad company's property at Yakima.

I was picked out as a shining mark by the commonwealers and citizens, for the day before I had given one of the former a clubbing for which I was ridiculed by both 'wealers and deputies and when the break came Wednesday I wanted to show the people that I was prepared to do my duty. The report that I fired into the crowd is wrong, for my pistol had not been discharged.

After being shot I managed to regain my feet and drew my revolver, but the men were so thick it would have been murder for me to have fired into them, and I returned the pistol to my pocket.[23]

In an effort to clarify the differing accounts, a Yakima newspaper reporter held interviews with several of the deputies, including Chidester, and the doctor who treated the wounded men.

Chidester vividly described a wild melee. He said he saw Jolly receive "a vicious blow on the shoulders," just before he himself was attacked and had to fight for his life.

> I was then set upon by three of them, was thrown down, struck twice in the head, and they endeavored to choke me. . . . In falling I caught one of my antagonists under me. . . . The man on top of me caught my cane, at the same time seized my left hand, which enabled the man under me to work himself out. . . . He dropped his club and pulled his gun, on seeing which I succeeded in raising upon my right knee and three men still on me. I then drew my pistol with my left hand, knocked up my opponent's gun, but before I could recover myself, he had fired. The ball passed to my left and struck Jolly. . . . I then tried to shoot the [shooter], but as I pulled the trigger, the men who were on top of me pulled my arm, knocking my hand down, sending the bullet through my left thigh.

Chidester said that a number of shots were fired, some of them from guns in the hands of members of the crowd around the train. He did not believe there were more than five shots fired by the deputies, who had received explicit orders not to fire their weapons unless in defense of their lives.

Deputy Marshal William Welsh stated flatly: "Chidester did not shoot Deputy Marshal Jolly. . . . There was only one bullet shot out of the revolver carried by Chidester and that went in his leg. I saw his revolver after the fight and there was only one cartridge that had been discharged."

A deputy marshal named Crosby blamed the throng gathered around the train for inciting the commonwealers to violence. When the officers attempted to release the brakes, he said, "the citizens began to throw stones and clubs at the deputies and shouted, 'Shoot them! Cut them! Kill them!' . . . The first shot was fired by a citizen . . . and then the commonwealers drew their guns and commenced to fire."

Dr. G. J. Hill, who ministered to the wounded, was convinced that Chidester could not have shot Jolly and himself, as the two wounds

Mug shot of Jack Jolly when he was incarcerated in the Montana
territorial prison at Deer Lodge. From the author's collection.

were made by bullets of different caliber. "Here is the ball that I cut from Chidester's leg," he said, exhibiting a .38 slug, "and I am confident that Jolly's wound was made by a .45."[24]

After the situation had cooled somewhat, the Yakima paper still speculated about the shooting of Jolly, who was still expected to die: "Who shot Jolly? is the question. The [commonwealers] claim that he was shot by one of his own companions. Some say he was shot by a hobo spectator while a number of the marshals maintain that he was shot by a Coxeyite. The truth may never be known."[25]

There was every reason to expect Jack Jolly to die. Intestinal gunshot wounds were almost invariably fatal in the nineteenth century, and the doctors attending Jolly held out little hope for his recovery. He himself told the reporter interviewing him that he did not expect to survive.

But survive he did. By the following summer he was back in Butte, where almost immediately he got into another fracas.

By 1895 open gambling had been outlawed in Butte, but a few games still operated in the backrooms and upper floors of saloons. A professional gambler named William W. Byther, a native of Maine, ran one of these illegal games in rooms over the Mint Saloon on Main Street. Byther was, according to a newspaper, "as square a man in his business as ever opened a jackpot or shuffled a card."[26]

About nine o'clock in the evening of August 9, 1895, Jolly entered Byther's clubrooms. Obviously intoxicated, he tried to pick a fight with several of the players. When the proprietor interfered, Jolly pulled a knife and stabbed him several times. The wounds were serious, and Byther remained bedridden for some time. In his weakened condition he contracted typhoid fever. Then, in a fit of delirium, he threw himself out the window and fell three stories. A few days later he died.[27]

Jolly reportedly fled after stabbing Byther and hid out overnight, but officers found him the next day, charged him with assault, and lodged him in the county jail.[28] Tried and convicted in September, he was sentenced to three and a half years in the territorial prison at Deer Lodge.

When he was received there on September 26, 1895, the prison doctor examined him and made notes of distinguishing marks. Jolly had a tattoo of a wreath and the initials "J. S." on his right forearm.

There was evidence of previous battles: a one-inch scar at his hairline, a scar on the knuckle of his left hand, a three-inch scar over his navel, and a two-inch scar below the left nipple.[29]

Jolly served a little more than half his sentence; he was pardoned and released from prison on August 18, 1897.[30] He returned to Butte for a short time and then joined the great gold rush to the Klondike.

Among the thousands also headed north to Alaska in the last great western mining stampede was Jefferson Randolph "Soapy" Smith, con man par excellence of Colorado, with his criminal gang of crooked gamblers. There were reports in the press, repeated later by some writers, that during the exodus of sporting men and women north, Soapy Smith and Jack Jolly clashed, and Smith put a bullet in the one-time lawman.[31] It is unlikely this ever happened, for none of Smith's several biographers mention the incident, and Jack Jolly was certainly not killed at this time.

Another story circulated that he was killed in Alaska in December 1898. A dispatch from Vancouver, British Columbia, Canada, dated January 5, 1899, and reprinted in several American papers, said that passengers on the steamer *Rosalie*, arriving in Vancouver from the northern country, reported that Jolly, "a saloonkeeper and gambler," had collected a gang of toughs around him at Eagle City, Alaska, and terrorized the surrounding camps. A vigilance committee "of twelve determined men" called on him and ordered him to leave. When he defied them, they overpowered him on December 11 and strung him up. His gang then scattered.[32]

This report, also untrue, sounded remarkably similar to the fate of Soapy Smith, who did take over the Alaskan town of Skagway and, with his gang, preyed on miners until vigilantes took action against him. On July 8, 1898, Smith and vigilante Frank Reid exchanged gunfire, and both were killed. With their leader dead, the Soapy gang members took to the hills.

Jack Jolly did not die at the end of a rope in 1898. He was alive and well and still in Alaska five years later. By 1903 he had turned once again to law enforcement. With the assistance of his friend Frank Richards, U.S. marshal for Alaska, he assumed the position of chief of police at Nome. There he was the central figure in another bizarre event; he shot one of his own policemen dead.

Indicted and tried in June 1903 for this killing, Jolly took the witness stand in his own behalf. The sordid tale all began, according to his testimony, when a prostitute named Lottie Wilson called Jolly to her rooms and demanded payment of $75 she claimed Sam James, a Nome policeman, owed her for professional services performed. Jolly went on:

> I says to her, "I can send him to McNeil Island, and I will if he don't pay me this $75."
>
> I says, "Why do you want to send this man to McNeil Island? What has he done?"
>
> James, she said, had stolen coal, coal oil and pistols.
>
> I says, "That's kind of funny you should keep tabs on him like that." She flew at me then, [saying that] I ought to pay $75. I told her to go and do her best. I goes to James' room immediately. I says, "James, this woman Lottie sent for me this morning and accuses you of stealing coal." I says, "God knows what you haven't stolen." I says, "James, I am going to lay you off and investigate these charges.... Jim, you have been drinking a good deal lately, you have been gambling a good deal lately and I am afraid you have been neglecting your duty as a policeman."[33]

When he heard the next day that James had spent the night with the woman who had leveled these serious charges against him, Jolly reproached him, saying, "You are going to the dogs as fast as you can."[34]

A few days later the two men met on the street. The situation had cooled down, James assured his former boss, as Lottie had taken no further action. Jolly said he again warned the ex-officer, "You better sober up. I believe that woman."[35]

Later James, very inebriated, braced Jolly and threatened to kill him unless he got his job back. "He called me a horse thief and a SOB," said Jolly. There were other confrontations on the street and in saloons in which James threatened his life before witnesses, but Jolly said he dismissed the calumny as the rantings of a drunken man.

When the two met again in front of the Hunter Saloon on a snowy, windy afternoon, James pulled a derringer from his pocket, jammed the muzzle into Jolly's midsection, and shouted: "I'm going to blow your belly out now!"

If that was his actual intention, he should have pulled the trigger at that moment, but he did not, and the hesitation cost him his life.

Jolly backed off a few feet. Then his hand darted beneath his coat and instantly reappeared with a revolver. He fired once, and James went down. Stepping closer, Jolly poured several more rounds into the fallen man's body to make sure he was dead.

As a crowd quickly gathered, Jolly loudly assured everyone it had been a matter of self-defense and pointed to the derringer lying close to the dead man's hand. He turned himself in to a deputy U.S. marshal. A week later he resigned his police position and prepared to defend his action in court. At the trial, Lottie Wilson corroborated Jolly's testimony, and the prosecution, led by acting U.S. Attorney George Grigsby, had little to refute it. The jury acquitted Jolly.

But many in Nome believed there was a great deal more to the story, that Jolly, as well as James, was guilty of larceny, and the shooting actually resulted from a falling-out among thieves. Unhappy with Jolly's acquittal, another grand jury reviewed the trial, and a majority of the jurors censured prosecutor Grigsby for his handling of the case. No additional charges were lodged against Jolly, but he was not reinstated in his chief of police position, and soon departed Alaska.[36]

Following his return from the north country, the trail of Jack Jolly grows quite dim. It is known that he was living in Seattle in the fall of 1907. He was arrested at that time by Captain A. S. Read of the Tacoma police department, who stated that he narrowly escaped being shot by the man he described as "a notorious gunman with a record of seven kills, men shot in self-defense or murder."[37]

By September 1912 the old battler had fallen on evil days; he was arrested by police in Centralia, Washington, for skipping out of Hoquiam, in Gray's Harbor County, without paying his board bill.[38]

Jack Jolly was sixty years old in 1912. For twenty-seven years since the tragic death of his family, he had lived his life on the raw edge as a gambler, a drinker, a consort of prostitutes, a sometime peace officer, and a wielder of deadly weapons. He had survived, but he and the frontier had grown old. Like the frontier that spawned him, he simply faded away and today is forgotten.

— 10 —

ZACK LIGHT
1853–1891

Zack was another tough man who would rather fight than do anything else, and when they got to exchanging words Les [Dow] drew his gun and shot him dead.

— Ed Harral

Two shots were heard and my Father [Les Dow] walked outside and mounted his horse and Zack Light was found with his pistol in his hand, lying face downward upon the bar room floor. He asked for it and he got it.

— Bob Dow, "Daybreak All Over the World"

The name Zack Light somehow has a western frontier ring to it. The name, composed of two short, clipped, one-syllable words, like many another — Sam Bass, Bob Ford, Tom Horn, John Larn, Luke Short — the list goes on and on — conjures up images of the romanticized West, vast prairies, rugged mountains, galloping horses, and hard-faced men brandishing pistols in the dusty street of a frontier town.

Light was given the biblical name Zachariah at birth, but nobody ever called him anything but Zack. He was the youngest of six Light brothers, natives of New York State, who heeded Horace Greeley's advice and went west at the conclusion of the Civil War to seek fame and fortune. Evander "Van" Light was the first of the brothers to head west; brothers John Wesley, Norman, Leonard, Coleman, and Zack followed.[1] They settled first in Kansas and took whatever work they could find. But driven by an entrepreneurial spirit, they quickly turned to private business ventures, trading with the Indians, farming, contracting with the railroads to supply wood and stone, and finally cattle ranching, a business at which Evander and John Wesley Light achieved notable success after moving to Texas in the mid-1870s.[2]

Several of the Light brothers experienced exciting adventures with the Indians during those early years in Kansas. Van and John Wesley, while on a trading expedition with "Buffalo Bill" Mathewson and Fred Jones, were captured by a mixed band of Kiowa and Cheyenne raiders. They lost their trade goods and equipment and almost their scalps. After six weeks in captivity, the Kiowa chieftain Satanta passed through the camp of their captors, recognized Van as one who had rendered him assistance years earlier, and allowed them to escape.[3] On another occasion, Norman "Doc" Light, while running a wood-cutting camp for the Union Pacific Railroad, was attacked by a party of Cheyennes near Bunker Hill, Kansas. In a life-and-death, hand-to-hand struggle he received a bullet wound in the thigh but survived.[4]

Any Indian-fighting experiences Zack Light may have had were never recorded. He first came to notice at Zarah, Kansas, in 1872 when he shot and killed a white man in what was probably the first of his gun-fighting encounters.

On June 8, 1871, town company promoters chartered a new community at a site one mile east of Fort Zarah in the central Kansas county of Barton, and named their creation after the nearby fortification.[5] From the first the town was designed primarily as an entertainment venue for the soldiers at the adjacent military installation. Its few buildings were mainly a collection of hastily constructed saloons, gambling houses, and "hog ranches," as frontier brothels were indelicately called.

Among the original members of the town company were two brothers-in-law, Titus J. Buckbee, a cattleman from neighboring Ellsworth County, and Perry Hodgden, an Ellsworth dry goods merchant.[6] They and their fellow town promoters had visions of outdistancing Great Bend, another new Barton County village, in the competition to become the most prominent community in the county.

On June 23, 1870, a sister of the Light brothers, Henrietta, married Titus Buckbee, and thus the Light brothers became brothers-in-law of the Zarah town promoter.[7] When Buckbee became postmaster at Zarah and built a home and general store there, his new in-laws — Van, John, Leonard, and Zack Light — moved in with him. The Light brothers now became boosters for the town of Zarah. For a time their dream of the village becoming a real prairie metropolis seemed possible. Zarah became a supply replenishment stopover for wagon trains heading west, and for trappers and traders returning east with animal hides and Mexican commodities. Livery stables, a post office, and stores began sprouting up alongside the saloons and bawdyhouses.[8]

On April 30, 1872, Zack Light was minding the Buckbee store when a man named Perry,[9] described as "a rough-and-ready cowboy," came in and asked for crackers. After Zack took down a box from the shelf, Perry ordered cheese to go with the crackers. Light said he had no cheese. Then, as the story was later related, there was this exchange:

> "This is a hell of a town," [said Perry]. "You're letting this other town [meaning Great Bend] get away with things. You don't even have cheese."
>
> "Damn you," Zack countered. "If you don't shut up, I'll shoot you."
>
> "You wouldn't shoot?" Perry queried Zack.
>
> "Yes, by God, I would," the young man replied, at the same time drawing his pistol and firing into Perry's forehead and he fell to the floor dead.[10]

Zack Light fled the scene, leaving Perry's dead body where it had fallen. Taking Titus Buckbee's fastest horse from the stable, he saddled up and rode hard for Ellsworth, the nearest town, where he gave himself up to the authorities.

Meanwhile, sometime after the shooting, a man entered the Buckbee store, and seeing a body on the floor, exclaimed, "What's going on here — somebody's dead!" Turning the corpse over, he gasped, "My God, that's my brother! Who killed him?" Learning that the killer was Zack Light and that he had lit out for Ellsworth, the victim's brother started after him to exact revenge. At Ellsworth, he found that Light was in custody and under the protection of the local police. By now night had fallen. The Ellsworth authorities decided to hold Light until the next day and then take him to back to Zarah for a preliminary examination into the shooting. Brother Perry spent the evening in the Ellsworth saloons, loudly proclaiming what he would do with Zack Light when he got a crack at him.

In the morning Zack was taken to Zarah under heavy protective escort. The party stopped briefly at the fort to pick up a Mr. Strong, justice of the peace there, who was to conduct the hearing. The body still lay undisturbed on the floor of Buckbee's store, and it was over the body that Justice of the Peace Strong held the examination, assisted by E. J. Dodge, a justice of the peace from Great Bend. After hearing very limited testimony, Strong bound Zack Light over for further action by the district court. No indictment was ever brought against him, however, and Zack Light never stood trial for the killing.[11]

The dead man's brother had followed at some distance behind the party taking Zack Light from Ellsworth to Zarah for the hearing, but the man never reached his destination. He simply disappeared and was never seen again.

Fifty-five years later, workmen excavating a basement at Ellinwood, a new community near the site of old Fort Zarah, found a human skeleton. District old-timers, including the son of E. J. Dodge, nodded their heads knowingly, for it had long been suspected that Zack's brothers had killed the vengeful Perry brother and buried his body somewhere along the trail.[12]

It wasn't long after the "cheese and cracker" killing that the Zarah dream began to fade. The threat of Indian raids had greatly diminished, and Fort Zarah was abandoned in 1872. Then came a second blow; the Santa Fe Railroad announced that its surveyors would take the line more than a mile from the town site. With the fun-seeking soldiers gone, and prospects dim for an influx of equally thirsty and libidinous gamblers from railroad construction gangs, the proprietors of the saloons, whorehouses, and gambling hells moved on. When in July 1872 Great Bend won an election to determine the seat of Barton County, Zarah was doomed. Other businessmen moved their houses and buildings to Ellinwood and Great Bend, where the railroad had established depots, and by 1873 Zarah was a ghost town.[13]

Titus Buckbee moved to Ellinwood when Zarah died, but did not reopen his store there, choosing instead to work for the merchants of Ellsworth as a trail guide, meeting Texas cattlemen driving longhorns north to the Kansas market and steering them to Ellsworth. Several of the Light brothers seem to have joined him in this work. In a letter to his wife, Henrietta, sister of the Light brothers, written from a camp on the trail on April 28, 1873, Buckbee mentions Zack and her other brothers:

> We have had a good trip thus far, have been as far south as Salt Fork [of the Brazos River] where we intended to stop for a short time. We have made a nice camp where we have plenty of wood and water. . . . How did Zack make it getting home, I hope well. The [Light] boys was afraid that the Indians would capture him. I did not anticipate any danger or I would have kept him along. . . . Write me at Sewell Ranch[,] Indian Territory[,] and I will get it. I will try and come up with first herd.[14]

These excursions into Texas evidently impressed the Light brothers, particularly John, for by 1874 he had taken up residence on a ranch in Mason County, Texas, where he was later joined by brothers Leonard and Zack.[15]

When John Light left Kansas for Texas in 1874, he had only $8 in his pocket. He took employment on the ranch of Ben F. Gooch of Mason County at $40 a month and quickly learned the cattle-raising business. Smart and industrious, he gained the trust of wealthy cattleman Seth Mabry of Austin, secured his financial backing, and by the following year was able to buy the Gooch spread and its twenty-five hundred head of cattle. Within two years he had doubled the size of his original herd. In the spring of 1876 he drove five thousand longhorns north to Ogallala, Nebraska, and sold them at a handsome profit. It was the beginning of a prosperous and successful career in the cattle business.[16]

While his brother John was getting his start as a cattleman, Zack Light was taking part in the great buffalo hunt then reaching its peak in western Kansas. Always adept with weapons, he quickly established a reputation as one of the foremost hunters on the plains. In a letter to the Sharps Rifle Company dated September 12, 1874, one young hunter named Sumner "Cimarron" Beach praised the Sharps weapons and singled out Zack Light for special approbation:

> I think that the Sharps that we use for killing buffalo need no improvement, as they are the perfect gun. I saw Zack Light (who is one of the best buffalo hunters, and acknowledged to be

the best shot on these Western prairies) last winter, while on a buffalo hunt, one day squat down in a buffalo wallow (after crawling and getting a stand on a herd of buffalo), kill 74 head of buffalo just where he sat in the wallow. He killed that winter twenty-three hundred head of buffalo. The rest of us killed about twelve hundred head. He used a Sharps' 50 caliber.[17]

Following the decimation of the buffalo herds, Zack Light joined his brothers John and Leonard at their ranch in Mason County, Texas. The older Light brothers had entered into a business association with prominent Texas cattlemen Charles Schreiner, John Lytle, and Tom McDonald and were now highly respected citizens of the county, but Zack soon acquired a reputation as a hard-drinking rounder and saloon bully. His notoriety as a quick-shooting and deadly gunman, which had its genesis in the fatal affair at Zarah, Kansas, only grew in Texas. He was said to have been wounded in a gunfight in Mexico, but details are lacking.[18] A peaceable and likable sort when sober, he became quarrelsome when in his cups. He was reputed to be absolutely fearless, an expert shot with pistol or rifle, and a very dangerous man in a fight.[19]

Titus Buckbee worked with the Light brothers during the early 1880s and in his letters to his wife often mentioned them:

> John wants me to buy Leonard's interest in the outfit, they are in good shape to make money.[20]
>
> John W. is out buying all the time. . . . Leonard and Zack are building fence and I am helping them to pass the time. . . . I rode fence today. I do all I can to help the boys as they are very good to me. I let John have three hundred dollars. He says he will pay me anytime I want it, he is trying to buy a herd to bring up but I guess he can't make it. He is well thought of here. . . .[21]
>
> I and Zack has been buying fat cows for Austin. We took down one bunch, made forty dollars apiece and we start in the morning with some more and that will be the last as this is too late for fat cows. I have not bought any cattle yet as John has been putting me off and says there is plenty of time. They are worth seven dollars a head now.[22]
>
> I came in today to take care of Zack, he is sick with new monia [*sic*]. I am afraid it will go hard with him, he looks bad. Dr. says that he will be alright, but I don't know.

John has gone below and when he comes back he will know weather [*sic*] he will go up the trail, if he comes up, I will come with him. Van was down here, but I did not get to see him as I was in Austin.[23]

In a letter written on March 22, 1881, Buckbee still expressed concerns about Zack's health: "Zack is well and back to the ranch, but looks bad yet. I wrote to him to bring his outfit and I will drive my own, as we can't get anyone to bring them under $3.00 per head. The boys are very busy getting up their herd for the trail."[24]

Zack finally recovered completely and did help drive Light herds to the northern markets. One of those drives, according to veteran drover Wyatt Anderson, was particularly difficult because the steers tended to stampede. "I helped John and Zack Light put up one herd to Llano County for driving to Kansas," Anderson wrote. "They were all steers and I was with them two or three weeks, but they ran almost every night, and I quit the outfit."[25]

Always impetuous, short-tempered, and quick to anger, Zack Light was not the best of trail bosses, as is illustrated by a story told by A. P. Black, another Texas cowhand. Black remembered Light from a Wichita River crossing incident in May 1884. While working for the Hashknife outfit, Black had been given the duty of "trail cutter inspector," looking for cattle without road brands. "In one instance," he said,

I saw a JD herd of 2,500 steers milling on the bank of the Wichita for three hours and refusing to cross the river. There was a herd of about 800 head just behind from the Nueces country waiting to cross. The JDs had a full crew of eight men. The man with the small herd rode down to the river bank and asked the JD man, Jack [*sic*] Light, why he didn't cross and get out of the way. The JD boss, a big, tough-looking, red-faced, mustached man, was sweating and swearing all up and down the riverbank. He looked around and said he was damned if anybody could cross them.

The boss of this other outfit was a long, lean cowpuncher, soft spoken as a woman. He looked like a boy and never carried a gun. Light looked around and asked the stranger, "Where you from?" The stranger smiled in kind of a slight way and said, "Oh, I've got a little cockle-burr outfit down on the Nueces. I'm heading north a-lookin' for grass." He looked the cattle over for a minute, then turned round and faced the JD man: "If you send four of your men up to my herd so I can get four of my boys down here, I'll have your herd across in half an hour."

Light sent four men back to the little herd and four "cockle-burr" riders came up to join their boss. Everybody dropped back and those five riders had charge of the herd. They just sat on their horses, smoked cigarettes and let the cattle quiet down. One steer got down to smell the water, then came another; in another few seconds several of them were in the water. One of the steers set his ears straight out and saw the other bank. In twenty-five minutes the whole herd was stepping across the river. Old Jack Light sat on his horse scratching his head. He glanced over at the long cow-puncher and said, "Well, I'm damned! I've been punchin' cows a long time, but I never thought a 'cockle-burr' boss from the Nueces could show me how to take a herd across a river."[26]

In November 1884 Zack Light and Eugenia Hainel were wed in the Methodist church in Mason,[27] but married life had no pacifying effect on this volatile man. Only a month after the wedding, on Christmas Day, 1884, he and a pal named Sebe Jones got into an altercation with Joe Kyle in the Tom Kinney Saloon in Mason. Hot words were exchanged, followed by hot lead. Kyle fell dead, report-edly the victim of Light's gun. Light and Jones were arrested and charged with murder.

Joe Kyle came from a prominent Texas family. His grandfather, Claiborne Kyle, was an early settler who served in the Texas House of Representatives. An uncle, Fergus Kyle, was a Civil War hero and a highly respected rancher, politician, and founder of the Hays County town that bore his name.[28] Feeling in Mason ran strongly against the accused murderers, and their defense attorneys sought a change of venue for the trial.

Even while he was out on bail awaiting trial, Zack Light could not stay out of trouble. When he created a disturbance in a Mason saloon, County Judge G. L. D. Adams intervened. Adams, whose real name was Albert S. Harrell, was as hotheaded and tough as Light. A veteran of the Civil War, he had fought with Quantrell's guerrillas and was known as a formidable fighter, even though he had only one eye and one arm. After administering a verbal thrashing to Light in the sa-

Les Dow, the man who put out Zack Light's light. Drawing by Joan DeArment Hall from a photograph in the author's collection.

loon, he pulled out a pistol and slammed the barrel over the trouble-maker's head. Stunned by the blow and partially blinded by a torrent of blood streaming down his face, Light roared with anger, jerked his own revolver, and shot Adams in the shoulder. The two men then emptied their weapons at each other without effect. Adams staggered out the door to get more ammunition, but collapsed from loss of blood. Apparently charges were not brought against either man, and the affair was shrugged off in rough-and-ready Mason as just another rather boisterous argument between fighting men.[29]

Lawyers for Light and Jones in the Kyle killing succeeded in get-ting a change of venue to the town of Brady in McCulloch County. There, on December 13, 1886, almost two full years after the shoot-ing, they convinced a jury that Light and Jones committed the killing in defense of their lives and secured an acquittal.[30]

Leonard Passmore was a young boy in Mason during this period, but he remembered Zack Light well forty years later.

> He was quite a prominent character in and around Mason in the 'eighties. He and his two brothers, John and Leonard, were prominent cattlemen. . . . When sober, Zach [sic] was kind in his disposition and very accommodating. He would go his "entire length" as the cow-boy expression has it, for a friend. The Lights and their outfit often penned their herds in my father's pens. Zach would come down to the house and get me, then a small child, and take me out to their camp. There I was petted and made the hero of the camp. The first silver dollar I ever possessed was given to me by Zach Light. . . . He handed me a bright silver dollar and to me it looked as large as a full moon.
> But Zach got into a great deal of trouble owing to strong drink. When drunk he was desperate.[31]

An incident that took place at Fort Stockton, Pecos County, Texas, in September 1886 did not end in bloodshed, but it was another illustration of Zack Light's propensity for violence when under the influence of alcohol. Bossing a trail drive to New Mexico that fall, Light held his herd for a few days outside Fort Stockton while he indulged his taste for drinking and gambling. On September 23 he was in Herman Koehler's saloon dealing monte to John Holland and J. W. Prude, two cattlemen who also had trail herds grazing outside town. When newly appointed county attorney Howell Johnson, only twenty-two years old, attempted to place a bet, Light rudely refused him, saying it was a private game. "He had a hard look on his face and appeared to be inebriated," Johnson recalled.[32]

Later that day the monte game moved down the street to Billy Young's saloon. About dusk shots rang out and Sheriff John Edgar, accompanied by Johnson, ran to the Young saloon, from whence the sound had come. There they found a very intoxicated Zack Light, gun in hand. No one seemed to have been hit, but the situation was still tense. Said Johnson: "Just as I appeared in front of the large door entrance, Zack Light, standing just beyond the door. . . , said sharply, 'That is the sheriff,' and threw his gun on me. I immediately halted and a man behind Light, [Bill Clark,] grabbed Light's pistol and said, 'That ain't the sheriff, there he is behind the post.' He, Light, immediately turned his attention to the sheriff and had him go into the saloon for a talk and drink."[33]

Having almost been shot by the drunken Light, Johnson, in a rising state of fury, went and got a shotgun. He loaded it and returned to the saloon, intending, as he freely admitted, "to poke the gun down on Light and give him both barrels." But Sheriff Edgar intervened and prevented the young attorney from becoming a killer.

After much cajoling by Edgar, Clark, Holland, and Prude, Zack Light finally agreed to return to his cattle camp for the night and come back in the morning to face the court of Pecos County Judge F. W. Young. Zack was in no condition to ride back into town the next day, however, and one of his cowboys appeared for him, entered a plea of guilty of disturbing the peace, and paid a $10 fine.[34]

Zack Light made several cattle drives to New Mexico and in December 1887 settled permanently with his wife at Seven Rivers, a rough little burg notorious in the territory as a rendezvous of outlaws and gunmen since the days of the Lincoln County War. It was, said old-timers, "as tough as the toughest. Nearly all of the town's early residents were either outlaws or borderline cases."[35] Located at the convergence of seven creeks "dancing their way to the Pecos,"[36] Seven Rivers was little more than a few shacks when Billy the Kid and other Lincoln County warriors frequented the area. By the middle 1880s, however, it had grown into a prosperous little community of three hundred, with a post office, a hotel complete with restaurant, a boot and saddle shop, a blacksmith shop, a drugstore, and two mercantile stores.[37] There were, of course, the inevitable saloons — two of them — to provide liquid refreshment and recreation in the form of gambling tables for cowboys from the surrounding ranches.

One of the saloons was owned and managed by transplanted Texan Les Dow, who had come to the Seven Rivers area with his wife and two young sons in 1885. An energetic and industrious man, Dow kept a ranch a few miles outside Seven Rivers and, in addition to his saloon, owned a wagon yard and stagecoach livery stable in town. He also was employed as a stock detective for cattle raisers' associations in both Texas and New Mexico and held a commission as a deputy U.S. marshal.[38]

Early in October 1889 Zack Light was involved in a shootout in the Dow saloon. He was drinking and gambling with Will T. Henderson and Jack Shelby when a dispute arose and guns flashed. Light put a bullet in Henderson's shoulder and creased Shelby's scalp with another shot before going down with a wound in the fleshy part of his abdomen. Justice of the Peace Fred H. Peitz of Lookout held a hearing into the matter on October 12. Light and Henderson were charged on two counts: carrying deadly weapons and assault with intent to kill. Both entered a plea of guilty on the deadly weapons charge, and each was fined $50 and costs. The second charges were dismissed for lack of evidence.[39]

Light quickly recovered from his wound, but the seeds of his demise may have been sown by this incident. Saloonkeeper Les Dow testified against him at the court hearing, and the hotheaded Light never forgave him for it. Additional bad blood developed between the two when Light drove a bunch of cattle to Clayton, New Mexico, and failed to pay Dow for a few of his cows that had drifted along with the herd.[40]

James Leslie Dow, known as "Les" by friend and foe alike, was a formidable adversary indeed. A newspaper described him as "a typical Texas cowboy, brave, quick in quarrel, a hard fighter and exceedingly gun handy. He . . . had earned a reputation as a gun fighter, which he seemed to enjoy."[41] Said another paper: "He was a man who feared nothing except assassination. None were so quick with a revolver as Les Dow. His aim was perfect and his nerve always steady."[42]

Zack Light and Les Dow would clash eighteen months later in the Dow saloon, and Light's violent career would end abruptly. But before that final confrontation, Light disrupted a trial presided over by Justice Frank Rheinboldt at Seven Rivers. In September 1890 he was called as the principal witness for Cicero Stewart, the plaintiff in a civil suit against defendant Joseph Taylor. After Stewart's attorney, J. O. Cameron, had finished examining Light, Taylor, acting as his own attorney, began asking questions that the witness found insulting. Light responded in an equally abusive manner. As lawyer Cameron told the tale years later:

> Taylor leaned over toward Light with a stern, offensive glare, shaking his finger towards him, and said, "Zack Light, do you dare to sit there and swear that this trade was made at the corral and not in my house?" Thereupon Light raised up from his chair, took a step towards Taylor, and said, "Yes, and that is the truth and you can't infer that I am lying, you damn lying son-of-bitch," and hit him a swift clout in the jaw with his fist. Taylor dodged another jab and ran out of the building.[43]

The *Eddy Argus* reported that Light pursued Taylor, who headed straight to his home, where he secured a Winchester. Light also armed himself. "Things looked mighty squally for a time, but finally everything settled down. In the meantime, however, the jurymen scattered and one of them had started for his home twenty-five miles away. Not until evening next day was the jury recorraled, when the trial was quickly concluded, Stewart winning the case. Light was fined $5.00 for contempt of court and $7.50 for carrying a pistol."[44]

Legal problems for the unpredictable Light mounted. Only a week or so later he was arrested again, charged this time with intent to murder and housebreaking. He was released on $1,000 bond when witnesses were not immediately available to testify. It is clear that the man at this time was out of control. During this same period he was charged in Lincoln County with two other cases of assault to murder John Y. Hewitt, an attorney from White Oaks who had defended Light in court, but whose work evidently did not meet with his client's satisfaction.[45]

These cases were still pending the first week of April 1891, when Zack Light went on a prolonged drinking spree. The binge began in Eddy, where Light reportedly bragged in the saloons that he was going to Seven Rivers to kill Les Dow. On April 3 he saddled up and set out to accomplish his purpose. As Dow's son Bob later told the story:

> It is several hours ride from there to Seven Rivers, a distance of about eighteen miles, and Light evidently did not reach Seven Rivers until along about night. My father was at home asleep. We lived across the street west of the two saloons. . . .
>
> About daylight the men who were employed to feed and care for the stage horses came over to our house and awakened Dad, saying, "You had better watch out. . . . There has been a crowd over in the saloon who have been drinking and playing poker all night and I heard Zack Light tell them that he had come up here to kill you."
>
> . . . My father stayed at home until shortly before the stage was due, but he knew that the stage horses should be fed. He went across the street and fed and watered the horses, then he saddled his own horse and rode back down the street and dismounted his horse, tying him to the hitch rack in front of the other saloon. He walked into the saloon and found no one present.
>
> In a few moments Zack Light came from over at the other saloon and walked in. Two shots were heard and my Father walked outside and mounted his horse and Zack Light was found with his pistol in his hand, lying face downward upon the bar room floor. He asked for it and he got it.[46]

Dow would later testify that Light walked into the saloon and demanded $100 from him. "I told him I could let him have twenty-five but not a hundred," he said. "He then drew his revolver, but I threw my hand under it and the discharge went over my head. I shot at the same time and killed Zack."[47] There was a bullet hole high on the wall of the saloon that seemed to confirm Dow's story.[48]

Dow's son said that when his father emerged from the saloon,

> Zack's friends were waiting for him in front of the other saloon, and they were no doubt disappointed when they saw my Father come out and get on his horse. One of them had a Winchester in his hand. He shot at my Father as he rode across the street and my Father's horse began bucking and disappeared around back of the Rheinboldt Store. My Mother had heard the

first shots and had run to the front door of our house just in time to see the man shoot at him. She then went to the back and saw my Father's horse running off with the saddle on. The horse had thrown my Father and he had entered the back door of the Rheinboldt Store, but Mother thought he had been killed. When he entered the store he immediately sent a message to tell her that he was all right. He also sent a message to the other saloon to advise the crowd that had been with Zack Light the night before not to come to the Rheinboldt Store; also that he would not submit to arrest if they came over there after him. "Tell them," he said to the messenger, "I am an officer myself and I will catch the stage and go to Eddy and give up to some proper authorized official."[49]

Lafe McDonald, who was in Seven Rivers at the time, related the story of the aftermath of the shooting a little differently. "I helped guard Dow that day," he said.

I told them I would help if they would disarm Dow. I knew he was very quick. At first he refused to give up his arms. Finally he said he would do so provided we would give them back to him in the case of a mob attacking him.

I told him if any crowd of men appeared that we could not control, we would return his arms to him. He then handed them over. We guarded him all that day till late in the evening, when the Judge came over and Dow stood an examining trial. He was released, as there was no evidence in the case save his own.[50]

The stage came in, and Dow boarded without further incident. He went on to Eddy, where he was released on bond to await grand jury action. No one had been in the saloon at the time of the shooting other than the two participants, and one of them was dead and could not testify at the grand jury hearing. The jurors accepted Dow's story. Given Light's reputation, it was no doubt a case of "good riddance."

Zack Light was buried at Seven Rivers. There were few mourners.

Les Dow, the man who closed out Zack Light's murderous career, went on to gain fame as a tenacious and fearless lawman and man hunter. In 1895 he arrested Bill McNew, the dangerous henchman of the equally dangerous rancher and feudist Oliver Lee.[51] In 1896 he was a member of the posse that fought a battle with members of the notorious High Five Gang and killed outlaw Bob Hayes.[52] That same year he was elected sheriff of Eddy County and took the oath of office on January 1, 1897. Only seven weeks later, on February 18, 1897, Dave Kemp, an old foe and former Eddy County sheriff, shot him to death on the streets of Eddy.[53]

— 11 —

TOM TUCKER
ca. 1866–1920

There wasn't a gamer man lived than Tom Tucker.
— Sheriff Cicero Stewart

The most controversial figures of the Old West, perhaps, were gun-fighters. Because of their skill with weapons and lack of hesitancy in using them against their fellows, gunmen were inevitably drawn into the family feuds, range wars, mining claim battles, struggles to establish the rule of law, and economic and political conflicts that raged on the advancing frontier. Gunfighters were controversial in their time and remain so today. Contemporaries branded them as "cold-blooded killers" or extolled them as "fearless fighting men," depending on whether the gunfighter was "fer" or "agin" the observer's side of an issue. Popular writers and historians of the Old West, influenced by personal bias, still portray noted six-shooter characters like Billy the Kid, Wyatt Earp, Doc Holliday, Tom Horn, Frank Canton, et al. as either heroes or villains. What is true of the way famous gunmen have been depicted is equally true of lesser lights, gunfighters who, for one reason or another, never achieved gun-smoke immortality and are virtually forgotten today.

No less controversial in his time than his better remembered contemporaries was a big, rugged character named Tom Tucker, who cowboyed in Texas, Arizona, and New Mexico; played a prominent role in a number of contentious clashes; and gained gunfighter noto-riety. Admired by his friends and feared by his enemies, Tucker always lived close to the six-shooter. A man who camped out with him on many occasions said he never went to sleep without "his pistol on his chest."[1] One governor of New Mexico branded Tucker a "professional killer,"[2] while another expressed admiration for him as "a leading gunman [who] proved his mettle as a brave man of good judgment."[3] Characterized in a contemporary newspaper as "a man of exemplary habits [who] never drinks, uses an oath or associates with bad men,"[4] he was vilified by a later writer as "deadly when sober and dangerous when drunk."[5] An imposing figure of a man, standing over six feet tall and weighing more than 220 pounds, Tucker has been described as looking like "a cross between a deputy sheriff and a cattle rustler."[6] Arizona cattleman Will Barnes rated him "a first class cow hand . . . , a big, good-natured chap, not hunting for trouble of any kind,"[7] and rancher Cole Railston, who employed Tucker for a time, remembered him as being very tough on cow thieves. "He was a special man. Hell, he was a good man in any outfit to break up the stealing. He done it because he wasn't afraid and would meet you face to face and would say: 'You can't get away with that.' "[8] Cicero Stewart, a New Mexico sheriff who employed Tucker as a deputy, summed up his opinion of the man succinctly: "There wasn't a gamer man lived than Tom Tucker."[9]

Tucker was born at the close of the Civil War into a notable Texas family. He was one of sixteen children fathered by Thomas F. Tucker, a native of South Carolina who settled in Shelby County, Texas, in 1841. After service in the Mexican War under the legendary Texas fighting man John Coffee "Jack" Hays, T. F. Tucker enlisted in the Confederate army during the Civil War and rose to the rank of colonel. Following the war he ranched in north Texas and was elected the first county judge of newly organized Haskell County.[10] He and his wife, Frances, along with six sons remaining at home, were enumerated in the U.S. Census at Haskell in 1880. The occupation of the father and all his sons, down to the youngest, eight-year-old George, was given as "cattle herder." One son, Alex D., was elected the first sheriff of Haskell County, serving from 1884 to 1890.[11] Lightning killed one of the boys, Mike, in 1888. George served in the New Mexico territorial legislature around the turn of the century.[12]

Thomas, Jr., was still in his teens when he went to work for the Aztec Land and Cattle Company, the famous Hashknife brand. In 1885 and

1886 he helped drive Hashknife herds from the plains of north Texas to new ranges in Navajo and Coconino counties, Arizona. The Hashknife cowboys would round up a manageable herd in Texas, drive the cattle to Arizona, return by rail, and begin the process again with another batch. A number of notable trail hands worked with him in those years, including Walter Durham, Hank Sharp, Jeff Lefors,[13] Bud Jones, Jim Saunders, Charlie Bryant, George Begnal, Charlie Baldridge, Mose Tate, Tom Beach, Mel Chapman, Bob Gillespie, and John Payne.[14] The last two named, Gillespie and Payne, would play prominent roles in Tom Tucker's first recorded clash of arms.

When the drives were completed, Tucker remained in Arizona, working for the Hashknife. He was stationed at a line shack near a watering hole and given the responsibility of keeping the surrounding section of range clear of unwelcome intruders, rustlers, and sheepherders. Nearby Mormon settlers, who raised sheep, tried to run their flocks onto the Hashknife range, but were unsuccessful, thanks to the diligence of the man the Mormons called "Tom Tuck."[15]

In March 1887 Sheriff Commodore P. Owens of Apache County, Arizona, arrested Tucker and James Stott, owner of the Circle Dot ranch at Bear Springs, for theft of a horse. The charge was apparently motivated by enemies of the cattlemen, for a magistrate at Globe could find "not a particle of evidence" to support the allegation and quickly discharged the pair.[16] This was an early incident in a lengthy dispute between cattlemen and sheepherders that was to escalate into violence and become nationally known as the Pleasant Valley or Tonto Basin War, one of the most sanguinary conflicts in Old West history.

The smoldering feud between the Grahams, a family of cattlemen, and the sheep-herding Tewksbury clan heated up considerably in June 1887 when "Old Man" Blevins, a cowman and Graham partisan, suddenly disappeared. Foul play was immediately suspected, and both sides prepared for war. Since the trouble was basically a fight between cattlemen and sheepherders, the Hashknife cowboys, including Tom Tucker, sided with the Grahams.

Early in August 1887 Tucker, Payne, and Gillespie rode out with Bob Carrington and Hampton Blevins, a son of the missing man, with the intention to start, they said, "a little war of our own." The embattled quintet showed up at a Hashknife roundup camp, borrowed all the surplus ammunition in the camp, and, despite the admonitions of foreman Ed Rogers, set out to do battle.[17] They were joined during the next several days by a few other Graham adherents.

On August 9 the war party approached an isolated cabin where a party of Tewksbury partisans had holed up. The riders halted outside the cabin, and, in the tradition of the West, Tucker called out an announcement of their arrival. Jim Tewksbury edged the door open and asked what they wanted. Tucker said they were hungry and would like something to eat.

"No sir. We do not keep a hotel here," Tewksbury snapped.

Suddenly, without warning, gunfire exploded from the windows of the cabin. A bullet struck Hamp Blevins in the head, and he fell, dead as he hit the ground. Another slug hit Payne's horse, and the animal fell, pinning the leg of its rider. Payne struggled free, snapped a shot at the cabin, and began to run. A bullet struck him, and he went down, mortally wounded. A shot ripped through Carrington's clothing, inflicting a minor wound. Gillespie was hit in the hip. A bullet whizzed by Tucker's head, clipping off a piece of his ear.[18] Another slammed into his chest just above the nipple, pierced his lung, and went out his back. Carrington, Gillespie, and the others spurred their mounts and galloped off in a cloud of dust.[19]

Reeling in the saddle, Tucker also took flight. His companions had disappeared. Sometime later, weak and dizzy from shock and loss of blood, he passed out and tumbled from his horse.

A sudden rainstorm that night revived him. His horse was nowhere in sight. He began to move doggedly on, sometimes walking, sometimes crawling, sometimes losing consciousness altogether. As he told the story later, at one point he had to beat off a mother bear and two cubs who, drawn by the smell of blood, blocked his path.

Finally he reached the cabin of rancher Robert Sigsby, who took him in. His wounds were in a frightful condition, swarming with maggots. Using a concoction of axle grease and sheep dip, the standard cowboy cure for flyblown cattle sores, Sigsby treated the wounds, and, amazingly, Tucker recovered.[20]

The man must have had remarkable recuperative powers, for within a month he was back in the saddle. Will Barnes recalled seeing him pass through his Big Dry Lake camp in September with Bob Gillespie, who was riding "sideways in the saddle from the effects of his wound." Barnes said the "chastened and sobered warriors" had enough of Arizona and its range wars and "drifted yonderly" eastward toward New Mexico.[21]

The neighboring territory offered Tucker many opportunities for his talents as a cowman and gunman, mostly through his association with Oliver M. Lee, another tough Texan. With his half brother, Perry Altman, Lee had driven a herd of horses to New Mexico in 1884 and stayed on to establish a ranch in Dog Canyon in the Sacramento Mountains of Doña Ana County. When Tucker fetched up in that country in 1887, he cowboyed for Lee and in time became his employer's friend, confidant, and trusted bodyguard.

Soon after his arrival, Tucker became embroiled in another range war when Oliver Lee tangled with a hard case Texas cattleman named John Good.

After a series of scrapes with the law in Texas, Good, together with his son Walter, a six-foot six-inch giant of a man, had trailed a herd of cattle to New Mexico's Lost River country and established a ranch near the White Sands. In 1888 the Goods began running cattle on ranges claimed by Jim Cooper, another Texan and a neighbor of Oliver Lee. Ever pugnacious and spoiling for a fight, Lee was vociferous in his support for Cooper, and his hired men, including Tom Tucker, were soon drawn into the controversy.[22]

On June 12, 1888, shortly after Walter Good and George McDonald, wagon boss for the Cooper outfit, had a shouting match at a roundup, McDonald was found shot to death. The position of the body indicated the man had been murdered while taking a nap. Cooper and Lee immediately blamed Good for the murder, although there was little evidence to implicate him. Lee obtained the bullet that had gone through McDonald's head and flattened against a rock. He attached it to his watch chain as a reminder of the vengeance he planned to exact.

In August a pony belonging to Walter Good came up missing. Acting on a report that the animal had wandered off to the Perry Altman place, Good rode over there to retrieve his property. He never returned.

When John Good learned that Jim Cooper, Oliver Lee, and Tom Tucker had been at Altman's house the day his son disappeared, he concluded immediately that they had done him in. While fifty men

Tom Tucker, the big man on the right, with his pal Billy Wilson.
Courtesy of the Arizona Historical Society, Tuscon.

searched for Walter, his father swore out a warrant for the arrest of Altman, Cooper, Lee, and Tucker and led a posse to the Altman home. He found the owner there, but the others were gone, camped out, said Altman, somewhere on the Agua Chiquita.

Good's posse took Altman to La Luz and subjected him to intensive questioning all that night. When they had gotten no additional information about Walter's disappearance from him by morning, John Good advocated an immediate hanging of the prisoner, but cooler heads prevailed, and Altman was released.

John Good then announced he would post a reward of $300 for his son's return, dead or alive. If Walter was found dead, he offered another $1,000 for the arrest and conviction of his killers.

While John Good and his gunmen searched the mountains for their enemies, Lee and Altman slipped into El Paso for munitions. They came back with five-gallon cans loaded with cartridges. Open warfare seemed imminent. "The whole country is up in arms," reported one newspaper, "and such a reign of terror has not been known since the Lincoln County War."[23]

Two weeks passed before Walter Good's coyote-ravaged body with two bullet holes in the skull was discovered in the White Sands. His exceptional height and personal pieces of clothing and jewelry made identification certain. His revolver with two empty chambers lay beside him, mute evidence that Walter had not gone down without a fight.

After viewing the remains, John Good and a company of angry relatives, friends, and employees started back to La Luz. On the way they were ambushed by gunmen, later identified as Oliver Lee, Tom Tucker, Perry Altman, Bill Earhart,[24] and "Cherokee Bill" Kellam, who were deployed behind a ditch bank. One of the ambushers nervously triggered off a shot before the Good party got within accurate shooting range, and, although more than a hundred shots were fired, the only casualties were two horses dead and one wounded.[25]

A coroner's jury on September 7 found that Walter Good came to his death at the hands of Jim Cooper, Oliver Lee, Perry Altman, Cherokee Bill Kellam, and Tom Tucker. Colonel Albert Jennings Fountain, lawyer, newspaper publisher, and former head of the New Mexico militia, was named special prosecutor to pursue the case. In October a Doña Ana County grand jury, convened by Fountain, heard damning testimony from a young black boy employed by Charlie Graham, Altman's brother-in-law. The boy said he had heard those accused plot the murder of Walter Good and watched them carry it out. The reported recovery of Good's lost horse, he said, had been only a ruse to entice the big man to the Altman place. He testified that when Good arrived, "Altman and Tucker went out to greet him, and as soon as they had hold of his hands, pulled him off his horse. They then carried him back of the corral, tied him to a fence, spoke a few words to him, and then stepped off about ten steps and emptied their pistols into his body. The body was untied, wrapped in a wagon sheet, and carried into the house." The killers, he said, later took the body of Walter Good twelve miles out into the White Sands and left it.[26]

When a fire destroyed the Altman house shortly afterward, Fountain contended that it had been deliberately set to eradicate traces of Walter's blood staining the wooden floor. He told the jury his investigation of the Altman corral had disclosed a bullet-riddled board, blood spots, and patches of hair, identified by family members as Walter's. Based on this evidence, the grand jury handed down murder indictments against the five principals, and they were arrested and jailed.

Like many other sensational cases, the prosecution of the accused murderers of Walter Good took on political coloration. It was a well-known fact that the John Good ranching operation had been backed financially by Republicans Thomas B. Catron, head of the so-called Santa Fe Ring, and John H. Riley, a principal figure in the Lincoln County War a decade earlier. The prosecution of Good's enemies by Albert Fountain, a Republican, was perceived by many to be the act of a legal hired gun to protect the financial interests of his Republican bosses. Southeastern New Mexico Democrats, led by Albert B. Fall of Las Cruces, quickly responded to what they claimed was a partisan attack on the staunchly Democratic Texans. Someone got to the young witness whose testimony had been so damaging, and at a habeas corpus hearing he retracted his story. Friendly Democrats posted bond in the amount of $10,000 for each of the accused, and they were released from custody. The case dragged on in the courts, and after continuances, delays, and a change of venue to Socorro County, was finally dismissed.

There were sporadic flare-ups in the feud. One night John Good and several cohorts threatened Oliver Lee at a dance in La Luz. Lee jumped out a window, leaped on a horse, and lit out for his ranch. The Good party rode in pursuit, but when they found Jim Cooper, Tom Tucker, and six other Lee partisans on hand, they reined up out of rifle range and chose not to fight. Not long after this incident John Good lost much of his support, abandoned his war on Lee and Cooper, and left the country.[27]

The Good-Cooper feud was only one of many battles pitting Democrat Albert Fall against Republican Albert Fountain. During the 1890s the two Alberts fought bitterly in the New Mexico territorial legislature and in the courts. On the range, where conflicts often resulted in bloodshed, Fall could always count on the support of Oliver Lee and a coterie of gun-fighting cowboys that included Tom Tucker, Bill Carr, Jim Gililland, and Billy McNew, a brother-in-law of Lee.[28]

On September 9, 1892, Fountain's newspaper, the *Rio Grande Republican*, singled Tucker out for scorn, saying he strutted the streets of Las Cruces "looking like a traveling arsenal." It accused him of assaulting Ed Brown, bartender at the Arcade Saloon, and throwing a rock "that shattered two of the handsome glasses." Brown claimed that when he refused to serve him liquor, Tucker threatened to shoot him. The story went on to say that when Albert Fall interceded with Sheriff Guadalupe Ascarate on Tucker's behalf, the officer "promptly arrested Brown and let Tucker go home." Left unmentioned was the fact that Ed Brown was a sworn enemy of Oliver Lee and a political ally of Albert Fountain.

Sheriff Ascarate, who was clearly in Fall's camp, issued deputy commissions to Lee, Tucker, McNew, Gililland, and Philip Fall, Albert's brother, even as Fountain and the *Republican* openly accused these same men of cattle rustling. Fall also used his influence in Santa Fe to secure deputy U.S. marshal appointments for his loyal gunmen.[29]

Trailing two suspected rustlers, Charles Rhodius and Matt Coffelt, in early 1893, Lee, Tucker, and McNew caught up with them four miles across the Texas line on February 12. The small herd of cattle the two men were driving appeared to have burned-over brands. When challenged, Rhodius pulled a gun, and Lee shot him dead. Tucker and McNew dispatched Coffelt. At a hearing Albert Fall represented the three gunmen and gained their release on the age-old plea of self-defense.[30]

Later that year Tucker was called to the New Mexico capital at Santa Fe on special assignment. The political battles of the territory, always rancorous, had become even more virulent, with the introduction of secret societies into the contests. Several killings and beatings culminated in the brutal murder of former Santa Fe County sheriff Frank Chavez on May 29, 1892. Democrats charged Republicans with supporting a secret society that had committed the sensational killing. William T. Thornton, a former mayor of Santa Fe, appointed territorial governor by Democratic president Grover Cleveland, acted quickly to move against the violent secret societies. He established a task force of fighting men under the direction of newly appointed U.S. Marshal Edward L. Hall and Santa Fe County Sheriff William Price Cunningham. One of these picked gunmen was Tom Tucker, who arrived in Santa Fe to pin on another deputy sheriff's badge.

During the next year Thornton's task force broke up several criminal secret societies, but the lawmen were convinced that peace could not be attained until the killers of Frank Chavez were brought to justice. After a lengthy investigation, Sheriff Cunningham obtained warrants for the arrest of five men believed to be principals in that murder. The five were Francisco Gonzales y Borrego, a former coroner of Santa Fe County commonly known as Frank Borrego; his brother, Antonio Gonzales y Borrego; Lauriano Alarid; Patricio Valencia; and Hipolito Vigil, a city policeman and former justice of the peace in whose office the Chavez murder plot was allegedly hatched.[31]

On January 9, 1894, Sheriff Cunningham and Deputies Tucker, Juan Delgado, and Page B. Otero (a brother of future New Mexico governor Miguel A. Otero) set out to make the arrests. They took four suspects into custody without incident, but Hipolito Vigil resisted arrest. As Cunningham later testified,

> Deputy Sheriff Tucker and myself advanced toward [Vigil] and when about 40 yards from him I ordered him to hold up his hands as I had a warrant for his arrest. At the same moment Deputy Tucker, in a clear tone of voice, gave the same order. This order was repeated at least three times and was disre-

garded. Vigil instantly drew his 45-caliber revolver, jumped behind an electric light post and fired at us. . . . We returned the fire. . . . When Vigil fell dead he held his 45-caliber pistol at full cock in his hand.[32]

The circumstances of the shooting immediately became a political football. Ex-governor L. Bradford Prince, a political foe of Thornton, was in Albuquerque at the time of the incident, but he spoke out quickly, condemning the killing of Vigil as cold-blooded murder. Tucker, he asserted, had shot Vigil dead even as Cunningham read the arrest warrant to him. He was quoted in an interview in the *Albuquerque Democrat* as saying: "What has created great feeling in Santa Fe is the fact that the sheriff has had his deputies, strangers, understood to be professional killers from Texas, brought here solely for the purpose of intimidation and quick shooting. . . . [Tucker], who is reported to have [first] fired on Vigil has been understood to be of like character."[33]

In an editorial headed "Tell The Truth," the *Santa Fe New Mexican* took issue with Prince's remarks, calling them "gross misstatements." In order to bring order and the rule of law to Santa Fe, the paper's editors argued,

> heroic treatment was necessary. The work was dangerous—and none but brave men would undertake it. It was absolutely necessary that the sheriff and his deputies should be parties unconnected by blood, friendship or party affiliation with anyone in Santa Fe . . . , that they should have no local influences to hinder them in the performance of their duties. [The lawmen] should be men of known courage, fearless and determined, who would not be hasty to shoot, but not afraid to do so when the demand became necessary. Such men were found and appointed. . . . Governor Prince can not show that Deputy Sheriff Tucker has the reputation of being a "professional killer," or that he ever shot a man or was engaged in any difficulty except when hunting thieves and murderers and in the performance of his official duty when arresting them. He is a man of exemplary habits, never drinks, uses an oath or associates with bad men.[34]

Rumors of reprisal against Cunningham and Tucker circulated in the city, and U.S. Marshal Hall found it necessary to hold the officers in protective custody.[35] At a coroner's hearing a jury concluded that Tucker had killed Vigil "in an unlawful and illegal manner," but Oliver Lee soon arrived with bail, and he and Tucker returned together to Doña Ana County.

After a lengthy and acrimonious trial in which the accused murderers of Frank Chavez were vigorously defended by Thomas B. Catron himself, the Borrego brothers and their confederates, Alarid and Valencia, were convicted and sentenced to death. On April 2, 1897, in what has been called "one of the most celebrated hangings in the Southwest,"[36] all four were hanged in Santa Fe.[37]

Meanwhile, after the Vigil shooting affair in Santa Fe, Tucker had returned to southern New Mexico, where life was not in the least dull. He continued to work for Oliver Lee and Lee's mentor and supporter Albert Fall, while still retaining his position as deputy U.S. marshal.

Tucker was one of thirteen federal officers, together with three companies of Texas Rangers, who were sent to El Paso, Texas, in February 1896 to prevent the heavyweight title match between Ruby Bob Fitzsimmons and Peter Maher.[38] George Curry, later governor of New Mexico, was also a deputy U.S. marshal assigned to the El Paso affair. In his memoirs, Curry recorded an incident involving Tucker and Albert Fall that might well have led to tragic consequences:

> As Fall was leaving for his home in Las Cruces, I went with him to the Santa Fe depot . . . , where Tom Tucker, a real gunman, joined us. As the train was about to depart, I noticed Ben Williams, then a deputy sheriff at Las Cruces and Fall's bitter personal enemy, with three others, all carrying rifles and about to board the train. Tucker and I boarded the train with Fall. . . . Just outside the El Paso city limits the train stopped and Williams and his men got off. Tucker and I, both U.S. deputy marshals, and required to be back in El Paso, returned there. It is my belief that if Tucker and I had not been with Fall, he might not have reached Las Cruces alive.[39]

Political battles, always acrimonious and personal in New Mexico, were particularly bitter in 1896, a presidential election year. When in February Albert Fountain, representing the New Mexico Cattle and Horse Growers Association, secured indictments in Lincoln County against a number of suspected cattle thieves, including Oliver Lee and Billy McNew, many Democrats were furious, believing the charges against Lee and McNew were politically motivated. Albert Fall and other lawyers fought the allegations vigorously, and, as the cases dragged on, the bitterness grew in intensity.

En route home from the Lincoln court, Fountain and his eight-year-old son, Henry, mysteriously vanished. Pinkerton detectives and celebrated man-hunter Pat Garrett were brought in to solve what seemed to be a double murder. But the bodies could not be found, and the mystery deepened.

Lee and his coterie of gunmen were immediately suspected. Pinkerton detective J. C. Fraser, assigned to the case, reported to his home office on March 7, 1896, that the case sounded a great deal like the murder of Walter Good a few years earlier. On his arrival in Santa Fe, Governor Thornton and others had informed him that Oliver Lee, Tom Tucker, and Cherokee Bill Kellam had murdered Good and buried his body in the White Sands. It appeared that Fountain and his young son had met the same fate.[40] A few days later Agent Fraser reported from Doña Ana County:

> Things are certainly in very bad shape around Las Cruces. . . . We have had eleven murders here and no convictions. Oliver Lee, McNew, Tucker and the balance of the gang are all deputies under the present sheriff and several cold-blooded murders are credited up to Oliver Lee and his friends, McNew, Tucker, and others. All of these killings they claim were done in self defense, but in each case Oliver Lee jumped the ranch of the man he killed.[41]

In April the Pinkerton office in Denver pulled Fraser off the case and replaced him with W. B. Sayers, a more experienced operative. Before leaving, Fraser "warned his colleague that he would be watched. Sayers noted that after he arrived in Santa Fe his every movement was under surveillance; his stalker was identified as Tom Tucker."[42] Despite this cat-and-mouse play, the investigation into the mysterious disappearance of Fountain and his son continued.

The Democratic Party of New Mexico held its convention in Las Vegas in May 1896 to select a slate of delegates to attend the national Democratic convention in Chicago. The New Mexico Democrats were deeply divided over several issues, and with many fighting men, including Tom Tucker, in attendance at Las Vegas, the potential for violence was ever present. Although still regarded as a dangerous man and a deadly gunman, Tucker at that convention developed something of a reputation as a peacemaker, according to George Curry. There were tense moments when a fight erupted over Governor Thornton's administration. Arrayed in support of Thornton were such gun-fighting notables as Charlie Perry, Les Dow, Charlie Ballard, and Buck Guyse, while prominent in the anti-Thornton forces were Albert Fall and Bill Cunningham, Tucker's old boss in Santa Fe. But, said Curry, when tempers flared, Tucker, with close friends on either side, acted as a mediator and calmed things down.[43]

In that month of May the Pinkerton Detective Agency pulled its operative from the Fountain disappearance investigation, but over the next months and years Pat Garrett continued to build a case against Lee and two of his men, Billy McNew and Jim Gililland. By April 1898 he had enough circumstantial evidence to get bench warrants for their arrest. But Lee refused to surrender to Garrett, and for months he and his cohorts hid out in the hills. On one occasion, by force of arms they beat off an attempt by a Garrett-led posse to arrest them at their Wildy Well hideout.

Garrett, however, was able to take Bill McNew into custody. While McNew was being held in the Las Cruces jail, a rumor swept the town that Albert Fall himself had been placed behind bars. To verify or disprove this report, George Curry and Tom Tucker went to the jail. Said Curry: "John Meadows, one of Garrett's deputies, threw down his Winchester rifle on Tucker who, like myself, was unarmed. Garrett soon appeared. When we told him we were there to ask if Fall was in jail, Garrett replied, 'No, but he ought to be.' It is my belief that had I not been with him, Tucker might have been killed, as he was known as Lee's close friend and ally."[44]

Oliver Lee resolutely refused to surrender to Pat Garrett. The impasse was finally resolved when Albert Fall and other sympathetic politicians worked out an arrangement. A new county called Otero was created and George Curry appointed sheriff. Curry, in turn, appointed Tom Tucker as his chief field deputy. Surrender terms for Lee and Gililland were negotiated by Tucker and Eugene Manlove Rhodes, a rancher and noted author who had sheltered the fugitives.[45]

But before the suspects in the Fountain case ever came to trial, Tom Tucker was faced with his own court challenge. The murder charge against him in the Hipolito Vigil slaying still remained open. Prosecutors dragged their feet, but in April 1898, more than four years after the shooting, new testimony by a man named Anselmo Armijo, who claimed to be an eyewitness to the incident, moved them to action. On information sworn to by Armijo, a Santa Fe judge issued a bench warrant for Tucker's arrest. Santa Fe County Sheriff Harry C. Kinsell went to Las Cruces, took Tucker into custody on April 7, 1898, and returned him to Santa Fe.[46]

The importance of the case is evidenced by that fact that Chief Justice William J. Mills of the New Mexico Supreme Court presided over the hearings and Solicitor General E. L. Bartlett conducted the prosecution. Attorneys D. A. Spiess and H. L. Warren defended Tucker.[47]

Testimony began on April 26. The star witness, of course, was Anselmo Armijo, who said that Sheriff Cunningham and Tucker arrived at the scene of the shooting in a hack and arrested Borrego without any difficulty. But when Tucker, who was armed with a repeating rifle, spied Vigil, he walked toward him. At a distance of about thirty yards he called out for Vigil to halt, raised the rifle, and fired at the same time. Cunningham "and others" ducked behind the hack and also began firing. At the first shot from Tucker, Vigil stepped behind a light post. After "six or seven shots were fired [Vigil] pulled a pistol, but did not shoot. . . . After Vigil fell, the officers pulled the body off a porch and another shot was fired." When asked why he had waited more than four years to come forward with this information, Armijo thought long and hard before answering: "Because I desired to."[48]

Other witnesses—Bruno Romero, Cosme Alarid, and Benigno Ortega—corroborated Armijo's testimony to some extent. They said Tucker was armed with a Winchester rifle and the other officers with shotguns. Tucker, they said, fired two shots before Vigil jumped behind the post. They testified that Tucker, after the shooting, "threw Vigil's body from the porch into the street."[49]

Contradictory testimony was given by Tucker himself and by fellow deputy sheriff Page Otero, who had been on the scene. Both swore that as Tucker walked toward Vigil, he shouted, "I have a warrant for you. Throw up your hands." Vigil then pushed back his overcoat, pulled a pistol, jumped behind a post, and fired. Tucker returned the fire and ordered Vigil to drop his weapon. "I remember very distinctly," said Otero, "of hearing Cunningham and Tucker ask him, between shots, to drop his pistol, which he refused to do." Otero and Tucker both denied that Vigil was thrown from the porch, but fell into the street after he was shot.[50]

After hearing the conflicting testimony, Justice Mills announced he would study the case and adjourned the hearing. Released on $2,500 bond, Tucker in May was bound over for consideration of his case by the next grand jury.[51]

Santa Fe, like the rest of the nation, during these weeks was in a great state of excitement over the news that war with Spain had been declared. Recruits for Theodore Roosevelt's Rough Rider cavalry unit made up of western volunteers were flocking into town. Tom Tucker was among the first to try to enlist, but his application was rejected because he was still under bond on the murder charge.[52]

A story later circulated that one of the other army volunteers gave Tucker a severe thrashing in Santa Fe. As one historian told the tale, Tucker's

> reputation as a fighting man meant nothing to a twenty-two-year-old cowboy who rode into Santa Fe in the early spring of 1898 to enlist in the Rough Rider company then being recruited at that place. While sitting in the plaza of the ancient capital of the conquistadores one day enjoying the war excitement, he became involved in a quarrel with this youth, and, according to the story related to me by an eyewitness, the fearless Tom Tucker received a severe beating at the hands of the young Rough Rider. It was the opinion of my informant that the old fighter lost his nerve when his deputy's star was removed; but in all probability it was just a case of youth against an older man; and then Tucker's reputation as a fighter was made with a six-shooter, not his fists.[53]

In January 1899, five years after the shooting of Hipolito Vigil, Tucker finally went on trial for that murder. He was quickly acquitted on the time-honored plea of self-defense.[54]

Lee, Gilliland, and McNew, the accused murderers of Albert Fountain and his son, were tried at Hillsboro, Sierra County, five months later. Albert Fall was their lead attorney, and Thomas Catron acted as special prosecutor. Tom Tucker, who in true cowboy fashion arrived at Hillsboro with no other baggage than his saddle and six-shooter and made camp outside of town, was an important witness for the defense.[55]

According to George Curry, Tucker was more than a witness. "The situation throughout the trial was tense," said Curry. "Tom Tucker, regarded as a leading 'gunman' among Lee's friends, proved his mettle as a brave man of good judgment throughout the trial, always alert to keep order."[56]

The case for the prosecution suffered from a major weakness — the absence of bodies — and the jury took only ten minutes to acquit the defendants.

Another murder charge still was pending against Lee and Gililland, however. During Garrett's unsuccessful attempt to arrest them at Wildy Well, they had shot and killed posseman Kent Kearney. Under indictment for this killing, they were held briefly at Alamogordo, Otero County, where their friends Sheriff George Curry and Chief Deputy Tom Tucker were the law. The district attorney, realizing he had little hope of impaneling a jury that would convict them, dropped the charges.

The years after the turn of the century were much less exciting for Tom Tucker. He continued to cowboy for Oliver Lee and worked with Lee, Gililland, McNew, Bill Carr, and Gene Rhodes on the construction of an ambitious project, a water line from the Sacramento River to Orogrande, a new gold camp.[57] In 1905 he was a cattle inspector at Socorro.[58] When the New Mexico Mounted Police was formed that year, he was one of the first to apply for membership, but his application was rejected, perhaps because of his unsavory reputation, but more likely because of his advancing age.[59]

His most notable gun-fighting exploit during these years was participation with Eddy County Sheriff Cicero Stewart and cattle inspector Dee Harkey in a 1908 battle with horse thieves near Sacramento Sinks, in which the officers succeeded in apprehending the Jim Nite outlaw gang without casualties on either side.[60]

In 1912 Tucker and Oliver Lee were guests of ex-governor George Curry at the Mexican government's military headquarters in Juarez, across the border from El Paso, to witness one of the major battles of the Mexican Revolution.[61]

Tucker remained a lifelong friend and supporter of Oliver Lee, George Curry, and Albert Fall, all of whom rose to high levels of political prominence. Lee was a representative and state senator in the New Mexico legislature for a dozen years.[62] Curry served as governor of New Mexico from 1907 to 1909 and later represented his district in the U.S. House of Representatives.[63] In 1912 New Mexico voters elected Fall to the U.S. Senate, where he served until 1921, when he accepted appointment as secretary of the interior in the cabinet of President Warren G. Harding.[64]

Tom Tucker was married once, sometime prior to 1910, to a woman named Mary, who had previously been wed to a man named Gordon. The union was childless. Five years after Tucker's death at Alamogordo in 1920, Mary Gordon Tucker married again, taking as her third husband John Meadows, the Pat Garrett deputy who twenty-seven years earlier had threatened to turn his Winchester loose on Tucker when he visited the Las Cruces jail. Given this history, the marriage of John Meadows to the widow Tucker was, as one historian has pointed out, "a curious alliance."[65]

But then Tom Tucker had been a controversial figure his entire life.

— 12 —

ED SCARBOROUGH
1879–?

He is a determined fellow and much like his father. . . . Scarborough was brought up in the saddle and is an excellent marksman. He don't know what fear is.

— *Tucson Citizen*

[Ed] was a bit on the harum-scarum side, and traveled quite a bit on his father's reputation.

— Burt Mossman

No young man entering the field of frontier law enforcement was ever given a greater advantage than Ed Scarborough, for he was taught by his father, one of the finest peace officers in the history of the West. As a county sheriff, deputy U.S. marshal, and range detective in Texas, New Mexico, and Arizona, George Adolphus Scarborough was a terror to lawbreakers and evildoers in the last two decades of the nineteenth century. During the course of his career, he dispatched in six-shooter encounters at least three men, none of them a gun-fighting slouch. But his remarkable life was brought to an abrupt end by an outlaw gang in an April 1900 shootout.[1]

Son George Edgar, always called "Ed," grew to manhood riding at his father's side in pursuit of outlaws and rustlers. Following George's tragic death, Ed seemed for a time to be living up to the admirable standard set by his father. But then his behavior became increasingly erratic. He lost one lawman's job after another, and finally he was convicted of cold-blooded murder and sentenced to prison.

The first of seven children born to George and Mary Francis "Mollie" Scarborough, Ed was born January 12, 1879, in McCulloch County, Texas, and raised at Anson, Jones County, where his father served two terms as sheriff, 1884–88. When George accepted appointment as a deputy U.S. marshal at El Paso in 1893, the family moved there.

El Paso was loaded with hair-trigger gunfighters in the 1890s, and Ed Scarborough, an impressionable teenager during those years, was undoubtedly affected by the atmosphere of violence pervasive in the town. His father killed two men there in 1895 and 1896. The first was Martin Mroz, a wanted fugitive from New Mexico. The second was John Selman, who had recently gained national attention by shooting to death the notorious gunfighter and killer John Wesley Hardin in El Paso. George Scarborough, charged with murder in both of these killings, stood trial and was exonerated on pleas of self-defense.[2]

But having come into some disrepute for his quickness to use deadly force, George had his commission as deputy U.S. marshal revoked. He moved his family to Deming in southern New Mexico Territory, where he continued chasing criminals as a stock detective for the Southwestern New Mexico Cattle Protective Association. His value to law enforcement was quickly recognized, and he soon received another deputy U.S. marshal commission as well as deputy sheriff appointments in several New Mexico and Arizona counties. To aid him in the work, he formed a group of tough, seasoned riders that came to be known as "Scarborough's Rangers." Members included Grant County Deputy Sheriffs William D. "Keechi" Johnson and Miles Marshall, as well as Deputy U.S. Marshal Frank McMahan, Scarborough's brother-in-law. Young Ed was soon brought into the group to learn the ropes.

As early as 1897, when he was only eighteen, Ed was riding alone into the wilds of old Mexico on missions for his father. Tough old lawman Jeff Milton, a deputy marshal who had sided George Scarborough in many a brush with gunmen and outlaws, was down in that country to meet with Colonel Emilio Kosterlitzky of the *Gendarmeria Fiscal* and investigate a report that the infamous "Black Jack" Ketchum gang was holed up down there. Milton's train was flagged down by Ed, who had a message from his father. George had been detained on other business, but had sent his son to assist Milton in any way required. "He was just a kid," Milton recalled, "[but] I took him with me."[3] George later caught up with Milton, and Ed and was with them when they found the outlaw camp, but the birds had flown. For Ed Scarborough, however, it was an invaluable experience; he had met the legendary Colonel Kosterlizky and had spent many hours with Jeff Milton, who, like his father, was one of the most respected lawmen of the West.

Fully grown to manhood now, Ed in 1898 took a wife. On December 13 he married sixteen-year-old Ruby Angelina Fuqua of Silver City. Justice of the Peace Louis J. Marshall presided over the ceremony performed in the home of the bride's parents.[4] The couple settled in Deming, where Ed's uncle, the Reverend Lee Scarborough, the following August baptized both of them "in a water hole at the east end of town." During his stay in Deming, the visiting Baptist minister "delivered a series of sermons resulting in several Demingites seeing the error of their ways and becoming Christians," according to the *Deming Headlight*. "The Reverend left Monday, accompanied by brother George and nephew Edwin [*sic*] on a 10-day trip."[5]

Less than a month after being dunked in the water hole and becoming a Christian, Ruby gave birth on September 9, 1899, to a baby girl that she and Ed named Corrine.[6]

During this period George Scarborough kept his son busy ranging far and wide in the hunt for outlaws. They even rode together as far west as California, according to a report in the Deming paper:

> George Scarborough and his son Edwin [*sic*] returned home last Wednesday from a trip through the southern part of California. While out, accompanied by a deputy sheriff of Cochise County, Arizona, they arrested Tom and Mat Birch for stealing cattle from the San Simon Cattle Co., and Jim Anderson and a man named Cooper, who are charged with stealing horses from ranchmen in the same territory. All of these fellows are now in jail at Tombstone, Arizona, awaiting trial. Mr. Geo. Scarborough left again yesterday for the ranges.[7]

On April 3, 1900, the senior Scarborough and a friend, Walt Birchfield, fought a long-distance pitched battle with an outlaw gang high

George Edgar Scarborough as a handsome child with three of his younger sisters. From the author's collection.

in the Chiricahua Mountains on the New Mexico–Arizona border. A rifle bullet struck Scarborough in the leg, smashing the bone. He lay behind a rough rock barrier the rest of that day and night while Birchfield made his way to the railroad station at San Simon, where he wired Deming for a doctor and sought help to bring his friend down from the mountains. Early the next morning Birchfield led some cowboys with a buckboard to the scene of the fight. Together they carried the badly wounded lawman back to the railroad, where they found a Deming doctor and son Ed waiting. George was taken to Deming, where surgeons removed his badly shattered leg. He died on the operating table.

The loss of George Scarborough, who had been a real nemesis for the outlaw gangs of the southwestern territories, was a blow to the law-abiding element of the region. A few days after the funeral the cattlemen of Grant County announced that George's brother-in-law, Frank McMahan, would replace him as the leader of the their association's rangers. "Mr. McMahan has been in the detective work on the frontier for a number of years and comes highly recommended," said the *Silver City Independent*. "He will be assisted by Edward [*sic*] Scarborough, who was his father's trusted assistant while serving the cattlemen of this district."[8] If he was irritated by the seeming inability of the press to get his name right or, because of his youth, being passed over to replace his father as the head of the rangers, Ed's actions over the next few months gave no such indication. He spent long days in the field as a member of posses that for weeks searched unsuccessfully for his father's killers.[9]

In July 1900 he was lauded in the press for his capture of Jerome Adams, wanted for the murder of Oliver Gruell at the Mormon colony at Luaz, Mexico. "After an exciting chase after his man in the Dree Creek country [Scarborough] came to Deming with his prisoner [who] was taken to Silver City by Sheriff [James K.] Blair to await extradition by the Mexican authorities. The murder is said to have been a cold blooded affair. . . . Scarborough displayed great courage in arresting Adams."[10]

In August two former Scarborough's Rangers, Grant County Deputy Sheriffs Keechi Johnson and Miles Marshall, were in the Upper Gila country after cattle rustlers. The lawmen parted at a split in the trail, Johnson taking one fork and Marshall the other. Finding nothing on his trail, Marshall returned to Silver City.

Johnson, meanwhile, arrested a man named Ralph Jenks and started back with his suspect. On the morning of August 27 Jenks showed up alone at a ranch, saying that Johnson had been shot and killed by bushwhackers. When the news reached Silver City, Sheriff Blair led a posse out to locate the body and investigate the shooting. Riding with him were Don Johnson, the son of the dead deputy; Miles Marshall; and range detectives Frank McMahan, Ed Scarborough, J. Marvin Hunter, and two others named Doak and Collier.

Arriving at the scene of the murder, Sheriff Blair found that authorities from the town of Mogollon had already held an inquest and buried the body. After questioning residents of the area, Blair decided that Ralph Jenks, his brother Roy, and a man named Henry Reinhart, partners in a rustling operation, were responsible for the death of Keechi Johnson. He sent McMahan and his rangers to Mogollon to arrest Ralph Jenks and Reinhart, while, accompanied by Marshall and Don Johnson, he went in search of Roy Jenks.

McMahan's posse successfully took Ralph Jenks and Reinhart into custody at Mogollon and started back for Silver City. As they rode along Duck Creek about nine o'clock on the night of September 3, Jenks suddenly reached over, jerked Ed Scarborough's shotgun from its scabbard, and began working its pump action in a feverish attempt to ram a shell into the chamber. Scarborough whipped out his pistol and shouted at Jenks to drop the weapon. When his repeated order was ignored, Scarborough opened fire, triggering off three rounds into the body of Jenks. Any one of the shots would have been fatal.

J. Marvin Hunter later wrote:

> I was present when Edgar Scarborough killed Ralph Jenks on Duck Creek near the White House. . . . Jenks managed to jerk Edgar Scarborough's pump gun from the scabbard as we were riding along, but in trying to work the gun it must have jammed. Jenks jumped from his horse and kept trying to work the gun. Scarborough called on him several times to drop the gun, and then shot him three times with his six-shooter — twice in the breast and once in the head, and as Jenks fell he threw the shotgun at Scarborough. . . . We covered the corpse with a tarp and went on to Silver City . . . , arriving there the next day.

McMahan had placed Scarborough under arrest and when we reached Silver City placed him in jail. District court was in session, and the grand jury no-billed Scarborough immediately and he was released.[11]

The coverage in the press was essentially the same. The headline in the *Silver City Independent* of September 4 read: "JENKS IS KILLED BY A RANGER. HE PULLED A GUN FROM THE SCABBARD OF ONE OF THE MEMBERS OF THE POSSE AND IN AT-TEMPTING TO GET THE SAME IN CONDITION TO DO BUSINESS WAS FIRED UPON AND KILLED." The story included a communication Sheriff Blair had received that morning by special messenger from McMahan:

> We started in from Mogollon this morning with Reinhart and Jenks, and tonight about 9 o'clock, about a mile above the White House on Duck Creek, Ralph Jenks tried to pull Edgar's shotgun and Edgar killed him. He pulled Ed's gun out of the scabbard and threw a cartridge in. We covered him with a "tarp" and left him as we did not feel safe to split the crowd. Please get Justice and other arrangements out to him soon as possible. We will bring Reinhart in.[12]

The arrests of the suspects in the Keechi Johnson murder and the subsequent shooting of Jenks were not looked upon with approval by all the residents of Grant County. The Jenks killing focused attention on what many considered the high-handed actions of the privately funded ranger organization, and especially Ed Scarborough. Although George Scarborough, the original head of the group, had not been universally liked in Grant County, he had commanded everyone's respect. His son had not earned that respect and consequently came under severe criticism by many who believed he had unnecessarily gunned down Ralph Jenks and used his position of authority to "bulldoze" suspects.

Sheriff Blair also received a share of that criticism. When Blair was attacked in some quarters for his practice of issuing deputy commissions to ranger members, the editor of the *Silver City Independent* rose to his defense. "The commissions," he said, "were applied for by the executive committee of the cattle association in order that its men might have proper authority to carry out the work they were employed to do." He also pointed out that the rangers held deputy commissions issued by the sheriffs of Sierra, Doña Ana, and Socorro counties in New Mexico and Cochise County in Arizona "in order to complete the circuit of the territory over which the men might have to work."[13]

Partly as a result of the uproar over his deputy's behavior, Sheriff Blair lost his bid for reelection in November. On taking office, his successor promptly canceled young Scarborough's commission as deputy.

All in all, that autumn was a bad season for Ed Scarborough. In October, while camping in the Hatchita Mountains on a scout for cattle thieves, he tangled with a skunk and received something more serious than the usual odious spray. As the press reported,

> Late in the night he was awakened by a grumbling noise under his blanket.
>
> He struck at the object by instinct, and a large skunk caught his wrist in its teeth and clung fast to it. After shaking it as only a frightened man can for about five seconds, he made the animal let go its hold, but it still made fight. He then grabbed his pistol and fired into his bed and the animal fled. Thinking it was all over, he returned to bed and no sooner had he lain down than the skunk made another attack. As the skunk went under the blanket on one side, Mr. Scarborough went out on the other and opened fire on his antagonist. The skunk fled again, but soon made another attack. In the third engagement the officer killed the animal with his Winchester.[14]

A bite by an overly aggressive skunk was a matter of concern, for always present was the possibility that the animal carried rabies. Ed went all the way to El Paso to receive a "mad stone" treatment.[15] He apparently suffered no lasting ill effects of the bite, although some of his enemies might have attributed his later erratic behavior to the bite of that truculent skunk.

He was becoming increasingly controversial. Even members of the cattlemen's association had differing views of the effectiveness of the rangers since the death of the leader, George Scarborough, and the emergence of his son as a major figure in the organization. Arguments between association members at a meeting held in Silver City in January 1901 grew so heated a fistfight nearly broke out, and the dispute led to the resignation of President William Jack. Reported a Lordsburg paper:

> The chief point of discussion seemed to have been the ranger system. Up to the time of the death of George Scarborough there was no trouble about the way the system was worked, but after he was killed and his son took the position there has been considerable trouble. Young Scarborough has arrested many men for stealing cattle but was unable to present enough evidence to warrant indictments, and the men arrested had to be turned loose. It looked to the citizens as though the rangers were trying to bulldoze men more than they were trying to secure convictions of cow thieves. The appointment of young Scarborough as a deputy sheriff was one of the main things brought against Sheriff Blair during the last campaign. Properly enough Sheriff Goodell refused to appoint him as a deputy when he assumed office. How matters will be arranged and how the cattle men will be protected is one of the problems for future solution.[16]

As controversy about his ability as a lawman swirled around him, Ed made a half-hearted try at a more mundane kind of work. In January 1901, with his cousin Tom McMahan as partner, he opened a wood and coal yard in Deming. But within a week his volatile personality was more than McMahan could stand, and the partnership was dissolved.[17] Scarborough tried to run the operation by himself for a time, but when in April he got the chance to pin on a badge again as a town constable, he grabbed it. Soon thereafter the cattlemen's association rehired him as a detective, his commission as a Grant County deputy sheriff was restored, and he was back in the law enforcement business.[18]

In the months following the murder of George Scarborough, law officers throughout the Southwest had searched in vain for those responsible for that crime. Certainly none of them had a greater incentive to bring the killers to justice than the dead officer's son, and more than a year after his father's death Ed captured one of the leading suspects.

Tod Carver was believed to be a member of the vicious gang that shot and killed two pursuing possemen from St. Johns, Apache County, Arizona, a few days before mortally wounding George Scarborough. Following those violent clashes, Carver laid low in Texas for a year before drifting back into the New Mexico–Arizona border country. Ed Scarborough, tipped off to his reappearance by informants, kept on his trail for several months. With a fellow officer named Ed Halverson, he finally located Carver's camp in the mountains. According to a newspaper report, when he stepped out with a drawn revolver, there was a verbal exchange that sounded very much like dialog from a western dime novel:

Scarborough: "Up with your hands!"

Carver: "Not for any officer!"

Scarborough: "Up with your hands or you'll soon be in hell!"

"Then," said the paper, "the outlaw's hands went up."[19]

The officers took their prisoner to St. Johns, Arizona, where he was charged with the murder of the two possemen. "There is not much doubt that this criminal [was] one of the murderers of our beloved townsmen Frank LeSueur and Augustus Gibbons fifteen months ago today," said the *St. Johns Herald*. "That he is Tod Carver there is no doubt. There is a pretty clear case against him."[20]

Although the folks in St. Johns were more concerned that punishment be meted out in the matter of their murdered friends, over in Grant County, New Mexico, there was greater interest in bringing to justice one of the killers of George Scarborough. Said the *Silver City Enterprise*: "Deputy Sheriff Ed Scarborough of Deming . . . seems very modest and reticent over his famous capture, [but] it is believed Carver is the man who shot and killed the father of young Scarborough."[21]

The capture made news as far away as Sonora, Texas, where the *Devil River News* reported that as one of the late Black Jack Ketchum gang, Carver had been chased all over Texas, Arizona, and New Mexico. Charged with the murder of the two possemen in Arizona, he was also suspected of being one of the murderers of George Scarborough, and for more than a year the dead officer's son had "unremittingly" been on Carver's trail.[22]

Under his true name, T. C. Hilliard, Carver was bound over at St. Johns for action of the Apache County grand jury, but he also faced a charge of killing two other lawmen in Utah in May 1900. The Arizona officials turned the prisoner over to the Utah authorities, but six months later the charges in Utah were dropped because of insufficient evidence, and Carver was released. He disappeared and never answered to the pending murder charges in either Arizona or New Mexico.[23]

In 1901 the legislature of Arizona approved the formation of a company of rangers to combat increased outlawry in the territory. The first captain appointed to head up this new force of lawmen was Burt Mossman, a tough cowman from the vast Aztec Land and Cattle Company, or Hashknife outfit, as it was better known. On August 30 Mossman began interviewing applicants for the Arizona Rangers, and on September 6 Ed Scarborough was one of the first four men to sign enlistment papers.[24]

His enlistment was hailed in a Tucson newspaper, which noted that "the daring young Arizona Ranger" had recently been on the trail of a notorious rustler gang led by Bill Smith. "If necessary, I will devote the rest of my life to the capture of the Smith outlaws, one of whom is the slayer of my father," Scarborough was quoted. "He is a determined fellow and much like his father," said the newspaper. "When he joined the Arizona Rangers this fall it was considered one of Captain Mossman's best acquisitions. Scarborough was brought up in the saddle and is an excellent marksman. He don't know what fear is and when he succeeds in coming up with the Smith outlaws, a lively scrap can safely be promised."[25]

But Scarborough did not catch up with the Smith gang, and his service with the Rangers was short and undistinguished. Captain Mossman soon discovered that the young man was very different from his father, whom Mossman had respected as "one of the most efficient peace officers the Southwest ever had." Ed, the captain learned, "was a bit on the harum-scarum side, and traveled quite a little on his father's reputation."[26]

Ed Scarborough had previously given the captain some trouble with minor infractions, but when Mossman rode into Tombstone one day in May 1902 and found that the hotheaded young man had started a fight in the courthouse, he knew it was time to crack down. County officers had subdued Scarborough but, reluctant to jail an Arizona Ranger, had turned him loose.

Mossman confronted Scarborough in a livery stable and barked: "You're under arrest!"

Startled by this unexpected announcement by his superior, Scarborough's quick temper erupted, and he started to draw his gun. Mossman knocked him down with a single blow. Scarborough fell under the horses, and Mossman later said the young man was lucky he did not get kicked to death.

Mossman, just preparing to leave on a scout, turned Scarborough over to Sheriff Del Lewis, with instructions to jail him until he returned.

The scout lasted almost three weeks, during which time Scarborough pulled every string he knew, including an appeal to the Arizona governor, to get out of the Tombstone calaboose, but Sheriff Lewis followed the Ranger captain's directive and kept Scarborough locked up. When Mossman returned, he escorted Scarborough to Ranger headquarters at Bisbee, where on May 31 Scarborough was formally discharged from the service. The captain was generous, at the last, indicating "services no longer required" as the reason for the discharge, and evaluating the young man's character as "good."[27]

In an interview many years later, Mossman said that "[Ed Scarborough] was one of our Rangers for a while. I gave him a bob-tail discharge. He was a worthless kind, dangerous too, would kill a man."[28]

This would not be the last time that Ed Scarborough found lodgings in the Tombstone jail, but for the present he was a free man, and he quickly took a job in the Tombstone area, working as a range inspector for the Boquillas Land and Cattle Company, popularly known as the "Wagon Rods." The very next day following his discharge from the Rangers the *Tombstone Epitaph* noted: "Detective Ed Scarborough was to the city today. Ed is now permanently located on the San Pedro."[29]

But from the time of Scarborough's discharge from the Arizona Rangers, the once-promising lawman's life spiraled ever downward. By December 1902 he was back in Deming, where officers arrested him on a charge of "unlawfully carrying a deadly weapon." Prominent New Mexico attorney James S. Fielder, who represented him in this case, managed to gain one continuance after another, and the charge was formally dropped four years later.[30]

New Mexico authorities issued a warrant for his arrest on a bunco charge in the fall of 1903, and Arizona officers got on his trail. In reporting the story, the *Phoenix Republican* pointed out once again the continually widening disparity between George Scarborough's exem-

Prison photograph of George Edgar Scarborough as a thirty-seven-
year-old convict incarcerated at the Arizona State Prison, Florence.
Courtesy of the Lamborn Collection, Kansas State Historical Society, Topeka.

plary career in law enforcement and the tarnished record his son was creating:

> Ed Scarborough, a former resident of this city, is wanted in New Mexico on a charge of buncoing a man out of $150. He is the son of the late George Scarborough, who made such a good reputation in New Mexico as a brave and efficient officer, and was afterward murdered by a gang of outlaws. [Ed] Scarborough, it is said, accepted $150 from a New Mexico man for recovering a bunch of strayed cattle. After he took the money nothing more was seen of him. While in Bisbee he is reported to have cashed several checks of his own on the bank of Douglas without ever having had funds in the bank. For several days thereafter he was known to be in Aqua Prieta, Mexico, just over the line from Douglas, thinking Mexico a healthier place for him than Arizona, but the officers were unable to get him across the line. Friday he took the train for Nacozarlo.[31]

Somehow dodging that alleged illegality, Ed some months later even managed to secure an appointment as constable at Douglas, Arizona. But in March 1904 he became involved in an incident at Douglas that newspapers across the Southwest picked up and reported, making him an object of ridicule.

The newspaper in Deming, the town that had been his home for years, began its story with the mandatory mention of the stark difference between the behavior of the almost sainted George Scarborough and his son:

> The following graphic account of an encounter between Ed Scarborough and a valiant bicycle rider at Douglas will be read with great interest by our readers, to many of whom Ed is well known. Scarborough's father, George, was at one time a respected citizen of Deming and probably had more friends in this community than any man who, as a pronounced "gun man" ever lived here. But not so with Ed. His conduct has for years led the people to look upon him as one with whom they want little to do.[32]

Headlining its story: "SCARBOROUGH HUMILIATED. ATTEMPTS A BULLDOZING GAME AS AN OFFICER AND COMES TO GRIEF," the Deming paper printed the report out of

Douglas, relating how "Bad Man Scarborough," the "erstwhile terror," had been "tamed" by Rube Shields, a trick bicycle rider:

Scarborough has lived upon his bad-man reputation for a long time. He has never walked out without a big revolver strapped to him, and backed up with his weapon, his language has flowed freely. He has howled many tenderfeet into the idea that he was more dangerous than Alkali Ike or a regiment of Indians, and that whipping his weight in wildcats was like eating hot cakes for breakfast. So when Rube Shields, a mild mannered bicycle rider, rode into town, Scarborough, the village cut-up, planned his downfall.

Shields was on his wheel riding fancy figures in front of the Cattle Exchange wet goods store. An admiring crowd stood around him. Scarborough, the unbridled scourge of the plains, introduced himself.

"Get off the highway, young feller," he said, addressing himself to the pale-faced bicycle rider.

"Don't bother me, please," said the boy. "I'm doing a difficult trick."

"Don't talk back to me," roared Scarborough. "I'm the constable here, and I won't stand for any foolishness. Jump!"

To enforce his remarks Scarborough drew his nine-pound gun and began to shoot at the front wheel of Shields' bicycle. The crowd looked on in terror lest the constable should shoot the poor stranger. "Bang, bang, bang!" rang out the pistol shots upon the clean air. Scarborough, laughing heartily at his fun, continued to shoot until something occurred to him. The bicyclist was the cause of it.

Young Shields had turned suddenly on his wheel, put his head down, thrown all his strength into the pedals, and smashed directly into the constable. Scarborough was rolled over and over, cursing enthusiastically.

Shields jumped from the wheel, grabbed the constable by the throat, took his gun away from him, and then, taking his time about the matter and proceeding skillfully, he kicked Scarborough into a state of utter submission. Justice of the Peace Johnson then took charge of Scarborough and fined him. He let Shields go. Shields is now the hero of the hour and Scarborough goes around looking like a broken man with a secret sorrow.[33]

Completely humiliated by this incident, Scarborough quickly departed Douglas and Arizona Territory as well. He returned to Deming to lick the wounds to his injured ego, only to become involved a few months later in a stunt even more damaging to the shreds of his dignity. He fell to the level of a common stickup man, and attempted his heist disguised in a woman's dress.

He walked into the Harvey House restaurant at the Deming railroad depot at two o'clock on the morning of August 20, 1904, wearing a Mother Hubbard dress, a woman's silk stocking over his head, and his face obscured by a handkerchief. At the point of a Colt's six-shooter, he relieved the clerk on duty of $24, all the money in the till, which he stuffed into another stocking. He then marched the clerk and another man present several hundred yards up the track, where he released them with a warning not to sound an alarm or they would be killed. He then disappeared into the shadows.

Ignoring the threat, the two men sent for the law. Sheriff D. B. Stephens arrived to find Ed Scarborough, characterized in one paper as "a well known character throughout the southwest,"[34] seated at the lunch counter with two other men, calmly eating. He was now dressed normally, but the robbery victims claimed they recognized him as the holdup man. The sheriff arrested Scarborough and his companions on suspicion. When officers searched a room in the rear of the Ranch Saloon where Scarborough had been staying, they found the dress and stocking cap used in the holdup. The other stocking was found in a water closet behind the saloon, but the money was gone. Later the dress was identified as belonging to Oro Little, a woman with whom Scarborough had "been quite intimate of late."[35] When questioned, this woman admitted the dress was hers, and she had loaned it to Scarborough. On the basis of this evidence, authorities bound Scarborough over for action by the grand jury, and on August 22 he was released on $5,000 bail.[36] A man named Lester Noah, who had recently arrived in Deming from El Paso with Scarborough, was also charged as being an accessory to the crime. Appearing in the press was a wild, totally unfounded report that Ed was the leader of a "gang of seven men who had planned to hold up one of the Southern Pacific trains."[37]

In December a grand jury brought in indictments against Ed Scarborough, charging him with robbery, assault with intent to rob, and two counts of assault with a deadly weapon.[38] His attorney, James

Fielder, requested and was granted a change of venue. The case was moved from Deming to Silver City, where the wily Fielder employed his stalling tactics, requesting and receiving continuances for several years until the charges were eventually dropped.[39]

Ed Scarborough's troubles with the law continued. In the spring of 1909 officers from Socorro County, New Mexico, sought his arrest as a common horse thief. On June 22 of that year the county's district attorney, John E. Griffith, wrote Fred Fornoff, captain of the recently organized New Mexico Mounted Police: "A recent grand jury returned two indictments against your friend Ed. Scarborough for larceny of a horse. If you can find him the service will be appreciated." A wanted notice was issued for Ed Scarborough and Jesse Ely for horse theft. Scarborough, it said, was about thirty-two years of age (he was thirty), had relatives in El Paso, and was "known all over the southwest and has been in trouble before."[40] It seems Scarborough once again escaped the clutches of the law on these charges, probably by staying out of New Mexico Territory.

By 1912 he was living in Los Angeles and working as a carpenter. His residence was listed in the Los Angeles city directory for that year as 326 East Fifty-fifth Street, next door to his widowed mother and his eighteen-year-old brother, Ray, whose occupation was listed as "apprentice."

Twelve years after the death of his father, Ed was still obsessed with bringing the killers to justice. In March 1912 he read in a paper that Ben Kilpatrick, a member of the gang Ed believed responsible for his father's murder, had been killed in a botched train holdup near Sanderson, Texas.

Arrested in 1901 and sent to prison, Kilpatrick gained his release in 1911, but returned to his criminal ways and, together with a bandit companion named Ole Beck, met his demise at the hands of a tough and determined express messenger at Sanderson. The messenger, D. A. Trousdale, brained Kilpatrick with an ice mallet and killed Beck with Kilpatrick's rifle.

On March 29, 1912, Ed wrote the warden of the federal penitentiary at Atlanta, Georgia, where Kilpatrick had been incarcerated:

> I was surprised a few days ago to hear that one of the men
> that was killed in attempted train robbery in western Texas was

Ben Kilpatrick whom you had in your prison for handling some unsigned currency that was claimed to have got in a train robbery in Colorado in 1901 or 1902.

As I was under the impression that he was to serve 20 yrs. in your prison.

I don't recognize the dead train robber picture as Kilpatricks [*sic*], but have not seen him since 1900 in New Mex.

This man Kilpatrick and some others of his gang waylayed [*sic*] and killed my father who was an officer at the time.

If you would kindly send me one of Kilpatricks pictures taken at the time of his release I would consider it a great favor as it would enable me to identify him from the picture taken of the dead bandit that is claimed to be Kilpatrick.

P.S. There was never a warrant sworn out for him for my father's murder but I know he did and if I can get on his trail if he is alive I can be able to prove it. My father was sheriff in Jones Co Tex from 85 until 89. Deputy U.S.M. under Dick Ware from 92 until 94.

On April 5 the warden responded to Ed's inquiry, informing him that the man of interest "was John Arnold, a man of many aliases, but whose true name was Ben Kilpatrick, a resident of Concho County, Texas."[41]

After receiving this letter, and with the knowledge that other members of the gang he held responsible had been killed or fled to Central and South America, Ed Scarborough may have finally abandoned his twelve-year quest to hunt down his father's killers; his later record, at least, gives no indication that his obsession drove him on.

He was, however, too restless to remain in a city, employed in the mundane occupation of a carpenter. By 1915 he was back punching cattle for the Boquillas Land and Cattle Company, and it was here that his volatile temperament and propensity for gunplay embroiled him in his most serious difficulty with the law.

John Clinton, who had settled on a small spread nine miles south of Hereford and only two miles from the Mexican border, ran his little herd of cattle on land adjacent to the Boquillas pasture. When Scarborough accused him of allowing his steers to graze over onto the neighboring property, words were exchanged. At one point Scarborough "had drawn a gun upon Clinton, who laughed the cowboy out of the notion of shooting."[42]

On the evening of June 18, 1915, Scarborough and a cowboy named Cal Cox rode up to the Clinton place. Scarborough dismounted, approached the house, and asked Clinton to step outside. Having just finished supper, the rancher had pulled off his boots in preparation for bed, but he donned a pair of moccasins and walked outside with Scarborough. A few minutes later Clinton's wife and young daughter heard the men's voices rising in anger. There was swearing and shouting and then the roar of gunshots. They ran into the yard to find Clinton, with four gunshot wounds in his body, breathing his last. Scarborough and Cox had galloped off, trailing a cloud of dust that indicated they were headed south, toward the nearby international line.

Rose Clinton sent word to Cochise County Sheriff Harry C. Wheeler in Tombstone that her husband had been gunned down by parties unknown.[43] Wheeler dispatched two deputies to the scene. After viewing the body and talking to the wife and daughter, the officers followed the trail left by the suspects and found that they had separated, one continuing on south, while the other had reversed directions and ridden north toward Benson and the main line of the Southern Pacific Railroad. They telephoned ahead, and the next morning officers apprehended Ed Scarborough as he rode into Benson. They took him to Tombstone, where he was jailed on suspicion of murder.[44]

Judge George R. Smith of Lowell later that day conducted an inquest at the scene of the shooting. An examination of the body revealed that Clinton had been shot four times—twice in the stomach, once in the right side, and once in the right leg. Rose Clinton and her daughter, Rosie, testified that Ed Scarborough was the man who came to the door, but they did not recognize his companion. The coroner's jury heard testimony regarding Clinton's previous confrontations with Scarborough. Based on the evidence revealed at the inquest, Scarborough was held without bail pending a preliminary hearing scheduled for the following week.[45]

Cal Cox was also found and arrested. Faced with an accessory to murder charge, he joined Scarborough in the Tombstone jail.

In response to rumors that the Wagon Rods outfit had sent Scarborough to deal with Clinton and that the killing had been done to further the interests of the big cattle company, Henry K. Street, ranch superintendent, a few days later published a letter in the Bisbee newspaper intended to quash the suspicion. "None of the employees of this company," he said, "has ever had a dispute with Mr. Clinton over the rights of his property or over any other question until this affair came up between him and Scarborough last Friday." He advised everyone to wait to see what Scarborough's preliminary examination revealed, as the false reports circulating were doing his company "a great injustice."[46]

That examination was scheduled to be held at Lowell on June 28 before Judge Smith. But Scarborough's attorney, Eugene S. Ives of Tucson, was not able to appear in his client's behalf. After a long-distance telephone conversation with his counsel, Scarborough declined to testify and was returned to his cell in Tombstone.

Cal Cox had been taken by automobile from Tombstone to Lowell to testify as a witness at the hearing. He sat in the front seat, and Clinton's sister, who had also been called to testify, rode in the back. During the trip the woman suddenly reached forward, grasped Cox by the throat, and attempted to throttle him. Only with great difficulty were officers able to release Cox from the grip of the enraged woman.[47]

The preliminary hearing for Cox's involvement in the Clinton shooting was held in Tombstone before a Judge Fowler on July 7. Witnesses testified they had heard Cox make threats against Clinton. Taking the stand, Cox said he had gone to the Clinton place at Scarborough's request, had not dismounted when Scarborough approached the house, and had heard an argument but could not make out the words as he was partly deaf. He heard the shots and saw the flash of a gun in the darkness. Scarborough had then "ordered" him to ride for the Mexican border. Both suspects were held without bail in the Cochise County jail at Tombstone.[48]

The two were arraigned separately. The arraignment for Scarborough was conducted on November 13, with trial set for superior court on December 2. Judge Alfred C. Lockwood presided at the trial, with the prosecution led by County Attorney John F. Ross, assisted by Bruce Stevenson and special prosecutor William B. Cleary, said to be the "best known criminal lawyer in the southern part of the state."[49] Representing Scarborough were Eugene S. Ives and Frank W. Doan.

A number of witnesses were called by the state, including Rose Clinton, but undoubtedly the most effective was little Rosie, the daughter, who answered all questions "without falter" and appeared to gain much sympathy from the jury members for the prosecution's case.[50]

Several well-known lawmen, including Jeff Milton and Harry Wheeler, were called by the defense to testify as to Scarborough's contributions as a peace officer, but the most important witness was the defendant himself. Ed was on the stand for most of two days and was subjected to severe cross-examination. He said he believed Clinton had stolen some of his calves and had argued with the man over this issue on several occasions. When he confronted Clinton in the yard of his house that fateful evening, they had argued again. Only when Clinton called out to his wife, "Mamma, get the rifle and kill him!" had he drawn his pistol and fired, as he believed his life was in danger.[51]

At the specific request of defense counsel, Judge Lockwood instructed the jury:

> If you believe that Clinton seized the defendant and prior to any shot by the defendant or effort by the defendant to shoot, said in effect, referring to Mrs. Clinton, "Mamma, get the rifle and kill him," referring by killing him to the defendant, and that at such time the defendant, as a reasonable man, believed himself in danger of death or great bodily injury, and acting under such belief, shot and killed Clinton, the homicide was justified and your verdict should be not guilty.[52]

The jury, however, did not buy this story. Retiring at five o'clock on the evening of December 10 to deliberate, it returned at eleven the next morning with a verdict of murder in the second degree. Judge Lockwood that afternoon sentenced Ed Scarborough to a term of ten years to life in the state penitentiary.[53]

One Arizona editor approved of the verdict and sentence, saying that it was an indication that the days of judicial lenience toward western frontier violence were finally over:

> The other day a man was convicted at Tombstone of murder in the second degree. The killing took place at the house of the victim when he was called out in the nighttime and shot down. The settings of the crime were those of the old Arizona days, of the days of Curly Bill. It looked like plain assassination and

there was nothing to remove that appearance except the word of the murderer and another man who was jointly indicted with him for the crime. Nine of the jurors believed it was assassination and they voted for a verdict of murder in the first degree. One juryman thought that second degree murder had been committed and one favored manslaughter. The remaining juryman, who must have been a person of superior superhuman intelligence, voted for acquittal. A compromise verdict was then agreed upon. Considering the verdicts of Cochise County jurors in the recent past in murder cases, where cold-blooded slayers have been acquitted because they stated that they thought their unarmed victims had "motioned toward their hip pockets," we think this verdict of second degree murder is something of an advance.[54]

The following week Cal Cox stood trial for complicity in the murder of John Clinton and was acquitted.[55]

Meanwhile, while his attorney appealed the verdict on technical grounds, Scarborough languished for five months in the county jail. The Tombstone calaboose was packed with a total of fifty-one prisoners, four of whom, including Scarborough, were charged with murder.[56] Tiring finally of the delay and anxious to get out of the cramped facilities, Scarborough in May 1916 instructed lawyer Ives to drop the appeal.[57] On May 19, 1916, he entered the Arizona State Prison at Florence and became Inmate No. 4787.[58]

Within months after Scarborough went to prison his wife, Ruby, filed for divorce. As soon as the decree became final, she married a railroad conductor named Omar A. Ash and moved to Douglas. When he heard this, Scarborough reportedly swore "vengeance on both his former wife and on Ash and vowed he would escape from the pen and kill them both."[59]

Another story also circulated that Ed felt betrayed by politicians who had promised an early pardon if he would withdraw his appeal, a pardon that never came.[60]

In any case, on the night of May 25, 1917, a little over a year after entering the prison, Ed Scarborough went over the wall with two other convicts, Bob Pitts and George Townsend. Officers recaptured Pitts and Townsend near Roswell, New Mexico, but Ed eluded them.[61]

Lawmen in Douglas, Arizona, and environs were especially alert. Said the *Tombstone Epitaph*: "Being a gunman of the worst known type, it is feared that [Scarborough] will make his way to Douglas where Mr. and Mrs. Ash now reside and attempt to carry out his threat. Officers all along the line have been warned to be on the lookout and Ash has been notified to be on his guard while efforts are being made to effect his capture."[62]

Ed Scarborough apparently never attempted to harm Ruby or her husband, nor does it appear he ever tried to contact his daughter, Corrine. In 1920 Omar and Ruby were still living peaceably in Douglas with Ash's fifteen-year-old son, George, and Corrine, now twenty and working as a stenographer. Whether or not Ash had legally adopted her, Corrine had dropped the surname "Scarborough" and was using the name "Ash."[63]

Ed broke off contact with his family and disappeared into old Mexico, where he cowboyed and eventually established a ranch. As late as 1928 the superintendent of the Arizona Penitentiary at Florence, former Cochise County sheriff Scott White, was still offering a reward of $100 for information leading to his capture.[64]

His mother, Mollie, lived out her last years in the home of Eva, one of her daughters, in southern California. According to family tradition, Ed would "sneak over every once in a while from his ranch — he had a Mexican ranch over there — and stay with [his mother] some and then scoot back because he still hadn't been pardoned."[65] After his mother died in 1949, the family lost all track of him.

Afterword

During the age of the western gunfighter, an era that lasted from the Civil War until the early years of the twentieth century, the state of Texas was widely recognized as a spawning ground for the breed. Some of the most celebrated gunmen — John Wesley Hardin, Ben Thompson, Luke Short, Bill Longley — were native Texans, as were many of the less publicized. Note was made in the first volume of *Deadly Dozen* that the Lone Star State contributed a disproportionate share of the subjects studied, as a quarter of the twelve were born in the state.

The disproportionality holds true in this volume, as a total of four, or a third of the dozen reviewed, were Texas born. John Owens, Jesse Rascoe, Tom Tucker, and Ed Scarborough were all born in Texas, although most of their lethal activity took place in other states and territories. Conversely, many of the remaining eight, born in five other states and one foreign country, gained their gun-fighting notoriety in Texas. Zack Light of New York, Jack Watson of Tennessee, Joel Fowler of South Carolina, and Jim Sherman and Burk Burnett of Missouri were always thought of as Texans, for it was there that they gained notoriety as gunmen.

Fearless men of demonstrated gun-wielding ability were called on to enforce the law on the turbulent frontier, so not surprisingly, many of the subjects pinned on a badge at some stage of their careers. Seven of the twelve studied (Watson, Owens, Rascoe, Sherman, Jolly, Tucker, and Scarborough) were lawmen of some sort. John Owens and Jesse Rascoe spent the final years of their checkered careers as honored and respected peace officers in their communities.

Other than law enforcement, the business of cattle raising attracted the majority of the twelve. Seven (Fowler, Rascoe, Sherman, Light, Tucker, Scarborough, and most notably, Burnett, who acquired a fortune) spent much of their adult lives ranching or tending cattle.

Watson and Jolly were blacksmiths by trade, Moon and Owens pursued the sporting life (although Owens also ranched on the side), and Currie was a railroad engineer.

The terrible War between the States and the tumultuous Reconstruction period in the South following the war played a significant part in the development of the characters of the men who grew to adulthood during this period, for the war and its aftermath undoubtedly inured them all to violence. Four of the men chronicled here were veterans of the Civil War, two on each side: Jim Moon and Jim Currie served in the Union army; Jack Watson and John Owens wore the gray of the Confederacy.

Before the war even began, ten-year-old Jim Sherman saw men maddened by the bitter North-South issue shoot his father dead before his eyes, and the traumatic event scarred him emotionally for life.

Jesse Rascoe, too young to fight for the Confederacy, came of age during the bloody Reconstruction period in Texas and, like John Wesley Hardin and Bill Longley and other unreconstructed Texans, was drawn into outlawry.

Ironically, the war may have had a beneficial effect on the character of Burk Burnett, who, when his father went off to war, was left at the age of eleven as the male head of his family. He soon developed strong virtues of self-reliance and independence, qualities that served him so well in later years as he acquired a fortune. But those early turbulent years also hardened him so that he did not flinch when faced with a gunfight, as he proved on two occasions.

Education for most of the twelve was rudimentary, probably limited to elementary school; several left home at an early age, either to join the military or seek a fortune in the West. Joel Fowler, however, was said to have read for the law in the offices of his lawyer uncle.

All but two, Jim Currie and Jack Watson, were married, and at least half of them fathered children.

Three of the twelve spent time in prison, sent there for murder or attempted murder. Jim Currie did time in the New Mexico territorial penitentiary at Santa Fe, Jack Jolly at the Montana territorial penitentiary at Deer Lodge, and Ed Scarborough at the Arizona State Penitentiary at Florence. None of them completed their sentences.

As might be expected, given the hazards of the gun-fighting life, five of the men chronicled here died violently. Moon, Watson, Sherman, and Light were shot to death, and Fowler was lynched for his crimes by an angry mob. Two were crippled for life by gunshot wounds — Watson, with a leg wound suffered in the Civil War, and Rascoe, who had an arm shot off in a gun battle. Jolly and Tucker, severely injured by gunfire, were expected to die, but surprised everyone by surviving and going on to further adventures.

Most surprising, perhaps, was the longevity these twelve gunfighters managed to achieve. The youngest to die was Zack Light, shot dead at the age of thirty-eight. He was the only one not to reach the age of forty. Moon, Fowler, and Sherman were in their forties when they died violently; Currie and Watson were in their fifties. Tucker lived to be sixty-four, and Jolly was in his sixties when last heard from. Burnett died peacefully at the age of seventy-three and Rascoe at age seventy-seven. Ed Scarborough is believed to have lived at least into his seventies.

And so these twelve men, heroes and villains, lived by the gun and played out their parts in the drama of the American frontier, in a time and place where violence was often the norm. Feared and hated by some of their contemporaries, respected and admired by others, they contributed to the western gunfighter mystique that fascinated people of their time and continues to fascinate many today.

Notes

INTRODUCTION

1. Arthur Shoemaker, in the *Tulsa* (Oklahoma) *World*, January 4, 2004.
2. Garton, "Book Reviews."
3. *San Angelo* (Texas) *Standard-Times*, December 15, 2003.
4. Massey, "Book Reviews."
5. O'Brien, "Book Reviews."
6. Brown, *No Duty to Retreat*, 39–41.

CHAPTER 1

1. Cowan, "Memories."
2. *Rocky Mountain News* (Denver), June 17, 1881.
3. There are conflicting reports of the unit in which Moon was said to have served during the war. One newspaper reported that he enlisted in the Forty-fourth Iowa Infantry (*Denver Republican*, June 17, 1881). A later article quoted Moon's wife as saying he "served throughout the Civil War with the 12th Illinois Cavalry" (Guinn, "Timely End of Jim Moon," 31). Attempts to verify either report in the National Archives have failed.
4. *Denver Daily Times*, June 17, 1881.
5. *Denver Republican*, June 17, 1881.
6. *Rocky Mountain News* (Denver), June 17, 1881.
7. *Denver Daily Times*, June 17, 1881.
8. *Topeka* (Kansas) *Daily Commonwealth*, September 17, 1871.
9. *Rocky Mountain News* (Denver), February 13, 1899. After a long and eventful career, Joe Lowe would be gunned down in Denver, the same town in which Jim Moon met his end in the same fashion eighteen years earlier.
10. *Rocky Mountain News* (Denver), June 17, 1881.
11. *Denver Republican*, June 17, 1881.
12. Ibid.
13. Ibid.
14. Ibid.; *Denver Daily Times*, June 17, 1881.
15. *Denver Daily Times*, June 17, 1881.
16. Ibid.
17. *Rocky Mountain News* (Denver), June 17, 1881.
18. For an account of John Bull's career, see DeArment, *Deadly Dozen*, 6–18.

19. *Rocky Mountain News* (Denver), November 30, 1880.

20. Ibid., October 15, 1880.

21. Ibid.

22. Ibid.

23. Ibid., November 30, 1880.

24. *Butte* (Montana) *Daily Miner*, June 24, 1881.

25. Cowan, "Memories."

26. *Butte* (Montana) *Daily Miner*, June 24, 1881.

27. Collier and Westrate, *Dave Cook of the Rockies*, 207. Another member of the sporting fraternity who assisted the city police in putting down the riot was Clay Wilson, who a year later was to play a major role in the Jim Moon story (ibid).

28. Cowan, "Memories."

29. Frank Marshall, the wayward son of a former Kansas governor, ten years later would shoot John Clow, a prominent prizefighter, to death in another notorious Denver resort, Murphy's Exchange, and at trial be acquitted by a jury. Bat Masterson, Clow's erstwhile manager, would comment bitterly "that it was no crime for the degenerate son of wealthy parents to kill a prizefighter without cause or provocation" (Parkhill, *Wildest of the West*, 92; W. B. Masterson column in the *New York Morning Telegraph*, April 26, 1914).

30. *Rocky Mountain News* (Denver), November 25, 1880; *Denver Daily Times*, June 17, 1881.

31. *Rocky Mountain News* (Denver), November 25, 1880.

32. *Denver Daily Times*, June 17, 1881.

33. Ibid. Moon's notoriety received national attention at this time when he was featured in an issue of the *National Police Gazette*. The *Rocky Mountain News* of January 15, 1881, took note: "James Moon was 'illustrated' between two murderers in a recent copy of the Police Gazette. The portrait does him proud, but he is entitled to be seen in much better company."

34. She was enumerated on June 8, 1880, at Salt Lake City. She gave her name to enumerator William McCurdy as "Emma DeMarr," which would suggest that she was never married to Moon as she claimed, or that she was so angry with him she adopted her maiden name. Also it is curious that both she and her sister, Perl, said they had been born in "Libia" to German parents (U.S. Census, Salt Lake County, Utah, 1880).

35. *Denver Republican*, June 17, 1881.

36. Ibid.; *Rocky Mountain News* (Denver), June 17, 1881; Guinn, "Timely End of Jim Moon," 28.

37. Lundin told a reporter that he had known Moon in Texas and Virginia City, where Moon had always been known as a "fighting man." Moon, he said, had once told him that his real name was James Hickok, who, of course, as "Wild Bill" was probably the most celebrated "fighting man" of the West. "Never knew of his killing any one except Hall," Lundin admitted, "but had seen him draw a gun" (*Denver Daily Times*, June 17, 1881).

38. Ibid.

39. Ibid.

40. Ibid.

41. *Denver Republican*, June 17, 1881.

42. *Rocky Mountain News* (Denver), June 17, 1881.

43. Ibid.

44. *Denver Republican*, June 17, 1881.

45. *Denver Daily Times*, June 17, 1881; *Rocky Mountain News* (Denver), July 8, 1881; *Denver Daily News*, September 17, 1881.

46. *Butte* (Montana) *Daily Miner*, June 24, 1881.

47. *Denver Daily News*, September 17, 1881; *Rocky Mountain News* (Denver), September 17, 1881. In an interview with a reporter a few months later, a Sergeant Foulkes of the Denver police department said: "There are hundreds of these small confidence men and tin-horn gamblers in the city. There are not so many of these hard characters as there used to be, though. Jim Moon is dead and Slim Jim and Denver have been driven out of town. If we can get rid of 'Doc' Baggs now, I think we shall have got rid of all the worst ones" (*Rocky Mountain News* [Denver], January 24, 1882).

48. *Colorado Springs* (Colorado) *Daily Gazette*, September 18, 1881.

49. Ibid., September 23, 1881.

50. *Denver Daily Times*, June 17, 1881.

51. *Rocky Mountain News* (Denver), June 17, 1881.

52. Guinn, "Timely End of Jim Moon," 31.

53. *Denver Republican*, reprinted in the *Butte* (Montana) *Daily Miner*, March 21, 1882; Guinn, "Timely End of Jim Moon," 28.

54. *Colorado Springs* (Colorado) *Daily Gazette*, March 18, April 8, 30, 1882; February 13, 1883.

55. Guinn, "Timely End of Jim Moon," 31.

CHAPTER 2

1. The name often appears as "Curry," even in documents signed by James, but the man was only semiliterate. His better-educated brother, Andrew, mayor of Shreveport, Louisiana, spelled it "Currie," which is believed to be correct and is employed throughout except when used in direct quotes. Researchers into the life of Currie have experienced considerable difficulty because there were at least three Jim Currys (or Curries) working as railroad men in the West during the 1870s and 1880s, two of them gamblers and known gunmen and killers (Rasch, "Killer Next to Wild Bill"; Criqui, *Fifty Fearless Men*, 80).

2. Masterson, "Famous Gunfighters, Ben Thompson"; Masterson, "Famous Gunfighters, Luke Short."

3. *Biographical and Historical Memoirs of Northwest Louisiana*, 60; Criqui, *Fifty Fearless Men*, 65. An early chronicler of Currie's misadventures said that he "was of a prominent and well known Southern family, schooled and educated in the customs and traditions of his illustrious ancestors" (Seymour, "Shooting of Maurice Barrymore," 1), but there is no evidence to support this assertion.

4. *Marshall* (Texas) *Tri-Weekly Herald*, March 20, 1879.

5. *Fort Worth* (Texas) *Daily Democrat*, April 3, 1879; O'Neal, "Jim Currie vs. Maurice Barrymore," 55.

6. Curry, "Declaration for Original Invalid Pension," May 17, 1890; Curry, "Declaration for Invalid Pension"; *Fort Worth* (Texas) *Daily Democrat*, April 3, 1879; Criqui, *Fifty Fearless Men*, 66–67.

7. John F. Dickson, former general superintendent of the Texas Pacific Railroad, in a letter to the *New York Herald*, reprinted in the *Marshall* (Texas) *Tri-Weekly Herald*, January 1, 1880.

8. *Fort Leavenworth* (Kansas) *Daily Commercial*, October 21, 1870; Connelley, *Wild Bill*, 127; Rasch, "Killer Next to Wild Bill."

9. Miguel Otero, an early visitor to Ellsworth and Hays City, identified a few of these women by their "working" names: "Lousy Liz," "Stink-foot Mag," and "Steamboat." It would appear they were far from attractive (Otero, *My Life on the Frontier*, 11).

10. Bascom, "Early Sketches," 14.

11. Ibid., 3.

12. Otero, *My Life on the Frontier*, 9.

13. Ibid., 11.

14. Montgomery, "Fort Wallace," 17:234.

15. Criqui, *Fifty Fearless Men*, 67.

16. Grover (ca. 1825–69), a thirty-year plains veteran, was named chief of scouts for the expedition. He was still recovering from a wound received in a fight with Cheyennes a few weeks earlier in which another famed scout, Will Comstock, was killed. Grover himself was killed less than a year later at Pond City, Kansas, "in a row" with a man named John Morrissey (Thrapp, *Encyclopedia of Frontier Biography*, 2:593–94).

17. The notable career of Jack Stilwell (1849–1903) as a scout for the army for more than thirteen years, and later deputy U.S. marshal, police judge, and U.S. commissioner in Oklahoma, stood in sharp contrast to his brother, Frank, a gunman shot and killed by Wyatt Earp at Tucson, Arizona, in March 1882 (Thrapp, *Encyclopedia of Frontier Biography*, 3:1370–71).

18. Thayer (1821–1905) was an adventurer who at the age of sixteen ran off to sea and made four trips around the world. A veteran of the California and Colorado gold rushes and the Civil War, he was later elected sheriff at Hays City (Thrapp, *Encyclopedia of Frontier Biography*, 3:1415).

19. Whitney (1842–73) had been constable at Ellsworth before the Beecher Island fight. Later he was city marshal and sheriff at Ellsworth, where on August 15, 1873, he was accidentally shot and killed by Billy Thompson, the ne'er-do-well younger brother of the celebrated gunfighter Ben Thompson (Thrapp, *Encyclopedia of Frontier Biography*, 3:1561).

20. Jaastad, *Man of the West*, 29–30; Grinnell, *Fighting Cheyennes*, 277–78; Thrapp, *Encyclopedia of Frontier Biography*, 4:122–23.

21. Twenty-seven-year-old Fred Beecher was a nephew of the famous cleric Henry Ward Beecher.

22. Jaastad, *Man of the West*, 31. The fight came to be known as the Beecher Island Battle to honor the young officer who died there.

23. Whitney's diary is quoted in Grinnell, *Fighting Cheyennes*, 279–80. Whitney's entry for August 20 gives the killed and wounded figure. Other sources differ. Wilbur Sturdevant Nye in *Plains Indian Raiders* (125) wrote that in addition to Beecher and Mooer, six enlisted scouts were killed. Thrapp (*Encyclopedia of Frontier Biography*, 3:1299) lists the scout casualties as five killed and sixteen wounded.

24. Bascom, "Early Sketches," 9.

25. Shlesinger, "Battle of the Arikaree," 15:541. Shlesinger himself was described by scout G. W. Oaks as "a little New York Jewish lad . . . , about sixteen years old," really too young and inexperienced for the undertaking, but he begged Forsyth "so hard to go with us that the major turned to Beecher and said, 'Oh hell, Beecher, sign him up'" (Jaarstad, *Man of the West*, 29). In later interviews, several other Forsyth Scouts, including Allison Pliley, Thomas Ranahan, George Green, Howard Morton, and E. A. Gilbert, attested to Currie's participation in the battle. Pliley said Currie was to his immediate right all during the fight. All those interviewed agreed Currie was a "desperate fighter" (Criqui, *Fifty Fearless Men*, 65).

26. Criqui, *Fifty Fearless Men*, 68. Veteran scouts Thomas Ranahan and W. F. "Buffalo Bill" Cody were also on the Fort Hays rolls at $75 a month. Scouts Louis McLaughlin, Jack Stilwell, and Sharp Grover were on "special assignment" at $100 a month (ibid.).

27. War Department Records, quoted in ibid.

28. Ibid.

29. *Fort Leavenworth* (Kansas) *Daily Commercial*, October 21, 1870; Rasch, "Killer Next to Wild Bill."

30. *Kansas Daily Tribune* (Lawrence), April 18, 1869.

31. Criqui, *Fifty Fearless Men*, 68, quoting a semifictional piece, "A Romance of the Plains," by Colonel James A. Hadley, appearing in the *Sidney* (Ohio) *Sentinel*, July 26, 1906.

32. *Hays City* (Kansas) *Republican*, January 10, 1903.

33. *Kansas Daily Commonwealth* (Topeka), May 4, 1869; Beach, "Old Fort Hays," 580; Rasch, "Killer Next to Wild Bill"; Drees, "Curry." Beach wrote that "it does not appear that any citizens were killed," although "according to local memory," as many as six soldiers lost their lives in the fight. After nightfall, he said, a mob collected and "drove every negro citizen of the place" out of town (580). A famous photograph of two dead bodies lying near the doorway to Currie's Star Restaurant may well have been taken after this shooting.

34. DeMattos in a footnote (p. 24) to his 1982 edition of *Famous Gunfighters of the Western Frontier*, a reprinting of Bat Masterson's 1907–1908 magazine articles; Reynolds, *Trouble in New Mexico*, 2:345.

35. Drees, "Curry." This writer suggests that Snow may have been one of the black victims of the race riot of May 3 and 4.

36. Criqui, *Fifty Fearless Men*, quoting an item in the *Junction City Union*.

37. *Hays City* (Kansas) *Sentinel*, March 28, 1879; Andreas and Cutler, *History of the State of Kansas*, 1291; Criqui, *Fifty Fearless Men*, 72. According to Andreas and Cutler in their *History of the State of Kansas*, Currie made a habit of tossing dead bodies around: "He killed several colored men, some of whom he threw into a dry well" (1291). Presumably these were blacks, either soldiers or civilians, killed in the racial clashes of May 3 and 4, 1869.

38. Drees, "Curry."

39. *Fort Leavenworth* (Kansas) *Daily Commercial*, October 21, 1870; *Hays City* (Kansas) *Sentinel*, March 28, 1879.

40. Andreas and Cutler, *History of the State of Kansas*, 1291; *Marshall* (Texas) *Tri-Weekly Herald*, April 1, 1879.

41. Drees, "Curry." This researcher pointed out that Estes's actual name was Edward, Jr., and not James, as reported in the press.

42. Roenigk, *Pioneer History of Kansas*, 204.

43. *Fort Leavenworth* (Kansas) *Daily Commercial*, October 21, 1870.

44. Wilcox, "Street Duel."

45. *Junction City* (Kansas) *Union*, July 31, 1869; Burkey, *Wild Bill Hickok*, 5; Rosa, *Wild Bill Hickok*, 103. A. B. Webster later went to Dodge City, where he became mayor and a bitter enemy of Bat Masterson (see DeArment, *Bat Masterson*).

46. Cowan, "Memories of the Bad Man."

47. *Fort Worth* (Texas) *Daily Democrat*, March 29, 1879, quoting the *Cincinnati Inquirer*.

48. Connelley, *Wild Bill and His Era*, 127.

49. *Kansas City Star*, June 13, 1915.

50. Criqui, *Fifty Fearless Men*, 70.

51. *Denison* (Texas) *Daily News*, March 25, 1879.

52. *Leavenworth* (Kansas) *Times and Conservative*, December 5, 1869; Roenigk, *Pioneer History of Kansas*, 204.

53. Roenigk, *Pioneer History of Kansas*, 204.

54. Ibid.; Rasch, "Killer Next to Wild Bill."

55. *Fort Worth* (Texas) *Daily Democrat*, March 29, 1879, quoting the *Cincinnati Inquirer*.

56. Bascom, "Early Sketches," 4.

57. *Fort Worth* (Texas) *Daily Democrat*, March 29, 1879, quoting the *Cincinnati Inquirer*; Roenigk, *Pioneer History of Kansas*, 204; Bascom, "Early Sketches," 4.

58. *Fort Leavenworth* (Texas) *Daily Commercial*, October 21, 1870; Rasch, "Killer Next to Wild Bill." It is curious that Lute Wilcox, in his wild tale of the street duel between William H. H. McCall and Currie in Hays City, credited McCall and not Currie with shooting the women: "A few years later in Wichita while indulging in the luxury of a little brawl General McCall shot Ida May and another woman. . . . Subsequently he was killed in Arizona" ("Street Duel"). McCall was indeed a brevet brigadier general in the Civil

War, and he died in Arizona, but hepatitis killed him at Prescott in 1883, and not a bullet (Thrapp, *Encyclopedia of Frontier Biography*, 2:890).

59. *Wichita* (Kansas) *Vidette*, October 27, 1870. Ida May, alive and well, later moved her operation to Wichita. The *Wichita* (Kansas) *Eagle* of May 22, 1873, reported that "Rowdy Joe" Lowe was thrown from his horse in that city. "Picked up insensible, [he was] carried into the house of Ida May and a doctor sent for." On August 5, 1874, the *Wichita Beacon* reported that Ida May, "a woman of sin," paid a $10 fine for disorderly conduct. In Wichita, Ida May was said to be the paramour of a man named Gordon (Bartholomew, *Wyatt Earp*, 116–17).

60. *Fort Leavenworth* (Texas) *Daily Commercial*, October 21, 1870.

61. *Leavenworth* (Kansas) *Times and Conservative*, November 11, 1870.

62. *Austin* (Texas) *Daily Democratic Statesman*, March 23, 1879.

63. Possibly a relative of some kind.

64. King, "Maurice Barrymore," 34; Rasch, "Killer Next to Wild Bill."

65. John F. Dickson's letter to the *New York Herald*, reprinted in the *Marshall* (Texas) *Tri-Weekly Herald*, January 1, 1880.

66. *Goodland* (Kansas) *News-Republic*, February 17, 1927. Chester D. Potter, who later knew Currie in New Mexico, enhanced this story, writing that "it was charged [Currie] *on several occasions* increased the steam pressure by burning negroes for fuel" ("Reminiscences," 51).

67. Miller, *Sam Bass*, 153–54; Martin, *Sketch of Sam Bass*, 90–92; Gard, *Sam Bass*, 128–29.

68. Barrymore was his mother's maiden name.

69. Davis-Kotsilibas, *Great Times, Good Times*.

70. *Denison* (Texas) *Daily News*, April 2, 1879; *Fort Worth* (Texas) *Daily Democrat*, April 3, 1879.

71. Warde, *Fifty Years of Make Believe*, 173.

72. The dialogue presented here is from the testimony of Nathaniel A. Harvey as reported in the *Marshall* (Texas) *Tri-Weekly*, March 22, 1879.

73. Currie was armed with two .38-caliber Smith and Wesson pistols (Davis-Kotsilibas, *Great Times, Good Times*, 129).

74. *Daily Arkansas Gazette* (Little Rock), March 24, 1879.

75. Ibid., March 22, 1879.

76. *Denison* (Texas) *Daily News*, March 21, 1879.

77. Seymour, "Shooting of Maurice Barrymore," 2.

78. Davis-Kotsilibas, *Great Times, Good Times*, 131. When asked many years later about the veracity of this tale, Lionel Barrymore said, "The story that I cut my teeth on a bullet extracted from my father's back is another of those figments about the Barrymores too happily told for me to deny at this late date. I was one year old at the time, so the yarn is at least possible" (Lionel Barrymore, as told to Cameron Shipp, *We Barrymores*, 29).

79. Seymour, "Shooting of Maurice Barrymore," 3.

80. *Waco Telephone*, reprinted in the *Denison* (Texas) *Daily News*, March 27, 1879.

81. *Marshall* (Texas) *Messenger*, March 21, 1879.

82. *Marshall* (Texas) *Tri-Weekly Herald*, March 22, 1879.

83. *Fort Worth* (Texas) *Daily Democrat*, March 29, April 3, 1879.

84. *Daily Democratic Statesman* (Austin, Texas), March 23, 1879.

85. Quoted in the *Hays City* (Kansas) *Sentinel*, March 28, 1879.

86. *Atlanta Constitution*, May 17, 1879.

87. Quoted in ibid., July 11, 1879.

88. Quoted in ibid., July 27, 1879.

89. Quoted in Davis-Kotsilibas, *Great Times, Good Times*, 134.

90. Quoted in ibid., 134.

91. *Marshall* (Texas) *Tri-Weekly Herald*, March 22, 1879.

92. Andrew Currie, mayor of Shreveport, 1878–90, was born in Ibrecken, County Clare, Ireland, in 1843 (Brock, "Shreveport's Mayoral History"). He was very familiar with Marshall; Currie's wife, the former Annie Foot Gregg, was from a prominent Marshall family (Rasch, "One Killed, One Wounded," 11).

93. King, "Maurice Barrymore," 36; Seymour, "Shooting of Maurice Barrymore," 3.

94. Davis-Kotsilibas, *Great Times, Good Times*, 133. Both men being from Cincinnati, they presumably had much to discuss about old times in the Queen City.

95. Ibid., 140.

96. Ibid.

97. *Marshall* (Texas) *Tri-Weekly Herald*, July 3, 1879.

98. Ibid., January 1, 1880.

99. Quoted in Rasch, "One Killed, One Wounded," 12.

100. Quoted in the *Marshall* (Texas) *Tri-Weekly Herald*, June 24, 1880.

101. Ibid.

102. Ibid.

103. Ibid.

104. Ibid.

105. Quoted in Davis-Kotsilibas, *Great Times, Good Times*, 149.

106. Cited in the *Marshall* (Texas) *Messenger*, June 25, 1880.

107. *Marshall* (Texas) *Tri-Weekly Herald*, July 8, 1880.

108. Ibid., June 26, 1880.

109. *Marshall* (Texas) *Messenger*, July 23, 1880. Ellen Cummins never recovered from the shock of the shooting and retired from acting. Maurice Barrymore, however, went on to a distinguished career on the stage. In later years he became increasingly irrational, even homicidal, and was committed to an asylum for the mentally deranged at Amityville, New York, where he died on March 25, 1905 (*Fort Wayne* [Indiana] *Journal-Gazette*, March 26, 1905; Rasch, "One Killed, One Wounded"; O'Neal, "Jim Currie vs. Maurice Barrymore," 55).

110. Interestingly, Jim Currie was enumerated twice in the U.S. Census conducted that summer. On June 10, the day his trial began, he was enumer-

ated at the jail in Marshall. His occupation was given as "detective" and his age, erroneously, as thirty-six. Two weeks later, on June 24, he was in his brother's home at Shreveport, and the census taker there also listed him, giving his occupation as "engineer" and his age, again erroneously, as forty-three.

111. *Fort Worth* (Texas) *Daily Democrat*, April 2, 1881.

112. Reprinted in the *Atlanta Constitution*, April 3, 1881.

113. Rasch, "Killer Next to Wild Bill"; *Las Vegas Daily Optic*, March 23, 1881. A full account of this shooting is in L'Aloge, *Knights of the Sixgun*, 143–50.

114. *Fort Worth* (Texas) *Daily Democrat*, April 6, 1881.

115. Rasch, "Killer Next to Wild Bill;" *El Paso* (Texas) *Lone Star*, August 16, 1882.

116. Potter, "Reminiscences," 51. Potter's memory was faulty, as he wrote his account of these events more than thirty years later. He consistently called his subject "Jim Curley," but there is no doubt he meant Currie, the man, he said, "who killed Porter, the actor, at Marshall, Texas."

117. Rasch, "Killer Next to Wild Bill."

118. Ibid.; *El Paso* (Texas) *Lone Star*, February 17, 1883.

119. Potter, "Reminiscences," 51–52.

120. Rasch, "Killer Next to Wild Bill."

121. See Chapter 5.

122. Lorentz, " 'Colorado Charley.' "

123. Potter, "Reminiscences," 52.

124. This was not John A. Foley, a master mechanic at the mill and a graduate of the Massachusetts Institute of Technology (Parker, *White Oaks*, 99–101).

125. Rasch, "Killer Next to Wild Bill;" Criqui, *Fifty Fearless Men*, 79. Currie's prison record as Convict Number 271 described him as of the Irish race, age forty-seven, weight 181 pounds, height five feet nine and a half inches, brown eyes, gray hair, fair complexion, size eight shoes, bad teeth, and wearing a mustache. Identifying body marks were: end of middle finger cut off, J. C. in India ink on right wrist, small scar on right side of nose, head bald. Born in Clare, Ireland, an engineer by trade and a Catholic, he was single with no children. His father and mother were not living. He had been self-supporting since the age of nine. His drinking habit was "moderate," and he used tobacco. He had a common school education — no high school or college — and could read and write. He had not been previously imprisoned. He named "A. Curry of Shreveport, Louisiana," as his nearest living relative (James Currie, Number 271, Record of Convicts, New Mexico Penitentiary).

126. *Graham* (Texas) *Leader*, September 27, 1888.

127. Curry, "Declaration for Original Invalid Pension," May 17, 1890.

128. Ibid., July 22, 1890; Frick, "Surgeon's Certificate."

129. James Currie, Number 271, Record of Convicts, New Mexico Penitentiary. Money may have changed hands to effect this pardon. Miguel Otero,

who six years later would accept appointment as governor of New Mexico Territory, had little respect for Prince, a fellow Republican. Prince, he said, "was not well liked and was regarded as a hypocrite, besides being well known as a 'lady admirer.' He had been indicted for fraud by an Erie County, New York, grand jury. . . . Just why President Harrison wished to inflict such punishment on the territory, no one seemed to know" (Otero, *My Life on the Frontier*, vol. 2, *1882–1897*, 230–31).

130. Drees, "Curry."

131. Cowan, "Memories of the Bad Man"; *Salt Lake Herald*, November 14, 1898.

132. Criqui, *Fifty Fearless Men*, 82.

133. Pension Files, National Archives.

CHAPTER 3

1. Shores, "Jack Watson," 1.

2. According to information in the Watson family Bible, John Watson, the eldest son of James Lemuel and Margaret Russell Watson of Hardin County, Tennessee, was named for his grandfather, a Methodist preacher who settled in Hardin County in the early 1800s. His great-grandfather, Samuel Watson of York County, South Carolina, served in the Revolutionary War (Jane Watson Ellis, great-grandniece of J. A. Watson, who holds the family Bible, to R. K. DeArment, April 25, 2000; U.S. Census, Hardin County, Tennessee, 1850).

3. Garrett, *Fort Worth*.

4. Confederate Military Service Records, John A. Watson, National Archives.

5. Shores, "Texas Ranger," 2.

6. Ibid.

7. Yost, *Boss Cowman*, 48.

8. Ibid., 303.

9. G. E. Lemmon to E. P. Lamborn, ca. August 1935. Thomas J. Smith was so identified with the gunfight at Bear River City that he was known in his later career as a lawman at Kit Carson, Colorado, and Abilene, Kansas, as "Bear River Tom." He was city marshal at Abilene before Wild Bill Hickok gained fame in that post, and was murdered there in November 1870.

10. Other than in the brief remarks of Ed Lemmon, the name of Jack Watson does not appear in any of the sketchy published accounts of the Bear River City riot. Some of Jack Watkins's Wyoming adventures are related in Gorzalka, *Wyoming's Territorial Sheriffs*, 105–106, 118–19; and Pence, *Boswell*, 89–92. It is certain, however, that a man named John Watson who, while intoxicated, shot and killed a restaurant owner in Austin, Texas, on July 11, 1870, was not the big, bewhiskered Confederate cavalry veteran with the gimpy leg, although he shared several of John A. Watson's characteristics—an ambition to pursue a career in law enforcement and a penchant to resort to firearms when under alcoholic influence. This John Watson was a thirty-five-

year-old farmer from Washington County, Texas, married to a woman named Sallie. John A. Watson was twenty-seven in 1870 and unmarried (U.S. Census, Washington County, Texas, 1870; Parsons and Hall Little, *Captain L. H. McNelly*, 55–56).

11. Muster Pay Roll of Company A, Frontier Men, Erath County, Texas, May 25, 1874 (Texas State Archives, Austin). This record shows Watson served in Waller's company for a year. But the muster rolls of the Rangers are incomplete, and other records indicate he may have seen Ranger service as early as 1870. N. A. Jennings, a former Ranger who published his reminiscences in 1899, recalled a member of Captain J. R. McNelly's company as "a lame fiddler but a man of reckless bravery" named Watson, but thought his first name was David (Jennings, *Texas Ranger*, 120, 124). The lame Ranger was probably Jack Watson.

12. Muster Pay Roll of Company A, Frontier Men, Erath County, Texas, May 25, 1874 (Texas State Archives). One of the privates listed was Dallas Studenmire, who would achieve fame in later years as the deadly gun-fighting city marshal of El Paso, Texas. Like Jack Watson, Studenmire fell victim to "demon rum" and on September 18, 1882, was shot to death in that city (Metz, *Dallas Studenmire*).

13. Report of Company A, Captain Waller Commanding, for the Month of May 1874 (Texas State Archives).

14. *Corsicana Observer*, June 17, 1874, quoted in Metz, *John Wesley Hardin*, 245.

15. Company A Monthly Report for June 1874; "Record of Scouts" Monthly Return, June 30, 1874 (Texas State Archives).

16. The Juvenall brothers, J. C. "Cul" and Ben, from Williamson County, Texas, were early drovers to the Kansas markets (Gard, *Chisholm Trail*). They were natives of Indiana and employed a number of young Indiana men as herders for their drives, according to J. B. Pumphrey, a Texan who helped drive a Juvenall herd north to Kansas in 1872. The Texans called these Indiana young men "Short Horns" (Hunter, *Trail Drivers of Texas*, 27).

17. Shores, "Texas Ranger," 2.

18. Major John B. Jones to Texas Ranger Lieutenant G. W. Arrington, August 1, 1878 (Texas State Archives).

19. Haley, *Charles Goodnight*, 337.

20. Cooke County Cause No. 914, *State of Texas v. John Watson*, Assault to Murder, May 9, 1876; *List of Fugitives from Justice* (Adjutant General's Office, Austin, Texas), 1886, 1900. Cooke County did not provide a list for 1878.

21. The list of fugitives for 1878 shows that J. M. Ables was wanted in Robertson County for "theft of goods."

22. John B. Jones Correspondence, Texas State Archives. Nine years later, in April 1885, a man named John Watson was arrested and jailed in Gainesville, Cooke County, and charged with the assault. In a letter to the district judge written from jail on May 14, 1885, he adamantly proclaimed his innocence. The letter was signed "J. T. Watson," and the handwriting looks nothing like that of John A. Watson's (Cooke County Cause No. 914). It

seems the authorities had arrested the wrong John Watson. Evidently they realized their mistake, for he was released and the case continued. John A. Watson was still under indictment in Cooke County as late as 1900.

23. Cooke County Cause No. 914.

24. Ibid. John A. Watson was still appearing on the fugitive lists from Cooke County as late as 1900.

25. *El Paso* (Texas) *Lone Star*, March 3, 1883.

26. Shores, "Texas Ranger," 3; Rockwell, *Uncompahgre Country*, 93; Look, *Unforgettable Characters*, 125. Doc Shores remembered the amount of the reward offered for Watson as $600, but the minutes of the Montrose city council indicate the reward was much greater. The minutes for February 8, 1884, show that as "the City Marshal and Police Magistrate were maliciously assaulted by a desperado, one J. A. Watsen [*sic*]," a resolution was passed to "offer a reward of five thousand dollars for the apprehension of said Watsen and the delivery of said fugitive to the proper authorities." Watson was described as "a cripple, one foot being cut off at the instep," about five feet, eight inches tall, with stooping shoulders, heavy of build, with heavy black eyebrows and a black beard "growing up to his cheekbones." When last seen, he was riding a bay pony with a bald face. At a later meeting of the council it was agreed to "pay the town marshal his salary while he was recovering from a pistol wound and he being unable to perform his duties due to his disability" (Jane Ellis to R. K. DeArment, November 28, 2005).

27. Shores, "Texas Ranger," 8.

28. Ibid.; Rockwell, *Memoirs*, 221.

29. Rockwell, *Memoirs*, 222.

30. Shores, "Texas Ranger," 9.

31. Rockwell, *Memoirs*, 223.

32. Ibid., 233.

33. Ibid., 248.

34. *Rocky Mountain News* (Denver, Colorado), December 19, 1891.

35. Rockwell, *Memoirs*, 252–53.

36. Ibid., 254.

37. Ibid., 374; O'Neal *Encyclopedia of Western Gunfighters*, 283.

38. *Eastern Utah Advocate* (Price, Utah), July 1, 1897.

39. Shores, "Jack Watson," 7.

40. Ibid., 8.

41. Ibid.

42. Ibid.

43. Kelly, *Outlaw Trail*, 171–72. Surprisingly, one member of Sheriff Tuttle's posse was the notorious outlaw Gunplay Maxwell.

44. *Eastern Utah Advocate* (Price, Utah), May 19, 1898; Reynolds, *Centennial Echoes*, 189–90; Kelly, *Outlaw Trail*, 170–72.

45. *Eastern Utah Advocate* (Price, Utah), May 12, 1898.

46. Quoted in Kelly, *Outlaw Trail*, 175.

47. Frandsen, "Posse Shootout," 14.

48. *Salt Lake Tribune*, May 14, 1898.

49. Kelly, *Outlaw Trail*, 177; Frandsen, "Posse Shootout," 14–15; *Salt Lake Tribune*, May 15, 1898.

50. Kelly, *Outlaw Trail*, 178; *Eastern Utah Advocate* (Price, Utah), May 19, June 16, 1898; Frandsen, "Posse Shootout," 20.

51. Watson was so desperate for money that he volunteered to take on the onerous task of cleaning the bodies of the dead outlaws before burial. For this work he was paid $2.50 (Frandsen, "Posse Shootout," 20).

52. Copy of letter provided R. K. DeArment by Jane Watson Ellis. It is not known if Watson was "stretching the blanket" to impress his brother when he said he had killed six men since being at Crested Butte (presumably during the coal strike of 1891–92), or if his actual number of fatal encounters was much higher than has been reported. At any rate, he seemed quite proud of his death toll. He obviously was more expert with the pistol than the pen, as evidenced by his misspellings.

53. Copies of letters provided R. K. DeArment by Jane Watson Ellis. Watson sold his share to James Rooney.

54. *Eastern Utah Advocate* (Price, Utah), June 16, 1898.

55. Ibid., June 30, 1898.

56. Shores, "Jack Watson," 9.

57. *Salt Lake Tribune*, July 24, 1898.

58. Ibid. Similar accounts of the gunfight appeared in the *Eastern Utah Advocate* (Price, Utah), August 4, 1898; and Shores, "Jack Watson," 9.

59. *Eastern Utah Advocate* (Price, Utah), August 4, 1898.

60. Frandsen, "Posse Shootout," 27. Watson's slayer, J. W. Warf, also had a violent history. Twelve years later, in 1910, the state of Utah indicted the former attorney for Carbon County, charging him with an assault on a man named Alfred Hansen. The charge that he had committed "a violent injury" on the person of Hansen with "a pistol, commonly called a revolver," and that he did "strike, beat, wound and bruise" the victim sounds very much like the attack he made on Watson over the irrigation issue. Arrested and released on bond, Warf failed to appear for trial and was a fugitive for a year. He later returned and, perhaps by means of a financial arrangement with Hansen, succeeded in having the charges dropped (*State of Utah v. J. W. Warf*, filed November 3, 1910).

CHAPTER 4

1. The report of a score or more killings attributed to John Owens apparently first appeared in print in an article on Owens in the *Sheridan* (Wyoming) *Post-Enterprise* of August 26, 1927, which said, rather ambiguously, "While it is said that 26 killings could be credited to Owens, there is no authority to substitute [*sic*, substantiate] such a claim." The respected Wyoming historian Agnes Wright Spring, in her book *The Cheyenne and Black Hills Stage and Express Routes*, published in 1948, said that "his twenty killings were made in self-defense, chiefly as an officer of the law" (109). She repeated the

assertion in a 1970 magazine article, "Twenty Notches on His Gun." Editor L. G. Flannery, in the second volume of his John Hunton diaries, published in 1958, twice made the same allegation (25, 196). Elizabeth Griffith, in her 1990 monograph on Owens, *The House of Blazes: The Story of Johnny Owens*, repeated the twenty kill figure (26). The "notching" of pistols as a kill-record was generally a practice of outlaws and not lawmen, but Owens may have been an exception. The handle of his favorite revolver was apparently notched, although not likely with the oft-mentioned twenty. When a youthful Albert Nietfeld examined that gun and inquired of its elderly owner about the notches it held, he received only "a smiling evasive answer." The boy was quickly admonished by his father, who told him "it was not good manners to question old timers about such a personal matter" (Flannery, *John Hunton's Diary, 1876–'77*, 197).

2. Thorpe, "Frontier Justice."

3. Root, "John Owens."

4. Griffith, *House of Blazes*, 12.

5. According to Elizabeth Thorpe Griffith, who researched the Owens family, John's father, John E. Owens, was a Virginian. His mother, name unknown, was a native of Kentucky who died when John, Jr., was quite young. In 1852, when young John was nine, his father remarried (ibid., 5).

6. Ibid., 5–6. The extent of Owens's military service is not clear, as there were at least three members of the Missouri militia named John Owens. One enlisted (no location cited) on September 6, 1861, in C Company, Fourth Infantry Regiment, and served only three months, being discharged (for no stated reason) on December 6, 1861. Another enlisted in Company G, Fifth Cavalry Regiment, on January 8, 1862, at St. Louis; was mustered in on April 14, 1862; and was discharged on January 11, 1865. Another enlisted in Company B, Third Infantry Regiment, at Louisiana, Missouri, on March 24, 1862; was mustered in on April 8, 1862; and was discharged for disability on May 3, 1863 (National Archives).

7. John Owens to Tom Powers, June 16, 1915.

8. Thorpe, "Let the Record Show."

9. John Owens to Tom Powers, June 10, 1915.

10. Griffith, "Johnny Owens," 7.

11. Flannery, *John Hunton's Diary, 1873–'75*, 18; Thorpe, "Let the Record Show."

12. Griffith, *House of Blazes*, 12–13, quoting an early-day Laramie County resident named Wilkerson.

13. John Hunton, Owens's neighbor, noted the passing on the April 20, 1875, page of his diary (Flannery, *John Hunton's Diary, 1873–'75*, 55).

14. Spring, *Cheyenne and Black Hills Stage and Express Routes*, 109.

15. Weston County Heritage Group, *Weston County, Wyoming*.

16. Griffith, *House of Blazes*, 16–17; Brown, *Hog Ranches of Wyoming*, 77–80. As an indication of how precarious life was on this Wyoming frontier, it should be noted that both Hog Ranch founders, Julius Ecoffey and Adolph

Cuny, died violently within a few years. Ecoffey was attacked by a man named Stonewall and died of his injuries in November 1876. A notorious outlaw and road agent named Clark Pelton killed Cuny the following summer (Brown, *Hog Ranches of Wyoming*, 72–73).

17. Quoted in Brown, *Hog Ranches of Wyoming*, 30; and Butler, *Daughters of Joy*, 8.

18. Griffith, *House of Blazes*, 14.

19. Ibid., 14–15; Spring, *Cheyenne and Black Hills Stage and Express Routes*, 157.

20. Griffith, *House of Blazes*, 15.

21. Ibid.

22. The *Weekly Globe* of Golden, Colorado, reported in its issue of August 19, 1876, that " 'Persimmon Bill,' that renegade and horse thief who shot Sergeant Sullivan of Company F on the 3rd of last March near Fort Fetterman, is now with Sitting Bull. He is a bad man and a coward, too, for he shot Sullivan in the back without giving him a chance to defend himself."

23. David, *Malcolm Campbell*, 56.

24. Thorpe, "Frontier Justice"; Spring, *Cheyenne and Black Hills Stage and Express Routes*, 329–30; Griffith, *House of Blazes*, 17.

25. Griffith, *House of Blazes*, 19.

26. Ibid.

27. *Lusk* (Wyoming) *Herald*, October 15, 1886. Trumble was convicted of the murder of Red Bill and sentenced to hang, but the Supreme Court, on appeal, ordered a new trial. At a second trial in Converse County on December 14, 1889, he was convicted of manslaughter and sentenced to six and a half years in the penitentiary at Joliet, Illinois. He served four years and five months and was discharged August 31, 1894. Cerns was also convicted and served time (Frye, *Atlas of Wyoming Outlaws*, 268, 269, 296).

28. *Lusk* (Wyoming) *Herald*, October 22, 1886.

29. Griffith, "Johnny Owens"; Weston County Heritage Group, *Weston County*; Thorpe, "Let the Record Show"; Flannery, *John Hunton's Diary, 1885–1889*, 154.

30. Flannery, *John Hunton's Diary, 1885–1889*, 229–30, quoting the *Cheyenne Leader*.

31. *Lusk* (Wyoming) *Herald*, January 21, 1887; Raine, *Guns of the Frontier*, 127–28; DeArment, *Deadly Dozen*, 161.

32. *Cheyenne* (Wyoming) *Daily Sun*, September 3, 1887; Carroll, "Dan Bogan Was the Real McCoy," 11.

33. Raine, *Guns of the Frontier*, 128.

34. *Cheyenne* (Wyoming) *Daily Sun*, February 5, 1887; Carroll, "Dan Bogan Was the Real McCoy," 12.

35. Flannery, *John Hunton's Diary, 1885–1889*, 229; DeArment, *Deadly Dozen*, 152.

36. Quoted in Griffith, *House of Blazes*, 21.

37. Flannery, *John Hunton's Diary, 1885–1889*, 191.

38. Reprinted in the *Lusk* (Wyoming) *Herald*, October 7, 1887.

39. Flannery, *John Hunton's Diary, 1885–1889*, 261.

40. Griffith, *House of Blazes*, 26. In other versions of this tale, Owens had a saloon and gambling house in Crawford, and he "killed five negro soldiers and wounded two others when those gentlemen had been so indiscreet as to make a disturbance and start shooting up his saloon" (*Newcastle* [Wyoming] *News Letter Journal*, May 28, 1959). William MacLeod Raine, in his 1940 book *Guns of the Frontier*, wrote that Owens was wakened out of sleep in the back room of a gambling house he operated in Crawford when "wild colored soldiers" from Fort Robinson staged a riot. He ran out to find the town marshal, his hands raised, backed against the wall and the room filled with soldiers who had taken charge. "Owens grabbed a double-barreled shotgun from back of the bar. When hostilities had concluded the tale of casualties included most of the soldiers. Several were in the hospital for a week, but none was seriously wounded" (132–33).

41. Griffith, *House of Blazes*, 26.

42. Thomas Buecker, Curator, Fort Robinson Museum, in a letter to R. K. DeArment, June 23, 2005: "Trust me, no event as you are asking about *ever* happened in Crawford, or any place in the Northern Plains for that matter. It is obviously a case of someone passing on bad information, which does not make history." Belvadine Lecher, Director, Dawes County History Museum, in a letter to R. K. DeArment, June 21, 2005: "I am sure if this had happened, it would be something that would still be talked about and would have been publicized in the local papers."

43. *Newcastle* (Wyoming) *News*, July 10, 1890.

44. *Newcastle* (Wyoming) *Journal*, July 18, 1890.

45. Griffith, *House of Blazes*, 25; Weston County Heritage Group, *Weston County*, 29.

46. Root, "John Owens"; Griffith, *House of Blazes*, 24.

47. One game was faro, according to one report, and monte, according to another (*Newcastle* [Wyoming] *Journal*, January 2, 1891).

48. Ibid. William MacLeod Raine, in his book *Guns of the Frontier* (129–30), describes a confrontation Owens had with Doc Cornett in which Cornett threatened Owens with a gun when Owens was sheriff. Even with a pistol aimed at him, "the sheriff's weapon flashed to light. A bullet crashed into Cornet's [*sic*] forehead before he had time to fire." This appears to be a garbled account of the Davis shooting.

49. Griffith, *House of Blazes*, 1.

50. Addie, born May 22, 1853, in Baltimore, loved to dance and sing and drifted west, ending up in John Owens's House of Blazes. She was described by her son as "about five feet, four [with] blue eyes and brown hair. She had a good alto voice" (ibid., 30; Browning, *Violence Was No Stranger*, 79).

51. Griffith, *House of Blazes*, 30.

52. Kongslie (as told to him by M. D. Quick), "Anecdote of Johnny Owens."

53. Griffith, *House of Blazes*, 31–33; *Laramie* (Wyoming) *Boomerang*, February 17, 1896; *Spearfish* (South Dakota) *Queen City Mail*, February 19, 1896.

54. Griffith, *House of Blazes*, 33; Weston County Heritage Group, *Weston County*.

55. *Laramie Boomerang*, February 17, 1896.

56. There is a story that Harry Longabaugh, alias the Sundance Kid, sidekick of outlaw gang leader Butch Cassidy, escaped from the Deadwood jail in late October 1897 and hid out for several days in the loft of the newspaper office in Newcastle, right under the nose of Sheriff Owens, before making his clean getaway (Griffith, *House of Blazes*, 33–34). But Donna Ernst, who has spent many years researching and writing about Longabaugh, a relative by marriage, has serious doubts about the story: "Someone may have hidden in the attic but we doubt it was Sundance" (Donna Ernst to R. K. DeArment, July 12, 2005).

57. Richardson, *Battle of Lightning Creek*, 7.

58. Ibid.

59. The deputies, in addition to Owens, were Oliver Johnson, Jack Moore, James Davis, Frank Zerbst, Steve Franklin, Fred Howell, Ralph Hackney, Louis Falkenberg, Charlie Harvey, Henry Coon, and George Fountain (ibid., 14).

60. One report had it that Black Kettle jumped behind a cottonwood stump, and Owens pierced the stump with a bullet, killing the Indian (Griffith, *House of Blazes*, 35).

61. Ibid., 15.

62. Frink, *Cow Country Cavalcade*, 27.

63. As a deputy sheriff of Weston County in 1891, Fred Coates had been involved in the buildup to the famous Johnson County Cattle War of 1892. He had been suspected of complicity in the lynching of Thomas J. Waggoner, a suspected horse thief, on June 4, 1891, and the attempted murder of Nate Champion and Ross Gilbertson, rustler suspects, on November 1, 1891 (De-Arment, *Alias Frank Canton*, 89, 98).

64. Newcastle Justice Docket, 215.

65. The name is spelled Blissard in some accounts.

66. Testimony of John Owens at inquest into the death of Logan Blizzard, quoted in Griffith, *House of Blazes*, 39–40.

67. Ibid.

68. Reprinted in the *Newcastle* (Wyoming) *News Letter Journal*, January 10, 1908.

69. Ibid., April 6, 1906.

70. Quoted in Griffin, *House of Blazes*, 42.

71. Judgment in case of *John Owens v. Ralph B. Hackney*, State of Wyoming; *Newcastle* (Wyoming) *News Letter Journal*, January 9, 1913.

72. Griffith, *House of Blazes*, 43.

73. Coroner's inquest held at Cambria on February 17, 1911, and published in the *Newcastle* (Wyoming) *News Letter Journal* on February 24, 1911.

74. Ibid.; Griffith, *House of Blazes*, 47; *State of Wyoming v. John Owens*, December 11, 1911.

75. On January 10, 1919, former Wyoming governor Joseph M. Carey wrote his son, Governor R. B. Carey: "I enclose a letter from John Owens, whom I think you know personally, who desires to be appointed Manager of the Industrial Institute at Worland. John Owens is a good man in his way and I think quite competent to fill almost any place that he will undertake. His letter shows that he is not very good in orthography but there have been great men in this world who would not spell the same word twice the same way" (Wyoming State Archives, Cheyenne).

76. *Newcastle* (Wyoming) *News Letter Journal*, August 18, 1927, August 17, 1939; *Sheridan* (Wyoming) *Post-Enterprise*, August 19, 1927; Browning, *Violence Was No Stranger*, 80. Serena lived little more than a year longer than John. She died December 4, 1928, and was buried at Casper (*Casper* [Wyoming] *Herald*, December 5, 1928).

CHAPTER 5

1. Adams, *Burs Under the Saddle*, 391.

2. Fergusson, *Rio Grande*, 249.

3. Collinson, *Life in the Saddle*, 171.

4. Montague Stevens, interview by Lou Blachly, January 27, 1953.

5. *Freeborn County Standard* (Albert Lea, Minnesota), November 28, 1883.

6. Nash, *Encyclopedia of Western Lawmen and Outlaws*, 131.

7. Otero, *My Life on the Frontier*, vol. 2, *1882–1897*, 136; Stanley, *Desperadoes of New Mexico*, 262; Stanley, *Notes on Joel Fowler*, 2; Bryan, *Robbers, Rogues and Ruffians*, 88; Metz, *Encyclopedia of Lawmen, Outlaws and Gunfighters*, 87; Rasch, "Alias 'Whiskey Jim.' "

8. *Albuquerque Weekly Journal*, January 28, 1884.

9. Cline, "Cold Night for Angels," 32; "Socorro Killer," 26. Dan L. Thrapp, sketching the life of Joel Fowler in his *Encyclopedia of Frontier Biography* (1:514–15), repeats Cline's contention.

10. *Socorro Daily Sun*, November 16, 1883, quoted in L'Aloge, *Incident of New Mexico's Nightriders*, 101–102.

11. U.S. Census, Marshall County, Mississippi, 1850.

12. Ibid.; *Galveston* (Texas) *Daily News*, January 24, 1884; Woody Campbell to R. K. DeArment, June 17, 19, 23, 2006; Rasch, "Joel A. Fowler," 39. Joel had another uncle, John Peter Fowler, who was a prosperous lawyer. Elected mayor of Bastrop, Texas, in 1874, he served as county attorney and served two terms in the Texas State Senate.

13. Knight, *Fort Worth*, 36–37; Tise, *Texas County Sheriffs*, 483.

14. Rasch, "Joel A. Fowler," quoting the September 7, 1861, issue of the *Texas State Gazette* of Austin. Knight, in *Fort Worth* (37), quotes an account of the fight that appeared in the *Fort Worth Star Telegram* of December 15, 1912.

In this version, written half a century later, "both men drew and fired," and there was no mention of the part played by the nephew.

15. Stanley, *Desperadoes of New Mexico*, 263.

16. In his chapter on Fowler in *Desperadoes of New Mexico*, published in 1953, Stanley gives the date as 1875 (264). In "Notes on Joel Fowler," published ten years later, he says 1877 (4). The story also appeared in Otero, *My Life on the Frontier*, vol. 2, *1882–1897*, 136.

17. Stanley, *Notes on Joel Fowler*, 4.

18. Williams, *Texas Trails*, 84–88.

19. *Lampasas* (Texas) *Dispatch*, June 30, 1877; Reynolds, "Report of Operations"; Parsons and Brice, *Texas Ranger N. O. Reynolds*, 115, 134.

20. Cause No. 1461, Williamson County, Texas.

21. Cause No. 1548, Williamson County, Texas.

22. *List of Fugitives from Justice, from Records in the Adjutant-General's Office*.

23. *Galveston* (Texas) *Daily News*, January 24, 1884. Details of Fowler's reported attack on Leopold Franklin Bohny, operator of the William Tell House, a German boardinghouse in Dallas, and a member of the Dallas City Council, 1879–80, are lacking. It is known, however, that Bohny did not die; he lived until 1896 (Rick Miller to R. K. DeArment, June 20, 2006).

24. Stanley, *Desperadoes of New Mexico*, 264.

25. *Freeborn County Standard* (Albert Lea, Minnesota), November 28, 1883. The name has been sometimes given mistakenly as "Burns" (e.g., Walters, *Tombstone's Yesterdays*, 258). John B. Barnes, the associate of Joel Fowler, was confused in contemporary newspaper reports and by later writers with John A. Barnes, an Arizona desperado. See Walters, *Tombstone's Yesterdays*, 258; Fattig, *Wyatt Earp*, 539–41, quoting the *Tombstone Republican*.

26. Stanley, *Desperadoes of New Mexico*, 265.

27. Otero, *My Life on the Frontier*, vol. 2, *1882–1897*, 136.

28. As enumerated in the 1880 U.S. Census, taken at Silver City, New Mexico.

29. Potter, "Reminiscences," 40; Haley, *Jeff Milton*, 119.

30. Potter, "Reminiscences," 40

31. One Santa Fe paper, for instance, reported that Joel Fowler "associated" with Josie, who was, it said, "his equal in grit and general cussedness" (*New Mexico Weekly Review* [Santa Fe], November 5, 1883).

32. *Daily Nevada State Journal* (Reno), March 5, 1878.

33. Rasch, "Joel A. Fowler," 41.

34. *Santa Fe Daily New Mexican*, February 2, 1880; Stanley, "Notes on Joel Fowler," 5.

35. *Santa Fe Daily New Mexican*, February 28, 1880.

36. Hutchinson and Mullin, *Whiskey Jim*, 30.

37. *Las Vegas Daily Optic*, June 7, 1880.

38. Finley's name is spelled "Finlay" in some sources. The name of the third individual has been given as "Jim Forrest" (Cline, "Socorro Killer, 28),

"Forrest Neal" (Metz, *Encyclopedia of Lawmen, Outlaws and Gunfighters*, 87), "Jim Kay" (Rasch, "Alias 'Whiskey Jim'" and "Joel A. Fowler," 42), and "Jim Conley" (Hutchinson and Mullin, *Whiskey Jim*, 30). As an outlaw, he may have used many aliases.

39. *Socorro* (New Mexico) *Sun*, December 19, 1881.

40. Nolan, *Lincoln County War*, 464.

41. Collinson, *Life in the Saddle*, 167; Metz, *Encyclopedia of Lawmen, Outlaws and Gunfighters*, 100; Rasch, "Alias 'Whiskey Jim'"; DeArment, *Bravo of the Brazos*, 70.

42. Clement Hightower's account as recorded in Hutchison and Mullin, *Whiskey Jim*, 30.

43. Ibid., 32.

44. Ibid., 33.

45. Ibid., 34–35.

46. Ibid., 35–36.

47. *New Mexico Weekly Review*, August 14, 1882, quoted in L'Alonge, *Incident of New Mexico's Nightriders*, 81.

48. This individual has been identified erroneously as "Pony Diehl," a notorious Arizona outlaw, in Walters, *Tombstone's Yesterdays*, 258. The confusion of "Pony Neal," killed by Joel Fowler in September 1883, and "Pony Diehl," or, more commonly, "Deal," an alias of Charles T. Ray, a notorious character of Arizona and New Mexico, has often been made. Ray was convicted of cattle theft in New Mexico in April 1884 and sentenced to five years in the penitentiary (Rasch, *Desperadoes of Arizona Territory*, 33–39).

49. *Albuquerque Daily Democrat*, September 19, 1883.

50. Ibid.

51. Ibid.

52. *New Mexico Weekly Review* (Santa Fe), September 19, 1883.

53. *Silver City* (New Mexico) *Enterprise*, September 21, 1883.

54. Accounts appeared in the September 21, 1883, issues of newspapers as widely scattered as the *Trenton* (New Jersey) *Times*, the *Newark* (Ohio) *Daily Advocate*, and the *Butte* (Montana) *Daily Miner*. The *Dunkirk* (New York) *Evening Observer* carried the story in its September 22, 1883, edition, and it appeared in the *Indiana* (Pennsylvania) *Weekly Messenger* of October 3, 1883.

55. From an undated copy of the *Socorro Sun*, quoted in L'Aloge, *Incident of New Mexico's Nightriders*, 95–96.

56. *Silver City* (New Mexico) *Enterprise*, September 21, 1883; *Albuquerque Daily Democrat*, September 20, 1883; *Silver City* (New Mexico) *Southwest Sentinel*, September 29, 1883; Rasch, "Joel A. Fowler," 43.

57. *Socorro* (New Mexico) *Daily Sun*, September 21, 1883.

58. Despite the loss of his right arm in the Civil War, Reed trailed Texas longhorn cattle to the Kansas railheads and established large ranches in Texas and later New Mexico. By the 1880s he was known as "the best experienced and by far the wealthiest man about Ft. Worth" (Tyler, *New Handbook of Texas*, 5:501).

59. Reed later sold his half interest in the Fowler ranch to Bruton for $36,000 (Rasch, "Joel A. Fowler," 49).

60. Potter, "Reminiscences," 41.

61. Ibid., 41–42.

62. Ibid.

63. Stevens, interview.

64. Reproduced in Bryan, *Robbers, Rogues and Ruffians*, 99. In spite of eyewitness testimony and the victim's deathbed statement that Fowler wielded the knife that killed Cale, some apparently believed otherwise. Erna Fergusson wrote that bank cashier Will Hardy believed a "Texas cowboy" stabbed Cale. "The day after the killing that cowboy came into the bank with a knife he wanted to give away, a double-edged dirk about six inches long and with a handle shaped like a coiled snake. . . . Cale died from a wound six inches deep, while Fowler was armed only with his pocket knife." Hardy, "a cautious young man," did not offer this evidence at the trial. "Fowler should have been hanged anyway, he thought" (Fergusson, *Murder and Mystery in New Mexico*, 30)

65. Bryan, *Robbers, Rogues and Ruffians*, 99.

66. Potter, "Reminiscences," 42.

67. *Las Vegas Optic*, January 23, 1884; Otero, *My Life on the Frontier*, vol. 2, *1882–1897*, 138.

68. Hutchinson and Mullin, *Whiskey Jim*, 39.

69. Rasch, "Alias Whiskey Jim."

70. Hutchinson and Mullin, *Whiskey Jim*, 39–40. Also curious is the comment by Rhodes's biographer W. H. Hutchinson in another volume that Rhodes said the name was "Joseph" Yale (Hutchinson, *Bar Cross Man*, 32).

71. Not a brother as reported in the press.

72. If Barnes was only nineteen years old in 1883, it is unlikely he had been associated with Fowler in criminal activity in Texas as far back as 1879, as asserted in some press reports (*Freeborn County Standard* [Albert Lea, Minnesota], November 28, 1883).

73. Cause No. 299, Socorro County, New Mexico.

74. Cause No. 300, Socorro County, New Mexico.

75. Rasch, "Joel A. Fowler," 44.

76. Affidavit of John B. Barnes in Joel Fowler case file, Socorro County.

77. Rasch, "Joel A. Fowler," 44; *Las Vegas Daily Optic*, January 2, 1884; *Austin* (Texas) *Daily Statesman*, March 23, 1884.

78. Rousseau had married Kate Fowler, half sister of Joel Fowler's father (Woody Campbell to R. K. DeArment, June 20, 2006). Rasch, in "Joel A. Fowler" (39), confused father and son and said Kate was young Joel's half sister. The *Austin* (Texas) *Daily Statesman* of March 8, 1884, said that "Fowler was a relative of Capt. Rousseau's wife," and printed Rousseau's claim that he had been a deputy sheriff at Austin for a number of years. Chester Potter of the *Socorro Sun* characterized Rousseau as "an old pal of Fowler's" and he and his companions as "desperate characters" ("Reminiscences," 44). Rousseau,

like Joel Fowler, was hotheaded and quick to resort to violence. The *Galveston* (Texas) *Daily News* of August 7 and 9, 1884, reported that he had knocked down a waiter in a restaurant in a dispute over the quality of a glass of buttermilk.

79. *Las Vegas Daily Optic*, January 2, 1884.

80. Lansing B. Bloom, Historical Society of New Mexico, to E. P. Lamborn, May 9, 1927.

81. Potter, "Reminiscences," 42–43.

82. *Freeborn County Standard* (Albert Lea, Minnesota), November 28, 1883.

83. *Las Vegas Optic*, January 23, 1884; Otero, *My Life on the Frontier*, vol. 2, *1882–1897*, 136. Stanley, *Notes on Joel Fowler* (13–14), quoting a December issue of the *Las Vegas Optic*: "Fowler, the murderer, boasts that he has paid out to lawyers since his indictment for the murder of Cale, thirteen thousand dollars. He says he will not pay another cent if his neck has to break in consequence." Ferguson in *Rio Grande* (249): "Field practiced law in Socorro when that was the toughest town in New Mexico and averaged one homicide a week. He defended killers and he told me that to secure an acquittal it was only necessary to prove that the dead man had a fair chance for his life."

84. Stevens, interview.

85. *Socorro* (New Mexico) *Sun*, December 8, 1883.

86. Cause No. 299, Socorro County, New Mexico.

87. Rasch, "Joel A. Fowler," 47.

88. Ibid., 45; *El Paso Lone Star*, reprinted in the *Las Vegas Optic*, January 2, 1884.

89. Potter, "Reminiscences," 42–43.

90. Payrolls for territorial militiamen guarding the Socorro jail from November 10, 1883, to January 21, 1884, totaled over $3,000 (Bloom to Lamborn, May 9, 1927).

91. *Socorro Advertiser* of January 23, 1884, reprinted in the *Silver City* (New Mexico) *Enterprise*, January 25, 1884.

92. Fowler's last request was apparently misstated. He asked that his body be sent to be buried *by* his uncle at Fort Worth.

93. *Las Vegas Optic*, January 23, 1884.

94. Reprinted in the *Dunkirk* (New York) *Evening Observer*, January 25, 1884.

95. Potter, "Reminiscences," 40.

96. Ibid., 43–44.

97. French, *Recollections*, 33–34. French's remarks are suspect. No one else mentions shots being fired into Fowler's body. French seems to have a penchant for falsely placing himself on the scene of dramatic events. He also claimed to have been in Socorro when Fowler killed Cale, and gave a graphic account of the incident in his *Recollections* (26–28). But by his own admission, he was not even in the United States on November 6, 1883, having sailed from Ireland on November 4 (ibid., 1).

98. Stevens, interview; Haley, *Jeff Milton*, 121–22.

99. *Las Vegas Daily Optic*, January 25, 1884.

100. Potter, "Reminiscences," 44.

101. *Fort Worth* (Texas) *Gazette*, January 27, 1884.

102. *Albuquerque Weekly Journal*, January 28, 1884.

103. Crichton, *Law and Order*, 70, 72.

104. Potter, "Reminiscences," 44.

105. Stevens, interview.

106. *Galveston* (Texas) *Daily News*, January 24, 27, 1884; *Fort Worth* (Texas) *Gazette*, January 27, 1884. Fowler was not yet in his grave when haggling began over his estate. In a dispatch from Fort Worth dated January 23, 1884, the Galveston paper reported that "Fowler's widow is in this city. A big lawsuit is likely to grow out of the estate of the dead man. His widow had a duebill of Captain J. D. Read [*sic*] for $25,000, which she disposed of to a gentleman in this city for $8000. A counter claim is set up by relatives who claim the money" (*Galveston* [Texas] *Daily News*, January 24, 1884). Nine months later there was still wrangling over Joel's money; Belle brought suit against Reed and F. W. Ball for $18,500 (ibid., September 7, 1884).

107. *Austin* (Texas) *Daily Statesman*, March 8, 1884.

108. Ibid., March 23, 1884. Socorro's letter to the *Austin* (Texas) *Daily Statesman* pointed out that when the vigilantes determined to finish Fowler, "Texas Ed" Rousseau "was not quite as anxious to assist his friend as he would desire one to believe, but . . . hied [*sic*] himself away to a certain house of ill-fame and sought protection behind the petticoats of the inmates."

109. *Gringo and Greaser*, February 1, 1884, quoted in Cline, "Cold Night for Angels," 52.

110. *White Oaks Leader*, quoted in the *Las Vegas Daily Optic*, January 29, 1884.

111. *Galveston* (Texas) *Daily News*, January 24, 1884.

112. Stanley, *Notes on Joel Fowler*, 19. Erna Fergusson described Field as "a handsome man with reddish hair and mein [*sic*] somewhat portentious [*sic*] for one so young." She said he declaimed from the plaza wall: "If one hair of my client's head is touched, I shall leave Socorro forever." One of the vigilantes commented years later: "What else could we do? We just had to hang Fowler after that!" (*Murder and Mystery in New Mexico*, 30–31).

113. *Chloride* (New Mexico) *Black Range*, February 1, 1884.

114. Stanley, *Notes on Joel Fowler*, 19.

115. *Silver City* (New Mexico) *Enterprise*, July 11, 1884.

116. Ibid., October 3, 1884.

117. Rasch, "Joel A. Fowler," 48–49, quoting the *Santa Fe New Mexican* of July 14 and 17, 1884.

118. Stanley, *Desperadoes of New Mexico*, 273.

119. *Las Vegas Daily Optic*, August 19, 1886.

120. *Santa Fe New Mexican*, August 23, 1886.

121. Ibid., August 31, 1886.

122. *Freeborn County Standard* (Albert Lea, Minnesota), November 28, 1883.

In the letter from Socorro to the *Austin Daily Statesman* castigating "Texas Ed" Rousseau, published on March 23, 1884, the charge was made that Fowler had lived in Socorro County two years, "and during that short time he murdered no fewer than seven persons without any provocation whatever."

123. Otero, *My Life on the Frontier*, vol. 2, *1882–1897*, 136.

124. Crichton, *Law and Order*, 73, quoting a letter from Hardcastle.

125. Ferguson, *Rio Grande*, 249.

126. Ollie Bell, interview by Lou Blachly (n.d.). Bell said her father told her an incredible story of how he had once captured Fowler, who had hidden himself in a cave: "My father went down and . . . got ahold of his arms and he held him down for eight or ten hours and my father was just about at the end of his strength when a man . . . came and helped him. . . . My father said [Fowler was] quick on the trigger and that he was a much more desperate man than Billy the Kid ever dared to be."

127. Bryan, *True Tales*, 28.

128. Potter, "Reminiscences," 45.

CHAPTER 6

1. Fleming and Williams, *Treasures of History*, 104; Miller, *Bounty Hunter*, 134.

2. The first serious legal trouble Josiah W. "Joe" Horner (1849–1927) experienced occurred on October 10, 1874, when he engaged in a gunfight with black troopers at Jacksboro, Texas, in which one soldier was killed and another wounded. He then began a crime spree that included a bank robbery, a stagecoach holdup, two jail breakouts, and a prison escape. Following his last escape, Horner went to Wyoming and changed his direction and his name. As "Frank Canton," he entered into a remarkable career as an officer of the law, culminating in appointment as the first adjutant general of the state of Oklahoma (DeArment, *Alias Frank Canton*).

3. A murderous career in the years 1867 to 1876, directed to a great extent against black freemen and Reconstruction soldiers, earned William Presley Longley (1851–78) the appellation "Bloody Bill." He was hanged on October 11, 1878, five days after his twenty-seventh birthday (Miller, *Bloody Bill Longley*).

4. Now considered the most deadly of western gunfighters, John Wesley Hardin (1853–95) began a sanguinary career at the age of fifteen with the murder of a former slave in 1868. Before he was shot to death in an El Paso saloon in 1895, he had, by his own admission, killed upward of forty men. Shortly before he died, Hardin completed an autobiography, *The Life of John Wesley Hardin as Written by Himself*, originally published in 1896. Since then a number of books have recounted his bloody career, the best of which are Richard C. Marohn, *The Last Gunfighter, John Wesley Hardin* (1995), and Leon Metz, *John Wesley Hardin: Dark Angel of Texas* (1996).

5. Fleming and Williams, *Treasures of History*, 104; U.S. Census, Navarro County, Texas, 1860.

6. Miller, *Bounty Hunter*, 134.

7. Fleming and Williams, *Treasures of History*, 104–105.

8. Tise, *Texas County Sheriffs*, 389.

9. *Galveston* (Texas) *Daily News*, August 8, 1874, quoting a special dispatch from Corsicana dated August 7.

10. No. 1814, Governors' Records and Correspondence, Texas State Archives. Rascoe evidently hid out in DeSoto Parish, Louisiana, at least part of the time; his son, Charles, was born there in 1876 (Fleming and Williams, *Treasures of History*, 104).

11. *Executive Record Book*, Governors Coke and Hubbard, 212, 216.

12. Fleming and Williams, *Treasures of History*, 104. It was also told in the family that Texas Ranger William Rascoe assisted Jesse in one of his escapes from jail by concealing a saw blade in a pair of boots he presented his brother in his cell. Jesse, according to this story, promptly sawed his way out and again disappeared (ibid.). No supporting evidence of this escapade can be found in the contemporary records.

13. Bill Rascoe served with distinction in the Ranger service in the years 1877 and 1878. He was involved in at least one gunfight while in Captain Sparks's company. At Coleman County in March 1877, he attempted to arrest Dave Lehpart, for whom he had papers from Llano County. Lehpart and a pal, Charles Elston, resisted, and a gunfight broke out. Rascoe shot Elston in the left shoulder. Lehpart and Elston mounted horses and galloped off, with Rascoe and a deputy sheriff in pursuit. Elston was captured, but Lehpart escaped. Said a newspaper: "Mr. Rascoe exhibited great coolness and discretion, and has won the good will and support of the entire community" (dispatch from Coleman County in the *Galveston* [Texas] *Daily News*, March 3, 1877). Rascoe was later promoted to sergeant and served in the Ranger company of Lieutenant G. W. Arrington. On October 31, 1878, Arrington gave W. P. Rascoe an honorable discharge "on account of his father being old, infirm, and in feeble health, and his presence being required at home to take care of his father and his little sisters" (John B. Jones Correspondence, Special Order No. 142, October 21, 1878).

Galveston (Texas) *Daily News*, January 1, 1878, quoting a dispatch from Corsicana dated December 30, 1877; Certification of J. H. Southworth, Clerk of the District Court, Navarro County, March 17, 1882 (Governors' Records and Correspondence, Texas State Archives).

14. *Galveston* (Texas) *Daily News*, January 1, 1878.

15. Ibid.; *Waco* (Texas) *Examiner and Patron*, January 11, 1878, quoting the *Corsicana Index*; Miller, *Bounty Hunter*, 135–36; Fleming and Williams, *Treasures of History*, 105. A story in the January 1, 1878, edition of the *Dallas Daily Herald* is a prime example of how papers of the time often grossly distorted the news: "Saturday night Corsicana was the scene of a shooting affray between Henry Lacky [*sic*] and Jesse Roscoe [*sic*], which resulted in the latter being killed. Lacky . . . is said to be a very desperate character, this being the third man he has killed. . . . Roscoe was shot three times, twice in the abdomen and once through the lungs, living but thirty minutes after the shooting.

Lacky was arrested at once, and placed in jail." Tried in early 1880 for his part in the Lacky murder, Jackson entered a plea of self-defense and drunkenness, and on February 3 a jury in Corsicana returned a verdict of "not guilty" (*Dallas Daily Herald*, February 7, 1880).

16. Thomas Martin, private secretary to Governor Hubbard, to N. W. Read, Navarro County Attorney, January 23, 1878 (Letterpress Book, Records of Governor R. B. Hubbard, Texas State Library); *List of Fugitives from Justice, from Records in the Adjutant-General's Office*.

17. W. D. Ryburn was sheriff of Ellis County, Texas, from February 1876 to November 1882 (Tise, *Texas County Sheriffs*, 170).

18. N. W. Read to R. B. Hubbard, January 30, 1878 (Governors' Records and Correspondence, Texas State Archives).

19. Cause No. 2018, *State of Texas v. Jesse Rasco and Wm. G. Jackson*, murder.

20. *Galveston* (Texas) *Daily News*, June 29, 1878; *Denison* (Texas) *Daily News*, July 4, 1878.

21. *San Antonio* (Texas) *Daily Express*, March 5, 1879; *Galveston* (Texas) *Daily News*, March 5, 1879.

22. *San Antonio* (Texas) *Daily Express*, April 13, 1879.

23. Fleming and Williams, *Treasures of History*, 105; Bartholomew, *Wyatt Earp*, 145.

24. Bartholomew, *Wyatt Earp*, 171. The family at this time consisted of his wife, Mollie; daughter Belle, aged nine; and sons Jesse, Jr., eight, and Charles, six (Fleming and Williams, *Treasures of History*, 104).

25. Miller, *Bounty Hunter*, 137. Chroniclers of Arizona's violent frontier history have overlooked this shooting, as it was overshadowed by the well-publicized war between the Earp brothers and the "cowboy" faction that was raging at the time. Only four months had passed since the shootout on the streets of Tombstone that has come to be known as the "Gunfight at the OK Corral." In that sanguinary affair, three "cowboys" were killed, and two of the Earps and their sidekick J. H. "Doc" Holliday were wounded. Two months later bushwhackers gunned down Virgil Earp. Only thirteen days after Rascoe was shot, on March 18 assassins shot Morgan Earp to death, precipitating Wyatt Earp's famous vendetta campaign against the cowboy element. Dr. George Goodfellow was kept extremely busy during this period.

26. *Tucson* (Arizona) *Daily Star*, March 8, 1882.

27. Governors' Records and Correspondence, Texas State Archives,

28. Ibid.

29. Miller, *Bounty Hunter*, 136–37; *Fort Worth* (Texas) *Daily Democrat-Advance*, March 29, 1882.

30. Miller, *Bounty Hunter*, 137; *Waco* (Texas) *Daily Examiner*, April 5, 1882; *Dallas Daily Herald*, April 6, 1882. Rascoe would later say that he was lured from his home by Duncan with a false story that he was required as a witness in a Tombstone trial (*Dallas Daily Herald*, April 11, 1882; *Las Vegas Optic*, April 8, 1882).

31. *Fort Worth* (Texas) *Daily Democrat-Advance*, April 7, 1882; *Waco* (Texas) *Daily Examiner*, April 7, 1882.

32. *Fort Worth* (Texas) *Daily Democrat-Advance*, April 7, 1882; *Dallas Daily Herald*, April 7, 1882.

33. *Fort Worth* (Texas) *Daily Democrat-Advance*, April 7, 1882; *Waco* (Texas) *Daily Examiner*, April 7, 1882.

34. *Dallas Daily Herald*, April 11, 1882; Miller, *Bounty Hunter*, 138.

35. *Dallas Daily Herald*, August 10, 1882; Cause No. 2018, *State of Texas v. Jesse Rasco and Wm. G. Jackson*, murder.

36. *El Paso* (Texas) *Times*, February 23, 1950; Fleming and Williams, *Treasures of History*, 105.

37. Fleming and Williams, *Treasures of History*, 105.

38. *Eddy* (New Mexico) *Argus*, January 18, 1890.

39. Ibid., May 31, 1890. Said the editor: "Everybody hopes and believes that Mr. Goodlett will come out all right, for he is a very popular officer." Goodlett was also supported by Sheriff Nowlin and others who thought the dispatch of a horse thief was a civil service. Nowlin wrote: "My opinion is that there is no harm in killing the man Cofelt, as I am certain he is wanted badly" (ibid., June 7, 1890). At a preliminary examination, Goodlett was bound over to the district court and released on $1,500 bail. Further evidence was produced to show that Cofelt was indeed a horse thief, which in that time and place apparently was sufficient justification for homicide, and the grand jury did not convict (ibid., June 21, 1890). Goodlett continued on as deputy sheriff, but like many men of his type, spent increasingly more time with the saloon crowd. In March 1893 he was one of a group of Phenix saloon men indicted for violation of the Sunday sales law (ibid., March 24, 1893).

40. Ibid., April 16, 1892.

41. Ibid., September 5, 1895.

42. *Eddy* (New Mexico) *Current*, July 11, 1895.

43. Fleming and Williams, *Treasures of History*, 106–107.

44. Bonney, *Looking Over My Shoulder*, 24. Bonney was incorrect when he wrote that Rascoe "lost his right arm in a shooting scrape with several Mexicans at Seven Rivers" (ibid).

45. Fleming and William, *Treasures of History*, 107.

46. An old Texas panhandle ranch dating back to 1878, the Turkey Track expanded into New Mexico in 1893 when ranch manager Caleb B. "Cape" Willingham, former Oldham County, Texas, sheriff, purchased a tract of range land near Roswell (Tyler, *New Handbook of Texas*, 6:591).

47. Two of Katherine's defense lawyers were Hiram M. Dow and Robert C. Dow, sons of Les Dow, an old friend of Jesse Rascoe's from Seven Rivers and Eddy and the newly elected sheriff who was murdered in Eddy.

48. Bonney, *Looking Over My Shoulder*, 170–79; Ball, "Murder on Credit," *Frontier Times*, February–March 1978, 35–36, 42–43.

49. *Bakersfield Californian*, January 25, 1925.

CHAPTER 7

1. "Samuel Burk Burnett." The other children of Jeremiah and Nancy Burnett born in Bates County, Missouri, were Tib, Elizabeth, Bruce, and Mollie. Amanda and Ruth were born in Denton County, Texas. Two died in infancy ("Burnetts").

2. Quoted in Williams, "Old Fort Worth."

3. *Fort Worth* (Texas) *Record*, June 27, 1922; Williams, "Old Fort Worth."

4. Williams, "Old Fort Worth." One of the young cowboys riding with him was another daring nineteen-year-old, a boyhood friend and Denton County neighbor named Joe Horner. In later years Horner would turn to outlawry. He would engage in fatal gunfights, stage bank and stagecoach holdups, and twice escape from jails, before finally being brought to heel and incarcerated in the state penitentiary at Huntsville, Texas. He would escape again and flee to Wyoming. There, under the adopted name Frank Canton, he would begin a decades-long career in law enforcement. After two distinguished terms as a county sheriff, he became head of the Wyoming Cattlemen's Association range detectives and was a central figure in the famous Johnson County Cattle War of 1892. Extricating himself from accusations that he was responsible for two cold-blooded assassinations in Wyoming, he relocated in Oklahoma Territory. After enlisting the help of his old friend Burk Burnett to obtain a pardon from the Texas governor for his crimes as Joe Horner, he built a notable record as a deputy U.S. marshal in the pursuit of outlaws infesting the area, killing one of them in a standup street gunfight. He went to Alaska during the Klondike Gold Rush and served as a federal officer there. Returning to Oklahoma, he accepted appointment as the first adjutant general when statehood was achieved. He served in that capacity for more than eight years at the pleasure of three governors. He retired in 1916, and when he died in 1927 at the age of seventy-eight, his body lay in state in the capitol building. During all those turbulent years as cowboy, outlaw, and celebrated lawman, Canton maintained a close friendship with his boyhood friend and trail compadre, Burk Burnett (DeArment, *Alias Frank Canton*).

5. Williams, "Old Fort Worth."

6. "Samuel Burk Burnett," 2; Walker, "Legend of the Four Sixes," 13; Douglas, *Cattle Kings of Texas*, 351; O'Neal, *Historic Ranches of the Old West*, 67.

7. "Samuel Burk Burnett."

8. "Burnetts," 2.

9. Tyler, *New Handbook of Texas*, 6:417. The original name of the organization was Stock-raisers' Association of North-West Texas.

10. Halsell, *Cowboys and Cattleland*, 221.

11. Haley, *Charles Goodnight*, 111–12.

12. *List of Fugitives from Justice, from Records in Adjutant General's Office.*

13. *Fort Worth* (Texas) *Daily Democrat*, June 10, 1879.

14. See chapter on Jim Sherman.

15. *Fort Griffin* (Texas) *Echo*, June 21, 1879.

16. *Henrietta Journal*, June 14, 1879, reprinted in the *Fort Worth* (Texas) *Daily Democrat*, June 21, 1879.

17. Ibid.

18. *Fort Worth* (Texas) *Daily Democrat*, June 16, 1879.

19. "Burnetts," 3.

20. Williams, "Old Fort Worth." The story is repeated in Fairley, "Cattlemen Didn't Shy from Violence." This was said to have taken place in 1893.

21. Douglas, *Cattle Kings of Texas*, 355.

22. "Burnetts," 5–6; Shirley, *West of Hell's Fringe*, 347.

23. O'Neal, *Historic Ranches of the Old West*, 70.

24. *Fort Worth* (Texas) *Star-Telegram*, June 27, 1922; "Burnetts," 11.

25. *Wichita* (Kansas) *Daily Times*, July 24, 1913; U.S. Census, King County, Texas, 1910.

26. That hatred understandably extended to Sam Graves as well. Sayers employee Willis Evans later told of being on the road in a hack with his boss when they came upon Graves in a wagon. Sayers "said he was going to kill Sam Graves when he was near enough, but Sam had a Winchester in his wagon and when he heard the hack he came around with the gun pointed in their faces, so Sears [*sic*] just rode on" ("Burnetts," 10).

27. Ibid., 9; *Wichita* (Kansas) *Daily Times*, May 24, 26, 1912.

28. James Barkley was married to Burk's sister, Amanda.

29. This Tom Pickett was neither the outlaw of the same name who rode with Billy the Kid nor the Tom M. Pickett who was a gunman in Arizona's Pleasant Valley War.

30. *Wichita* (Kansas) *Daily Times*, May 24, 1912.

31. "Burnetts," 10.

32. A dialectic word meaning "lively" or "brisk."

33. *Wichita* (Kansas) *Daily Times*, July 23, 1913.

34. Ibid., May 24, 1912.

35. Ibid., May 26, 1912.

36. Ibid., May 24, 1912.

37. Ibid., May 1, 1913.

38. Ibid., July 22, 1913. The paper remarked that Burk's son, Tom, came "overland [from Fort Worth] by auto the same day, making the trip [of about 120 miles] in eight hours, after coming the last twenty-five miles on the rim."

39. Ibid., July 21, 1913.

40. Ibid., July 24, 1913.

41. *Fort Worth* (Texas) *Star-Telegram*, March 22, 1915; December 23, 1951; *Fort Worth* (Texas) *Record*, June 27, 1922; "Samuel Burk Burnett," 4–5.

In his will, drawn up on November 24, 1921, seven months before his death, Burnett was very generous to friends and family who had remained loyal to him throughout the years. To "certain old and faithful employees," including Tom Pickett and "a faithful negro," Oak Owens, "better known as 'Coley,'" he bequeathed a monthly payment of $30 to be paid throughout their natural lifetimes. Some of his foremen and ranch managers received lifetime payments of $100 a month in addition to $5,000 in cash. His wife, Mary, had been non compos mentis for years and was institutionalized. The major beneficiaries of his will, therefore, were Ollie Burnett, widow of his deceased son; Samuel Burk, Jr., who received a one-third share of his remaining estate; and Annie Burnett, a granddaughter, who received the other two-thirds. He emphasized in the will that his daughter-in-law Ollie had "been as much a daughter to me as if she were born of my flesh, who has ministered to my wants and guarded my health with a never-flagging and generous solicitude." The old man's closest living blood relative was Thomas L. Burnett, his son by his first marriage, but Tom had been a great disappointment to his father, as was plainly evident in the will. Burk left set-aside property sufficient to provide an income of $25,000 a year for Tom, but stipulated that his son was to have no interest whatever in the balance of the estate. "That he is denied a direct interest in the body of the estate is due to his misbehavior and to his failure to pay just regard to the proprieties of life," Burk wrote in his will. "While it is painful on the part of a father to pass censure on his son and that such censure should be expressed in a last will and testament, it nevertheless becomes my duty to do so as a means of preventing wasteful management and dissipation of the estate I have accumulated in my lifetime." He further specified that if Tom chose to contest the provisions of the will, he would "forfeit this bequest entirely and take nothing hereunder as a further penalty of his filial misconduct," and directed his executors to exclude Tom from "any participation in the management, control or supervision" of his estate (Last Will and Testament of S. B. Burnett).

42. Fairley, "Burnett Changed Cattle Industry."

43. *Fort Worth* (Texas) *Star-Telegram*, April 26, 1969.

CHAPTER 8

1. U.S. Census, Lawrence County, Ohio, 1820, 1830, 1840, 1850; Henry County, Iowa, 1850; and DeKalb and Buchanan counties, Missouri, 1860.

2. *Caldwell* (Kansas) *Weekly Advance*, October 18, 1894, reprinted from the *Sumner County Star*. This account indicates that the murder of Sherman took place after the beginning of the Civil War, but other records indicate both of Jim Sherman's parents died before 1860.

3. The older boys, Eugene and Edmund, went to live with George and Sarah Mumford on their farm near Platte, Buchanan County. Rollan was taken in by Ezra and Catherine Birt of Washington, DeKalb County, and Sylvester moved into the farm home of James and Nancy Hale of Polk, DeKalb County. For some reason, perhaps to protect her from the obvious dangers of the Missouri frontier, Flora was sent back to Lawrence County, Ohio, to be raised by J. A. and Nacy Sherman (U.S. Census, Buchanan and DeKalb counties, Missouri, 1860; and Lawrence County, Ohio, 1860).

4. *Caldwell* (Kansas) *Weekly Advance*, October 18, 1894, reprinted from the *Sumner County Star*.

5. Ibid.

6. Ibid.

7. *Wichita* (Kansas) *Eagle*, April 19, 1895; U.S. Census, Buchanan County, Missouri, 1870.

8. *Wichita* (Kansas) *Daily Beacon*, September 17, 1894.

9. Bexar County, Texas, marriage records.

10. *San Francisco Examiner*, December 21, 1881.

11. *San Francisco Chronicle*, August 13, 1896; *Ukiah* (California) *Republican Press*, August 14, 1896; Webb, "Some Experiences of Frontier Life."

12. Excerpted from Sherman's testimony at his murder trial and published in the *Wichita* (Kansas) *Eagle*, April 19, 1895.

13. Masterson and DeMattos, *Famous Gunfighters*, 13.

14. One wonders if Frank and Thad Williams may have been relatives—perhaps brothers—of the former Allie Williams, the wife of Jim Daniels.

15. Cause Nos. 1720 and 1721, Hill County, Texas; *List of Fugitives from Justice, Indicted for Felonies in the State of Texas.*

16. Black, *Long Horn Trail*, 12, 13, 15.

17. Biggers, *Shackelford County Sketches*, 29.

18. Webb, "Some Experiences of Frontier Life." Accounts of the gun battle at the Millett ranch headquarters have been given in Black, *Longhorn Trail*, 16; and Rye, *Quirt and the Spur*, 357–63. John Simpson and Sheriff Green Simpson were not related.

19. *Fort Griffin* (Texas) *Echo*, May 28, 1881. The bullet that struck Herron in the hip later came out his groin; he kept it as a souvenir (Webb, "Some Experiences of Frontier Life").

20. One was reportedly shot dead at a dance in an Oklahoma town by the father of a young man the outlaw had just killed. Two others were said to have also died violently in Oklahoma and another in Colorado (Webb, "Some Experiences of Frontier Life"). Ignoring the reports, authorities in Hill County kept the charges against all four open for thirty-nine years. Finally, in 1920 the cases were dropped at the request of the county attorney, as they had "been on the docket of this court for many, many years and no arrest has ever been made" (Cause Nos. 1720 and 1721, Hill County, Texas).

21. Cause Nos. 13, 14, 15, Baylor County, Texas. The *List of Fugitives from Justice*, however, in 1900 still listed James Daniels as wanted in Baylor County on the 1881 indictment for assault to murder.

22. *Wichita* (Kansas) *Beacon*, September 17, 1894.

23. The police dockets for most of 1881 have disappeared, but the arrest was mentioned in the *Caldwell* (Kansas) *Commercial* of December 22, 1881.

24. *Caldwell* (Kansas) *Post*, January 4, 1883; Freeman, *Midnight and Noonday*, 251. The family had been enumerated in the 1880 U.S. census at Jones County, Texas. The head of the family, obviously concealing his actual identity with misinformation, gave his name as "James Daniels," and said he was twenty-seven years old, a blacksmith by trade, born in Wisconsin. His wife was "Allie Daniels," age twenty, born in Texas. There were two children, James, age two, and Sarah E., two months old.

25. Description by Sumner County Sheriff Joseph M. Thralls published in the *Caldwell* (Kansas) *Post*, January 4, 1883.

26. Records, *Cherokee Outlet Cowboy*, 175.

27. *Wichita* (Kansas) *Daily Times*, December 20, 1881.

28. Ibid., December 1, 20, 1881.

29. Debo, *Cowman's Southwest*, 32.

30. Ibid., 33

31. McNeal, *When Kansas Was* Young, 226–27.

32. *Sumner County Weekly Press*, December 22, 1881, quoted in the *Wellington* (Kansas) *Daily Mail*, September 13, 1894; *Wichita* (Kansas) *Daily Eagle*, September 18, 1894.

33. *Caldwell* (Kansas) *Weekly Advance*, November 22, 1894.

34. From the testimony of three men at Talbot's trial in April 1895 (*Wellington* [Kansas] *Daily Mail*, April 16, 1895).

35. Freeman, *Midnight and Noonday*, 253–54. Laban Records, who was not an eyewitness to the Caldwell battle but heard the story from the gang members a few days later, said that Talbot sent Jim Martin to retrieve a buffalo gun and cartridge belt from his house. Martin found the gun but not the belt, so he left both. Gun and belt were later found in the house by the townsmen (Records, *Cherokee Outlet Cowboy*, 175).

36. Ridings, *Chisholm Trail*, 477.

37. Testimony of Wilson and Rathburn at the Meagher death inquest, reported in the *Caldwell* (Kansas) *Post*, December 17, 1881.

38. A man named S. Berry, who claimed to have been a witness to the gunfight in Caldwell, told an Atchison, Kansas, newsman that more than a thousand shots were fired. "The strangest thing in the whole matter," he said, "is the fact that only three persons were killed [*sic*], for every man in Caldwell who could raise a fire-arm of any kind had it out, and was banging away in every conceivable shape and direction." The leader of the cowboys, whom he called "Texas Bill," was "a bad man and he came to Caldwell for the purpose of killing Mike Meagher and he done it" (*Atchison* [Kansas] *Globe*, December 20, 1881).

39. *Wichita Daily Times*, December 17, 1881, quoted in the *Sumner County* (Kansas) *Weekly Press*, December 22, 1881.

40. The report in the *Caldwell* (Kansas) *Post* of December 22, 1881, that Campbell's clothing was perforated by twenty-seven holes made by five rifle balls, was undoubtedly an exaggeration (Freeman, *Midnight and Noonday*, 262).

41. *Caldwell* (Kansas) *Post*, December 22, 1881. G. D. Freeman was also a member of the posse and provided an account of the chase in his *Midnight and Noonday* (258–63).

42. *Caldwell* (Kansas) *Post*, December 22, 1881; Freeman, *Midnight and Noonday*, 263. The outlaws later said they got away when one of those guarding the dugout went to sleep (Colcord, *Autobiography*, 111).

43. *Wichita* (Kansas) *Daily Times*, December 20, 1881; *San Francisco Exam-*

iner, December 21, 1881; *Caldwell* (Kansas) *Post*, December 22, 1881; Colcord, *Autobiography*, 112.

44. *Caldwell* (Kansas) *Post*, December 29, 1881; *Cowley County* (Kansas) *Courant*, January 5, 1882; Freeman, *Midnight and Noonday*, 264–65.

45. Reprinted in the *Caldwell* (Kansas) *Commercial*, December 29, 1881.

46. Records, *Cherokee Outlet* Cowboy, 176.

47. Ibid., 178.

48. Colcord, *Autobiography*, 112.

49. C. F. Doan to J. Evetts Haley, October 8, 1926. Doan's claim that Captain Arrington was looking for the fugitives cannot be confirmed by the Texas Ranger records in the Texas State Archives at Austin. Arrington did not mention Talbot or his confederates in his reports of the period (Donaly Brice to R. K. DeArment, February 15, 1999).

50. A former city marshal at Caldwell, George Flatt, was the victim of a controversial, never solved murder in the town on June 19, 1880.

51. As reprinted in the *Caldwell* (Kansas) *Commercial*, January 26, 1882.

52. *Caldwell* (Kansas) *Post*, December 22, 1881; *Winfield* (Kansas) *Courier*, December 29, 1881.

53. *Wichita* (Kansas) *Daily Times*, December 20, 1881; *Caldwell* (Kansas) *Commercial*, December 22, 1881; *Caldwell* (Kansas) *Post*, January 26, 1882.

54. *Caldwell* (Kansas) *Post*, December 22, 1881.

55. Ibid.; *Wichita* (Kansas) *Eagle*, December 22, 29, 1881, quoting the *Caldwell Commercial*; *Cowley County* (Kansas) *Courant*, December 29, 1881, quoting the *Wichita Beacon*.

56. *Wichita* (Kansas) *Daily Times*, December 20, 1881.

57. *Caldwell* (Kansas) *Commercial*, December 22, 1881; *Caldwell* (Kansas) *Post*, January 19, 1882.

58. Laban Records said Talbot "got a job with a friend in the Texas Panhandle" (*Cherokee Outlet Cowboy*, 178), but he was also reported working at this time in the Neutral Strip or Public Lands, an ungoverned rectangle of land bordered by the Texas panhandle on the south, Kansas on the north, New Mexico Territory on the west, and the Cherokee Strip in Indian Territory on the east. It was a haven for outlaws, who called it "No Man's Land" (Chrisman, *Lost Trails*, 46, 228).

59. Records, *Cherokee Outlet Cowboy*, 178–80.

60. *Wichita* (Kansas) *Eagle*, April 18, 1895. Only one of Talbot's cohorts was ever apprehended and brought to trial for the Caldwell shootings. Sumner County Deputy Sheriff William Lee arrested Doug Hill at San Antonio in October 1886 and returned him to Wellington, where his court-appointed attorney, A. A. Richards, editor of the *Wellington* (Kansas) *Daily Mail*, negotiated a guilty plea to manslaughter in the fourth degree, and Hill received a sentence of six months in the county jail (*Wellington* [Kansas] *Daily Mail*, April 13, 1895; Freeman, *Midnight and Noonday*, 267; Sanders and Sanders, *Sumner County Story*, 154). The others—Martin, Bigtree, and Munson—disappeared.

61. *Wellington* (Kansas) *Daily Mail*, April 16, 1895; *Wichita* (Kansas) *Eagle*, April 18, 1895; San *Francisco Chronicle*, August 15, 1896; Great Register, Mendocino County, 1886, 1888, 1890, 1892.

62. *Mendocino* (California) *Dispatch Democrat*, June 23, 1893; *Ukiah* (California) *Republican Press*, June 23, 1893. The papers reported that Parker was forty-four years old, married, with four children. A native of Buffalo, New York, he had lived in Ukiah for eight years.

63. *Mendocino* (California) *Dispatch Democrat*, June 23, 1893.

64. Ibid.

65. Ibid., November 24, 1893.

66. Ibid., December 15, 1893.

67. *San Francisco Chronicle*, April 25, 1894.

68. *Mendocino* (California) *Dispatch Democrat*, April 27, 1894.

69. Ibid., July 27, August 3, 1894.

70. Ibid., January 26, 1894; San *Francisco Examiner*, January 24, 30, 1894; *San Francisco Morning Call*, January 25, 26, 30, 1894.

71. *Caldwell* (Kansas) *Journal*, December 27, 1883.

72. *New York Times*, September 15, 1895.

73. Ibid.

74. *Wichita* (Kansas) *Eagle*, April 28, 1916; Leahy, "Random Recollections." John Meagher apparently was not the only man who swore to avenge Mike Meagher's murder. Only days after the tragedy, eyewitness S. Berry loaned his gun "to a man who swore by the eternal that he would never return home until he brought [Talbot's] scalp with him." Said Berry: "He will do it, too, because he is just that kind of man, is an old cow boy himself" (*Atchison* [Kansas] *Globe*, December 20, 1881).

75. Cause No. 699, *State of Kansas v. James Talbott, James Martin, Bob Munson, Bob Bigtree*, murder.

76. *Wellington* (Kansas) *Daily Mail*, September 13, 1894; *Caldwell* (Kansas) *Weekly Advance*, September 13, 1894; *Mendocino* (California) *Dispatch Democrat*, September 14, 1894.

77. Papers in towns as distant as Sandusky, Ohio, carried the story of Talbot's return (*Sandusky* [Ohio] *Register*, September 19, 1894).

78. *Caldwell* (Kansas) *Weekly Advance*, September 13, 1894.

79. *Wichita* (Kansas) *Daily Beacon*, September 17, 1894.

80. Ibid.

81. *Wichita* (Kansas) *Daily Eagle*, September 18, 1894.

82. *Caldwell* (Kansas) *News*, April 4, 1895.

83. *Caldwell* (Kansas) *Weekly Advance*, January 31, 1895, quoting the *Wichita Eagle*. The *Wellington* (Kansas) *Daily Mail* of January 23, 1895, carried the same story.

84. *Wellington* (Kansas) *Daily Mail*, April 8, 1895; Freeman, *Midnight and Noonday*, 250. William J. L. Crank and his brother, John L., were partners in a Denver law firm (Denver city directories, 1893–99). Sherman's brother, Rollan, also lived in Denver, where he had multiple business investments.

Denver city directories for the years 1891 through 1899 indicate Rollan's involvement in hay and grain sales, meat markets, livery stables, wholesale mutton sales, hydraulic pump sales, mining, and stock raising. Brother Sylvester was a ranchman in Wyoming (*Caldwell* [Kansas] *Weekly Advance*, October 18, 1894).

85. *Wellington* (Kansas) *Daily Mail*, April 16, 1895.

86. Freeman, *Midnight and Noonday*, 186. A comment in a Caldwell paper is indicative of the low esteem in which Wilson was held; his wife and two children, said the *Journal* of December 11, 1884, "will probably be as well off without him as with him."

87. *Wellington* (Kansas) *Daily Mail*, April 18, 1895.

88. Ibid.

89. *Wichita* (Kansas) *Eagle*, April 19, 1895.

90. *Wellington* (Kansas) *Daily Mail*, April 16, 1895.

91. Ibid., April 18, 1895.

92. *Caldwell* (Kansas) *News*, April 25, 1895.

93. *New York Times*, September 15, 1895.

94. *Wichita* (Kansas) *Beacon*, April 19, 1895.

95. *Wellington* (Kansas) *Daily Mail*, April 22, 1895.

96. Ibid., September 16, 1895.

97. Quoted in the *Caldwell* (Kansas) *News*, September 19, 1895.

98. *San Francisco Call*, August 13, 1896.

99. *Wellington* (Kansas) *Daily Mail*, September 16, 1895.

100. *San Francisco Examiner*, November 12, 1895; *San Francisco Call*, November 12, 1895.

101. Carranco and Beard, *Genocide and Vendetta*, 259–80.

102. *Mendocino* (California) *Dispatch Democrat*, August 21, 1896.

103. *Caldwell* (Kansas) *Messenger*, April 19, 1954.

104. *San Francisco Chronicle*, August 13, 1896; *San Francisco Examiner*, August 13, 1896; *Ukiah* (California) *Republican Press*, August 14, 21, 1896; *Mendocino* (California) *Dispatch Democrat*, August 14, 21, 1896.

105. Longtime Covelo resident Whit Ham made this unequivocal claim in a July 1974 interview (Carranco and Beard, *Genocide and Vendetta*, 376).

106. *Mendocino* (California) *Dispatch Democrat*, August 21, 1896.

107. Drago, *Legend Makers*, 64.

108. Leahy, "Random Recollections."

109. *Hot Springs* (South Dakota) *Star*, March 6, 1930; Records of the Veterans Administration Medical Center, Veterans Cemetery, Hot Springs, S.Dak.

CHAPTER 9

1. Leeson, *History of Montana*, 1340.

2. Ibid.

3. Ibid. His competitors were the McMillan and Clayton blacksmith and wagon shop on Park Street, near Main, and Mulville and Giard (later Mulville and Doud), blacksmiths.

4. The name was spelled "Jolly" and "Jolley" in the newspapers, and even both ways in the man's own advertisements.

5. "Fire Warden Lon P. Smith and John Jolly, acting for the fire department, will make a general tour of the city for the purpose of examining flues and chimneys" (*Butte* [Montana] *Daily Miner*, September 17, 1882). Later Jolly was "First Assistant" to the Butte fire marshal, Jerry McCarty (ibid., January 15, 1885).

6. Ibid., June 24, 1883.

7. Ibid., September 22, 1883.

8. Ibid., September 25, 1883.

9. Ibid., December 9, 1883.

10. Ibid., January 15, 1884.

11. Ibid., January 9, 30, 1885; Glasscock, *War of the Copper Kings*, 96–97.

12. Butte City Council Records, 1887–88; David J. Johnson to Ronald Van Raalte, January 15, 1985.

13. Pete Hanson, a native of Denmark, came to Montana by way of Florida in the 1880s and was a leading figure of the Butte netherworld until his death there in January 1899 (*Anaconda* [Montana] *Standard*, January 11, 1899).

14. Ibid.

15. The unnamed judge bragged that he had "prepared the bride for the ceremony," and that Molly's "last indiscretion" had been with him. "Anyway, that is the judge's story, and what he says he sticks by" (Glasscock, *War of the Copper Kings*, 96–97).

16. Elman, *Badmen of the West*, 180.

17. Christopher Daly, Director, Butte–Silver Bow Public Archives, to R. K. DeArment, June 11, 1981. The last year Molly Demurska was listed in the city directory was 1893 (ibid.).

18. *Daily Inter Mountain* (Butte, Montana), January 5, 1899.

19. Butte City Council Records, 1887–88.

20. Glasscock, *War of the Copper Kings*, 97.

21. The story was front-page news in newspapers as widely separated as the *Fresno* (California) *Weekly Republican* of May 11, 1894, and the *Middleton* (New York) *Daily Argus* of the same date.

22. *Yakima* (Washington) *Herald*, May 12, 1894, reprinting a story in the *Tacoma News*.

23. Ibid., reprinting a story in the *Tacoma Union*.

24. Ibid.

25. Ibid., May 17, 1894.

26. *Daily Inter Mountain* (Butte, Montana), January 5, 1899.

27. Ibid.; *Anaconda* (Montana) *Standard*, December 18, 1898.

28. *Daily Inter Mountain* (Butte, Montana), January 5, 1899.

29. John Jolly, Montana Territory Prison Record. The prison record erroneously gave his age as forty-one (he was forty-three), and described him as a blacksmith by trade, healthy, literate, five feet eight inches tall, weighing 162 pounds, with dark complexion, blue eyes, and thinning black hair.

30. Ibid.

31. Hicks, *Adventures of a Tramp Printer*, 241; Elman, *Badmen of the West*, 180.

32. *Daily Inter Mountain* (Butte, Montana), January 5, 1899.

33. Court record, *U.S. v. John J. Jolley*, quoted in Hunt, *Distant Justice*, 141.

34. Ibid.

35. Ibid., 142.

36. Ibid., 142–43.

37. *History of the Tacoma Police Department*, 19, 27.

38. *Centralia* (Washington) *Chronicle*, September 24, 1912.

CHAPTER 10

1. The parents of the Light brothers and their sisters, Hanna Jane, Juliette, Clara, and Henrietta, were Hiram L. Light and Elizabeth Henion Light. Both died during the Civil War years (Yarmer, "John W. Light," 15).

2. Penn, "Light Brothers," 38–39.

3. Ibid.; Yarmer, "John W. Light," 16–17.

4. Penn, "Light Brothers."

5. Yarmer, "John W. Light," 18. Fort Zarah was named for Major H. Zarah Curtis, killed in the Civil War at the Baxter Springs Massacre of 1863 (Fitzgerald, *Faded Dreams*, 157).

6. Yarmer, "John W. Light," 18; Dykstra, *Cattle Towns*, 167, 226.

7. Yarmer, "John W. Light," 18.

8. Fitzgerald, *Faded Dreams*, 157.

9. The man's name has been given as "Newman" in some accounts (Rasch, "Zach Light," 1).

10. *Great Bend* (Kansas) *Tribune*, October 20, 1927, quoting pioneer Don Dodge.

11. Ibid.

12. Ibid.

13. Fitzgerald, *More Ghost Towns of Kansas*, 157–58; Yarmer, "John W. Light," 20.

14. Quoted in Yarmer, "John W. Light," 20.

15. Brothers Van, Norman, and Coleman Light remained in Kansas and established farms in Saline County (Penn, "Light Brothers"). In 1878 Van Light, described by a newspaper "as brave a man as ever looked down a gun barrel," worked as an undercover agent in the apprehension of the Roark gang of train robbers. On October 21, 1878, he shot and killed Dan Dement, one of the gang (Penn, "Rounding Up the Roark Gang," 34–40, 80–82).

16. Cox, *Historical and Biographical Record of the Cattle Industry*.

17. Gilbert, Reminger, and Cunningham, *Encyclopedia of Buffalo Hunters and Skinners*, vol. 1, *A–D*, 18.

18. Passmore, "Memoirs of Lafe McDonald," 173; Rasch, "Zack Light," 1.

19. Hunter, "Early Days of Mason County," 185.

20. Titus Buckbee to Henrietta Buckbee, November 28, 1880, quoted in Yarmer, "John W. Light," 22.

21. Ibid., December 26, 1880.

22. Ibid., February 7, 1881.

23. Ibid., February 24, 1881.

24. Ibid.

25. Wyatt Anderson, "Pioneer in West Texas," 14–15.

26. Black, *End of the Long-Horn Trail*, 35–36.

27. Yarmer, "John W. Light," 23. It has been erroneously reported that Zack married Margaret Riley, half sister to James M. Riley, who gained notoriety in Nebraska as a horse thief and outlaw, calling himself "Doc Middleton" (Hutton, *Doc Middleton*, 197).

28. Tyler, *New Handbook of Texas*, 3:1171–72; Hunter, "Early Days of Mason County," 185; "We Stand Corrected," 240.

29. Rasch, "Zach Light," 1. Evidently neither Light nor Adams learned a lesson from this incident, for both remained violence-prone. As a defendant in another trial in 1889, Judge Adams became infuriated with the courtroom tactics of the county attorney. Picking up a chair, Adams attempted to break it over the prosecutor's head, but succeeded only in breaking one of the man's fingers as he warded off the blow (ibid., 3, quoting the *Mason County News* of April 13, 1889).

30. Ibid., 3. The defense was successful but expensive. John and Leonard Light had helped Zack finance the defense lawyers, and, it is said, the cost drove them into bankruptcy (Hunter, "Early Days of Mason County," 185).

31. Passmore, "Memoirs of Lafe McDonald," 172–73.

32. Johnson, "Fatal Encounter," 351.

33. Ibid.

34. Ibid.

35. Quoted in Rasch and Myers, "Les Dow," 241.

36. Rasch, "Zach Light," 3; Stanley, *Seven Rivers*, 2.

37. Stanley, *Seven Rivers*, 7.

38. Rasch and Myers, "Les Dow," 242; Dow, "Daybreak All Over the World," 24–25.

39. Rasch, "Zach Light," 3; *Eddy Argus*, October 12, 19, 1889.

40. Rasch and Myers, "Les Dow," 242.

41. *El Paso* (Texas) *Daily Herald*, February 23, 1897.

42. *Eddy* (New Mexico) *Current*, February 20, 1897.

43. *Carlsbad Daily Current-Argus*, October 24, 1943, quoted in Rasch, "Zach Light," 4.

44. *Eddy* (New Mexico) *Argus*, September 6, 1890.

45. Rasch, "Zach Light," 4. John Y. Hewitt (1836–1932), a Union veteran of the Civil War from Ohio, was considered the "first citizen" of White Oaks, settling there in 1880 and taking a leading role in early New Mexico history as a lawyer, politician, mine owner, and newspaper editor (Parker, *White Oaks*, 44).

46. Dow, "Daybreak All Over the World," 25.

47. Passmore, "Memoirs of Lafe McDonald," 172.

48. Rasch, "Zach Light," 4.

49. Dow, "Daybreak All Over the World," 26. Bob Dow was not yet three years old when his father killed Light; his older brother, Hiram, was not yet six. Although the boys were in the Dow home at the time, they probably got these details from their parents.

50. Passmore, "Memoirs of Lafe McDonald," 172.

51. Rasch and Myers, "Les Dow," 244. See Chapter 11.

52. Ibid., 245–46.

53. Ibid., 246–50; DeArment, *Deadly Dozen*, 188–89.

CHAPTER 11

1. Hutchison, *Another Verdict for Oliver Lee*, 2.

2. Governor L. Bradford Prince, quoted in the *Santa Fe New Mexican*, January 12, 1894.

3. Hening, *George Curry*, 114.

4. *Santa Fe New Mexican*, January 12, 1894.

5. Gibson, *Colonel Albert Jennings Fountain*, 214.

6. Keleher, *Fabulous Frontier*, 267.

7. Barnes, "Pleasant Valley War" (January 1932), 36.

8. Cole Railston, interview by J. Evetts Haley and Harvey Chesley, February 26, 1945; Chesley, *Adventuring with the Old-Timers*, 124.

9. Cicero Stewart, interview by Lou Blachly, November 20, 1953.

10. Tyler, *New Handbook of Texas*, 6:103. Although it is not altogether clear, Thomas F. Tucker may well have been the legendary "ex-gunfighter Tom Tucker" who led a band of lawmen called "the New Mexico Rangers" in the early territorial days of New Mexico (Hornung, *Thin Gray Line*, 23).

11. Unidentified clipping from a 1954 newspaper; Tise, *Texas County Sheriffs*, 248.

12. Unidentified 1954 newspaper clipping.

13. Jeff Lefors was the brother of two notable western lawmen, Joe Lefors of Wyoming and Rufe Lefors of Oklahoma.

14. Carlock, *Hashknife*, 82. John Payne's name is often spelled "Paine."

15. Tinsley, *Hash Knife Brand*, 59.

16. Dedera, *Little War of Our Own*, 188–89. A year later, in August 1888, Jim Stott and two others, Jim Scott and Billy Wilson, were lynched as horse thieves. Wilson was a friend of Tucker's; the two appear together in the only known photograph of Tucker.

17. Barnes, "Pleasant Valley War" (January 1932), 25.

18. Cattlemen who knew Tucker in later years often remarked that he was missing a portion of one ear (Henry Brock and John Cox, interview by Lou Blachly, April 11, 1953; Stewart, interview).

19. A number of accounts have been written about this gunfight, many of them conflicting in important details. The version given here is drawn mainly from Barnes, "Pleasant Valley War" (January 1932), 25–26. Barnes saw

Tucker not long after the event and got the story directly from him. In another account, presumably based on statements of the cabin's occupants, Ed Tewksbury shot Tucker three times with a rifle: "Ed was trying to shoot Tucker but hated to shoot his horse. Tucker was trying to get his rifle from the saddle, reaching under the horse's neck. Ed was placing his shots well. He first got Tucker in the arm, then in the leg, and after that shot the horse. When the horse was down, he shot Tucker in the chest, bullet went clear through. Ed said Tucker turned the horse over in another attempt to get at his rifle. Failing . . . , Tucker grabbed a horse running free . . . and rode out of range" (Dedera, *Little War of Our Own*, 123). Tom Tucker was a large, powerful man, but it is unbelievable that with three bullet wounds, including one through his lungs, he could have turned over a fallen horse.

20. Barnes, "Pleasant Valley War" (January 1932), 26. The *St. Johns* (Arizona) *Herald* of August 18, 1887, mistakenly reported that Tucker, Gillespie, and Payne were all killed in the gunfight. Accounts of Tucker's escape and recovery differ. Dedera (*Little War of Our Own*, 121–22) quotes a Globe newspaper, the *Silver Belt*, which reported a "statement gleaned from Tucker, one of the wounded men, who after being shot through the lungs, reached Al Rose's ranch, a distance of about nine miles, in thirty-five or forty hours." In October 1887 Al Rose, another victim of the bloody war, was shot and killed at his ranch (Barnes, "Pleasant Valley War" [January 1932], 35).

21. Barnes, "Pleasant Valley War" (January 1932), 36–37. Years later, in 1905, when Barnes was secretary of the New Mexico Sanitary Board and Tucker was working for the board as a cattle inspector at Socorro, the two reminisced over those hectic days in Arizona. "When I crossed the line into New Mexico," Tucker confided, "this country over here looked awful good to me. I headed straight for the old Rio Grande and never again had any hankering to see Arizona" (ibid., 37).

Bob Gillespie cowboyed with Tucker for a time after reaching New Mexico, but did not seem to share his friend's antipathy for Arizona. He later returned to the territory and tended livestock in Cochise and Graham counties. At the age of eighty-six he died at Coolidge of natural causes (Dedera, *Little War of Our Own*, 252).

Although A. M. Gibson, the biographer of Albert Jennings Fountain, wrote that "homicide indictments in Arizona and Texas caused [Tucker] to flee to indulgent New Mexico Territory," there is no record of murder indictments against the man being issued in either place. Citing the *El Paso* (Texas) *Lone Star* of October 7, 1882, as his source, Gibson went on to say, erroneously, that "Tucker went on one spree at Silver City, New Mexico, which ended with the killing of an Anglo and several Chinese." Tucker later beat murder charges on a plea of self-defense (Gibson, *Colonel Albert Jennings Fountain*, 214–15). The writer apparently confused Tom Tucker with Dan Tucker, another gunfighter of note who was active as a lawman in Silver City and Grant County, New Mexico, in the 1880s (see Alexander, *Dangerous Dan Tucker*, 66–80).

22. Jeff Ake, who kept a saloon at Organ, New Mexico, at the time, recalled that Lee had "about fifteen men" allied with him: "Bill McNew, who married Oliver's niece; Cherokee Bill [Kellam]; Jim-Ike-Bob (I never can remember his last name) [Jim Gililland]; Tom Tucker, Jack Tucker, old one-eyed Bill Carr, Jim Cooper, a nigger named Ed, and some more. All these fellows was the kind that believed in doing the right thing when they could" (O'Neil, *They Die but Once*, 189). Jack Tucker may have been Tom's brother.

23. *Rio Grande Republican* (Las Cruces, New Mexico), August 25, 1888.

24. This was the same Bill Earhart who got involved in another deadly feud some years later and was shot to death in 1896 by Barney Riggs in a Pecos, Texas, saloon (Sonnichsen, *Tularosa*, 52; DeArment, *Deadly Dozen*, 145–46).

25. Sonnichsen, *Tularosa*, 43–44; *Rio Grande Republican* (Las Cruces, New Mexico), September 15, 1888.

26. *Rio Grande Republican*, June 29, 1889, quoted in Gibson, *Colonel Albert Jennings Fountain*, 216.

27. Hening, *George Curry*, 101–102.

28. Cherokee Bill Kellam disappeared about this time. In a confidential report, a Pinkerton detective would later allege that "Lee and Tom Tucker killed [Walter] Good and there was a man named Cherokee Bill who was with them. Lee was afraid that Bill, who had no interest in the country, would give it away, [and] took him on a trip to Old Mexico to get some cattle and when he got to a convenient place on the other side of the line he killed Cherokee Bill Kellam and returned to his ranch" (Gibson, *Colonel Albert Jennings Fountain*, 260, quoting a Pinkerton National Detective Agency report of April 22, 1896).

29. Ball, *United States Marshals*, 169.

30. Gibson, *Colonel Albert Jennings Fountain*, 217; O'Neal, "100 Years Ago in the West," 13. In 1890 W. L. Goodlett, an officer of Eddy County, had also been charged with the murder of a suspected horse thief named Cofelt or Coffelt (see Chapter 6). Perhaps the two victims were related, and horse theft was a family enterprise.

31. *Santa Fe New Mexican*, January 9, 15, 1894; Poldervaart, *Black-Robed Justice*, 155–56.

32. *Santa Fe New Mexican*, January 10, 1894.

33. Quoted in ibid., January 12, 1894.

34. Ibid.

35. Ball, *United States Marshals*, 155.

36. Ball, *Desert Lawmen*, 155.

37. The executions were conducted by a new Santa Fe County sheriff, Harry C. Kinsell, who a year later would arrest Tom Tucker for the Hipolito Vigil killing (Gilbreath, *Death on the Gallows*, 159–62).

38. For a complete account of this bizarre boxing promotion, see Miletich, *Dan Stuart's Fistic Carnival*.

39. Hening, *George Curry*, 91.

40. Pinkerton report of March 7, 1896, quoted in Gibson, *Colonel Albert Jennings Fountain*, 249.

41. Pinkerton report of March 10, 1896, quoted in Gibson, *Colonel Albert Jennings Fountain*, 246.

42. Gibson, *Colonel Albert Jennings Fountains*, 285.

43. Hening, *George Curry*, 94.

44. Ibid., 105. This is an interesting story in light of Tom Tucker's later marital history.

45. Ibid., 109; Sonnichsen, *Tularosa*, 170–72.

46. *Santa Fe New Mexican*, April 7, 1898.

47. Ibid., April 26, 1898.

48. Ibid.

49. Ibid., April 27, 1898.

50. Ibid. Citizens of Santa Fe were especially interested in the testimony of Page Otero, as he was the brother of Miguel A. Otero, who the previous year had been appointed governor of New Mexico by President William McKinley. In his study of justice and injustice during the New Mexico territorial period, Arie W. Poldevaart quotes a "Borrego sympathizer," then living (1948), as saying Vigil "was leaning against a post at the Gutierrez Bakery shop location" when he was shot. "As Tucker passed the fallen policeman, he kicked [him] out of the way from where he had fallen into the street." The author makes this story less credible by calling "the fallen policeman" Hipolito Dominquez, when earlier in his account of the Borrego case he had correctly identified him as Hipolito Vigil (Poldervaart, *Black Robed Justice*, 156, 178).

51. *Santa Fe New Mexican*, April 27, May 19, 1898.

52. Hening, *George Curry*, 105. Curry said that Pat Garrett also tried to enlist, but Governor Miguel Otero refused to give him a commission until he arrested Oliver Lee for the Fountain murders (ibid.).

53. Forrest, *Arizona's Dark and Bloody Ground*, 287–88. Tucker was in his early thirties, hardly an old man, at this time.

54. Hening, *George Curry*, 105; Keleher, *Fabulous Frontier*, 267.

55. Keleher, *Fabulous Frontier*, 267.

56. Hening, *George Curry*, 114.

57. Hutchison, *Bar Cross Man*, 91.

58. Thrapp, *Encyclopedia of Frontier Biography*, 4:516.

59. Chuck Hornung to R. K. DeArment, April 4, 1985.

60. Dee Harkey, *Mean as Hell*, 190–200.

61. Hening, *George Curry*, 278.

62. Thrapp, *Encyclopedia of Frontier Biography*, 2:834. "The old ways of the range clung to Oliver Lee and during the time of his service in the State Legislature it was an open secret among his brethren in the Senate that at every session he carried a forty-five in a leather holster, with a well-filled cartridge belt nicely concealed beneath the folds of the Prince Albert coat which he wore on all occasions of state" (Keleher, *Fabulous Frontier*, 244).

Oliver Lee died in Alamogordo on December 15, 1941. He was seventy-six (ibid).

63. Hening, *George Curry*. After a long and eventful life, George Curry died at the age of eighty-six in Albuquerque on November 24, 1947 (ibid., 317).

64. Keleher, *Fabulous Frontier*, 226–27. A central figure in the Elk Hills and Teapot Dome oil reserve scandals that rocked the Harding administration, Fall was convicted of taking a bribe in 1929 and sent to prison. He died at El Paso, Texas, November 30, 1944, a few days before his eighty-third birthday (ibid., 208).

65. Wilson, *Pat Garrett and Billy the Kid*, 12; John P. Wilson to R. K. DeArment, October 4, 2004. Mary J. Gordon Tucker Meadows died at Alamogordo, February 1, 1933, and her third husband, John P. Meadows, followed her in death in the same city on June 23, 1936 (*Alamogordo* [New Mexico] *News*, February 16, 1933; *Alamogordo* [New Mexico] *Advertiser*, February 2, 1933; *Otero County* [New Mexico] *Index to Births-Deaths*, Book #1).

CHAPTER 12

1. DeArment, *George Scarborough*.

2. When he was sheriff in Jones County, Texas, a jury had also acquitted him in the shooting death of outlaw A. J. Williams (ibid.).

3. Jeff Milton, interview by J. Evetts Haley, December 2, 1942.

4. *Silver City* (New Mexico) *Independent*, December 20, 1898; Marriage Register for Grant County, New Mexico.

5. *Deming* (New Mexico) *Headlight*, August 12, 1899. Edgar's name was often mistakenly given as "Edwin" in the press.

6. U.S. Census, Grant County, New Mexico, 1900.

7. *Deming* (New Mexico) *Headlight*, August 26, 1899.

8. *Silver City* (New Mexico) *Independent*, April 24, 1900.

9. *Silver City* (New Mexico) *Enterprise*, April 13, 1900; *Silver City* (New Mexico) *Independent*, April 17, 1900.

10. *Silver City* (New Mexico) *Independent*, July 24, 1900.

11. Hunter, *Lottie Deno*, 170–71.

12. *Silver City* (New Mexico) *Independent*, September 4, 1900.

13. Ibid., October 9, 1900. In another editorial, readers were reminded that "tax payers should consider the fact that these men are no expense whatever to the county, and judge accordingly" (ibid., October 23, 1900).

14. *Silver City* (New Mexico) *Enterprise*, October 5, 1900, quoting the *Deming Herald*.

15. Ibid.

16. *Lordsburg* (New Mexico) *Western Liberal*, January 18, 1901.

17. *Deming* (New Mexico) *Headlight*, January 12, 19, 1901.

18. Ibid., January 12, February 16, 1901; *Silver City* (New Mexico) *Independent*, April 12, 1901.

19. *St. Johns* (Arizona) *Herald*, June 29, 1901.

20. Ibid.

21. *Silver City* (New Mexico) *Enterprise*, August 16, 1901.

22. *Devil's River News* (Sonora, Texas), July 20, 1901.

23. Rasch, "Death Comes to St. Johns."

24. The other three initial enlistees were Bert Grover, Tom Holland, and Leonard Page (O'Neal, *Arizona Rangers*, 9). Ed Scarborough and Don Johnson, son of the late Keechi Johnson, who signed up a week later, were, at twenty-two years of age, the youngest members of the Arizona Rangers.

25. Undated story in the *Tucson Citizen* quoted in Miller, *Arizona Rangers*, 31.

26. Hunt, *Cap Mossman*, 183–84.

27. Ibid.; Enlistment Record, G. E. Scarborough, Arizona Ranger Files.

28. Burton C. Mossman, interview by J. Evetts Haley, July 25, 1945, Midland, Texas.

29. *Tombstone* (Arizona) *Epitaph*, June 1, 1902.

30. Cause No. 69, *Territory of New Mexico v. Ed Scarborough*.

31. *Arizona Republican* (Phoenix), November 19, 1903.

32. *Deming* (New Mexico) *Headlight*, March 26, 1904.

33. Ibid.

34. *Silver City* (New Mexico) *Independent*, August 23, 1904. In its story of the holdup on August 20, 1904, the *El Paso* (Texas) *Evening News* called Ed Scarborough a "noted badman." To the *Arizona Republican* (Phoenix) of August 25, 1904, he was a "former Arizona Ranger and son of a noted frontiersman."

35. *Deming* (New Mexico) *Headlight*, August 20, 1904.

36. *Silver City* (New Mexico) *Enterprise*, August 26, 1904.

37. *Silver City* (New Mexico) *Independent*, August 23, 1904.

38. Cause Nos. 239, 240, 241, 247, Luna County, New Mexico, Court Records.

39. Cause Nos. 239, 240, 241, 247, Luna County, New Mexico, Court Records.

40. Notebook of Reward Posters, Strayed or Stolen Stock, Wanted Men and Related Correspondence, 1906–1912, Territorial Archives of New Mexico, New Mexico State Records Center and Archives, Santa Fe.

41. Copies of Ed's letter and the warden's response provided to R. K. DeArment by Wild Bunch researcher Arthur Soule.

42. *Bisbee* (Arizona) *Daily Review*, June 20, 1915.

43. Before assuming office as Cochise County sheriff, Harry C. Wheeler had served in the Arizona Rangers and risen in the ranks to captain, but this was after Ed Scarborough's short stint in the organization.

44. *Tombstone* (Arizona) *Prospector*, June 19, 1915; *Bisbee* (Arizona) *Daily Review*, June 20, 1915. This was the same jail in which Arizona Ranger Captain Mossman had ensconced Scarborough back in 1902.

45. *Bisbee* (Arizona) *Daily Review*, June 20, 1915.

46. Ibid., June 27, 1915.

47. Ibid., June 29, 1915.

48. Ibid., July 7, 1915.

49. Ibid., June 29, 1915.

50. *Tombstone* (Arizona) *Epitaph*, December 12, 1915.

51. Cause No. 634, *State of Arizona v. George Edgar Scarborough*.

52. Ibid.

53. Ibid.; *Tombstone* (Arizona) *Epitaph*, December 12, 1915. The Scarborough family back in Texas had been following events in Tombstone closely, of course. Lee Scarborough, a prominent Baptist minister and Ed's uncle, tried to get another uncle, Will, to go with him to Arizona to help their nephew, but Will refused, saying Ed had created his own problems and should pay the penalty (Evelyn Linebery, daughter of Will Scarborough, interviews by R. K. DeArment, November 19, 1984, and May 6, 1989). Lee attended the trial and told the family he was disgusted as it was outrageous: "The thing was set before anything was said" (Moliere Scarborough, interview by Stuart M. Scarborough, December 1, 1984).

54. *Tombstone* (Arizona) *Prospector*, December 15, 1915, quoting the *Arizona Republican*.

55. *Tombstone* (Arizona) *Epitaph*, December 19, 1915.

56. Ibid., May 7, 1916.

57. Ibid.; *Tombstone* (Arizona) *Prospector*, May 10, 17, 1916.

58. Kay Dargitz, State of Arizona Department of Corrections, to R. K. DeArment, May 4, 1984.

59. *Tombstone* (Arizona) *Epitaph*, June 3, 1917.

60. Scarborough, interview; DeArment, *George Scarborough*, 294.

61. *Tombstone* (Arizona) *Epitaph*, June 3, 1917; *Florence* (Arizona) *Blade-Tribune*, June 2, 16, 1917.

62. *Tombstone* (Arizona) *Epitaph*, June 3, 1917.

63. U.S. Census, Cochise County, Arizona, 1920.

64. Scott White to E. P. Lamborn, February 24, 1928.

65. Scarborough, interview. Moliere Scarborough was Ed's first cousin. Other family members — Evelyn Linebery, another first cousin (interviews), and Marion Marshall, a niece (interview by R. K. DeArment, February 4, 1996) — confirmed this.

Bibliography

GOVERNMENT DOCUMENTS

Arizona Ranger Files, Arizona State Archives, Phoenix.

Butte City Council Records, 1887–88.

Caldwell, Kansas, Police Docket, 1879–96.

Carbon County Commissioners Minutes, Price, Utah, July 5, 1898.

Confederate Military Service Records, John A. Watson, National Archives.

Confederate Military Service Records, John Owens, National Archives.

Curry, James. "Declaration for Invalid Pension," March 10, 1890, National Archives.

———. "Declaration for Original Invalid Pension," May 17, July 22, 1890, National Archives.

Denver City Directories, 1893–99.

Executive Record Book. Governors Coke and Hubbard, Texas State Library, Austin.

Frick, A. S. "Surgeon's Certificate," February 5, 1891, National Archives.

Governors' Records and Correspondence, Texas State Archives, Austin.

Great Register, Mendocino County, California, 1886–96.

John B. Jones Correspondence, Texas State Archives, Austin.

Last Will and Testament of Samuel Burk Burnett.

Letterpress Book, Records of Governor R. B. Hubbard, Texas State Library.

Los Angeles City Directory, 1912.

Marriage Records, Bexar County, Texas.

Marriage Register for Grant County, New Mexico.

Monthly Reports, May, June 1874, Company A, Frontier Men, Erath County, Texas, Texas State Archives, Austin.

Muster Pay Roll of Company A, Frontier Men, Erath County, Texas, May 25, 1874, Texas State Archives, Austin.

Newcastle, Wyoming, Justice Docket.

Otero County (New Mexico) *Index to Births-Deaths*, Book #1.

Pension Files, James Curry, John Meagher, National Archives.

Records of the Veterans Administration Medical Center, Veterans Cemetery, Hot Springs, South Dakota.

Report, Company A of Frontier Forces, State of Texas, for the month of June 1874, "Record of Scouts," by Captain John R. Waller, Commanding, Texas State Archives, Austin.

U.S. CENSUS

Alabama: Talledega County, 1860.
Arizona: Cochise County, 1920.
California: Medocino County, 1870.
Iowa: Henry County, 1850.
Kansas: Coffey County, 1870.
Louisiana: Caddo Parish, 1880.
Mississippi, Marshall County, 1850.
Missouri: Buchanan County, 1860, 1870; DeKalb County, 1860.
New Mexico: Grant County, 1880, 1900.
Ohio: Lawrence County, 1820, 1830, 1840, 1850.
Tennessee: Hardin County, 1850.
Texas: Harrison County, 1880; Haskell County, 1880; Jones County, 1880; King County, 1910; Navarro County, 1860; Shackelford County, 1880; Washington County, 1870.
Utah: Salt Lake County, 1880.

COURT AND PRISON RECORDS

Arizona
Cause No. 634, *State of Arizona v. George Edgar Scarborough*.
Cause No. 684, *State of Arizona v. George Edgar Scarborough*, murder.
Cause No. 691, *State of Arizona v. Calvin Cox*, murder.

Kansas
Cause No. 699, *State of Kansas v. James Talbott, James Martin, Bob Munson, Bob Bigtree, Dug Hill*, murder.

Montana
John Jolly, Montana Territory Prison Record.

New Mexico:
Cause Nos. 69, 239, 240, 241, 247, Luna County, Court Records.
Cause No. 299, Socorro County, *Territory of New Mexico v. Joel A. Fowler*, murder.
Cause No. 300, Socorro County, *Territory of New Mexico v. Joel A. Fowler and John B. Barnes*, murder.
James Currie, Number 271, Record of Convicts, New Mexico Penitentiary, New Mexico State Records and Archives, Santa Fe.

Texas
Cause Nos. 13, 14, 15, Baylor County, *State of Texas v. James Daniels, Frank Williams, alias Pierce, Thad Williams and John Ray*, assault to murder.
Cause No. 914, Cooke County, *State of Texas v. John Watson*, assault to murder, May 9, 1876.
Cause No. 1461, Williamson County.

Cause No. 1548, Williamson County.

Cause Nos. 1720 and 1721, Hill County, *State of Texas v. James Daniels, John Ray, Thad Williams, Frank Williams*, theft of horse.

Cause No. 2018, Navarro County, *State of Texas v. Jesse Rasco and Wm. G. Jackson*, Murder.

Utah

State of Utah v. Clarence Marsh and J. A. Watson, September 11, 1898.

State of Utah v. J. W. Warf, November 3, 1910.

Wyoming

John Owens v. Ralph B. Hackney, State of Wyoming, County of Weston.

State of Wyoming v. John Owens, December 11, 1911.

ARCHIVES

Lou Blachly interviews, Zimmerman Library, University of New Mexico, Albuquerque.

J. Evetts Haley Collection, Nita Stewart Haley Memorial Library, Midland, Texas.

Notebook of Reward Posters, Strayed or Stolen Stock, Wanted Men and Related Correspondence, 1906–1912, Territorial Archives of New Mexico, New Mexico State Records Center and Archives, Santa Fe.

Wyoming State Archives, Cheyenne.

MANUSCRIPTS

Bascom, C. J. "Some Early Sketches on the U. P. Between Junction City and Sheridan, Now Lisbon." Manuscript Collection, Library and Archives Division, Kansas State Historical Society.

Browning, James A. "Violence Was No Stranger, Vol. II." Unpublished manuscript in author's collection.

"The Burnetts." Texas and Southwestern Cattle Raisers Association Museum, Fort Worth, Texas.

Dow, Bob. "Daybreak All Over the World." Unpublished 1946 manuscript in J. Evetts Haley Collection, Haley Memorial Library and History Center, Midland, Texas.

Howard, Jed. "Phenix and the Wolf: The Saloon Battles of Phenix and the Dave Kemp Saga." Unpublished manuscript in author's collection.

Kongslie, Olaf B. "An Anecdote of Johnny Owens." WPA File #1361, Weston County, Folklore, Wyoming State Archives, Cheyenne.

Myers, Lee C. "The Pearl of the Pecos." Unpublished manuscript in author's collection.

Owens, Mr., and Mrs. Charles R. Owens. "John Owens Chronology." Homesteader Museum, Torrington, Wyoming.

Pels, Monica. "Andrew Currie." Caddo Parish Web site, 2004.

Root, Curtis. "John Owens." Homesteader Museum, Torrington, Wyoming.

"Samuel Burk Burnett—1849–1922." Texas and Southwestern Cattle Raisers Association Museum, Fort Worth, Texas.

Shores, C. W. "The Story of an Old Fighting Texas Ranger." Denver, December 22, 1927. Western History Department, Denver Public Library.

———. "More About the Texas Ranger, Jack Watson." Denver, December 24, 1927. Western History Department, Denver Public Library.

Thorpe, Russell. "Frontier Justice: John Owens." American Heritage Center, University of Wyoming, Laramie.

Webb, J. R. "Some Experiences of Frontier Life as Told by Henry Herron to J. R. Webb, July 17, 1940." J. R. Webb Papers, Rupert Richardson Research Center, Hardin-Simmons University Library, Abilene, Texas.

LETTERS

C. W. Allred, Sheriff, Carbon County, Utah, to Heber M. Wells, Governor, Utah, May 27, 1898.

Susan K. Anderson to R. K. DeArment, October 10, 1984.

Lansing B. Bloom to E. P. Lamborn, May 9, 1927. E. P. Lamborn Collection, Kansas State Historical Society, Topeka.

Donaly Brice to R. K. DeArment, February 15, 1999; April 29, 2002.

Larry K. Brown to R. K. DeArment, June 30, 2005.

Thomas R. Buecker, Curator, Fort Robinson Museum, to R. K. DeArment, June 17, 23, 2005.

G. M. Calfee, Deputy Sheriff, Ellis County, Texas, to Texas Governor R. B. Hubbard, January 25, 1878. Governors' Correspondence, Texas State Archives, Austin.

Susan C. Callaway, Deputy Clerk, Cochise County, Arizona, to R. K. DeArment, February 26, 1985.

Woody Campbell to R. K. DeArment, June 16, 17, 18, 19, 2006.

Joseph M. Carey to Governor Robert D. Carey, January 10, 1919. Governor R. B. Carey's Records, Wyoming State Archives, Cheyenne.

Harry E. Chrisman to Gary L. Roberts, March 30, 1976. Roberts Collection, Tifton, Georgia.

Christopher Daly, Director, Butte–Silver Bow Public Archives, to R. K. DeArment, June 11, 1981.

Kay Dargitz, State of Arizona Department of Corrections, Phoenix, to R. K. DeArment, May 4, 1984.

C. F. Doan to J. Evetts Haley, October 8, 1926. J. Evetts Haley Collection, Nita Stewart Haley Memorial Library, Midland, Texas.

Jane Watson Ellis to R. K. DeArment, April 25, 2000; November 28, 2005.

Donna Ernst to R. K. DeArment, July 12, 2005.

Fred Fornoff to J. E. Griffith, April 22, 1909. Letters Sent, Territorial Archives of New Mexico, New Mexico State Records and Archives, Santa Fe.

John E. Griffith to Fred Fornoff, June 18, 1909. Letters Received, Territorial Archives of New Mexico, New Mexico State Records and Archives, Santa Fe.

J. C. Hancock to E. P. Lamborn, August 23, 1936. E. P. Lamborn Collection, Kansas State Historical Society, Topeka.

Chuck Hornung to R. K. DeArment, April 4, 1985.

David J. Johnson, Assistant Archivist, Butte–Silver Bow Public Archives, to Ronald Van Raalte, January 15, 1985. Author's collection.

Joseph K. Johnson, Capt., 36th Div., Texas National Guard, to Commissioner of Pensions, Washington, July 5, 1927. Texas State Archives, Austin.

Richard Johnston, Carson City, Nevada, to R. K. DeArment, September 5, 1981.

Major John B. Jones, Commanding Officer, Frontier Battalion, Texas, to Lt. G. W. Arrington, Commanding Co. C, Fort Griffin, Texas, August 1, 1878. Texas State Archives, Austin.

Hal S. Kerr to Jeff Milton, February 10, 1947. J. D. Milton Files, J. Evetts Haley Collection, Nita Stewart Haley Memorial Library, Midland, Texas.

Belvadine Lecher, Director, Dawes County History Museum, to R. K. DeArment, June 21, 2005.

G. E. Lemmon to E. P. Lamborn, June 6, 1935; circa August 1935. E. P. Lamborn Collection, Kansas State Historical Society, Topeka.

Charlotte Liddle, Clerk of the District Court, Sumner County, Kansas, to Gary L. Roberts, February 11, 1976. Roberts Collection.

Rebekkah Lohr, Texas Ranger Hall of Fame and Museum, to Jane Helvering, March 13, 2000. Author's collection.

"Marion" to Harry Litt, March 19, 1934. Meagher Files, Kansas State Historical Society, Topeka.

Rick Miller to R. K. DeArment, June 20, 2006.

Roger Myers to R. K. DeArment, July 11, 12, 30, 2001.

Bob G. O'Dell, Cowley County, Kansas, Sheriff, to Mary Ann Wortman, July 10, 2001. Wortman Web site.

John Owens to Tom Powers, June 16, 1915. Archives, Homesteader Museum, Torrington, Wyoming.

Ruth Owens, DeKalb County Historical Society, to R. K. DeArment, May 26, 1999.

Chris Penn to R. K. DeArment, January 12, February 9, 11, 2002.

N. W. Read to R. B. Hubbard, January 30, 1878. Governors' Correspondence, Texas State Archives, Austin.

Tom Rives, National Archives — Central Plains Region, to R. K. DeArment, March 1, 1999.

Gary Roberts to R. K. DeArment, September 21, 1998.

George E. Scarborough to Judge A. C. Lockwood, May 15, 1916. Author's collection.

George E. Scarborough to Warden, Federal Penitentiary, Atlanta, Georgia, March 29, 1912. Author's collection.

E. J. Simkins, District Attorney, Navarro County, Texas, to Texas Governor Richard Coke, March 2, 1876. Governors' Correspondence, Texas State Archives, Austin.

Warden, Federal Penitentiary, Atlanta, Georgia, to George E. Scarborough, April 5, 1912. Author's collection.

J. Wesley Warf, Prosecuting Attorney, Carbon County, Utah, to Heber M. Wells, Governor, Utah, June 15, 1898. Author's collection.

Scott White to E. P. Lamborn, February 24, 1928. E. P. Lamborn Collection, Kansas State Historical Society, Topeka.

John P. Wilson to R. K. DeArment, October 4, 2004.

Lt. Jim Woods, Sedgwick County, Kansas, to R. K. DeArment, August 16, 2001.

INTERVIEWS

Ollie Bell. Interview by Lou Blachly, n.d.

John Cox and Henry Brock. Interview by Lou Blachly, April 11, 1953.

C. F. Doan. Interview by J. Evetts Haley, October 8, 1926.

Dee Harkey. Interview by J. Evetts Haley, December 16, 1947.

Ed Harral. Interview by J. Evetts Haley and Hervey Chesley, June 13, 1939.

Evelyn Linebery. Interviews by R. K. DeArment, November 19, 1984; May 6, 1989, Midland, Texas.

Marion Marshall. Interview by R. K. DeArment, February 4, 1996, La Jolla, California.

Henry Meagher. Interview by Anna R. Berry, June 18, 1937.

Jeff Milton. Interview by J. Evetts Haley, December 2, 1942.

Burton C. Mossman. Interview by J. Evetts Haley, July 25, 1945, Midland, Texas.

Cole Railston. Interview by J. Evetts Haley and Harvey Chesley, February 26, 1945.

Moliere Scarborough. Interview by Stuart M. Scarborough, December 1, 1984.

Montague Stevens. Interview by Lou Blachly, January 27, 1953.

Cicero Stewart. Interview by Lou Blachly, November 20, 1953.

NEWSPAPERS

Alamogordo (New Mexico) *Advertiser*, February 2, 1933.

Alamogordo (New Mexico) *News*, February 2, 16, 1933.

Albuquerque Daily Democrat, September 19, 20, 1883.

Albuquerque Weekly Journal, January 28, 1884.

Anaconda (Montana) *Standard*, December 18, 1898; January 11, 1899.

Apache County (Arizona) *Critic*, March 26, 31, 1887.

Arizona Republican (Phoenix), November 19, 1903; August 25, 1904.

Atchison (Kansas) *Globe*, December 20, 1881.

Atlanta Constitution, March 21, 28, April 17, May 11, 17, June 22, July 11, 27, 1879; January 6, 1880; April 3, 1881.

Austin (Texas) *Daily Statesman*, March 8, 23, 1884.

Bakersfield Californian, January 25, 1925.

Bisbee (Arizona) *Daily Review*, June 20, 22, 27, 29, July 7, 1915.

Butte (Montana) *Daily Miner*, June 24, July 28, December 2, 1881; March 21, September 17, 1882; June 24, September 21, 22, 25, December 9, 1883; January 15, 1884; January 9, 15, 30, 1885.

Caldwell (Kansas) *Commercial*, June 24, July 1, 8, 1880; December 15, 22, 29, 1881; January 5, 19, 26, February 2, 9, June 29, October 12, 1882.

Caldwell (Kansas) *Journal*, December 27, 1883; December 11, 1884; October 14, 1886; June 16, 1887.

Caldwell (Kansas) *Messenger*, April 8, 19, 1954; April 30, 1956.

Caldwell (Kansas) *News*, April 4, 11, 18, 25, September 18, 19, 26, 1895; September 3, 1896.

Caldwell (Kansas) *Post*, July 1, 18, 1880; December 1, 17, 18, 21, 22, 29, 1881; January 19, 26, February 2, July 6, October 12, 1882; January 4, 11, 1883.

Caldwell (Kansas) *Weekly Advance*, September 13, October 18, November 22, 1894; January 31, April 4, 11, 18, 25, September 5, 19, 1895.

Carlsbad (New Mexico) *Daily Current-Argus*, October 24, 1943.

Casper (Wyoming) *Herald*, December 5, 1928.

Cheyenne (Wyoming) *Daily Sun*, February 5, September 3, 1887.

Chicago Chronicle, October 16, 1898.

Chloride (New Mexico) *Black Range*, February 1, 1884.

Colorado Springs (Colorado) *Daily Gazette*, September 17, 18, 23, 1881; March 18, April 8, 30, 1882; February 13, 1883.

Corsicana (Texas) *Observer*, June 17, 1874.

Cowley County (Kansas) *Courant*, December 29, 1881; January 5, 1882.

Daily Arkansas Gazette (Little Rock), March 22, 24, 25, 26, 1879.

Daily Democratic Statesman (Austin, Texas), March 23, 1879; March 8, 23, 1884.

Daily Inter Mountain (Butte, Montana), January 5, 1899.

Daily Nevada State Journal (Reno), March 5, 1878.

Dallas Daily Herald, January 1, 1878; February 7, 1880; April 5, 7, 11, August 10, 1882.

Dallas Weekly Herald, April 6, 1882.

Decatur (Illinois) *Review*, January 25, 1884.

Deming (New Mexico) *Headlight*, August 12, 26, 1899; January 12, 19, February 16, 1901; March 26, August 20, 1904.

Denison (Texas) *Daily News*, July 4, 1878; March 21, 22, 24, 25, 26, 27, April 2, 1879.

Denver Daily News, September 17, 1881; October 23, 1898.

Denver Daily Times, June 17, 1881.

Denver Field and Farm, April 4, 1914.

Denver Republican, June 17, 1881.

Devil's River News (Sonora, Texas), July 20, 1901.

Dodge City (Kansas) *Times*, May 10, 1879; July 20, 1882.

Eastern Utah Advocate (Price, Utah), July 1, 1897; May 12, 19, June 16, 30, August 4, 1898.

Eddy (New Mexico) *Argus*, October 12, 19, 1889; January 18, May 31, June 7,

21, September 6, 20, 1890; April 16, 1892; March 24, 1893; September 5, 1895.

Eddy (New Mexico) *Current*, July 11, 1895; February 20, 1897.

Ellsworth (Kansas) *Reporter*, May 2, 1872.

El Paso (Texas) *Daily Herald*, February 19, 23, 1897.

El Paso (Texas) *Evening News*, August 20, 1904.

El Paso (Texas) *Lone Star*, August 16, 1882; February 17, March 3, 1883.

El Paso (Texas) *Times*, February 14, 1893; February 23, 1950.

El Reno (Oklahoma) *American*, May 4, 1939.

Evening Observer (Dunkirk, New York), September 22, 1883; January 25, 1884.

Florence (Arizona) *Blade-Tribune*, June 2, 16, 1917.

Fort Griffin (Texas) *Echo*, June 14, 21, 1879; May 28, June 18, December 31, 1881.

Fort Leavenworth (Kansas) *Daily Commercial*, October 21, 1870.

Fort Wayne (Indiana) *Journal-Gazette*, March 26, 1905.

Fort Worth (Texas) *Daily Democrat*, March 29, April 3, 4, June 10, 16, 21, 1879; April 2, 6, 1881.

Fort Worth (Texas) *Democrat-Advance*, March 29, April 7, 1882.

Fort Worth (Texas) *Gazette*, January 27, 1884.

Fort Worth (Texas) *Record*, June 27, 28, 1922.

Fort Worth (Texas) *Star-Telegram*, March 22, 1915; June 26, 27, 1922; December 23, 1951; April 26, 1969; August 8, 13, 1997.

Freeborn County Standard (Albert Lea, Minnesota), November 28, 1883.

Fresno (California) *Weekly Republican*, May 11, 1894.

Galveston (Texas) *Daily News*, August 8, 1874; March 3, 1877; January 1, June 29, 1878; March 5, 25, 1879; January 24, 25, 27, August 7, 9, September 7, 1884.

Globe (Arizona) *Silver Belt*, August 20, 1887.

Goodland (Kansas) *News-Republic*, February 17, 1927.

Graham (Texas) *Leader*, September 27, 1888.

Great Bend (Kansas) *Tribune*, October 20, 1927.

Hays (Kansas) *Daily News*, April 26, 1984.

Hays City (Kansas) *Republican*, January 10, 1903.

Hays City (Kansas) *Sentinel*, March 28, 1879.

Hot Springs (South Dakota) *Star*, March 6, 1930.

Indiana (Pennsylvania) *Weekly Messenger*, October 3, 1883.

Junction City (Kansas) *Union*, July 31, 1869.

Kansas City Star, June 13, 1915; June 15, 1918.

Kansas Daily Commonwealth (Topeka), May 4, 1869.

Kansas Daily Tribune (Lawrence), April 18, 1869.

Lampasas (Texas) *Dispatch*, June 30, 1887.

Laramie (Wyoming) *Boomerang*, February 17, 1896.

Las Vegas Daily Optic, June 7, 1880; March 23, 1881; April 8, 1882; January 2, 23, 25, 29, June 3, 1884; August 19, 1886.

Leavenworth (Kansas) *Times and Conservative*, October 8, 1868; June 4, December 5, 1869; November 11, 1870.

Lordsburg (New Mexico) *Western Liberal*, January 18, 1901.

Lusk (Wyoming) *Herald*, May 1886–May 1887.

Marshall (Texas) *Messenger*, March 21, 1879; June 25, July 23, 1880.

Marshall (Texas) *Tri-Weekly Herald*, March 20, 22, 25, 27, April 1, 17, June 24, July 3, October 28, November 25, 27, 1879; January 1, June 15, 17, 22, 24, 26, July 8, 1880.

Mendocino (California) *Dispatch Democrat*, June 23, November 24, December 15, 1893; January 26, April 27, July 27, August 3, September 14, 21, November 30, 1894; August 14, 21, 1896.

Middletown (New York) *Daily Argus*, May 11, 1894.

National Police Gazette, March 3, 1883.

Newark (Ohio) *Daily Advocate*, September 21, 1883.

Newcastle (Wyoming) *Journal*, July 18, 1890; January 2, 1891.

Newcastle (Wyoming) *News*, July 10, 1890.

Newcastle (Wyoming) *News Letter Journal*, January 2, 1891; April 6, 1906; January 10, March 6, 1908; February 24, 1911; January 9, 1913; August 18, 1927; August 17, 1939; May 28, November 12, 1959.

New Mexico Weekly Review (Santa Fe), August 14, 1882; September 19, November 5, 1883.

New York Morning Telegraph, April 26, 1914.

New York Times, July 3, 1879; September 15, 1895.

New York Tribune, March 22, 27, 1879.

Ogden (Utah) *Standard*, July 1, 1890.

Phoenix Republican, November 19, 1903.

Queen City Mail (Spearfish, South Dakota), February 19, 1896.

Reno (Nevada) *Evening Gazette*, November 21, 1883.

Reno (Nevada) *Weekly Gazette and Stockman*, May 17, 1894.

Rio Grande Republican (Las Cruces, New Mexico), August 25, September 15, 1888; June 29, 1889; September 9, 1892; February 17, 1893.

Rocky Mountain News (Denver), October 15, November 25, 30, 1880; January 15, June 17, July 8, September 17, 1881; January 24, 1882; December 19, 1891; February 13, 1899.

Runnels County Record (Balinger, Texas), November 8, 1884.

St. Johns (Arizona) *Herald*, August 18, 1887; June 29, 1901.

Salt Lake Herald, November 14, 1898.

Salt Lake Tribune, May 14, 15, July 24, 1898.

San Angelo (Texas) *Standard*, June 27, 1901.

San Angelo (Texas) *Standard-Times*, December 15, 2003.

San Antonio (Texas) *Daily Express*, March 5, April 13, 1879.

Sandusky (Ohio) *Register*, September 19, 1894.

San Francisco Bulletin, January 24, 1894.

San Francisco Chronicle, April 25, 1894; August 13, 15, 1896.

San Francisco Examiner, December 21, 1881; January 24, 30, 1894; November 12, 1895; August 13, 1896.

San Francisco Morning Call, January 25, 26, 30, 1894; November 12, 1895; August 13, 19, 1896.

Santa Fe Daily New Mexican, February 2, 28, 1880; August 23, 31, 1886; January 9, 10, 12, 13, 15, 1894; April 7, 26, 27, May 19, December 28, 1898.

Santa Fe Weekly Democrat, August 10, 1882.

Sedalia (Missouri) *Daily Democrat*, December 18, 1879.

Sheridan (Wyoming) *Post-Enterprise*, August 19, 26, 1927.

Shreveport (Louisiana) *Times*, February 9, 1918; June 16, 1935.

Sidney (Ohio) *Sentinel*, July 26, 1906.

Silver City (New Mexico) *Enterprise*, September 21, November 9, 16, 1883; January 25, July 11, October 3, 1884; April 13, October 5, 1900; August 16, 1901; August 26, 1904.

Silver City (New Mexico) *Independent*, December 20, 1898; April 17, 24, July 24, September 4, 25, October 9, 23, 1900; April 12, August 16, 1901; August 23, 1904.

Silver City (New Mexico) *Southwest Sentinel*, September 29, 1883.

Socorro (New Mexico) *Daily Sun*, December 19, 1881; September 21, December 8, 1883.

Sumner County (Kansas) *Weekly Press*, December 22, 1881.

Tombstone (Arizona) *Epitaph*, June 1, 1902; December 6, 12, 19, 1915; May 7, 1916; June 3, 24, 1917.

Tombstone (Arizona) *Prospector*, June 19, 28, December 6, 9, 12, 15, 19, 1915; May 7, 10, 15, 17, 1916.

Topeka (Kansas) *Daily Commonwealth*, September 17, 1871.

Trenton (New Jersey) *Times*, September 21, 1883; March 30, 1905.

Tucson (Arizona) *Daily Star*, March 8, 1882.

Tulsa (Oklahoma) *World*, January 4, 2004.

Ukiah (California) *Republican Press*, June 23, 1893; August 14, 21, 1896.

Yakima (Washington) *Herald*, May 12, 17, 1894.

Waco (Texas) *Examiner and Patron*, January 11, 1878; April 5, 7, 1882.

Washington Post, March 26, 1905.

Weekly Globe (Golden, Colorado), August 19, 1876.

Wellington (Kansas) *Daily Mail*, September 13, 1894; January 23, April 6–22, September 6–16, 1895.

Wellington (Kansas) *Monitor-Press*, April 11, 18, 1895.

Wichita (Kansas) *Beacon*, August 5, 1874; September 17, 1894; April 19, 1895; April 28, 1916; October 21, 1923.

Wichita (Kansas) *Daily Times*, December 17, 20, 1881; May 23, 24, 26, 1912; May 1, July 21, 22, 23, 24, 25, 1913.

Wichita (Kansas) *Eagle*, May 22, 1873; December 22, 29, 1881; September 18, 1894; April 18, 19, 1895; March 1, 1908; March 12, 1912; April 28, 1916; April 3, 1932; May 3, 1990.

Wichita (Kansas) *Vidette*, October 27, 1870.

Winfield (Kansas) *Courier*, December 29, 1881.

Wyoming State Tribune (Cheyenne), December 2, 1926.
Yakima (Washington) *Herald*, May 12, 17, 1894.

MISCELLANEOUS
Lingenfelter Genealogy Extract, Kansas State Historical Society, Topeka.

BOOKS AND PAMPHLETS
Adams, Ramon F. *Burs under the Saddle: A Second Look at Books and Histories of the West.* Norman: University of Oklahoma Press, 1964.
———. *More Burs under the Saddle: Books and Histories of the West.* Norman: University of Oklahoma Press, 1979.
———. *Six-Guns and Saddle Leather: A Bibliography of Books and Pamphlets on Western Outlaws and Gunmen.* Norman: University of Oklahoma Press, 1969.
Alexander, Bob. *Dangerous Dan Tucker: New Mexico's Deadly Lawman.* Silver City, N.Mex.: High-Lonesome Books, 2001.
———. *Lawmen, Outlaws, and S.O.Bs.* Silver City, N.Mex.: High Lonesome Books, 2004.
Andreas, A. T., and W. G. Cutler. *History of the State of Kansas.* Chicago, 1883.
Baker, Pearl. *The Wild Bunch at Robbers Roost.* Los Angeles: Westernlore Press, 1965.
Ball, Eve. *Ma'am Jones of the Pecos.* Tucson: University of Arizona Press, 1968.
Ball, Larry D. *Desert Lawmen: The High Sheriffs of New Mexico and Arizona, 1846–1912.* Albuquerque: University of New Mexico Press, 1992.
———. *The United States Marshals of New Mexico and Arizona Territories, 1846–1912.* Albuquerque: University of New Mexico Press, 1978.
Barrymore, Lionel, as told to Cameron Shipp. *We Barrymores.* New York: Appleton-Century-Crofts, 1951.
Bartholomew, Ed. *The Biographical Album of Western Gunfighters.* Houston: Frontier Press of Texas, 1958.
———. *Wyatt Earp: The Man and the Myth.* Toyahville, Tex.: Frontier Book, 1964.
———. *Wyatt Earp: The Untold Story.* Toyahville, Tex.: Frontier Book, 1963.
Biggers, Don H. *Shackelford County Sketches.* Albany and Fort Griffin, Tex.: Clear Fork Press, 1974.
Biographical and Historical Memoirs of Northwest Louisiana. Nashville and Chicago: Southern Publishing, 1890.
Black, A. P. (Ott). *The End of the Long Horn Trail.* Selfridge, N.D.: Selfridge Journal, 1939.
Bonney, Cecil. *Looking Over My Shoulder: Seventy-five Years in the Pecos Valley.* Roswell, N.Mex.: Hall-Poorbaugh Press, 1971.
Brown, Larry K. *The Hog Ranches of Wyoming: Liquor, Lust and Lies under Sagebrush Skies.* Glendo, Wyo.: High Plains Press, 1995.
Brown, Richard Maxwell. *No Duty to Retreat: Violence and Values in American History and Society.* Norman: University of Oklahoma Press, 1991.

Browning, James A. *Violence Was No Stranger*. Stillwater, Okla.: Barbed Wire Press, 1993.

Bryan, Howard. *Robbers, Rogues and Ruffians: True Tales of the Wild West in New Mexico*. Santa Fe, N.Mex.: Clear Light, 1991.

———. *True Tales of the American Southwest: Pioneer Recollections of Frontier Adventures*. Santa Fe, N.Mex.: Clear Light, 1998.

Burkey, Blaine. *Wild Bill Hickok, The Law in Hays City*. Hays, Kans.: Thomas More Prep, 1973.

Butler, Anne M. *Daughters of Joy, Sisters of Misery: Prostitutes in the American West*. Urbana: University of Illinois Press, 1985.

Carlock, Robert H. *The Hashknife: The Early Days of the Aztec and Cattle Company*. Tucson, Ariz.: Westernlore Press, 1994.

Carranco, Lynwood, and Estle Beard. *Genocide and Vendetta: The Round Valley Wars of Northern California*. Norman: University of Oklahoma Press, 1981.

Chesley, Harvey E. *Adventuring with the Old-Timers: Trails Traveled—Tales Told*. Midland, Tex.: Nita Stewart Haley Memorial Library, 1979.

Choitz, John F. *A History of Ellsworth County, 1854–1885*. Ellsworth, Kans.: Ellsworth County Historical Society, 1967.

Chrisman, Harry E. *Fifty Years on the Owl Hoot Trail: Jim Herron, the First Sheriff of No Man's Land, Oklahoma Territory*. Chicago: Sage Books, 1969.

———. *Lost Trails of the Cimarron*. Denver: Sage Books, 1961.

Cochran, Keith. *American West: A Historical Chronology*. Rapid City, S.D.: Keith Cochran, 1992.

Colcord, Charles Francis. *The Autobiography of Charles Francis Colcord*. N.p.: privately printed by C. C. Helmerich, 1970.

Collier, William Ross, and Edwin Westrate. *Dave Cook of the Rockies: Fighting Sheriff and Leader of Men*. New York: Rufus Rockwell Wilson, 1936.

Collinson, Frank. *Life in the Saddle*. Norman: University of Oklahoma Press, 1963.

Connelley, William Elsey. *Wild Bill and His Era: The Life and Adventures of James Butler Hickok*. New York: Cooper Square, 1972.

Cox, James. *Historical and Biographical Record of the Cattle Industry and the Cattlemen: Texas and Adjacent Territory*. St. Louis: Wodward and Tiemam, 1895.

Crichton, Kyle S. *Law and Order, Ltd. The Rousing Life of Elfego Baca of New Mexico*. Glorieta, N.Mex.: Rio Grande Press, 1970.

Criqui, Orvel A. *Fifty Fearless Men: The Forsyth Scouts and Beecher Island*. Marceline, Mo.: Walsworth, 1993.

Daughters of the American Revolution, Eunice Sterling Chapter. *Illustrated History of Early Wichita: Incidents of Frontier Days*. Wichita, Kans., 1914.

David, Robert B. *Malcolm Campbell, Sheriff*. Casper, Wyo.: Wyomingana, 1932.

Davis-Kotsilibas, James. *Great Times, Good Times: The Odyssey of Maurice Barrymore*. Garden City, N.Y.: Doubleday, 1977.

DeArment, Robert K. *Alias Frank Canton*. Norman: University of Oklahoma Press, 1996.

———. *Bat Masterson: The Man and the Legend*. Norman: University of Oklahoma Press, 1979.

———. *Bravo of the Brazos: John Larn of Fort Griffin, Texas*. Norman: University of Oklahoma Press, 2002.

———. *Deadly Dozen: Twelve Forgotten Gunfighters of the Old West*. Norman: University of Oklahoma Press, 2003.

———. *George Scarborough: The Life and Death of a Lawman on the Closing Frontier*. Norman: University of Oklahoma Press, 1992.

———. *Knights of the Green Cloth: The Saga of the Frontier Gamblers*. Norman: University of Oklahoma Press, 1982.

Debo, Angie, ed. *The Cowman's Southwest: Being the Reminiscences of Oliver Nelson, Freighter, Camp Cook, Cowboy, Frontiersman in Kansas, Indian Territory, Texas and Oklahoma, 1878–1893*. Lincoln: University of Nebraska Press, 1953.

Dedera, Don. *A Little War of Our Own: The Pleasant Valley Feud Revisited*. Flagstaff, Ariz.: Northland, 1988.

Douglas, C. L. *Cattle Kings of Texas*. Dallas: Cecil Baugh, 1939.

Drago, Harry Sinclair. *Great American Cattle Trails: The Story of the Old Cow Paths of the East and the Longhorn Highways of the Plains*. New York: Dodd, Mead, 1965.

———. *The Legend Makers: Tales of the Old-Time Peace Officers and Desperadoes of the Frontier*. New York: Dodd, Mead, 1975.

———. *Wild, Woolly and Wicked: The History of the Kansas Cow Towns and the Cattle Trade*. New York: Clarkson N. Potter, 1960.

Dykstra, Robert R. *The Cattle Towns*. New York: Atheneum, 1972.

Elman, Robert. *Badmen of the West*. Secaucus, N.J.: Ridge Press Pound Book, 1974.

Fattig, Timothy W. *Wyatt Earp, The Biography*. Honolulu: Talei, 2002.

Fergusson, Erna. *Murder and Mystery in New Mexico*. Albuquerque, N.Mex.: Merle Armitage Editions, 1948.

Fergusson, Harvey. *Rio Grande*. New York: Alfred A. Knopf, 1940.

Fitzgerald, Daniel C. *Faded Dreams: More Ghost Towns of Kansas*. Lawrence: University Press of Kansas, 1994.

Flannery, L. G. ed. *John Hunton's Diary, 1873–'75*. Vol. 1. Lingle, Wyo.: Guide-Review, 1956.

———. *John Hunton's Diary, 1876–'77*. Vol. 2. Lingle, Wyo.: Guide-Review, 1958.

———. *John Hunton's Diary, 1878–'79*. Vol. 3. Lingle, Wyo.: Guide-Review, 1960.

———. *John Hunton's Diary, 1880–'82*. Vol. 4. Lingle, Wyo.: Guide-Review, 1963.

———. *John Hunton's Diary, 1883–'84*. Vol. 5. Lingle, Wyo.: Guide-Review, 1964.

———. *John Hunton's Diary, Wyoming Territory, 1885–1889*. Vol. 6. Glendale, Calif.: Arthur H. Clark, 1970.

Fleming, Elvis E., and Ernestine Chesser Williams. *Treasures of History II: Chaves County Vignettes*. Roswell, N.Mex.: Chaves County Historical Society, 1991.

Forrest, Earle R. *Arizona's Dark and Bloody Ground*. Caldwell, Idaho: Caxton, 1950.

Freeman, G. D. *Midnight and Noonday, or The Incidental History of Southern Kansas and the Indian Territory, 1871–1890*. Norman: University of Oklahoma Press, 1984.

French, William. *Some Recollections of a Western Ranchman, New Mexico, 1883–1899*. New York: Argosy-Antiquarian, 1965.

Frink, Maurice. *Cow Country Cavalcade: Eighty Years of the Wyoming Stock Growers Association*. Denver: Old West, 1954.

Frye, Elnora L. *Atlas of Wyoming Outlaws at the Territorial Penitentiary*. Laramie, Wyo.: Jelm Mountain, 1990.

Gard. Wayne. *The Chisholm Trail*. Norman: University of Oklahoma Press, 1954.

———. *Frontier Justice*. Norman: University of Oklahoma Press, 1949.

———. *The Great Buffalo Hunt*. New York: Alfred A. Knopf, 1959.

———. *Sam Bass*. Boston: Houghton Mifflin, 1936.

Garrett, Julia Kathryn. *Fort Worth: A Frontier Triumph*. Fort Worth: Texas Christian University Press, 1996.

Gibson, A. M. *The Life and Death of Colonel Albert Jennings Fountain*. Norman: University of Oklahoma Press, 1965.

Gilbert, Miles. *Getting a Stand*. Tempe, Ariz.: Hal Green, 1986.

Gilbert, Miles, Leo Reminger, and Sharon Cunningham. *Encyclopedia of Buffalo Hunters and Skinners*. Vol. 1, *A–D*. Union City, Tenn.: Pioneer Press, 2003.

Gilbreath, West C. *Death on the Gallows: The Story of Legal Hangings in New Mexico, 1847–1923*. Silver City, N.Mex.: High-Lonesome Books, 2002.

Glasscock, Carl B. *The War of the Copper Kings*. Indianapolis: Bobbs, Merrill, 1935.

Gorzalka, Ann. *Wyoming's Territorial Sheriffs*. Glendo, Wyo.: High Plains Press, 1998.

Griffith, Elizabeth T. *The House of Blazes: The Story of Johnny Owens*. Newcastle, Wyo.: News Letter Journal, 1990.

Grinnell, George Bird. *The Fighting Cheyennes*. Norman: University of Oklahoma Press, 1955.

Haley, J. Evetts. *Charles Goodnight: Cowboy and Plainsman*. Norman: University of Oklahoma Press, 1936.

———. *Jeff Milton: A Good Man with a Gun*. Norman: University of Oklahoma Press, 1948.

Halsell, H. H. *Cowboys and Cattleland: Memoirs of a Frontier Cowboy*. Fort Worth: Texas Christian University Press, 1983.

Hardin, John Wesley. *The Life of John Wesley Hardin as Written by Himself.* Norman: University of Oklahoma Press, 1961.

Harkey, Dee. *Mean as Hell.* Albuquerque: University of New Mexico Press, 1948.

Hening, H. B., ed. *George Curry, 1861–1947: An Autobiography.* Albuquerque: University of New Mexico Press, 1958.

Hertzog, Peter. *A Directory of New Mexico Desperadoes.* Santa Fe, N.Mex.: Press of the Territorian, 1965.

Hicks, John Edward. *Adventures of a Tramp Printer, 1880–1890.* Kansas City, Mo.: Mid-American Press, 1950.

History of the Tacoma Police Department. Tacoma, Wash., 1908.

Hornung, Chuck. *Fullertown's Rangers: A History of the New Mexico Territorial Mounted Police.* Jefferson, N.C.: McFarland, 2005.

———. *The Thin Gray Line: The New Mexico Mounted Police.* Fort Worth, Tex.: Western Heritage Press, 1971.

Hough, Emerson. *The Story of the Outlaw: A Study of the Western Desperado.* New York: Grosset and Dunlap, 1905.

Hunt, Frazier. *Cap Mossman, Last of the Great Cowmen.* New York: Hastings House, 1951.

Hunt, William R. *Distant Justice: Policing the Alaska Frontier.* Norman: University of Oklahoma Press, 1987.

Hunter, J. Marvin. *The Story of Lottie Deno: Her Life and Times.* Bandera, Tex.: Four Hunters, 1959.

———. *The Trail Drivers of Texas.* New York: Argosy-Antiquarian, 1963.

Hunter, J. Marvin, and Noah H. Rose. *The Album of Gunfighters.* Bandera, Tex., 1951.

Hutchinson, W. H. *Another Verdict for Oliver Lee.* Clarendon, Tex.: Clarendon Press, 1965.

———. *A Bar Cross Man: The Life and Personal Writings of Eugene Manlove Rhodes.* Norman: University of Oklahoma Press, 1956.

Hutchinson, W. H., and R. N. Mullin. *Whiskey Jim and a Kid Named Billy.* Clarendon, Tex.: Clarendon Press, 1967.

Hutton, Harold. *Doc Middleton: Life and Legends of the Notorious Plains Outlaw.* Chicago: Sage Books, 1974.

Ingmire, Frances T. *Texas Ranger Service Records, 1847–1900.* St. Louis: Ingmire, 1982.

Jaastad, Ben. *Man of the West: Reminiscences of George Washington Oaks, 1840–1917.* Tucson: Arizona Pioneers' Historical Society, 1956.

Jennings, N. A. *A Texas Ranger.* New York: Charles Scribner's Sons, 1899.

Keleher, William A. *The Fabulous Frontier: Twelve New Mexico Items.* Albuquerque: University of New Mexico Press, 1982.

Keller, John E. *The Saga of Round Valley, the Last of the West.* Ukiah, Calif.: Mendocino County Historical Society, 1971.

Kelly, Charles. *The Outlaw Trail: A History of Butch Cassidy and His Wild Bunch.* New York: Devin-Adair, 1959.

Knight, Oliver. *Fort Worth: Outpost on the Trinity*. Fort Worth: Texas Christian University Press, 1990.

L'Aloge, Bob. *The Incident of New Mexico's Nightriders: A True Account of the Socorro Vigilantes*. Sunnyside, Wash.: BJS Brand Books, 1992.

———. *Knights of the Sixgun: A Diary of Gunfighters, Outlaws and Villains of New Mexico*. Las Cruces, N.Mex.: Yucca Tree Press, 1991.

Ledbetter, Barbara A. Neal. *Marlow Brothers Ordeal, 1888–1892: 138 Days of Hell in Graham on the Texas Frontier*. Graham, Tex.: Lavender Books, 1991.

Lee, Wayne C. *Deadly Days in Kansas*. Caldwell, Idaho: Caxton, 1997.

Leeson, Michael. *History of Montana: 1739–1885*. Chicago: Warner, Beers, 1885.

LeFors, Joe. *Wyoming Peace Officer: An Autobiography*. Laramie, Wyo.: Laramie Printers, 1953.

A List of Fugitives from Justice, 1891. Part VII, Complied from Reports of Sheriffs Received at the Adjutant General's Office. Austin, Tex.: Henry Hutchings, State Printer, 1891.

A List of Fugitives from Justice, from Records in the Adjutant-General's Office. Austin, Tex.: Adjutant General's Office, 1878.

A List of Fugitives from Justice, Indicted for Felonies in the State of Texas and a Descriptive List of Escaped Convicts. Austin, Tex.: John P. Kirk, 1886.

A List of Fugitives from Justice for 1900. Austin: Texas State Library, 1900.

Look, Al. *Unforgettable Characters of Western Colorado*. Boulder, Colo.: Pruett Press, 1966.

Marohn, Richard C. *The Last Gunfighter, John Wesley Hardin*. College Station, Tex.: Creative, 1995.

Martin, Charles L. *A Sketch of Sam Bass, the Bandit*. Norman: University of Oklahoma Press, 1997.

Masterson, W. B. "Bat," and Jack DeMattos. *Famous Gunfighters of the Western Frontier*. Monroe, Wash.: Weatherford Press, 1982.

McLure, Lilla, and J. Ed Howe. *History of Shreveport and Shreveport Builders*. Shreveport, La., 1937.

McNeal, T. A. *When Kansas Was Young*. New York: Macmillan, 1922.

Metz, Leon C. *Dallas Studenmire, El Paso Marshal*. Austin, Tex.: Pemberton Press, 1969.

———. *The Encyclopedia of Lawmen, Outlaws, and Gunfighters*. New York: Checkmark Books, 2003.

———. *John Wesley Hardin: Dark Angel of Texas*. El Paso, Tex.: Mangan Books, 1996.

Miletich, Leo N. *Dan Stuart's Fistic Carnival*. College Station: Texas A&M University Press, 1994.

Miller, Joseph, ed. *The Arizona Rangers*. New York: Hastings House, 1972.

Miller, Nyle H., and Joseph W. Snell. *Why the West Was Wild: A Contemporary Look at the Antics of Some Highly Publicized Kansas Cowtown Personalities*. Topeka: Kansas State Historical Society, 1963.

Miller, Rick. *Bloody Bill Longley*. Wolfe City, Tex.: Henington, 1996.

———. *Bounty Hunter*. College Station, Tex.: Creative, 1988.

———. *Sam Bass and Gang*. Austin, Tex.: State House Press, 1999.

Miner, H. Craig. *Wichita: The Early Years, 1865–80*. Lincoln: University of Nebraska Press, 1982.

Mullane, William H., ed. *This Is Silver City, 1882, 1883, 1884*. Silver City, N.Mex.: Silver City Enterprise, 1963.

Nash, Jay Robert. *Encyclopedia of Western Lawmen and Outlaws*. New York: Paragon House, 1992.

National Cyclopedia of American Biography. New York: James T. White, 1921.

Nolan, Frederick. *The Lincoln County War: A Documentary History*. Norman: University of Oklahoma Press, 1992.

Nye, Wilbur Sturdevant. *Plains Indian Raiders*. Norman: University of Oklahoma Press, 1968.

O'Neal, Bill. *The Arizona Rangers*. Austin, Tex.: Eakin Press, 1987.

———. *Caldwell in the 1870s and 1880s: The Rowdy Years of the Border Queen*. N.p., n.d.

———. *Encyclopedia of Western Gunfighters*. Norman: University of Oklahoma Press, 1979.

———. *Historic Ranches of the Old West*. Austin, Tex.: Eakin Press, 1997.

O'Neil, James B. *They Die But Once: The Story of a Tejano*. New York: Knight, 1935.

Otero, Miguel A. *My Life on the Frontier, 1864–1882: Incidents and Characters of the Period When Kansas, Colorado, and New Mexico Were Passing Through the Last of Their Wild and Romantic Years*. New York: Press of the Pioneers, 1935.

———. *My Life on the Frontier*. Vol. 2, *1882–1897: Death Knell of a Territory and Birth of a State*. Albuquerque: University of New Mexico Press, 1939.

Paine, Albert Bigelow. *Captain Bill McDonald: Texas Ranger*. Austin, Tex.: State House Press, 1986.

Parker, Morris B. *White Oaks: Life in a New Mexico Gold Camp, 1880–1900*. Tucson: University of Arizona Press, 1971.

Parkhill, Forbes. *The Wildest of the West*. New York: Henry Holt, 1951.

Parsons, Chuck, and Donaly E. Brice. *Texas Ranger N. O. Reynolds, the Intrepid*. Honolulu: Talei, 2005

Parsons, Chuck, and Marianne E. Hall Little. *Captain L. H. McNelly, Texas Ranger: The Life and Times of a Fighting Man*. Austin, Tex.: State House Press, 2001.

Pence, Mary Lou. *Boswell: The Story of a Frontier Lawman*. Cheyenne, Wyo.: Pioneer Printing and Stationery, 1978.

Poldervaart, Arie W. *Black-Robed Justice*. N.p.: Historical Society of New Mexico, 1948.

Portrait and Biographical Album of Sumner County, Kansas. Chicago: Chapman Bros., 1890.

Raine, William MacLeod. *Guns of the Frontier*. Boston: Houghton Mifflin, 1940.

Rasch, Philip J. *Desperadoes of Arizona Territory*. Stillwater, Okla.: Western, 1999.

———. *Gunsmoke in Lincoln County*. Stillwater, Okla.: Western, 1997.

———. *Warriors of Lincoln County*. Stillwater, Okla.: Western, 1998.

Rathmell, William. *Life of the Marlows: A True Story of Frontier Life of Early Days*. Edited with an introduction and annotations by Robert K. DeArment. Denton: University of North Texas Press, 2004.

Records, Laban S. *Cherokee Outlet Cowboy: Recollections of Laban S. Records*. Norman: University of Oklahoma Press, 1995.

Reynolds, Bill. *Trouble in New Mexico: The Outlaws, Gunmen, Desperados, Murderers and Lawmen for Fifty Turbulent Years*. Vol. 2. Bakersfield, Calif.: Kinko's Copies, 1994.

Reynolds, Thursey Jessen. *Centennial Echoes from Carbon County*. Price, Utah: Daughters of Utah Pioneers of Carbon County, 1948.

Richardson, Ernest M. *The Battle of Lightning Creek*. Pacific Palisades, Calif.: n.p., 1956.

Ridings, Sam P. *The Chisholm Trail: A History of the Word's Greatest Cattle Trail*. Guthrie, Okla.: Co-Operative, 1936.

Robertson, Frank G., and Beth Kay Harris. *Soapy Smith: King of the Frontier Con Men*. New York: Hastings House, 1961.

Rockwell, Wilson. *Memoirs of a Lawman*. Denver: Sage Books, 1962.

———. *Sunset Slope*. Denver: Big Mountain Press, 1955.

———. *Uncompahgre Country*. Denver: Sage Books, 1965.

Roenigk, Adolph. *Pioneer History of Kansas*. Lincoln, Kans.: Adolph Roenigk, 1933.

Rosa, Joseph. *They Called Him Wild Bill: The Life and Adventures of James Butler Hickok*. Norman: University of Oklahoma Press, 1974.

———. *Wild Bill Hickok, Gunfighter*. College Station, Tex.: Creative, 2001.

Rosa, Joseph, and Waldo E. Koop. *Rowdy Joe Lowe: Gambler with a Gun*. Norman: University of Oklahoma Press, 1989.

Rye, Edgar. *The Quirt and the Spur*. Austin, Tex.: Steck-Vaughn, 1967.

Sanders, Gwendline, and Paul Sanders. *The Sumner County Story*. North Newton, Kans.: Mennonite Press, 1966.

Shirley, Glenn. *The Fighting Marlows, Men Who Wouldn't Be Lynched*. Fort Worth: Texas Christian University Press, 1994.

———. *West of Hell's Fringe*. Norman: University of Oklahoma Press, 1978.

Sifakis, Carl. *The Encyclopedia of American Crime*. New York: Smithmark, 1992.

Siringo, Charles A. *Riata and Spurs: The Story of a Lifetime Spent in the Saddle as Cowboy and Ranger*. Boston: Houghton Mifflin, 1927.

———. *A Texas Cowboy, or Fifteen Years on the Hurricane Deck of a Spanish Pony—Taken From Real Life*. New York: William Sloane, 1950.

Smith, Victor Grant. *The Champion Buffalo Hunter: The Frontier Memoirs of Yellowstone Vic Smith*. Helena, Mont.: Two Dot Books, 1997.

Sonnichsen, C. L. *Tularosa: Last of the Frontier West*. New York: Devin-Adair, 1963.

Spring, Agnes Wright. *The Cheyenne and Black Hills Stage and Express Routes.* Lincoln: University of Nebraska Press, 1948.

——. *Colorado Charley, Wild Bill's Pard.* Boulder, Colo.: Pruett Press, 1968.

Stanley, F. *Dave Rudabaugh, Border Ruffian.* Denver: World Press, 1961.

——. *Desperadoes of New Mexico.* Denver: World Press, 1953.

——. *Notes on Joel Fowler.* Pep, Tex., 1963.

——. *The Seven Rivers (New Mexico) Story.* Pep, Tex., 1963.

Streeter, Floyd B. *Prairie Trails and Cow Town.* Boston: Chapman and Grimes, 1936.

Thrapp, Dan L. *Encyclopedia of Frontier Biography.* 4 Vols. Glendale, Calif.: Arthur H. Clark, 1988–94.

Tinsley, Jim Bob. *The Hash Knife Brand.* Gainesville: University Press of Florida, 1993.

Tise, Sammy. *Texas County Sheriffs.* Albuquerque, N.Mex.: Oakwood, 1989.

Tyler, Ron, ed. *The New Handbook of Texas.* Austin: Texas State Historical Society, 1996.

Walters, Lorenzo. *Tombstone's Yesterdays.* Tucson, Ariz.: Acme, 1928.

Warde, Frederick. *Fifty Years of Make-Believe.* New York: International Press Syndicate, 1920.

Weston County Heritage Group. *Weston County, Wyoming—The First 100 Years.* N.p.: Curtis Media, 1988.

White, Virgil. *Index to Indian Wars Pension Files, 1892–1926.* Vol. 2. Waynesboro, Tenn.: National Historical, 1987.

Wilkins, Frederick. *The Law Comes to Texas: The Texas Rangers 1870–1901.* Austin, Tex.: State House Press, 1999.

Williams, Clayton W. *Texas' Last Frontier: Fort Stockton and the Trans-Pecos, 1861–1895.* College Station: Texas A&M University Press, 1982.

Williams, Harry. *Texas Trails: Legends of the Great Southwest.* San Antonio, Tex.: Naylor, 1932.

Wilson, John P., ed. *Pat Garrett and Billy the Kid as I Knew Them: Reminiscences of John P. Meadows.* Albuquerque: University of New Mexico Press, 2004.

Writers' Project of Montana. *Copper Camp: The Lusty Story of Butte, Montana.* New York: Hastings House, 1976.

Yost, Nellie Snyder, ed. *Boss Cowman: The Recollections of Ed Lemmon.* Lincoln: University of Nebraska Press, 1969.

ARTICLES

Anderson, Wyatt. "A Pioneer in West Texas." *Frontier Times,* February 1926.

Ball, Eve. "Murder on Credit." *Frontier Times,* February–March 1978.

Barnes, Will C. "The Pleasant Valley War of 1887: Its Genesis, History and Necrology." *Arizona Historical Review* (October 1931, January 1932).

Beach, James H. "Old Fort Hays." *Collections of the Kansas State Historical Society, 1909–1910,* 11:580.

Benfer, Maurice. "Early Law Enforcement Problems in Wichita." *Wichita* (Kansas) *Eagle Sunday Magazine,* January 21, 1929.

Brock, Eric J. "More Mystery in Shreveport History." *Forum*, November 24, 2004.

———. "Shreveport's Mayoral History." *Forum*, June 1, 2005.

Carroll, Murray L. "As an Outlaw and Escape Artist Dan Bogan Was the Real McCoy." *Journal of the Western Outlaw-Lawman History Association* (Spring–Summer 1992).

Christiansen, Paige W. "Reminiscences of the Socorro Vigilantes." *New Mexico Historical Review* 40, no. 1 (1965).

Cline, Don. "A Cold Night for Angels." *Real West*, December 1984.

———. "Socorro Killer." *Frontier Times*, February–March 1974.

Cowan, E. D. "Memories of the Happy Bad Man of the West." *Chicago Chronicle*, October 16, 1898.

DeArment, R. K. "Controversial Cowboy Gunman Tom Tucker." *Wild West*, April 2002.

———. "Doc's Deputy." *True West*, September 1996.

———. "Gunfighters and Lawmen: Jack Jolly." *Wild West*, February 2004.

———. "Gunfighters and Lawmen: Zack Light." *Wild West*, April 2003.

———. "The Gunfights of Pioneer Cattleman Burk Burnett." *Wild West*, August 2005.

———. "The Long Arm of the Law: But Only One." *True West*, January 2003.

———. "Revenge! A Tale of Murder and Mystery in the Old West." In *Revenge! And Other True Tales of the Old West*. Lafayette, Ind.: ScarletMask Enterprises, 2004.

———. "Toughest Cow Outfit in Texas." *True West*, April–May 1991.

———. "When Hell Was in Session in Caldwell." *True West*, September 1999.

Drees, James D. "Curry, an Early Bad Guy." *Hays*(Kansas) *Daily News*, April 26, 1984.

Fairley, Bill. "Burnett Changed Cattle Industry." Undated clipping from *Fort Worth* (Texas) *Star-Telegram*.

Frandsen, Joel. "The Posse Shootout — The Slaying of Jack Watson." *Outlaw Trail Journal* (Winter 2000).

Freeman, Frank M. "The Meanest So-and-So in Colorado." *Real West*, September 1981.

Garton, Bill, "Book Reviews." *Wyoming Rural Electric News*, April 2004.

Griffith, Elizabeth. "Johnny Owens: Gambler, Whoremaster, Rancher, Killer — Sheriff." *Journal of the Western Outlaw-Lawman History Association* (Spring–Summer 1991).

Guinn, Jack. "The Timely End of Jim Moon." *Denver Post Empire Magazine*, April 30, 1967.

Heizer, Chester C. "Heizer Writes Sequel to Meagher Murder Story." *Caldwell* (Kansas) *Messenger*, April 30, 1956.

Henderson, Sam. "Brothers of Fortune." *Golden West*, July 1965.

Hunter, J. Marvin. "Brief History of the Early Days of Mason County." *Frontier Times*, February 1929.

———. "We Stand Corrected." *Frontier Times*, March 1929.

Johnson, Howell. "An Almost Fatal Encounter." *Frontier Times*, May 1929.

Johnson, Edward W. "Deputy Marshal Johnson Breaks a Long Silence." *True West*, January–February, 1980.

Johnson, Lester Douglas. "Two Brothers Kept Order in Old West." *Topeka* (Kansas) *Pictorial-Times*, January 20, 1971.

Leahy, D. D. "Random Recollections of Other Days." *Wichita* (Kansas) *Eagle*, April 3, 1932.

Lorentz, Upton. " 'Colorado Charley,' Friend of 'Wild Bill.' " *Frontier Times*, May 1936.

King, C. Richard. "Maurice Barrymore and the Incident at Marshall." *East Texas Historical Journal* 1, no. 1 (July 1963).

Massey, Sarah, "Book Reviews." *Cowboys and Indians*, July 2004.

Masterson, W. B. "Famous Gunfighters of the Western Frontier: Ben Thompson." *Human Life*, January 1907.

——. "Famous Gunfighters of the Western Frontier: Luke Short." *Human Life*, April 1907.

Montgomery, Mrs. Frank C. "Fort Wallace and its Relation to the Frontier." *Collections of the Kansas State Historical Society, 1926–1928*, 17:234.

Morehouse, Charles H. "A City Marshal on the Frontier: A New Years Tragedy in Old Time Wichita." *Kansas Magazine*, September 1909.

——. "The City Marshall on the Frontier: How Wichita Celebrated New Year Over Forty Years Ago." *Midwest Bookman*, January 1921.

Myers, Roger. "Mike Meagher: Terror to the Pistol-Shooting Texans." *WOLA Journal* (Summer 2003).

O'Brien, Patrick G. "Book Reviews," *Journal of the West* (Summer 2004).

O'Neal, Bill. "Jim Currie vs. Maurice Barrymore and Company — March 19, 1879, Marshall, Texas." *True West*, September 1990.

——. "100 Years Ago in the West." *Old West*, Spring 1993.

Passmore, Leonard. "Memoirs of Lafe McDonald." *Frontier Times*, January 1929.

Penn, Chris, "The Light Brothers." *Wild West*, April 2003.

——. "Rounding up the Roark Gang." *Wild West*, April 2003.

Potter, Chester D. "Reminiscences of the Socorro Vigilantes." *New Mexico Historical Review* 40, no. 1 (1965).

Rasch, Philip J. "Alias 'Whiskey Jim.' " *Panhandle-Plains Historical Review* (1963).

——. "Death Comes to St. Johns." *Quarterly of the National Association for Outlaw and Lawman History* (January 1982).

——. "Joel A. Fowler, 'The Human Hyena.' " *Brand Book of the Denver Westerners* 21 (1966).

——. "A Killer Next to Wild Bill." *Real West*, April 1981.

——. "One Killed, One Wounded." *Quarterly of the National Association and Center for Outlaw and Lawman History*, (Autumn 1978).

——. "Zach Light, New Mexico Badman." *Quarterly of the National Association and Center for Outlaw and Lawman History* (June 1979).

Rasch, Philip J., and Lee Myers. "Les Dow, Sheriff of Eddy County." *New Mexico Historical Review* (July 1974).

Seymour, Clifton, "The Shooting of Maurice Barrymore." *Frontier Times*, April 1927.

Shlesinger, Sigmund. "Battle of the Arikaree." *Collections of the Kansas State Historical Society, 1919–1922*, 15:541.

Snell, Joseph W. "The Murder of Mike Meagher." *The West*, January 1965.

Spring, Agnes Wright. "Twenty Notches on His Gun." *True West*, April 1970.

Streeter, Floyd B. "The Millet Cattle Ranch in Baylor County, Texas." *Panhandle-Plains Historical Review* 22 (1949).

Tanner, Beccy. "Meaghers Kept the Peace." *Wichita* (Kansas) *Eagle*, May 3, 1900.

Thorpe, Elizabeth J. "Let the Record Show." *Bits and Pieces Magazine*, March 1969.

———. "The Gambling Sheriff." *True West*, July–August 1967.

Walker, Wayne T. "Burk Burnett and the Four Sixes." *Real West*, January 1981.

———. "Legend of the Four Sixes." *Golden West*, March 1971.

Weidman, Joe. "Early Days Cowboy Recalls Meagher's Death on City Street." *Caldwell* (Kansas) *Messenger*, April 30, 1956.

Wilcox, Lute. "A Street Duel." *Denver Field and Farm*, April 4, 1914.

Williams, Mack. "In Old Fort Worth." *Fort Worth* (Texas) *News-Tribune*, 1977.

Yarmer, Robert E. "The Life of John W. Light." *Cochise Quarterly* (Autumn 1994).

Index

Barnes, John B., 98, 106, 108, 112, 113, 115, 281n25, 283n72
Barnes, Will C., 220, 222, 223, 301n19, 302n19, 302n21
Barnum, I. E., 20
Barrow, J. M. ("Bud"), 156
Barry, W. F., 74
Barrymore, Ethel, 36
Barrymore, John, 36
Barrymore, Lionel, 36, 40, 269n78
Barrymore, Maurice Herbert (Herbert Blythe), 36–40, 42, 43, 44, 270n109
Bartholomew, Ed, 5
Bartholomew, E. W., 89
Bartlett, E. L., 233
Barton County, Kans., 204, 206
Bascom, Cal J., 27, 31, 33
Bass, Sam, 35, 134, 161, 203
Bassett, Charley, 23
Bastrop, Tex., 280n12
Bates County, Mo., 141, 290n1
Battle Mountain Sanitarium, Hot Springs, S.Dak., 189
Battle of Antietam, 23, 50
Baxter Springs Massacre, 299n5
Baylor County, Tex., 153, 162, 163, 164, 293n21
Beach, Sumner ("Cimarron"), 207
Beach, Tom, 221
Beale, R. C., 133
Beall, W. N., 108, 112
Bear River City, Wyo., 272n9
Bear River Riot, 54, 272n10
Bear Springs, Ariz., 221
Bear Springs, N.Mex., 103, 104, 106
Beard, E. T. ("Red"), 161
Beck, Ole, 253
Beckwith, A. K., 54
Beecher, Frederick, 25, 266n21, 267n23
Beecher, Henry Ward, 266n21
Beecher Island Fight, 25–27, 266n19
Begnal, George, 221
Belcher (police officer), 16
Bell, Joseph, 114, 115, 116
Bell, J. Ross, 153
Bell, Ollie, 125, 286n126
Benjamin, Tex., 150
Benson, Ariz., 134, 255
Berekman, Alec, 55

Berney, J. H., 153
Berry, S., 294n38, 296n74
Best, Jack, 113
Big Dry Lake, Ariz., 222
Big Pasture, I.T., 149
Bigtree, Bob, 167, 171, 172, 176, 178, 295n60
Biographical Album of Western Gun-fighters, 5
Birch, Mat, 239
Birch, Tom, 239
Birchfield, Walt, 239, 241
Birt, Catherine, 292n3
Birt, Ezra, 292n3
Bisbee, Ariz., 248, 250, 255
Bishop, John, 188
Bitter, John, 24
Black (Butte blacksmith), 190
Black, A. P., 162–63, 209–10
Black, Barney, 18
Black Hills, 32, 73, 75, 84, 90, 91
Black Kettle, 88, 279n60
Blair, James K., 241, 242, 243, 244, 245
Blevins ("Old Man"), 221
Blevins, Hampton ("Hamp"), 221, 222
Blizzard, Logan, 88–90
Bogan, Dan ("Bill McCoy," "Bill Gatlin"), 78–79, 81
Bohan, Barney, 24
Bohny, Leopold, 98, 281n23
Bonney, William H. ("Billy the Kid."), 4, 6, 47, 103, 173, 176, 213, 219, 286n126, 291n29
Book Cliffs, 66
Boonville, Calif., 179
Booty, A. J., 43–45
Boston, Mass., 23
Boswell, Nathaniel, 81
Boulder Hot Springs, 191
Bourke, John Gregory, 74
Brady, Charles T., 29
Brady, Tex., 211
Brands: "10," 73; "818," 145; "6666," 143, 145, 148, 149, 150, 154, 156; "COD," 103; "DE," 73; "JD," 209, 210
Breakenridge, Colo., 14
Brice, Charles R., 139
Bridger, Jim, 54
Brocius ("Curly Bill"), 257

Charles, Dick, 82
Charleston, Ariz., 132
Charleston, S.C., 23
Chaves County, N.Mex., 138, 139
Chavez, Frank, 228, 230
Cherokee County, Tex., 127
Cherokee Strip, 295n58
Cheyenne, Wyo., 10, 11, 53, 54, 71, 72, 73, 75, 77, 79, 81, 82, 90
Chicago, Ill., 40, 193, 231
Chidester, J. C., 195–97, 199
Childes ("Butcher Knife Bill"), 106, 108, 112, 113, 115
Childress, Tex., 153
Chisholm Trail, 142, 161, 165, 174
Christian brothers (outlaws), 148
Chug Springs, Wyo., 73, 74, 75, 76
Chug Water Valley, 73, 75
Church (murder victims), 87
Churches: Baptist, 239, 307n53; Methodist, 110, 210, 272n2; Mormon, 221, 241
Cincinnati, Ohio, 23, 43, 270n94
Civil War, 3, 9, 12, 32, 37, 50, 53, 72, 127, 128, 142, 159, 160, 161, 189, 203, 210, 220, 260, 261, 262, 263n3, 266n18, 282n58, 292n2, 299n1, 299n5, 300n45
Clark (cowboy), 147
Clark, Bill, 213
Clark, Dick, 9, 10
Clay County, Tex., 173
Clayton, N.Mex., 214
Cleary, William B., 256
Clermont County, Ohio, 190
Cleveland, Grover, 228
Cleveland, Harper, 77
Cleveland, Larkin, 77
Clifton, W. C. ("Diamond L. Slim"), 87
Clinton, John, 254–58
Clinton, Rose, 255, 256, 257
Clinton, Rosie, 255, 256
Clow, John, 264n29
Coates, Fred, 88, 279n63
Cochise County, Ariz., 132, 133, 239, 244, 255, 256, 258, 259, 302n21, 306n42
Coconino County, Ariz., 221
Code of the West, 4

Cody, W. F. ("Buffalo Bill"), 267n26
Cofelt (Coffelt), Matt, 137, 227, 289n39, 303n30
Coke, Richard, 54, 129
Colcord, Charles, 174
Coleman County, Tex., 287n13
Collier (posseman), 242
Collins, Joseph, 113
Collinson, Frank, 94
Colt's pistol, 17, 25, 138, 144, 151, 156, 252
Columbus, Ohio, 23
Comanche, Tex., 55, 58
Comanche County, Tex., 55
Companies: Aztec Land and Cattle Company ("Hashknife" outfit), 164, 209, 220, 247; Boquillas Land and Cattle Company ("Wagon Rods"), 248, 254, 255; Cambria Fuel Company, 91, 92; Coe & Carter Company, 54; Colorado Coal and Iron Company, 62; Denver and Rio Grande Express Company, 63; Globe Express Company, 63; McMillan & Clayton blacksmiths, Butte, Mont., 297n3; North Homestake Company, 49, 50; Pleasant Valley Coal Company, 65, 66; Price Trading Company, 70; San Simon Cattle Company, 239; Sharps Rifle Company, 207; Texas Express Company, 35; Wells Fargo Express Company, 125
Comstock, Will, 266n16
Concho County, Tex., 254
Confederate Army, 53, 56, 72, 85, 142, 261, 272n10
Conklin, C. A. D., 106
Cook (railroad worker), 32
Cook, David J., 13–14, 18, 20
Cooke County, Tex., 58, 273n22
Coombs, W. M., 156
Coon, Henry, 279n59
Cooper (horse thief suspect), 239
Cooper, J. A., 180
Cooper, Jim, 223, 225, 227, 303n22
Cork, Ireland, 23
Cornett ("Doc"), 77, 83–84, 278n48
Corsicana, Tex., 55, 127, 128, 130, 132, 133, 136, 287n15

George (farmer), 150
Georgetown, N.Mex., 101, 125
Germany, 10
Gibbins, Aaron, 128, 129
Gibbons, Augustus, 246
Gibson, A. M., 302n21
Gilbert, E. A., 267n25
Gilbertson, Ross, 279n63
Gillespie, Bob, 221, 222, 302n20, 302n21
Gilliland, James R. ("Jim"), 227, 232, 234, 235, 303n22
Gillman, Bob, 30
Gilmo, John, 106
Globe, Ariz., 221
Goddard, Cy, 24
Goebel, Arthur, 119
Gold Rush: California, 266n18; Colorado, 266n18; Klondike, 200, 290n4
Gonzales y Borrego, Antonio, 228, 230
Gonzales y Borrego, Francisco, 228, 230, 233
Gooch, Ben F., 207
Good, John, 223, 225, 226, 227
Good, Walter, 223, 225, 226, 231, 303n28
Goodell, Sheriff, 245
Goodfellow, George, 133, 288n25
Goodlett, W. L., 127, 137, 289n39, 303n30
Goodnight, Charles, 56, 144
Gordon, 269n59
Goshen Hole, Wyo., 75
Graham, Charlie, 226
Graham, Tex., 143
Graham County, Ariz., 302n21
Graham family, 221, 222
Grand Junction, Colo., 63
Grant, William, 62
Grant County, N.Mex., 101, 125, 238, 241, 243, 245, 246, 302n21
Graves, Sam, 150, 154, 291n26
Gray's Harbor County, Wash., 202
Great Bend, Kans., 204, 205, 206
Greathouse ("Whiskey Jim"), 101–105, 113
Greathouse's Tavern ("Red Cloud"), 102
Greeley, Horace, 203
Green, George, 267n25

Greenwald, Henry, 45–46
Greenwood Cemetery, Newcastle, Wyo., 93
Gregory, Joe, 187
Grenier (pugilist), 192
Griffin, Ab, 58
Griffith, Elizabeth, 276n1, 276n5
Griffith, John E., 253
Grigsby, George, 202
Grimes, A. W., 97
Grover, Abner S. ("Jack Sharp"), 25, 27, 266n16, 267n26
Grover, Bert, 306n24
Gruell, Oliver, 241
Gunderson, Robert, 89
"Gunfight at the OK Corral," 288n25
Gunn, Charles, 77, 78, 79
Gunning, George G., 29
Gunnison, Colo., 60, 62, 63
Gunnison County, Colo., 52, 59, 60, 61, 63
Guthrie, Tex., 156
Gutierrez Bakery Shop, Santa Fe, N.Mex., 304n50
Guyse, Buck, 232
Gymnasium Arena, Butte, Mont., 192

Hackney, Fred, 279n59
Hackney, Ralph, 91
Hagerman, W. W., 136
Hale, James, 292n3
Hale, Nancy, 292n3
Hall, Edward L., 228, 229
Hall, John, 172
Hall, Samuel, 14–15
Halsell, H. H., 144
Halsey, Fred, 139
Halverson, Ed, 246
Ham, Whit, 297n105
Hamburg, Germany, 10
Handy, Fred C., 180
Hansen, Alfred, 275n60
Hanson, Pete ("King of Galena Street"), 193, 298n13
Hardcastle, Alfred, 122, 125
Hardin, John Wesley, 4, 6, 55, 127, 137, 161, 238, 260, 261, 286n4
Hardin County, Tenn., 272n2
Harding, Warren G., 236, 305n64

Peitz, Fred H., 214
Pelton, Clark, 277n16
Pemberton, J. E., 180, 183
Pendergast, Mike, 83–84
Prisons: Arizona State Prison, 258, 259, 261; Montana Territorial Prison, 199, 261; New Mexico Territorial Prison, 49, 262; Texas State Penitentiary, 290n4
Pennick, Quint, 79
Pepoon, Silas, 27
Perry (brother of Zack Light victim), 205, 206
Perry (Zack Light victim), 205
Perry, Charlie, 232
Perry, Solomon, R., 40
Perry, Watt, 163–65 Petaluma, Calif., 181
Peterson, Carl, 11
Phenix, N.Mex., 136–37, 138, 289n39
Philadelphia, Pa., 9, 21, 40
Phillips (police sergeant), 18
Pickett, Tom, 150–53, 156, 291n29
Pickett, Tom (outlaw), 291n29
Pickett, Tom M., 291n29
Pine Ridge Indian Agency, 87
Pinkham, W., 191–92
Pitts, Bob, 258
Platte, Mo., 292n3
Pleasant Valley War (Tonto Basin War), 221, 291n29
Pliley, Allison, 267n25
Poage, S. C., 180
Poldevaart, Arie W., 304n50
Political Parties: Democratic, 191, 226, 227, 228, 231; People's, 137; Republican, 159, 191, 226, 227, 228, 271n129
Polk, Mo., 292n3
Pond City, Kans., 266n16
Pope, Alexander, 43
Pope, W. H., 43
Porter, Benjamin C., 36–39, 41–42, 47, 50, 271n116
Portland, Ore., 51
Potter, Chester D., 47, 48, 49, 108, 110, 114, 118, 121, 122, 126, 269n66, 271n116, 283n78
Powell, Henry, 159
Powell, Jacob, 159

Powell, Sylvester, 160, 167, 169, 184
Powers (jail guard), 132
Prescott, Ariz., 269n58
Price, Sterling, 85
Price, Utah, 63, 64, 65, 66, 68, 70
Prince, L. Bradford, 50, 229, 272n129
Provo, Utah, 63
Prude, J. W., 212, 213
Pumphrey, J. B., 273n16
Putnam, Captain, 20

Quantrill, William Clark, 210
Queensbury Cup, 36
Quick, M. D., 85

Railroads: Atchison, Topeka and Santa Fe, 47, 49, 98, 114, 206; Burlington and Missouri, 77, 83; Denver and Rio Grande, 63; Kansas Pacific, 23–24, 27–28, 35; Little Miami, 23; Little Rock, 35; Memphis and Charleston, 35; New Orleans, St. Louis and Chicago, 35; Quanah, Acme and Pacific, 151; Southern Pacific, 252, 255; Texas Pacific, 35, 36, 39, 41, 43; Union Pacific, 53, 54, 72, 204
Railston, Cole, 220
Rallia, Grace, 99
Ranahan, Tom, 32, 267n25, 267n26
Ranches: Alamo, 104, 106, 112, 125; Circle Dot, 221; Four Sixes, 143; Kimmel, 137; Marks and Newfield, 179; Sewell, 207; Shaw, 101; Triple C, 132; Turkey Track, 139, 289n46; Willow, 181
Rascoe, Belle, 288n14
Rascoe, Charles, 287n10, 288n14
Rascoe, Francis, 127
Rascoe, George, 136
Rascoe, Jesse J. (Peavey House), 4–5, 127–40, 260, 261, 262, 287n10, 287n12, 287n15, 288n15, 288n25, 288n30, 289n44, 289n47
Rascoe, Jesse, Jr., 288n14
Rascoe, Katherine, 136, 139–40, 289n47
Rascoe, Laban, 127
Rascoe, Lydia, 136
Rascoe, Mary Jane Duncan ("Mollie"), 128, 138, 139, 288n14